SGEULACHDAN GOIRID AGUS BÀRDACHD À ASTRÀILIA

(SHORT TALES AND POEMS FROM AUSTRALIA)

GAELIC VOICES FROM AUSTRALIA IN THE NINETEENTH CENTURY

Edited by Kerry Cardell and Cliff Cummin

First published in December 2020

This is a work of nonfiction. No names have been changed, no characters invented, no events fabricated. It depicts actual tales, poems and songs as truthfully as recollection permits and/or can be verified by research.

Published by Peter Diggins

E-Mail: outsider@eftel.com.au

Cover design by Peter Diggins

Cover Image: Lithograph showing the Emigrant Ship *Hercules* at anchor in Cambelton Harbour, Isle of Skye, 1853 [*Illustrated London News Ltd*/Mary Evans Picture Library].

The *Hercules* was the first of the emigrant ships to carry emigrants from the Highlands and Islands under the Highland and Islands Emigration Scheme which operated between 1852-57. The *Hercules* turned out to be a 'hell ship' as far as Highland emigrants were concerned and generated a prejudice towards such emigration vessels which never really disappeared. The *Hercules* was visited by smallpox and then typhus before it even left Scottish waters and was put into quarantine at Cork, Ireland for almost three and a half months during which 59 deaths took place. Of the original 758 emigrants, 380 continued with the *Hercules* and just over 300 of the remainder were divided over a number of other ships. A few more deaths occurred during the voyage before the *Hercules* finally arrived at Adelaide over seven months after first leaving Scotland!

More info can be found online at:

https://gaelicvoicesfromaustraliainthenineteenthcentury.wordpress.com/

ISBN-10: 0-6450314-1-0
ISBN: 978-0-6450314-1-6

CONTENTS

Section Seven - Folklore - Tales and Songs 240

Section Eight - Humour and Satire 304

Acknowledgements

Our grateful thanks go to all of those individuals who happily shared relevant letters, diaries and information regarding their Gaelic-speaking forebears who, in the nineteenth century, either willingly or forced, faced the long and dangerous voyage to Australia on the other side of the world. Some of this material was a fruitful source of poems and songs, as well as prose, all composed in Gaelic.

Highland Newspapers such as the *Oban Times* (Oban) and *The Highlander* (Inverness), the many Gaelic literary magazines which, overall, came and went with regularity, were all sources, though hard won, for Gaelic material from Australia. For a short period of ten months, in 1857, there was a Gaelic publication (*An Teachdaire Gaidhealach - The Gaelic Messenger*) published at Hobart in Tasmania. This provided an outlet for 'local' contributors of poems, songs, stories and essays all composed in Gaelic and coming from most of the Eastern States, particularly Victoria and New South Wales. There was also the occasional Gaelic item appearing in some local newspapers.

All of this confronted the editors with a massive job of teasing out of the potential sources, material demonstrating that Gaelic use in Australia was continuous and creative. It was, however, a slow process and much of the overseas material could only be retrieved during infrequent research trips to libraries, newspaper offices and archival collections while on study leave from our places of employment.

We are thus grateful for the patience, helpfulness and genuine kindness shown to us by the various institutions and archival personnel who, observing our helplessness on occasions, unobtrusively suggested various approaches which led us to discoveries which would otherwise have been missed.

To Rab, who showed himself to be as deft at handling a scanner as he is in sorting out politicians, we owe our usual debt of gratitude which is, of course, cheaper than owing a debt of money.

And to Peter – what more can we say but thank you again. The cheque is in the post.

And to 'E', the world champion 'pusher and prodder' – "for Scotland I'll not tell her name." (apologies to Irish trad.)

Kerry Cardell and Cliff Cummin
(Editors)

Introduction

Sgeulachdan Goirid agus Bàrdachd à Astràilia

Tales, Poems and Songs from Australia

> "They will be telling us what they ate, what everything cost, how they got from place to place, what they wore, what illnesses they had and how they were dealt with, how marriages were arranged, what weddings and funerals were like, what they did in their spare time (if they had any), the songs they sang, the games they played, the books and newspapers they read, their gardening interests, the way politicians behaved, about the prevalence of quarrelling, stealing and superstition ..." (Quoted in M. Flinn Scottish Population History, Cambridge University Press, 1977)

The Gaels' impressions of leaving, journeying, arriving and settling in the new land, and of their attempts to fit all of these experiences into a Gaelic cultural context, are related with full candour. Many expressed these experiences through prose and poetry all in their own tongue and it is from these that we have assembled this, the first anthology of Gaelic-writing from Australia.

In offering an initial collection of Gaelic-writing from Australia since the large-scale immigration of Highlanders, primarily in the nineteenth century, the editors have rejected any notions that Gaelic ceased to exist almost from the time Gaels set foot in the new land. If the given wisdom about the existence of spoken Gaelic in the Australian colonies is dismissive, references to original "written material" are rare indeed, almost to the point of denying such an 'animal' existed.

This volume contains only a sample of the written Gaelic material which the editors have collected and it is meant to be an introductory volume to the subject. It mostly omits certain categories of Gaelic-writing such as that found, for example, in sermons, minutes of Gaelic societies, routine diary entries and so on. While recognizing the importance of this sort of material in constructing a full social history of Highland culture in Australia, the editors felt that it would have fitted uneasily within the context of an anthology designed more to highlight the creative and imaginative aspects of Gaelic writing through prose and poetry. This omission will be redressed in a later Anthology.

If evidence exists for the survival of spoken and written Gaelic material well beyond the initial arrival of those from the Highlander and Islands, it might well be asked why a collection such as the present one has never been presented. One factor appears to have been the general belief by social and cultural historians that Gaelic, either spoken or written, did not survive the initial generation of settlers. It is true that the dispersal of much of the Highland emigration led to few viable Gaelic cultural communities being established and, from this, historians and other researchers have generalized the rapid disappearance of the culture, except in its token forms.

To a large extent this has meant that little has been done by researchers to search out the possibilities of Gaelic cultural survival. Scottish research continues largely to be besotted by the Canadian experience. Thus, as far as Australia was concerned, the material which has survived in written form has largely been ignored and none of the anthologies of colonial verse or prose contains any awareness of the existence of such material. Even in more recent studies of multicultural writing in Australia, there still persists a seeming ignorance of Gaelic material.

The absence of any collection of Gaelic writing* from Australia before this present volume might well, therefore, be explained by the foregoing major reasons as well as other factors such as the necessity of finding out which Scottish papers and journals printed overseas Gaelic contributions and then engaging in the time-consuming 'treasure' hunt of trolling through the thousands of pages of such publications. There was the added problem that some of the poetry reproduced in these newspapers etc., often was unsigned. This latter fact has led the editors of this collection to exclude material where there was no direct identification of its origin or its originality.

*This has to be qualified to some extent. Ewan Cameron, after much bother, managed to have a collection of his Gaelic verse published in 1860's. The poor compositing led him taking the publisher to court! Cameron's volume 'N Righalach le Eughan Camathrom, Masterman Printers, Brunswick, 1868, was dedicated to the Duke of Edinburgh who had, in 1867, visited Victoria in the first ever first royal visit to Australia. Cameron's verses are almost entirely given over to exaggerated praise of royalty, especially to the persons composing the royal family of Cameron's time.

The search for Gaelic writing originating from Australia has to be undertaken on many fronts. A number of poets and folklorists chose to send their compositions direct to Gaelic journals, and to those few newspapers in Scotland which carried Gaelic material, eschewing a colonial audience in any direct sense. The Hamilton Advertiser and a few Tasmanian papers did carry some Gaelic material but the amount was trifling compared to what went overseas.

One exception to this was the Gaelic periodical, *An Teachdaire Gaidhealach*, which was published at Hobart Tasmania in 1857, and which included original poems, letters, songs, stories and other creative material, totally in Gaelic, from Gaels in Australia. In addition, this journal also included excerpts from the works of past famous Gaelic bards of Scotland.

Manuscript sources in Australia certainly reveal letters and poems, but the location of these required a measure of time-consuming concentrated searching and, as with all research, a dash of serendipity! Such material may turn up in quite unlikely places. The farmer Donald MacKinnon, for example, was wont to write many of his verses in the margin of the pages of his farming diary. Institutional records, systematically kept in Gaelic by certain churches and Gaelic cultural and sporting societies, are more predictable in this regard, but their survival has often been more than a little haphazard! Material, handed down through generations of families, has also been located through responses to advertising in Australian newspapers for any such material.

The editors are conscious of the fact that their own researches in Australia and overseas have been more thorough in some archives than in others and that much, therefore, still remains to be carried out. However, it is hoped that the items collected and presented in this present volume will stimulate readers to sift through their own 'handed-down' personal records and, perhaps, tease out Gaelic riches whether they are in the form of letters, diaries and journals..

To an extent the editors have 'artificially' arranged their material to follow a certain progression. Firstly, the verse and prose have been grouped under self-explanatory thematic headings with short introductions provided to each. Where it is known, the date on which an item first appeared, and its author, is given. With some few exceptions the majority of the material was written by the assisted emigrant from the Highlands - the shepherd, the rural worker, the labourer – and thus there does not appear to be any particular 'style' which was followed in much of this writing. Many of the pieces were written as songs and set to familiar tunes and it is obvious that the authors expected, at least in the intimacy of their previous home or local neighbourhood, that their words would be sung and their sentiments made known to family and to neighbours.

Secondly, while it is a reasonably simple matter to establish the chronology of most of the pieces in this anthology, there is a broader chronology of the course of immigrant life to be discerned through the range and scope of the sample of writings given here. The pen of the newly-arrived immigrant drips nostalgia in every word of his contributions. In a new land it becomes important to 'fix' and celebrate the landscapes and activities of home – things that few ever expected to see again in the course of their lives. Thus, even when the theme may be a daily activity in Australia, the point of reference may often be set firmly in the time and space of the homeland. Donald MacKinnon, for example, was especially adept at turning an Australian time and space activity, such as a harvest, into a contemplation of life and activity back in his native Coll at that same time.

While many of the early immigrants to Australia consisted of Highlanders and Islanders who had been 'cleared' from their homeland, this was not the whole story. However, the experiences of many of these Highland settlers at having been 'cleared' continued to simmer even after many years in the colonies and barbs directed at clan chiefs and landowners, continued to appear in their poetry. Angus Beaton's graphic account in Òran an Eilthirich along with the anger and bewilderment in Ewen MacIntyre's An Gaidheal a' Fàghail a Dhùthcha, demonstrate the depth of feeling which existed against what the landowners had done to their people.

While anger at being forced off their traditional plots provided inspiration for many of the initial poems, many more emigrants, assisted or otherwise, came looking for a better life for themselves and their children. As years passed, the acuteness of the nostalgia and the homesickness did abate to a certain extent to the point where some emigrants began to write in praise of certain features of their new land. A similar pattern is to be seen, too, in cultural matters. Initially it was intensely important to ensure on-going Gaelic worship, and to set up societies in an attempt preserve Highland sports and customs and language. This is the phase of establishing a psychological Gaidhealtachd. But life was being lived in Australia now, not in Scotland, and the Highlanders were a small proportion of the overall community within which they had to live and work and play.

Thus, over time, there were growing interactions with the new society and this was reflected in the type of Gaelic material being written and its subject matter. This included Gaelic advertisements appearing in newspapers urging Highlanders to vote for certain candidates in local and State elections. Social issues such as drunkenness and unemployment and land reform were also addressed through public and private Gaelic writings.

Outside of the local sphere, we find Gaelic engaging with international events. Poems in Gaelic relating to Crimea, the Boer War and An Cogadh Mhòr, and to other major, contemporary experiences, found their way into the local and overseas press. Events of concern, too, back in the homeland, such as the continuing clearances, the distress of the people and the demise of their traditional way of life, drew prose and poetical comment from Gaels in the Australian colonies. It is notable that when struggles for land in Australian began in earnest from the second half of the nineteenth century, such struggles were often set, in prose and through verse, in the context of fighting against the Australian equivalent of the greedy Highland landowners of the clearances.

Perhaps too, on the part of some, realising the uncertain future of Gaelic, there is the desire, such as that of Donald Beaton, originally from Mull, to take on the role of folklorist or story-teller as with Cù Dubh a' Chuain Ghuirm and Sgeulachd na Trì Saighdearan. Traditional tales in prose and poetry, customs and experiences of their past in the homeland are anxiously put into writing to preserve them. For example, Donald Beaton's regret, appended with his final contribution, that death will prevent him finishing a particular piece of traditional lore, illustrates how such Gaels saw the importance of their work.

The editors of this Anthology are conscious, then, that what has been gathered and what has been presented in this volume inadequately represents the labour of many individual Gaels in writing original material, in rehearsing long–remembered lore and in committing to writing stories and songs which may well have been lost. The editors owe a sincere expression of gratitude to those who, in their land of exile, sought to pass on elements of their Gaelic culture. We apologise for having neglected them for so long and for the inadequate efforts, so far, to uncover the totality of their contributions.

If any part of this initial anthology excites the interest of readers, the editors hope that the same measure of enthusiasm and excitement which inspired them in their research will spur others, in Scotland and Australia, to continue the search to fill an important gap which exists in our Antipodean Gaelic heritage and history.

The editors' work in collecting and translating material should also be explained. Neither of the two editors is a native Gaelic-speaker, although both have been learning for some time. As learners, the editors are aware that there is a vast gulf between simply translating each of the words and understanding idioms, and other literary devices, which poets and writers use in their creative work. It must be realised, too, that not all Gaelic-speaking Highland emigrants were literate in writing Gaelic.

Formal schooling was not equally available for all across the Highlands and Islands and this led to many of the Highland settlers being unable to write or spell their own tongue. There are examples, for instance, of some of the writers composing in a form of phonetic Gaelic spelling. Others offer up apologies that the years had robbed them of their competence in Gaelic spelling and requesting the editor of the particular journal or newspaper to correct their composition before printing it. It was also the case that many of the original documents, such as letters and diary entries, had deteriorated over the years and this, together with some poor penmanship, made it difficult to read certain words or passages when it came to transcribing and translating them.

For these reasons, the editors have, where necessary, engaged in using a method of 'free translation' for many of the poems included in this Anthology. This does not imply that the meaning of words or lines has been changed but only that a strict literal, word for word, translation has not been followed. Instead, it is the meaning of the line which has been presented and, as far as possible, the integrity of the verse structure has been retained. The editors have followed, therefore, the basic rule of translation in not reading into the translation anything that was not in the original nor omitting anything from the translation which was in the original.

Lastly, what this initial offering does not do is to offer any judgment as to the quality of the Gaelic verse presented. The editors do not regard themselves qualified to be able to offer an assessment as to the quality, style, creativity or originality of the material contained in this volume. The nineteenth century saw a transition from the high 'classical' style of previous centuries of Gaelic poetry to a more 'modern' presentation of lines and rhythm. Even within the nineteenth century itself, there is a clear difference between early and later compositions.

Not all Gaelic poetry in this, or in any other period, dealt only with the grand themes of life. Thus, although the editors' selection does provide examples of musings on man's 'birth, life and death' trajectory, it also recognises the satirical, the whimsical and the humorous spirit in which other pieces were composed.

"It is from this 'Pedlar's Pack' of lore, as well as personal experiences, that items have been chosen for inclusion in this initial Sgeulachdan Goirid agus Bàrdachd à Astràilia – Short Tales and Poems from Australia. The editors, in offering this initial collection, hope that the reader will share the same spirit of one of the contributors when he appended to his story the sentiment, "agus ma 's breug bhuam i 's breug dam 'n ionnsuidh I" – ["and if any of this has entertained you I am pleased."]

Section One - Leaving

For those Gaels – the vast majority - whose emigration was forced, propelled by rural impoverishment or a desire for a better life - departure amounted to a final leave-taking of their traditional homeland, their friends and, often, close family members. Some of the poets conflated the lands and the kin they were leaving with the heroic landscapes and valiant warriors of Highland mythology (*An Gaidheal a' Fàghail a Dhùtcha*). All understood that their prospects of ever returning to familiar locales and settlements, of ever again seeing family and friends, were negligible, although some did express this hope, perhaps more out of personal reassurance than reality, in their verse. For those, such as Lochaberman (*An t-Abrach aig Uaighean a Dhìlsean*), whose path to his point of departure took him through his local church graveyard where many of his family and friends already lay, depopulation had already reduced the ties attaching him to his homeland. All, of course, felt apprehension about what they were sailing to although the extent, the danger and the conditions of the voyage were experiences for which few, if any, would have had any preparation either physically or psychologically.

Remembrances of the manner by which some of the Highlanders were treated and "herded" onto the emigrant ships left many, such as Angus Beaton, from Mull, with an attitude of bitterness. We can hear this especially in the early verses of his *Òran an Eilthirich.*

Other departures were accompanied with community-wide expressions of grief.

Donald Beaton's leaving, for example, along with many others from his native Mull, was accompanied by a community outpouring of grief as seen in "*An latha dh'fhàg Dòmhull Dearbhaig*"

Ewen McIntyre, Donald MacKinnon and the anonymous Gael leaving his homeland, all composed poems recalling vividly the places, the people, the hospitality, the fauna, the customs and so on from which the voyage had separated them. Not far below the surface, in a number of the poems and prose such as *An Gaidheal a' Fàghail a Dhùtcha*, is a note of resentment over the causes of their exile. For some, these causes included the clearances and the in-coming 'foreigners' bringing lowland sheep and sporting deer walks. All of this, including the general industrial and economic revolution which had transformed England, brought defeat to the (lingering) traditions of the ancient Highland heroes, and imposed a toxic mixture of language, customs, dress and attitudes, all of which formed an 'acid' which was, before the very eyes of the Highlanders, dissolving their culture.

It was the case, of course, that not all those who left did so because they were physically 'cleared' from their homes or crofts. Some left of their own volition, although 'Hobson's Choice' may be a better term to use. However, it would be correct to generalise that all those who left as "assisted" emigrants did so because of poverty, distress and a sense of hopelessness. It was also the case that not all departure poems were totally pessimistic. Duncan Campbell's *Guma Slàn do na Fearaibh* was a rousing call to optimism as it set out its list of the benefits awaiting the emigrants when they reached Australia. Some, too, saw in what was happening, the outworking of God's Providence and took a measure of comfort from this belief.

1 An t-Abrach a Fàghail a Dhùthcha

[le Eoghan Mac-an-t-Shaoir]

Gur muladach tha mi sgur cràiteach tha m' inntinn
Toirt soiridh gu bràtha gum chàirdean 's gum dhilsean
Toirt m' aghaidh air saile gu fàgail mo rìoghachd
'S gu dol thun na tìr as nach till mi ri m' bheò.

'S mi fàgail an àit' anns am b' àbhaist dom shinnsre
Bhi aon-ghilte, càirdeil, le nàbuigheachd dhìleas,
Gu h-ionmhasach, stòrasach, sòlasach, innt'neach,
Gun aimhreit, gun mhi-thlachd, gun mhi-rùn, gun ghò.

Gun mhi-ghean, gun bruaidlein, gun tuaireap,
Mur tigeadh luchd-fuadain thoirt uatha na bh' aca;
Nan tigeadh bu luath-chasach ruaig orra dhachaidh,
Nuair dh'èireadh na gaisgich bha sgairteil 's an tòir.

Bu tric chaidh ar sinnsearaibh dìleas 's an tuasaid
Thoirt cùis do fhir-Shasuinn le 'n glas-lanan cruadhach
Ach dh'fhaoghluim an linn so bhi sìobhalta,
Bhi strìochdadh d' an uachdrain mar thruaghain gun treòir.

Nuair thàinig Prìonns' Tearlach a nall thair an t-shàile,
'Sa sgaoil e 'san t-Slataich a bhrataichean àrda
Bha faraid a's sireadh air gillean an là sin
Aig daoine tha an-dràsta orra farail gu leòir.

'S nam biodh Mac an Toisich le chòmhlain do ghillean
An-diugh air Srath-Lochaidh 's e toiseach' ri iomairt
Bhiodh sodal gu leòir rinn, a's gleòramus milis,
Aig dream rinn ar milleadh le miodal am beòil.

'S nam b' ann chum an fheachda no ghleachd ri ar nàmhaid
Bhiodh uaislean ar cinnidh 'gar sirreadh mur b' àbhaist
Gu onair ar dùthcha a's cliù do na Gaidheil
Chan fhaict' aig an t-shluagh liuthad gruaidh fo na deòir.

Chan ann airson droch-bheirt no olcas ar giùlain
A tha iad 'gar bho 'r n-eolas 's bho 'r dùthchas
Ach meud 's tha don dhìonaich na cridheachan dùbailt
Tha riaghladh ar dùthcha 's nach dùbhraichd dhuinn lon.

Ged thèid sinn gur n-innleachd le dìchioll 's le saothair
Toirt falais ar fèithean troimh 'r leinntean na bhraonabh

Cha chum sinn sinn-fèin ach air èiginn bhon daonachd
Gun bhiadh na gun aodach mar dhaoine bhi oirnn.

'S mar sin sann is èiginn dhuinn gèill thoirt gu bràth
Do shocair fon ghrèin mur a d' thèid sinn thar sàil
Far am faigh sinn am fearann na mhachraichean fàsail
'S nach iarr am fhèill-Martuinn na màil oirnn nì 's na.

'S chan fhaicear mi tuilleadh lem ghunna ri làmhaich
Air srath na air mullach toirt fuil air an làn dàmh
Cha siubhail mi Ghiubhsach lem chù no lem spàinntich
'S cha dùisg mi mun Bhan-Ath'm fear àrd fa 'm bi chroic.

Chan fhaicear gu bràth mi mar bha mi lem nighnaig
Ag èisdeachd na h-àbhachd 's a mhanrain bu mhilse
Cha phaisg mi 'n am achlais i 'm bhreacan fo 's n-ìosal
'S cha socraich mi m' intinn air brìodal a beòil.

Lochabar, Lochabar, Lochabar, nan àrd-bheann,
Nan stùchd-bheanna casa, 's nan glacagan fàsaich,
'S e dh'fhàg mi fo èislein gur èiginn dhomh t-fhàgail
S' bhi triall as an àite rinn m' àrach 's mi òg!

Taobh Loch Liobhunn.

A Lochaberman Leaving His Country
[by Ewan MacIntyre]

Cease your melancholy grief, my mind,
Say farewell for ever to friend and family.
My face is set to the sea, to leave my homeland,
To go to a land from which I will never return.

I am leaving my traditional land,
Sincere, kind, with genuine neighbourliness,
Without wealth, comfort, stores or conceit,
Without contention, without resentment, without deceit.

Without complaint, or strife, without tumult, or rashness,
Fellow exiles come bringing nothing with them
In their swift banishment from their homes,
When no warrior arose to defend them.

Our loyal ancestors often went to battle
Taking issue with the English with their grey steel blades;
But we have learned in this generation to be peaceful, civil,
To be obedient to the rulers, as subjects without power.

When Prince Charlie came across the sea,
He raised the Stately banners high
Appealing to the young men of that day.
Now there are people aplenty.

And if it were MacIntosh with a company of young men
Today on Strath Lochy, and he in the van of the conflict,
There would be flattery enough and boasting,
But it was through flattery our people were destroyed.

And the army took the fight to our enemy,
The nobles of our clan leading as usual;
Honour to our country and praise to the Gael
Yet never was seen so many tearful countenances.

It was not for our wicked behaviour
That they exiled us from friends and country,
But because of the greed of deceitful hearts;
Our country's chiefs have no concern for our hunger.

Though toiling hard at what has been allotted to us,
Sweating and straining our every muscle in the rain,

It was with difficulty we kept ourselves from charity,
As a people who are without food, without clothes.

And because of this we have to yield for ever
Our peace beneath the sun, unless we go across the sea
Where we will get land, not desolate machairs*,
And none will require the Martinmas** rent from us.

I shall never more be seen with my shooting gun
On strath or on summit, taking the full-grown stag,
Nor crossing the Ghiubhsach*** with my dog and gun
Nor to awaken on Bhan-Ath'm the chief of the hills.

I shall never be as I was with my daughter
Listening to the music and play that was sweet,
Nor wrap my humble plaid around her
Tenderly expressing comforting words to her.

Lochaber, Lochaber, Lochaber of the high peaks,
Of the steep rocky mountains, and of desolate valleys,
In grief and under compulsion did I leave.
Leaving the place of my youth and rearing!

Beside Loch Leven.

Loch Leven, Scotland

2 Naidheachd bho *An Teachdaire Gaidhealach*

Tha iadsan a fhuair an arach ann an dutchaich na' fraoch-bheann, nan sluagh air leth. Ged a sgapar iad, mar na h-Iudhaich o shean, a-measg chearnaibh iomallach an domhain gheibhar iad a "Leanntuinn gu dlù ri cliù an sinnsear", a thaob a 'n daimh ris a Ghaeltachd gun lagachadh air bith.

Nach cruaidh, màta, gum biodh sluagh aig a bheril uiread spèis da 'n dutchaich air am fogradh air falbh o fhearann an athaireichean, le uachdrain an-iochdmhor; seadh gu cinnteach; ach tha a 'm Freasdal gu minic, a tionndadh ain-tighearnas nan daoine gu mor-bhuanachd don t-sluagh bhochd a tha iad a fuadach as an dutchaich.

Tha miltean, aig an am seo, ann an Astraillia, a chaidh, chan e mhain a bharlinneachdh, ach a chuir a-mach as an taighean, le maoir, anns a' Ghaeltachd, a tha moran nis fearr dheth na iadsan a thug a leithid do dhroch-abhaisteachadh dhaibh.

'S e 'ar durachdna gun èirich gu maith do gach Gael a chuireas a chas air tìr anns na ceàrnaibh seo; agus chan eil teagamh again nach èirich, ma bhitheas iad fèin dichiollach bunailteach-mar a tha sinn toillicht' fhaicinn, a tha iad an coitchionntas. Bithith sinne 'g oidhearpachadh, o am gu am, nis urrainn duinn a dheanamh airson sonas aimsireil agus spioradail nan Gael `ardachadh.

Cat-Thaobh

Ged a tha dlù air seachd mìle-thar fhichead, de shluagh ann an Siorramachd Chat-thaobh, cha robh, a-rèir a chunntais ma dheireadh a fhuair sinn as a chèarna sin den Ghaeltachd, ach aon neach ann am prìosan Dhoirnich, baile na Siorramachd.

Cha mhòr de na Gaidheil nach eil fiosrach air na fòirneartan a dh'fhulaing na Cataich 'o ceann iomadh bliadhna. Bha iad air an droch-ghnàthachadh le uachdrain an-iochdmhor ann an caochladh dhòigheanaibh – air an geur-leanmhuinn airson a bhi gu coguiseach a cuir cùl ris an Eaglais Stèidhichte agus a leanmhuinn na h-Eaglais-Saoire – gu minic air am bàirlinneachadh as an fhearann a shealbhaich iad on athairaichan, agus leis a sin tha iad a-nis air an cunntas nan sluagh siochail, deadh-bheusach, agus nan eiseampleir da 'n luchd-dùtcha anns gach cèarna eile den Ghaeltachd.

News from The Messenger

They were reared in the country of the heath covered hill; a separate people. Though they are scattered as the Jews of old among the uttermost regions of the world, they, "Follow the fame of their fathers," without, at all, weakening their connection to the Highlands.

Is it not distressing, then, that a people as much attached to their country are expelled from the land of their ancestors, by merciless rulers; indeed, it is; but Providence frequently turns oppression of the people to great advantage to the poor who were driven out of the country.

Thousands, who are at this time in Australia, who left not only by being given a warning to quit, but by being put out of their homes in the Highlands by the bailiff, are better off now than those who behaved viciously towards them.

We wish every Highlander well that puts foot in this region; and we have no doubt that they will succeed if they are diligently stable, in a community, as we are pleased to see they are. We will be endeavouring, from time to time, to do what we can to ensure the temporal and spiritual prosperity of the praiseworthy Highlander.

Sutherland

Though there are close to twenty-seven thousand people in the county of Sutherland, according to the last account we had from that region of the Highlands, there was only one person in prison at Dornoch, the county town.

There are not many Gaels who do not know of the oppression suffered by the Sutherland people over many years. They were badly treated by their merciless masters in changing the system of land holding – persecuting those who, for conscience sake, forsook the Established Church and adhered to the Free Church – frequently being given notice to quit from off the land they had inherited from their ancestors, and even in the face of that they are counted as a quiet and otherwise well-behaved people, and an example of their fellow-countrymen in every other region of the Highlands.

Fasachadh na Gaidhealtachd

Fasachadh na Gaidhealtachd:- Is ro bhrònach leinn e bhi again ri innseadh nach do sguir na tighearnam Gaelic fhathast do bhi fògradh nan Gael fo fhearann ann sinnsre. Fhuair gach teaghlach a tha an Achanaseileach, air strath Loch Caruinn bàirlinn gus an t-àite fhàgail air a' Chuingeis seo dh'fhalbh.

'S ann a sin a bha cheathairne choir fhialuidh, a bha tighinn beò cho math 's bu mhiann leò fo riaghaladh cluinn càirdeil, fhir na Comraich. 'Se na h-eunndairean a's coireach ris a seo le bhi toirt droch comhairle air an duin-uasal dom buin a t-àite.

Bithidh a-nis an srath bòidheach tàcarach seo na fhrìth fhàsail fo fhèidh 's fo eunlaith a's sliochd nan sonn air am fuadach …

Depopulation of the Highlands

We are very sad to relate that the Highland proprietors have not yet stopped ejecting Gaels from the land of their ancestors. Every family that is in Achanseileach, on strath Loch Carron, received a summons of removal requiring them to leave that place at Whitsuntide.

They were an honest and hospitable peasantry becoming prosperous, and they chose to settle under a friendly patron. It is the factors who are to blame for this by giving bad advice to the gentleman to whom the place belonged.

Now this beautiful valley, a byword for fertility, will be deserted and put under deer and birds and the descendants of the heroes banished …

Luchd-Imric Ghaidhealach

Dh'fhàg long da 'n ainm am *Persia*, Sasunn, deireadh Juli, le da cheud de luchd-imric Ghaidhealach, airson Hobart Town, Tasmania. Cha d' ràinig an long seo ceann h-ùidhe fhàthast, ach tha fiuthair rithe a h-uile latha.

A-rèir a chunntais a fhuair sinn mun luchd-imric seo, 's croiteirean a chuid 's mo dhiù, bho chaochladh cheàrnaibh de Ghaeltachd 's de dh'Eileanna na h-Alba, agus faoidaidh e bhi gu bheil nam measg Teaghlaichean dìchiollach, oidhirpeach, a dh'fhulaine mora nana-cothrom bho nach drain chruaidh-chridheach mhi-sheirceil a bha gam feannadh le mail fad bhliadhnachan, agus nuair nach b' urrainn dhaibh na "h-eucoraich olc" sin a dhìoladh, gun deachdaich am barlinn eachadh as an fhearann a bha 'ig an athaireachean, agus cead an coise a thoirt dhaibh a dh'iarruidh dachaidh anns an ceàrnaibh an domhin.

Taing don Fhreasdal tha farsuingeachd gu leòir an Tasmania, air an son …

Highland Immigrants

A ship, of the name *Persia*, left England at the end of July, with two hundred Highland immigrants, for Hobart Town, Tasmania. The ship has not reached this destination yet, but she is expected any day.

According to the accounts we got about these immigrants, many of the men are crofters, from the changing regions of the Highlands and Islands of Scotland, and it may be that among some of the enterprising families many will have suffered from the grim-faced, hard-hearted, uncharitable landlords and burdened with rents all year, and when they were not able to pay that "unjust evil", without warning they got summons of removal from the land of their fathers and sought permission to request a home in the remote corners of the world.

Thanks to Providence there is plenty of room in Tasmania, for their sake …

3 Slàn le Beanntan

[Neo-Ainmichte]

Slàn le beanntan an fhraoich
Dhosach, ghucagach, chaoin,-
Badan suaicheantais dheadh Chloinn-Dòmh'uill,-
Le shugh meala a's cèir,
Tàladh 'n t-seillein, 's an fheidh
A's 'g an sàsach' dheth fèin le sògh;
'S a toirt fasgaidh ri fuachd
Do chaoraich 's do dh-uam,
'S, do na cearcagan ruadh, an lòn
'S a' toirt fasgaidh … etc,

'S le Gleanndaruail mo chridh',
Righ gach glean tha 's an tìr!
Far an d' araicheadh mi bho m' òig-
Gleann nan coilltean 's nam raon,
Gleann nan glacag 's nan craobh,
Gleann nan aighean, nan laogh, 's nam bò;
Gleann nam bradan 's nan greis,
Gleann nan cam-lùba min,
Gleann is pailte 's cinn gach pòr!
Gleann nan bradan … etc.,

Far am binne na h-eoin,
Far an grinne na h-oigh'n,
'S iad gu ceileireach, ceòlmhor, coir;
Modhail, beusach, gun ghruaim,
Teisteil, cuirtteil, grin, suairc',
Tuigseach, fòghluimte, stuaim; gun phrois;
Dreachail, meachair, gun mheang,
Ann am pearsa 's an cainnt,
'S iad deas, nosail, gun sgraing, gun sgleò.
Dreachail, meachair, … etc,

A's na fleasgaich is àill',
Foinnidh, fearail, làn bàigh,
Uasal, smiorail, air sràid 's aig mòd;
'S iad àrd-inntinneach, dian;
'S anns an tìr am mòr mhiadh –
'S iad a sheasadh gun fhiamh a' choir!
'Reachadh foirmeil 's an strìth,
Bheireadh nàimhdean fo chìs,
A's nach gèilleadh gu sìorruidh beò.
Rachadh foirmeil, … etc,

M' an cuir gleanntan m' an cuairt
Dhiùbh cranndachd an fhuachd,
Bidh Gleanndaruail nam buadh 'n a ghlòir;
Bidh craobh-ubhal fo bhlàth,
Bidh an duilleach aig, fhàs,
'S ceileir cuthaig an sgàth nam fròg;
Mac-'S-'Illeathain le phìob,
'N àm na grein bhi a' dol sìos,
A' toirt fuaim as an tìr le 'cheol.
'S Mac-'Illeathain … etc,

A chaidh – teangain an àigh,
Soraidh slàn leat gu bnràth!
'S leis gach neach a tha'tamh air d' dhòd,-
Slàn le cuideachd mo ghràidh,
Slàn le m' athair 's le m' mhàth'ir,
Slàn le m' pheathraichean bàigheil, òg;
Slàn le m' bràithrean gu lèir,
Slàn le m' chàirdean 's luchd-spèis,
Slàn le uiseag nan speur 's a ceòl!
        Slàn le m' bràithrean … etc,

'S eiginn domhsa nis triall,
Dh'fhàgail dùthaich nan triath,
Nam filidh nam cliar 's nan seòd;
Na h-earba, 's an fheidh,
Agus iolair nan speur,
Na h-eala, nan peuc, a's nan còrr;
Nan sìthean, 's nan cruach,
A's nan dùn, a's nan bruach,
Nan doire, nan cluan, a's nan còs
        Nan sìthein … etc,

Ged tha 'n dùth'ch so làn bhuadh,
'S iomadh diomb tha rith' fuaight',-
Cha chum ceilear na cuaich rium lòn,-
Than a fearainn ro dhaor,
A's na tuarasdail saor,
'S chan eil farraid air saothair dhaoin' òg;
Ach tha sùil ris an long
Tha gu m' aiseag thar thonn,
Gu Australia, fonn an fheòir,
        Ach tha sùil … etc,

Farewell – Glendaruel
[Anon]

Farewell to the heather-clad mountains
Abundant, blooming, flowering-
Worthy ensign of Clan Donald-
With the sweetness of the honeycomb,
Enticing the bee; and the deer
Satisfying itself with the delicacies;
And providing shelter from the cold
To sheep and lambs,
And food to the little red hens.
    Providing shelter from … etc,

It is beside my dear Glendaruel,
King of all other glens,
Where I was raised from my youth-
Glen of the woods and the plain,
Glen of the dell and the tree
Glen of the deer, the calf and the cow
Glen of the salmon, and the hero
Glen of peaceful meandering waters,
Glen abounding in every kind of plant!
    Glen of the salmon … etc,

Where the music of the birds,
And the beauty of the maidens
Sing in harmony their melodious air
Delicate, gentle without melancholy,
Pure, respectful, elegant, kind,
Intelligent, learned, modest, without pride;
Comely, tender, faultless,
In [their] appearance and speech,
And, true to custom, they are without anger or darkness.
    Comely, tender … etc,

The pretty lassies, and the handsome lads
Elegant, manly, full of affection,
Noble, lively, whether walking or dancing;
And high-minded they are with keenness;
Greatly respected in their land-
And standing, without fear, for justice,
They would willingly enter the fray
And [would] bring their enemies under subjection
Never yielding while they lived.
    Would willingly … etc,

Other glens were round about
Witheringly cold and chill;
But Glendaruel is glorious
With the apple tree in bloom
And the foliage lush;
The cuckoo singing from its hidden nook
And McLean with his pipes
With the sun going down
Giving voice to the land with music.
    And McLean … etc,

The glorious tongue is gone
Farewell to you forever!
And to every one resting in the grave-
Farewell also to my love,
Farewell to my father and mother
Farewell to my affectionate young sisters;
Farewell to my many brothers,
Farewell my friends and esteemed people,
Farewell skylark of the heavenly song!
    Farewell my many brothers … etc,

It is necessary for me to depart
To leave the homeland of the hero,
Of the bard and the renowned warrior;
Of the roe, and the deer,
And of the eagle in the heavens.
The swan, the peacock and the heron;
Of the knolls and the peaks,
And the hill and the bank,
Of the grove, the green fields and the cave.
    Of the knolls … etc,

Though this country is full of endowments
There is much dissatisfaction against her;
She cannot provide me with food, drink or shelter;
The land is too dear,
And the wages too low,
And the young are not offered work;
But the eye is towards the ship
To my deliverance across the waves,
To Australia, the grassy land.
    But the eye … etc,

4 An Gaidheal a' Fàghail a Dhùthcha

[le Eoghan Mac-an-t-Shaoir]

A Ghlinn mo ghraidh! Rinn m' àrach òg,
An èiginn t-fhàgail 's mi gun treòir,
An èiginn, domh, 's do chloinn mo ghaoil,
Falbh gun dùil ri tionndadh chaoidh?

An èiginn domhs' fa dheireadh triall,
Is falt mo chinn na dhualaibh liath,
Èarr mo làithean ruith gu luath,
Mar chloich 'na dèan o àrd na cruaich.

Ceò na h-aois mum shùilibh dall
Mo chasan lag nach gluais ach mall;
Air chàileachd fhodha nach tog fonn;
'S mo chridhe fann air fàs ro throm.

Is faoin domh fèin bhi g' èisteachd ceòil,
Cha dùisgear tuillidh mi on bhròn;
Luigh mòr ghriann siar fo stuaidh,
'S cha till i dhomhsa chaoidh le buaidh.

A bhean mo ghaoil, 's beusa ciùin
Na biodh do dheòir a' ruith co dlùth;
Oir claoidhidh bròn do neart 's do chàil,
Gun neach 'm bheil iochd no dàimh a' d' dhàil.

Is goirt lem chridh do chor a ghaoil,
Aois gad chlaoidh mi fèin gun fheum
An t-àite an d' fhuair sinn riamh ar leòir
Chan ionad tàimh dhuinn e nis mò.

Tha muinntir eil air teachd dar tìr,
A's sìol san treun gan cur a dhìth,
Siol nan treun, a ghlèidh le buaidh
Air beanntan àrd, a's traigh a chuain.

Ach thrèig iad fèin a gach euchd a rinn,
'S tha sinn an-diugh an sliochd gun sgoinn
Mar chuiseag fhaoin fo th'aom gach sian,
Air call air neart ar meas, ar miagh.

Gluaisibh, chlann na muinghinn threin,
'S gum faigh sibh iochd fo chaochladh grèin,
Ge caomh leibh beanntan àrd ri ur n-òig,
'S gann gum faic sibh iad ri ur beò.

Triallaibh dh'ionnsaigh cuan nan stuagh
Ach och mo chreach cha b' e mo luaidh,
B' annsa luidh sìos gu ciùin
Mar ri m' dhaimhich anns an ùir.

'S tric o'm shùil na deura trom
'S mi sealltinn air gach làrach lom
Am faca uair mo chàirdean treun,
Ge fada n' diu gach aon a cheil.

Cha chluinn mi tuillidh 'n còmhradh gaoil,
Moch na feasgar air 'n raoin;
Tha 'n gleann a b' aoibhach fuaim as ceoil,
Gu tosdach balbh, mar neach ri bròn.

Càit an deach na h-ogair threun?
Càit an deach na h oighean caoin?
Càit 'm bheil n aois gun ghruaim?
Càit 'n ceòl b' àirde fuaim?

Càit am bheil na bòrdaibh fial
Bheireadh do gach acrach biadh?
Sgapadh iad le fòirneart geur
'S cha neil a h-aon 'n diu le chèil.

Fhir a shiubhlas glean mo ghaoil
Na meallar thu le buathraibh faoin,
Oigh cha ghlac do damh gu bràth;
'S chan iarr i thu gu h-ionaid tàimh.

Chan fhaic thu i le cuach fo chroic
Moch na feasgar teachd on chrò,
Nì mò chluinn thu ceòlan binn,
Tional ghabhrag bhreac sna ghlinn.

'S faoin bhi 'g iarraidh 'n aosda choir
A shuidh gu tric ri taobh an ròid

Sgeul chan iarr uat, no dàn,
Cuirm na fleagh cha sgaoil gu bràth.

Ge fann do cheum, 's ge faoin do dhòigh,
Caomh chan fhaic thu anns an ròd;
Tha àite an tàimh na làrach fhuair,
Fo eanndag ghlais-fo choinnich uaine.

Iarr 's an fheur an teach bha fial,
A's gheibh an stairsneach caitht' gu train;
Leac 'n teine, 's h-aogais ruadh,
Fraoich a's còinneach fàs mu bruaich.

Tha 'n cnocan glas gun ai na dhruim,
Far an tric a shuidh na suinn,
Far an rùisgeadh iad le chèil',
An rùn, 's am beachd, gun tlachd am beud.

Far an labhradh iad gu fial
Air gach treun bh' ann o chian
'S am macraidh òg le ioghnadh gràdh
A snaimh san sgeul a b' euchdach càil.

Ach feudaidh caochladh teachd ri àm,
'S gun iarrar sinne air feadh nam beann;
Ach beann na gleann cha toir a h-aon,
A leanas àrmuinn dh'ionnsuidh an raoin.

Aonaranach, fann, gun treòir,
Bithidh gach triath gun dàimh 'na choir,
Trèigear e le brosgul baoth
Nan gealtair cealgach ghlac a mhaoin:

Trèigear e 'na àmhghar geur,
Gun aon r' a thaic d' a chinne fèin:
Fada, fada thall thar chuan,
Sgaoilte gheibh e 'm fuigheall truagh.

Chì e 'n sin le deòir 'na shùil,
Am beud a chinnic leis an tùs,
'Nuair a dh'fhògair e o 'sgeith,
Na laochraidh b' fhèarr a bha fon ghrèin

Ach ged a shil an deòir gach ial,
Aon cha tìg, a chaoidh gan dìon:

Is cuimhne leò gach cràdh a's spìd,
A dh'fhuiling iad mun d' fhàg an tìr.

Dubhach cianail biodh an gleus,
Mar eun na h-oidhche 'n còs leis fèin;
Gus an claoidhear annt' le bròn,
Gaol an airgid ghlais 's an òir.

Gus an till an gràdh 's an t-iochd,
Is dual do athair thoirt da sliochd;
'S gum faic gach triath gur fèarr na trèin,
Na mìlte uan am mìle treud.

Ach 's cian mun lìonar rìs na glinn
A dh'oigridh ghlan, mar bh'ann ri m' linn:
Amhluidh darag 'thuit le gaoith,
Is fad mum fàs a faillein maoth.

Feudaidh sàmhladh teachd ri àm;
Ach 's lag an gaol, 's faoin an làmh;
Sliochd nan treun chan eighear dhiùbh,
San dàn cha chluinnear chaoidh an cliù.

An èigin duinn bhi triall, a ghaoil
Na sgaoileadh suas na siùil gaoith?
No m' feud sinn tàmh an nochd as ghleann,
San d' àraicheadh sinn fèin, sar clann?

Tha siùil ri croinn gan sgaoileadh shuas,
Is gaoth nam beann ag iarruidh chuain;
Tàmh nis faid chan fheudar leinn,
Ach iarramaid gun dàil na tuinn.

A chlann mo ghraidh! Cha dàil nis mò;
'S èigin falbh, 's chan ann dar deòn,
Ar cnuic ar glinn, sar beanntaibh àrd,
Fhàgail faoin gun chaoimh nan dàil.

Slàn le fèidh nam fraoch-bheann àrd,
On suain cha ghluais mi iad gu bràth,
Slàn le earbag bheag on raon,
'S faon a geilt mu meannan maoth.

Slàn le eoin is moiche seinn;
Slàn le beannaibh àrd, 's le coille,
Slàn le gabhraibh breac nam bruach;
Slàn le caoirich is le uain.

Slàn leis an teach bha farsuing fial,
Sa chòmhladh nach do dhrùideadh riamh
Slàn le leaca fuar na h-uaigh,
Fom bheil mo dhàimhich ciùin nan suain.

Slàn le Albainn ghleann is chnoc;
Oir 's èigin dhomhsa triall an nochd,
Gun dùil am feasd ri cois air t-fheur,
Mo chreach! Mo chràdh! 'S e fàth mo dheur'.

A Gael Leaving His Homeland

[by Ewan MacIntyre]

My beloved glens where I was reared;
Powerless, I was compelled to leave.
All of us, both young and old,
Forced to leave without hope of ever returning.

I was distressed at journey's end,
My fair hair turned grey as a result.
My last days are rushing to their end,
Like a stone speeding down a steep hill.

The mist of age dims my eyes,
My feeble legs are barely able to move.
My low spirit is unable to raise a song
And my heart grows increasingly heavy.

It is useless for me to listen to music,
Never more shall I be aroused from sorrow;
The full sun sets westward beneath the sea
And it shall never ever return for me.

My wife, my love, virtuous and gentle,
You should not weep tears so deeply;
Because such sad wearying saps your strength
Without friend or family for comfort.

My beloved, your condition is painful to my heart,
And though old and useless myself;
The place where we always had enough
Is no longer a place of rest for us.

Other people have come to our land
Banishing the children of the brave,
Descendants of the valiant, successful defenders
From the high mountains to the sea shore.

But they have gone, along with every deed they did,
And we today are the generation without power
like a helpless reed wilting under rough weather.
We have lost our strength, our respect, and our honour.

Rouse yourselves, children of the valiant brave,
You will find success under a different sun,
Though you loved the high mountains of your youth,
It is unlikely that you will ever see them again.

Travelling over the ocean waves
O my distress; were it not for my beloved
I would be glad to lie down in peace,
Like my friends in the grave.

Tears of grief are often in my eyes
as I picture every bare ruin.
My friends were once in full strength,
Though every one is long since buried.

I no longer hear the familiar conversation
early in the evening in the field;
Or the sound of beautiful music in the glen,
Quietly at peace, as a person in sorrow.

Where have the brave youths gone?
Where have gone the tender maidens?
Where are the cheerful aged?
Where is the echoing music?

Where are the tables of hospitality
that would feed the hungry?
They were scattered with cruel force,
There is not a single one today.

You will not see again the cuckoo below the hill
in early evening, coming from the sheep fold,
Or anymore hear the tinkling bells
of the goats gathering in the glens.

And it will be futile asking the old worthy,
Who often sits beside the road,
For a story or a song,
Neither feast nor hospitality shall ever again be offered.

Though your step is feeble, and your position hopeless,
You will not see hospitality on your path;
The place of refuge is now a cold ruin
Under withering nettles and green moss.

Search among the grass, the house was hospitable,
See how the threshold was quite worn with use;
And the hearthstone scorched brown with heat.
Now heather and moss grow about its edge.

The green hills are without sheep on their slopes,
Where often the men sat
clipping the wool together,
And recollecting, without pleasure, their fate.

Places where they much conversed
About every champion of old,
About youth and the wonder of love
And of swimming and tales of heroic feats.

But change has come with the passing of time;
And though we ask among the mountains,
Neither mountain nor glen can give an answer,
Except to follow the way of the hero.

Forsaken, feeble, without strength,
Every one will be friendless,
He will quit because of the vain flattery
of the deceitful coward who seized his property.

He will leave in painful sorrow,
Without anyone from his own clan to support him:
Far, far, across the ocean,
The poor remnant will become scattered.

He will see then through tearful eye,
The beginning of his nation's loss
When he was expelled without protection
from the best heroes under the sun.

But though tears continually fall,
No one will ever come to their defence:
The memory of every pain and tyranny remains,
But with forbearance they left the land.

Sad and sorrowful will be his state,
Like a bird in the night alone in its nest,
Until they are wearied with sorrow,
Longing for the golden dawn.

Until the love and the healing return,
Giving your father's inheritance to his descendants,
Then every chief will see that better than power
Is thousands of lambs from a thousand flocks.

But it will be long before the glens will be filled
By innocent youth, as it was in my day,
Like an oak tree felled by the wind,
The growth of tender shoots takes a long time.

Their likenesses may come in time,
But weaker will be their love, and vain their hand;
These will not be called descendants of the brave,
Their praise will never be heard in song.

What forced our departure
Spreading out like wind-filled sails?
May we not stay another night in the glens
Where we and our children were raised?

Sails on the masts are billowing out
And the mountain winds are asking the seas
to stay longer, but we may not,
And we would ask the waves not to linger.

My beloved children do not delay more;
It is painful, unwillingly leaving
our hills, our glens, and our high mountains,
Left lonely without a friend close by.

Farewell the deer and the mountain heath,
From abroad they are forever beyond my reach,
Farewell young roe from the plain,
And the skittish young goats.

Farewell birds and their dawn chorus;
Farewell the high mountains and the woods,
Farewell taking salmon by the river bank;
Farewell the sheep and their lambs.

Farewell the hospitable home
Whose door was never closed,
Farewell cold grave stone
Beneath where my gentle relatives sleep.

Farewell Scotland, glen and hill;
I will never tread your paths again
Because I am forced to depart this night.
Alas! My pain! This is the reason for my tears.

The Falls of Dochart, Killin, Scotland

5 Òran – Slàn Leat Albainn

[le Seumas Mac 'Ille-Mhaoil]

Slàn leat Albainn nan garbhlach, 's nan gleann;
Nam beantainnean binneach, nam fireach, 's nam meall;
Nam fuaran, nan easan, nam preasan, 's nan crann;
'S nan coireinnean uaine, le 'n cuid uan agus mheann.

Ged theirear gur cruaidh thu, greannach fuar agus lom,
Stùchdannach, sgòrrach, uchdach, corrach, làn thom;
Leam fhèin tha thu àluinn, sùgh'or, tlàth, bileach, donn,
Dubh-ghorm, guganach, àirneagach, Tìr thug bàrr air gach fonn.

'S iomadh tìr agus fearann 's an robh mi air chuairt
Làn ioghnaidh, miann ghaithean, agus choilltichen, uain',
Air nach seargadh an duilleach ri teas, turadh no fuachd,
Ach b' fhaoineis leam fhèin iad làmh ri slèibhtean mo luaidh.

Bha mi 'n rìogh'dan ainmeil air 'm bheil seanchas bho chian,
'An eachdraidhean sgrìobhta, maiseach, mìnealt' 'an sgiamh,
Le 'n craobhannan fige, us ciders 's deirg' fiamh:-
Cha choi'meas leam fhèin iad làmh ri d' shlèibhtean donn, ciar.

Nuair thig Samhradh a' Chèitein le ceutachd mun cuairt
Mu d' bheanntaibh slèibhteach, lusach, geuganach, uain',
B' e 'n t-aighear 'san t-èibhneas bhi siubhal rèidhleach 'us bhruach.
Moch 's a' mhaduinn 's mi 'g èisdeachd ceòl binn, èibhinn 'am chluais.

Ged nach fhaicear leam tuillidh do bheanntainnean fraoich,
'S nach cluinn mi do chuthag ann an dubhar nan craobh,
No do smeoraichean binne seinn gu fileanta, caoin,
'Chaoidh, chan fhuaraich mo spèis dhuit gus an gèill mi don Aog.

Farewell Scotland
[by James MacMillan]

Farewell my Scotland of rocky rivers and glens,
Of high peaked mountains, of moors and heights;
Of springs and cascades and thickets and trees,
And of lamb and kid in the green dells.

Though it is said that you are hard, cold and bleak,
Rocky, craggy and marshy, and full of thickets;
To me you are beautiful, strong, gentle, green and brown,
Abounding in dark-blue flowers and sloe. A land above all others.

I have lived in many a land and country
Full of wonder, with strong straight branches, and green woods
Whose leaves were not withered from heat or drought or cold,
But they were trifling compared to my own beloved mountains.

I have been in famous kingdoms with antiquities from afar,
Whose beauties are recorded in the old histories.
With fig trees, and red-tinged cedars-
They cannot, in my opinion, compare to the dark, brown mountains.

When summer comes with its pleasant weather all around
An abundance of plants grow green about the hills and mountains,
Joy and pleasure line every border of them,
And in early morning I hear the sweet music of happiness.

Though I will not see the mountain heather again,
Nor hear the cuckoo in the shadows of the tree,
Or the mavis, sweetly singing its soft melody,
My love for you will not wane until I yield to Death.

6 Cead le Dùthaich

[Neo-Ainmichte]

Fo' throm mhighean 's leisg mo ghluasad,
Gur a cruaidh lium bhi fàgail,
Tìr mo shinnsir, tìr na h-uaisle
A bha dual do chlann nan Gàidheal.

Tha mi fàgail na tìr Abraich
Agus caidreamh mo chàirdean
Chan eil m' aigne ach neo shùrdail
A's chan ioghnadh bhi ma'r tha mi.

Ciamar dh'fhaodas mi bhi sunndach
'S mi ag ionndrain nam beann àrda
Far an cluinnte damh na cròice
Ri àrd-dreòcam dol 's n damhair.

Tìr nam beanntaibh àrda fuar-ghlas,
Tìr nan gleanntaibh lurach tlàthail
Far am faighte sprèidh am buailidh
'S panal ghruagach measg an slaich.

'S cliùteach ainm nan Gàidheal gasda
Seòrsa reachd'or ri uchd nàmhaid
Luchd nam breacanibh gun ghealtachd
Uasal smachdail làn do dh'àrdan.

Seòladh air an fhairge dhubh-ghorm
An cuan ùdlaidh farsuinn gabhaidh
Fuachd a's teas mu seach a mùthadh
Ach na Dùilean chì sin sàbhailt.

Dol gu taobh mu dheas a chruinne
Far nach cluinear lium mar b' àbhuist
Fonn na smeòraich air na h-ògain
Ceòlmhor anns' a mhaduin mhàighe.

Bidh mi cuimhneachadh nan gleannaibh
Anns' an fhearan sin 's an d' àraicht'
Anns an d' ionnsaicht' lium na leanas
Rium gus 'n càirear mi fo chlàraibh.

O! mo bheannachd leis na stùcaibh
Mun tiugh dhuineas ceò nan àrdaibh
'S mu'r a faicear iad le m' shùilean
Bidh cuimhn' agam gu bràch orr'!

Farewell to the Land of the Mountains
[Anon]

In deep sadness, with reluctant step,
I am distressed at leaving
The land of my ancestors, land of the proud,
Birthright of the children of the Gael.

I am leaving the land of Lochaber
And the bosom of my friends.
My spirit is unwilling
And it is no wonder that it so.

How can I be cheerful?
I, longing for the high mountains.
Where is heard the antlered stag
With its high rutting cry.

Land of high mountains, grey-cold,
Land of the lovely, tranquil glens,
Where the cattle are in the fold
And young women at the threshing.

And the honoured name of the noble Gael,
A strong race, braving the enemy,
People of the tartan, untainted with cowardice,
Noble, lordly, full of pride.

Sailing on the black-blue ocean,
The gloomy sea perilous to us,
Cold and hot, changing by turn
But our Faith will see us safe.

I am going to the other side of the world
Where I shall not hear, as before,
The song of the thrush on its branch,
Melodious in the pleasant morning.

Memories of the glens,
And of the land where I was reared,
Will continue with me
Until I am laid beneath the earth.

Oh! my blessings on those hills,
A thick mist about their peaks,
And because my eyes have seen them
The memory of them will ever be with me.

7 An latha dh'fhàg Dòmhnall

[*The Celtic Monthly*]

An latha dh'fhàg Dòmhull Dearbhaig, b' e sin an latha; mu dhà-fhichead pearsa, eadar bheag is mhòr a' triall gu cladach 's Gilleasbuig Mac Pheadearain air on ceann, leis a' phìob a' seinn, "mo chùl, mo chùl, mo chùl ri Muile."

Mun d' ràinig e ceann a' bhaile b' fheadar dha a' phìob a phasgadh. B' e sin an sealladh! Cha robh fear, no bean no pàisde 'sa' bhaile nach robh a sileadh nan deur gu frasach, a' fàgail beannachd aig gach aon a bha trial.

8 Òran an Eilthirich

[Aonghas Peutan]

[Tha an t-òran a leanas a tabhairt mion chunntas air gach ni a thachair don luchd-imric 's don luing leis an do sheòl an t-ughdair, anns an Fhogaradh, 1852, 'on a dh'fhàg iad a Ghaeltachd gus an d-ràinig iad Astraillia, far an do dhealich e ri a' luchd-dùtcha ionmhainn – cuid diubh, theagamh, nach fhaicear leis tuillidh gu bràth.]

'S iomadh aon a bha brònach nuair a sheòl sinn fon chala
'S beag a bha, aca ri iunndrainn dhiult an grunnd ri 'n cuid barra;
Bha na mail riu ag èirigh, iad gun sprèidh air an fhearann,
Maoir a tighin 's bàirlin iad a dh'fhàgail a 'n taighean.

Bha sinn deasaich 's tuathaich eadar Cluaidh 's Lochcarruinn,
Agus dùthaich Shàir Seumas agus Slèibhte nam bradan,
'Sinn 's an luing ud le chèile mar threud air an aiseag,
'S gann gun gabhair ar n-àireamh thug am bàs uainn am deachamh.

The Day Donald left Dervaig

[*Celtic Monthly*]

The day Donald left Dervaig, there were that day about forty persons, small and big, that travelled to the beach and Archibald Mac Pheadrais was at the head, with pipes singing, "mo chùl, mo chùl, mo chùl ri Muille."

When he reached the top of the town he put down his pipes. It was quite a sight. There was not a man, or woman, or child from that town that was not shedding showers of tears, bestowing a blessing on each one who was leaving.

Song of the Exile

[Angus Beaton]

[Eds Note:- The following song gives a detailed account of everything that happened to the immigrants on board the ship on which the author, Angus Beaton, sailed in the autumn of 1852, when they left the Highlands until they reached Australia, parting from their beloved countrymen, some of them, doubtless, never to be seen again.]

Many were sad when we sailed from the harbour;
Though they had little to miss given their unproductive land;
Their rents were increasing, and they were without livestock,
While officers served notice that they must abandon their homes.

We were northern and southern Highlanders;
Between the Clyde and Loch Carron,
And the land of Sir James and Sleat of the Salmon,
Like animals ferried on to the ship we could scarcely be counted,
But, on board, death removed a tenth of our number.

9 An t-Abrach aig Uaighean a Dhìlsean

[le Eoghan Mac-an-t-Shaoir]

Tha m' aigne fo throm luasgan,
'S cha shuarach fàth mo shuim;
Mo spiorad tha air ghluasad
Ri cuimhneachadh nan uasal
Tha taisgte an cnuaic an tuim-
Agus cnuasachd tigh'n fom chuimne.
Na fir bha toirteil suaicheant'
'S am buaidhean mòr air chuimhn'.

An Cill-a-Chairioll uaignidh
Fodh leacibh fuaraidh 'n tamh,
Nan cadal anns' na h-uaighibh
Fo ghlasibh buan a bhàis;
Tha suinn a bha glè bhuadh'or
Le lùgh a's cruaidh's an làmh,
Ged tha iad anns an uair seo
Gun smior no smuais nan cnàimh.

Tha 'n teach 's an robh mo chàirdean
Na fhàrdaich air bheag sunnd;
Gun chridhealas, gun mhànran,
Gun àbhachd, 'se gun mhùirn,
Cha cluinnear pìob no clàrsach
Mar àbhaist, anns an dùn:-
Gun duin' an diugh a làthair dhiù
'Se 's fath dhomh bhi ga thùrs'.

Tha 'n Tuillaich a bha cluainear
A sealltain fuaraidh lom;
Chan fhaicear fiù an ruadh-bhuic,
Air fuaran no air tom,-
'San àit nan àrmunn uasal
Do'm bu dual a bhi 'san fhonn,
Chìthear Goill lem buachailean
Luchd fuadaich nan greigh-donn.

Nuair bheirt' a truaill na claidhean,
B' e 'n àbhaist bhi air thus;
A sheasamh suas ri nàmhaid,
Gun ghiorrag bhi nan gnùis:-
Bha mòran iochd agus bàigh annt',
Bu ghràdhach miann agus rùn,
Le cridhe fialaidh pàirteil
Nach iarradh sàs an cùis.

B' iad sliochd Iain Luibh an t-seòrsa,
'S bu mhòrchuiseach an cliù
'S ged a rinnt' orr' fòirneadh,
'S an còirichean thoirt diù,
Gu bheil mi ann an dochas
Gun d' orduicheadhadh na b' fhiù
Gach anam-dhiù bhi 'n solas
An glòir de Righ nan Dùl!

A Lochaberman at the Graves of his Kinfolk
[Ewan MacIntyre]

My mind is under heavy dread,
And not without good cause;
My spirit is agitated,
Recollecting what is in my mind
Commemorating the worthy people
Who are buried on the hill side;
Men notable for their generosity
And remembered for their great victories.

Resting beneath cold flagstones
In solitary Cill-a-Chairioll,
Asleep in their grave -
Under pale, eternal death -
Are Heroes who were mighty in victory,
Powerful with spear in hand,
Though they are now
without strength or vigour in their bones.

In what was my friend's house
There is little joy now around the hearth;
Without cheerfulness, without music,
Without merriment and without hospitality.
Now, neither pipes nor harp shall be heard,
As was customary at the castle:-
Without the presence of a man of worth today.
This is the cause of my great sorrow.

Tullaich*, which was peaceful,
Looks cold and bare;
The worthy roe-buck shall not be seen
At pool or on hillside-
In the place of the noble chief,
Who held the hereditary right of land,
Is now seen Lowlanders with their shepherds.
The people have been expelled for brown deer.

When sword blades were unsheathed
They were in the van as usual;
Standing up to the enemy,
Without fear on their faces:-
They were overwhelmingly generous and merciful,
With loving intention, kindly and affectionate
With bountiful hearts,
Not seeking anything in return.

They were descendants of Iain Luibh,
Renowned for their heroism,
And though this intrusion was forced on them,
As the records bear witness,
I am in hope,
Though no one is worthy,
That every noble soul will be a light
To the glory of the God of All!

*Part of the Buachaille Etive Mòr range, Glen Coe, in the Scottish Highlands.

10 Guma Slàn do no fearaibh

[Dòmhnall Caimbeul]

Guma slàn do no fearaibh,
Thèid thairis a' chuan
Gu talamh a' gheallaidh
Far nach fairich iad fuachd,
Gum a sl`an do na fearaibh
Thèid thairis a' chuan.

'Nuair dh'fhàgas s 'n t-`ait' so,
Cha chuir iad mòr-mhàl oirnn
'S cha bhi an Fheill Màrtainn
'Cur nàire 'n ar gruaidh.
Gum a sl`an do na fearaibh
Thèid thairis a' chuan.

Gum fàg sinn an tìr so
Cha chinnich aon nì ann
Tha 'm buntat' air dol 'dhìth ann
'S cha chin iad le fuachd.
Gum a slàn do na fearaibh
Thèid thairis a' chuan.

Gheibh sinn sìod' agus sròl ann
Gheibh sinn pailteas de 'n chlòimh ann
'S ni na mnathan dhuinn clò dheth
Air seòl an Taoibh-Tuath.
Gum a slàn do na fearaibh
Thèid thairis a' chuan.

Cha bhi iad 'g ar dùsgadh
Le clag Chinne-Ghiùbhsaich
Cha bhi e gun diùbhras
Ged nach dùisg sinn cho luath.
Gum a slàn do na fearaibh
Thèid thairis a' chuan.

Gu talamh a' gheallaidh
Far nach fairich iad fuachd,
Gum a slan do na fearaibh
Thèid thairis a' chuan

To the Health of the People.
[Donald Campbell]

To the health of the people,
Who are crossing the sea
To a land of promise
Where they'll not feel cold.
Here's to the health of the people,
Who'll be crossing the sea.

When we have left this place,
No longer can our rents be increased;
And Martinmas will no longer
Bring shame to our faces.
Here's to the health of the people
Who'll be crossing the ocean.

Without anything we left this place
Where not a thing would grow;
Even the potato is diseased
And will not flourish in the cold.
Here's to the health of the people
Who'll be crossing the sea.

We will get silk and satin there
We will get plenty of wool;
And the women will make cloth
As they did in the North.
Here's to the health of the people
Who'll be crossing the sea.

They'll not awaken us
With the bell of Kingussie;
Nor will it make any difference,
That we not awaken soon.
Here's to the health of the people
Who'll be crossing the sea.

To a country with promise
Where they will not feel cold,
Here's to the health of the people
Who'll be crossing the sea.

Section Two - The Journey - On the Seas

For most of the emigrants, especially those who had been 'cleared' from the land, an ocean voyage was a first-time experience. Conditions on many of the assisted emigrant ships, especially those relating to steerage passage, for a journey which could extend to five months, added to the misery of these Highlanders. Death rates, from some emigrant ships such as the *Hercules*, especially among children, was quite high, and disease could be devastating. The heart-breaking news, in letters home, of the deaths of their children on the voyage, or from ill-health as a result of the voyage, makes sad reading even today.

As well as the unhygienic conditions, overcrowding, poor food, and rough weather, other dangers such as fire at sea and the presence of ice-bergs, were ever-present fears.

Angus Beaton's *Òran an Eilthirich*, Rev. Alexander MacIntyre's account of the ship the *Typhoon*, the eyewitness account of the fire on an Emigrant barque, the India (*Losgadh na Luinge*) provide examples of dangers on the long voyage to Australia. Even surviving the four to five months journey, and being within hailing distance of their destination port, did not guarantee safe docking. The shipwreck of the *Dunbar* and that of the *Champion*, within Australian waters (the *Dunbar* at Sydney Heads and the *Champion*, between Melbourne and Portland Bay), are among examples which demonstrated the dangers which faced ships.

Many aspects of the long (four to five month), voyage to Australia, are recorded by these writers. The beauty of the ship in full sail, seasickness, shipboard fever, impromptu music and dancing, and cards and sport to relieve the tedium of endless days at sea, are all recorded one way or another by emigrants from Scotland. It is hardly surprising that it is the exceptional events punctuating the voyage – storm or fire at sea, the rituals observed when crossing the equator and so on – which transfix the attention of the Highland emigrants. Angus Beaton's *Òran an Eilthirich*, for example, would have encapsulated, for many, the attitudes of resentments at leaving, the means by which they left and the threats to their health and safety which such a long voyage posed. Upon arrival, the sense of loss did not abate quickly. Rev Alexander MacIntyre's, *Air Bòrd an t-Saoithich 'Typhoon'* also illustrates the tensions which existed between the different classes of emigrants on board.

Even the attempt to lighten the mood of the long journey by diversions, such as Neptune's visit when crossing the equator, as portrayed, in *Mu She'oladh Thairis air Crios-Meadhoin*, proves to be more of a horror story than harmless fun and games!

Others, such as James MacMillan (*Mo Mhàthair*), who was wracked with emotion at leaving his home and his mother, could find beauty and comfort in the passage of his ship over the waves, and of its sails, in *Òran-Tha 'n oidhche ciùin.* Even having to relinquish wearing the kilt he can rationalise, recognising that Australian conditions would not suit his Highland mode of dress.

11 Òran an Eilthirich

[le Aonghas Peutan]

Nuair a dh'fhàg sinn Rutha Clearach cha robh tìr ann ri lèirsinn,
Ach an cuan as a thoiseach, molach robach ag èiridh,
Dh'èirich tinneas 's bochdainn a bha goirt da luchd deuchainn,
Dol a dh'iarraidh an fhortain taobh toisgeal na grèine.

Bha mnathain a's clann ann 's iad gun sannt air an aran,
Iad ri tuireadh 's ri caoineadh — a' glaodhaich 's ri gearan,
Iad a' caoidhrean gun tamh mu ànradh na mara,
'S cha robh leigheas 's a' chàs ud ach fuireach sàmhach 's an leabaidh.

Tha mi seo air an fhairge fatheadh onfhadh na mara,
Fuaim sheòl agus ròpan fead aig corcaich 's aig ballaibh,
A siùil àrd air an reubadh — a croin reidh air am bearradh,
'S ged bu làidir an sèisdeadh cha do gheill i na darach.

Rinn na saoir i cho làidir 's nach robh lamh air pìob-thaomaidh,
Siùil ùr orr' on tàilleir gun chàradh gun sgaoileadh,
Iad gu teann air am beannamh a gabhail na gaoithe
Brace's bowline gan tharruing 's cha be 'n teannachadh faoine.

La Dònaich 'n dèidh searmoin thàinig stoirm oirnn bha làidir,
Bha 'n joboon air a bhristeadh 's chuir sid clisgeadh nar nàdur,
Cha robh guth air an t-soisgeul, na na sochairean gràsmhor,
Ach a' caoidh 's gearan nach robh fearann ri thàrsinn.

Nuair a chuala mi 'n fhuaim ud mar gum buaileadh i sgàrnach,
Chaidh mi suas chum na guallainn feuch dè fuathas a thàinig,
Cladach mara mun cuirt di mar bheinn a' fuasgladh a h-àite,
'S cha ghleidhinn mo chasan ach ri taice mar phàiste.

'S iad na gillean bha gleusda chaidh don a reidh chrannaibh àrda,
'S nach tilleadh le sochair ged bu choltach rim bàs e,
Bho rèiteach nan ròpan bha gach seòl air a fàgail,
'S ged bha Neptune na dhùsgadh chaidh siùil ùr chuir nan àite.

'S iomadh òganach briarach mu ghriasaich a mhàthar,
Dhèanamh treabhadh a's iasgach, dhèanamh gnìomh ann am bàta,
'S e th' agam ri innseadh gur e 'n fhìrinn domh ràitinn,
Iad aig òrais 's a dìobhairt 's nan sìneadh gun slàinte.

Nuair a chunnaic iad fearann, urad feannaig de 'n àite
Dh'fhalbh am bròn 's thàinig misneach 's dh'fh às iad cridheil mar b' àbhaist,
Bha iad toillichte an uair sin gun, d' fhuair iad teachd sàbhailt,
Seach laidhe 's a chuan dol am poc 's luaidhe 's a mhas aig.

Song of the Exile

[Angus Beaton]

When we left Cape Clear, we lost sight of land,
And from the outset the sea rose, rough and stormy;
Sickness and misery gave pain to those suffering them,
Who had left to seek good fortune on the far side of the sun.

There were women and children without a desire for bread,
Lamenting and keening they were - crying and complaining,
They were whimpering, without stop, about the ocean tempest,
There was no remedy for their distress but to stay quiet in bed.

I am here on the sea, feeling the battering of the ocean,
With the noises of whistling sails and hempen ropes and rigging.
Her top sails torn - her smooth masts shorn of their sails,
Though greatly under pressure, the ship's oaken frame did not give way.

She was made strong by her builders, no hand was needed at the pump,
New sails from good makers, unpatched and well-stitched,
Were fixed on the beam, correcting for the wind,
And Brace's bowline, peak halyard sheets were effectively straightening.

During the Lord's Day sermon, a strong tempest broke,
The jib boom was splintered creating great fear within us,
There was no mention of the gospel, nor of gracious blessings,
But only weeping and sighing, that no land was in sight.

When I heard the noise as if she had struck a rock,
I went towards the beam to see what spectre had come –
A coast-line* around her like a mountain breaking free from its place,
I could not keep my feet but was holding on tightly like a child.

But well-trained young men went up the lofty masts,
Not shirking their job, though they risked death.
By unravelling the small ropes each sail was unfurled,
And though Neptune was stirring each new sail was fitted.

Many a young man brave at his mother's fireside,
Who would plough and fish, and work in a boat,
I am telling the truth when I say
They were nauseous and vomiting and stretched out ill.

When they saw land, as much as a lazybed's size,
The mourning left and good cheer returned,
They were pleased then that they had arrived safely,
And were not lying on the ocean floor like a bag of lead ballast.

*This is probably a reference to an ice-berg.

12 Òran Tha'n Oidhche

[Seumas Mac 'Ille-Mhaoil]

Tha 'n oidhche ciùin, 's a' ghaoth nar dèigh;
Tha 'n long ag èirigh air bhàrr tuinn;
Tha ghealach chliuiteach snàg 's an speur,
Is na reultan dealrach os mo chionn,
Tha siùil a' crochadh 's roip gu feum
A' ruith gu rèidh air roilein cruinn,
'Us iad 'g a m' fhuadachadh le chèil',
Bho Thìr gu bràth nach tèich 'a m' chuimhn'.

Aig marbh na h-oidhche 's mi leam fhèin
A' cumail fàir' bho sgèith nan crann,
Gur, tric mo smaointean dol am dhèigh
Far 'n chaith mi òg an t-èideadh cruinn;
Na pleatan suainteach, cuachach, fèileach,
Uallach, eutrom, rèidh ri m' chom;-
A ruith, no 'ruaig no bhuidhinn rèis,
'Se sud an t-èideadh thaghta leam.

Ach faic gach nì dhiùbh sud 'g a m' thrèigsum,
Chaidh an t-fhèileadh chur air chùl,
Tha 'n triubhas mhogannach mum shlèisdean,
A chumas moill air ceum a' ghlùin;
'An àit' bhi siubhal bheann 'us rèidhleach,
A' ruith 's a' leum, 'cur rèis fo stùchd,
Chan fhaic 's an uair seo luach fon ghrèin
Ach cuan 'us speuran oirnn mun cuairt.

Ged a's bòidheach long fo h-èideadh
'S i mar pheucaig 's àillidh com,
Tha sgaoileadh 'itean ri lath' grèine,
Mar dèarrsadh reult air feadh nan tonn:-
Siùil cho geal ri canach shlèibhtean
Gaoth 'n ar an uair bhi 'g èiridh
Fo sgàth nan geug, bun Chnoc-nan-long.*

*This is the name the poet gave to his home in Western Australia.

A Song
[James MacMillan]

It is a still night and the wind is behind us;
The boat is rising on the waves;
A magnificent moon creeps across the sky,
And the stars shine above my head.
Sails are billowing as they should,
The ship running leisurely on crown rollers,
Carrying into banishment me and my wife
Forever from a land that won't fade from my memory.

It is the dead of night and I am alone
Observing the horizon through the cut of the mast,
Until, suddenly, my thoughts go to the past
Where as a youth I wore the well-gathered kilt;
The plaid with bountiful pleats,
Airy, light and comfortable round my waist,
Running, chasing or winning a race
It is that garment I would prefer to wear.

But see, everyone with whom I am leaving,
Has discarded the kilt,
Trousers are now about my thighs,
That would hinder the free movement of my knees;
As I crossed mountain and plain,
Running and jumping and racing around the hill.
Its value under the sun can't be seen at this time
With sea and sky all around us.

It is the most beautiful ship under sail,
She is like a pea-hen, with resplendent breast,
Spreading her morning feathers to the sun,
Like a radiant star along the length of the wave -
Sails as white as mountain cotton sedge.
The wind will presently be rising
Under the shadow of the branches,
At the foot of Cnoc-nan-long.

13 An t-Abrach Air Chuan

[Eoghan Mac-an-t-Shaoir]

Seo deoch-cuimhne na h-alba garbh chrìoch 's nam beann,
As deoch-slàinte nan gaisgeach gun ghealtachd a th'annt',
Fhad 's a chinneas a' fraoch a th' air aodann an t-sleibh,
Nar robh dì-meas no tàir air na dh'fhàg sinn nar dèidh,
Air na dh'fhàg sinn nar dèigh.

Fhad 's bhios eunlaith air gheugan no iasg air traigh,
Fhad 's a dh'ionnailtreas fiadh air feadh shliabh agus bhlas.
Fhad 's bhios cuthag no smeòrach ri ceòl anns a mhagh,
Nar robh dearmad no di-chuimhe air tìr nam beann àrd,
Air tìr nam beann àrd.

Tha ar càirdean 's ar dìlsean an tìr nam beann àrd.
Sid an tìr ar n-àrach 'n ar pàisdeinean maoth,
Sid an tìr anns an d' fhàs sinn le càirdeas as goal,
'S ann tha chuid ud dhiùbh bhàsaich 's a chàireadh fon fhòid,
Chaidh a chàireadh fon fhòid.

'N sid tha màthraichesan dhleasnach bha beadrach mun cloinn,
'S a bha 'n iartas 's an togradh le toraidh an coim,
Far an d' fhàg sinn fo bhròn iad 's na deòir air an sùil,
Nuair a theann sinn gu sùil cuir gu bràth riù ar cùil,
Cuir gu bràth riù ar cùil.

Nuair bhios stoirmean a gheamhraidh feadh chrann agus thom
Sa bhios spionnadh na gaoith cuir nan craobh as am bonn
Bi'dh iadsan fo smuairein as gruaim air an gnùis
'S iad a saoilsinn nach beò sinn 's na deòir air an sùil
Bidh na deòir air an sùil.

Nuair bhios òigridh ar dùthcha gu sunndach mun bhòrd,
(Ged nach èisd sinn ri 'n abhachd ri 'n dàin no ri 'n ceòl.)
Nì iad luaidh oir le gaol agus craobh ac air cuaich
'Siad ag òl sid air slàinte na thar thair a chuan
'Siad ag òl sid air slàinte na thar thair a chuan.
Air na thair a chuan.

'S ann na h-àitean 's na chleachd sinn bhi tachairt ri chèile
Air la sàbaid as seachdain air clachan 's air fèill,
Ni na h-igh'neagan faoilte ri faotainn ar sgèil
'S ri bhi cluinntinn gun a thàinig sin sàbhailt gun bheud
'S bho 'n tha sinn gun bheud bho 'n a tha sinn gun bheud
Gheibh iad sgial air gun a thàinig sinn sàbhailt gun bheud.

A Lochaberman on the Ocean

[Ewan MacIntyre]

A toast to the memory of Scotland, land of rugged mountains,
And a toast to the heroes that are in the highlands,
While the heather blooms on the face of the hill
Neither shame nor contempt caused us to forsake our past,
Caused us to forsake our past.

While birds are on branches or fish on the shore,
While strong deer graze amid mountains and plain;
While there is snipe or mavis to sing in the field,
Neither neglected nor forgotten will be the land of high mountains;
Nor our friends or loved ones still in that land.

Yonder is the land that nurtured and reared us,
The land where we grew amid kindness and love,
Yonder are our friends, some we left still living,
While others are now dead and lie buried there;
Dead and lie buried there.

Yonder were affectionate mothers surrounded with children
Their prayers and wishes for protection were granted.
In sorrow we left, with tearful eye,
As we gradually lost sight of our country for ever;
Lost sight of our country for ever.

When winter comes it will be stormy amid tree and bush
With the powerful wind uprooting trees.
Our families will be anxious, with gloomy faces
And with tearful eye they will imagine us dead;
Will imagine us dead.

When the youth of our country are happy around the table,
(Though we cannot hear the joyful song or music),
They will make mention of us with love, and with foaming cup
Will drink to our health, those of us now across the sea;
Now across the sea.

And in our region, as usual, folk will meet together
On the sabbath each week, and in town on market day,
The young women will be delighted to receive news of us.
They will hear news that we arrived safe and without harm;
Safe and without harm.

14 *Air Bòrd* an t-Saoithich '*Typhoon*' ann an Acarsaic Lisboin

[le An t-Urramach Alasdair Mac-an-t-Shaoir]

Air feasgar là grianaich;
Bu chianail an sealladh!
Ann am Baile mòr Ghrianaig,
A' tha cian uaith seo fada:
A bhi faicinn nan ciadan
A bha triall chum na mara;
S' gu siubhal thair sàile
O 'n càirdean 's o 'n dachaidh,
Gu fearann Australi,
Gun sùil gu bràth ri tighinn aiste.

Bha 'n long bha gur giulan
A-mach air a h-acair;
Fo làn uidheam an òrdugh
Le cuid seòl agus achdfhuinn.
Tha cuid làmhan tha lìonmhor
Fo riaghlach a Chaiptein,
Cuid duineil 'us dàicheil
Nach eil dàna no gealtach
S' mòr a mhisneach le càch sud,
Dol gun dàil air an astar.

Air a bòrd sud gun cheum iad
Mar a steach ann nan dachaidh;
Oir gu ceann thair thrì mìosan
Cha robh suil ac'tighinn aiste;
Bha gach neach mar a thàr iad
Ri cuir àird air am fachail;
S' ann a sin a bha 'n ùbraid
Ma ri mùisead 's mi-thaitneas,
Troimh chèile 's eas-òrdugh
S' gun dòigh air am pachdadh.

S' ann na deireadh bha bhuidhean
A b' urramaich fada;
Mas a riadhaill na phàigh iad
Airson fardaish 'us leaba
Bha iad spailpeil 'us tàireil
Co thug bàr air aon neach dhuibh,
Ach fuirich car ùine

'S le 'd shùilibh gum faic thu;
Na suinn ud a gèilleadh
Nuair thig feum air air an tapadh.

Ann a meadhoin na luinge
S' na toiseach le pachdadh;
Tha an dream tha gun mheas diù
Ma chreideas tu facal;
Na dream tha san deireadh
Oir se their iad gun fhaitchas,
Nach buin meas doibh na urradh,
S' iad gun rudeigin aca;
Air na chroch iad an uaisle,
Ris nach d' fhuair iad an taice.

Ach cha b' fhada bha mise
Tabhail beachd air an cleachdadh,
Gus a faic mi nì leòir dhiubh
Agus cor na bu mhaith dhomh;
Thilg iad òrdugh us riaghailt
Chum nan ialtag s' nam famhuadh,
Chuir iad uigh san easùmhlachd
Chor s' nach drùigh orr a 'm facal;
Ris a sgib ud an taice.
Sud a chreud a bh' aig mòran.

Sud a chreud a bh' aig mòran
Nuair sheol sinn a Cala;
Gun robh an longe seo òrdail
S' co sònraichte snasda,
S' nach feudadh gun èireadh
Beud da crè no da h-acum;
Ge do thogair iad gluasad
Rèir an smuaintean s' am beachdan;
Bhi an-diadhaidh gun so-gràdh,
Sud an obair a chleachd iad.

Chan eil sùil air an t-sàbaid
No 'n àithne thug Esan;
Thug a steach iad don t-saoghal
S' a chaoimhn' iad ann fathast.
Thug dhoibh biadh agus aodach
Gun mhaoidheadh gun ghainne;

Thog suas ann san tìr iad
S' an robh 'm Bìobal ra fhaighinn.
S' iomadh sochair ro phriseil
Gar 'm bu ni leò an gabhail.

Ge do dheònaich an t-àrd Righ
Iomadh fàbhar na Fhreasdal;
S' ge do ghlèigh E sinn sàbhailt
Nar' fàrdaich car ghreise,
Ann an àite bhi taingeil
S' ga àideachadh gu cleachdail,
Bhi ga iarraidh le dùrachd
Araon moch agus feasgar;
S' ann a thug iad gu gnàthail
Gu fidhil tàileasg 'us cairtean.

On Board the '*Typhoon*' in Lisbon Harbour
[Rev Alexander MacIntyre]

On a sunny evening
It was a sad spectacle
In the great town of Greenock,
Far distant from here,
That created these impressions
Of journeying towards the sea;
And travelling across the ocean
Away from friends and from home,
To the land of Australia
Without expectation of ever returning.

The ship carried us
Out of the harbour,
Full sails was the order
And there were numerous hands
On the sail and rigging
Under the Captain's direction.
Some of the passengers were manly and keen
Without being overconfident or fearful,
And others showed great courage
Taking this journey without hesitation.

They stepped on board
As though entering a house
Because for more than three months
There was no hope of leaving it.
Every person, as he boards,
Struggles to get prepared;
And there was upset,
Together with fear and unpleasantness,
And a mixture of confusion and disorder
The luggage being handled without any system.

And in the stern was a group
Who were respectful throughout;
Those in the bottom of the ship did not pay
For lodgings or for bed,
They were proud but despised
Brought out with one atop the other.
But stay for a time

And with your eyes you will see,
Should there be a crisis.
They would demonstrate their courage.

In the middle of the ship;
And in front, with the luggage;
Were some people considered worthless,
If you believe my word.
These people are in the stern
Because, as is said without contradiction,
No one respects them.
Nor do they possess anything;
Having to depend upon charity
Without which they have no support.

It didn't take me long,
Observing their habits,
To see enough of their behaviour
To consider their condition deserved;
They rejected order and rule
And were detained as the titmouse and the mole.
They deliberately chose disobedience,
The word of Him upon whose hand they depend
Made no impression on them.
And that was the opinion of many.

When we sailed into the Harbour
This ship was in an orderly state;
And it was specially decorated.
But it was necessary to avoid
Harm to the ship's keel or to its rigging,
Though they wished otherwise,
According to their thoughts and desires,
Which were ungodly and without sincere love,
They behaved according to their usual nature;
That is, the way of life they were used to practising.

They had no eye for the Sabbath
Nor the commandments given by God
Who brought them into the world
And whose kindness still maintains them,
Giving them food and clothes
Without reluctance and without stinting.
They were raised in the land
Where the Bible was so precious,

And with many valuable privileges
For our and their acceptance.

Because the Almighty imparts
Many Providential favours;
And though He preserves us from harm,
In what is our dwelling for a while,
There should be thankfulness
And continual confession
Where we would worship with sincerity
Together both morning and evening;
Instead, they brought out, as usual,
The fiddle, sports and cards.

15 Losgadh na Luinge *India*

[Tha fear a bha air bòrd air an àm a' toirt a' chùnntais a' leannas air a' ghnothuch mhuladach seo:]

Air Di-Luain, an 19mh là do mhios deiridh an t-samhraidh, bha ar soitheach goirid bho dheich ceud mìle an taobh mu dheas do chearcall-meadhoin na talmhuinn. An dèigh àm braiceis, thàinig aon don luchd-aisg a dh'innseadh gun robh long nach b'aithne don sgioba san t-sealladh; agus o nach fhaca sinn soitheach sam bith o chionn ceithir-là-deug, bha gach aon gu grad air clàr na luinge. Bha i tuille 's fad' air falbh chum aire thoirt air na sanusan a thairg sinn; ach o 'n a bha i a' seòladh air an aon slighe ruinn, chum sinn sealladh air a cheile fad na maidne; agus aig dà-uair-dheug, mhothuich sinn gun robh sinn beagan na bu teinne air a chèile.

Chaidh mi sìos don t-seòmar-luinge; agus an ceann h-uair, chuala mi treas-oifigeach na luinge a' glaodhaich airson uisge, le mionnan agus mallachadh oillteil! Ghrad leum mi suas, agus chunnaic mi mòran toit agus lasrach a' tighin o 'n tigh-thaisg. Cha robh mionaid r'a chall. Dh'orduicheadh an sgioba gu ceann-deiridh na luinge, leis gach seòrsa soithich a b'urrainn iad fhaotainn, a thogail uisge. Rinn iadsan an dleasnas mar is gnàth le maraichean Breatunnach, gun tiomadh gun athadh; ach ged a dh'oibrich iad gu foghainteach, agus len uile neart, cha robh e nan comas ni bu leòir a dh'uisge thogail. Bha inneal-taosgaidh againn deireadh na luinge; ach bha a' phìob tuille 's cumhann, agus cha d'rinn e ach beag feum. Fad na h-ùine seo, bhan teine meudachadh agus a' buidhinn oirnn gu h-uamhasach.

Bha e nis soilleir nach robh e comasach an long a shàbhaladh, agus bha gach aon a' smuainteachadh ciamar a thèarnadh e a bheatha fèin. Thug mi ceann-toisich na luing orm, agus 's ann an sin a bhan sealladh muladach - na boirionnaich a' bas-bhualadh, 's a' caoineadh, 's a' sgreadail, air an dòigh a b'eagalaiche; agus cha b'iad a' chlann òg bhochd bu lugha eagal. Bha nis na gunnacha-mòra a' losgadh shanas-teinn, an dòchas gu'm mothuicheadh an long eile dhoibh; agus chuir sinn air falbh coig maraichean ann am bàta g'a h-ionnsuidh, oir bha e cinnteach mur tigeadh i gar teasraiginn, gun caillteadh gach creutair a bha air bòrd. Thòisich na lamhan an sin air mucan, agus gobhair, agus beathaichean eile bham bata-mòr na luinge a thilgeil thar bòrd. Bham bàta so làidir, trom; agus cha b'ann gun spàirn a fhuair iad thar taobh an t-soithich i.

Cha luaithe bha i thairis na lìonadh i le cloinn agus a liuthad do na mnathan 's a thiochdadh innte, le ceithir maraichean gan iomran chum na loing a bha san t-sealladh. Mhothuich sinn a-nis le sòlas agus taingealachd, a thuigeas iadsan amhàin a bha na leithid seo do chruaidh-chas, gun do thuig muinntir na luinge ar staid, agus gun robh iad a' greasad dar n' ionnsuidh leis gach luathas a bha nan comas, ged a bha iad fhathast, air a' chuid bu lugha, naoi mìle bhuainn; agus ged a bha i air an fhuaradh dhinn, bha aobhar eagail nach snàmhadh an India gus an ruigeadh i sinn; oir bha iochdar an t-soithich a-nis na aona mheall teine, agus na lasraichean a' bristeadh a mach troimh 'n dorus, agus a' streip ris na croinn agus ris an acuinn le luathas uamhasach.

Na bu lugha na uair an uaireadair o thoiseach an losgaidh, chaidh an crann-mor thar taobh-fasgaidh an t-soithich; agus thuit an dà chrann eile, ged nach deachaidh iad thairis. Bha nis cuid don sgioba agus don luchd-aisig, a b'urrainn snàmh, a' deanamh ionnsuidh na luinge coigrich; agus bhan crann-spreòid cùirnichte le luchd-aisig, ag oidhirpeachadh an teas a sheachnadh. Leum an sgiobair 's am mate thar an taobh gu snàmh, agus bha ao-dòchas anns gach gnùis; gidheadh, ge neònach r'a inns' e, chìteadh cuid a dhaoine bha, do reir coltais, gun smuairean gun iomaguin, gun nì a' cur dragh orra ach an teas! - ach am bitheantas, chìte gun robh aire gach aon air an tèaruinteachd fèin - athraichean, màthairean, agus clann, gach aon air leth ag iarraidh meadhon-tèarnaidh dhoibh fein; agus chite mun àm seo mòran a' gramachadh ri mirean fiodha a thuit no a thilgeadh thar bòrd. Nam measg seo, chaidh crann a bhan caomhnadh aig an luing, a thilgeadh thar bòrd, agus ghramaich mu dhusan pearsa ris; ach, gu mi-fhortanach, o 'n bha iad cha mhòr uile air aon taobh dhe, bha e daonnan a' tionndadh san uisge, agus bha iadsan a' tuiteam dheth; agus, a reir coltais, chailleadh iad so uile.

Bha nis clàr-uachdair na luinge loisgte, agus bàtaichean na luinge-coigrich air ar ruigheachd. Bha na h-uile h-àite far am b'urrainn creutair beò an teas fhulang làn don luchd-aisig, gu h-àraid na croinn a thuit tarsuing an t-soithich; agus nuair chunnaic iad na bàtaichean aig taobh na luinge, leum gach aon mar a b'urrainn iad a stigh annta. Air an dòigh seo chuir iad aon do na bàtaichean thairis, agus bhàthadh leth-dusan fear. Ràinig am bàta fein a-nis iad; agus le cùram agus seòltachd dara-mate na luinge Breatunnaich, chaidh gach aon a bhan crochadh rithe chur gu sàbhailte sa' bhàta."

'S ann don Fhraing a bhuineadh an long choigreach. Bha i dol gu iasgach nam muca-mara sa' chuan mu dheas, agus bha pailteas bidh aca. Bha i mu mheudachd an India, mu choig ceud tunna; agus thaisbean iad gach caoimhneas dar luchd-dùthcha mi-fhortanach a bha nan comas, ged a bha mòran diubh dearg-rùiste, 'chionn nach b'urrainn iad nì air bith a thèarnadh o 'n teine. Bha air bòrd an India 214; dhiubh sin, chailleadh 18.

Thòisich an teine air an dòigh seo:- Bha dara-mate na luinge agus aon do na balachain a' tarraing dibhe-làidir a togsaid; agus a chionn gun robh a' choinneal a bha aca tuille 's goirid airson an lanntair, thug iad as i; agus thuit i eadar dà bhuideal, far an deach deoch a dhòrtadh, agus ann am prioba na sùl bhan t-àite na lasair.

Thug an long Fhrangach a-stigh iad do chala Rio Janeiro, agus chan fhiosrach sinn dad tuille mun deibhinn air an àm; ach tha e soilleir, mur biodh am Freasdal air cur an t-soithich Fhrangaich nan carabh, gun caillteadh iad gu lèir.

The Burning of the Ship *India* on her Maiden Voyage to Australia in 1841

[A man that was on board at the time gives the following account of this sad matter]

On Monday, 19th day of the month at the end of summer, our vessel was about a thousand miles south of the equator. After breakfast time, a person came with news from the skipper that another ship had been sighted, and since we had not seen another vessel for fourteen days everyone suddenly went on deck. It was too far away to notice the greeting that we gave; but from its direction it was on the same course as us. We held it in view all the morning; and at twelve o'clock, we noticed that a few among us were sick.

I went down to the cabin; and at the end of an hour, I heard the ship's third officer shouting for water, with frightful oaths and curses! I quickly leapt up, and I saw much smoke and flame coming from the hold. There was not a minute to be lost. The skipper ordered the crew to the rear of the ship, with every sort of container they could find, to collect water.

They carried out their tasks as befits British seamen, without fear and without cowardice; but though the workmen were efficient and strong it was beyond their power and not enough water was able to be carried. We had pumping machines in the stern of the ship, but the pipe was too narrow, and it was of little use. All this time, the terrifying fire was increasing and gaining on us but more of the pipe was contracted and was useless.

It was now clear that it was not possible to save the ship, and every-one was thinking how he could save his own life. I took to the prow of the ship, and it was a sad sight - the women wrung their hands in grief, and were wailing and shrieking in a manner that was frightening; and no less afraid were the poor young children. The large guns were now firing a signal of distress, the hope being that this would attract the other ship to them. We put away five sailors in a boat in its direction, because it was certain that unless rescue would come, every person on board would be lost. Pigs, goats, and other animals were, together with a large boat, thrown overboard by the crew. This was a strong, heavy boat; and it was not without a hard struggle that they got it over the side of the vessel.

She was not swift across the swell as she was carrying children and several women who could also fit in her, with four sailors rowing towards the ship that was in view. We observed now, with consolation and thankfulness, that they had recognised what was our danger and the condition of the people on the ship, and that they were hastening towards us with every speed that was in their power. They were still more or less nine miles from us; and she was on the windward side of us. There was the fear that the India would not continue afloat until she reached us because the bottom of the ship was now one mass of fire, and flames were breaking out through the hatch and, with terrible speed, were climbing up the mast and towards the rigging.

Time was running out. Since the fire began the lee-side main mast fell across the vessel; and the second mast fell also, yet they did not go over. Some of the crew, and those passengers who could swim, were making towards the foreign ship; and the bowsprit was crowded with passengers attempting to avoid the heat. The skipper and the mate leapt over the side to swim, and despair was on every face though, surprising to say, some of the men were, in all likelihood, without fear, without anxiety and without any concern except the heat! But what was frequently seen was that everyone sought their own safety - fathers, mothers, and children, separately seeking to escape; and many were to be seen at this time fastening themselves to little pieces of wood that fell, or that were thrown, overboard. Among this debris was the reserve mast that went over-board, and about a dozen persons fastened to it; but unfortunately, since they were all on one side of it, it was always turning in the water, and they were falling off it; and, in all likelihood, they were all lost.

The deck of the ship was now burnt and the boats of the foreign vessel were within our reach. Every place where the live animals were suffering the heat was full of passengers, masts especially fell across the vessel; and when they saw the boats beside the ship, every one leapt into them as they were able. In this manner they turned one of the boats over, and half a dozen men drowned. They now reached the ship itself; and with the care and skill of the first mate of the British ship, everyone that was hanging on to her went safely into the rescue boat.

The foreign ship belonged to France. She was going to fish for whale in the south seas, and was well provisioned. She was the same bulk as the *India*, about five hundred tons; and the crew showed every kindness that was in their power to do to our unfortunate countrymen, though many of them were burned raw, because they were not able to escape from the fire. There were 214 on board the *India*, 18* of them were lost.

The fire began like this:- The ship's first mate and a small boy were drawing a hogshead of strong drink; and because the candle they had was too short for the lantern, they took it out; and it fell between two casks, where drink had been spilled and in the blink of an eye the place was aflame.

The French ship took us to the Rio de Janeiro harbour, and we did not know anything more at the time; but it is clear that had not Providence put the French vessel in our path, many would have been lost."

*All but one came from the lowest class in the steerage section reserved for the poorest Highlanders.

The barque *India (1840)* – setting out for its first journey to Australia in 1840

Samuel Elyard, S. (1817-1910) Australian artist.
The Burning of the Barque *"India", off Greenock in the South Atlantic Ocean,* 19th July 1841

16 Sgiorraidhean Muladach

[*An Teachdaire Gaidhealach*]

Tha e na aobhar bròin duinn a bhi again r aithris gun do thachair, ann a mhìos a chaidh seachad dà sgiorradh ro mhuladach air oirthir Astraillia.

An *Dunbar*

Air oidhch' an fhicheada' latha chaidh an *Dunbar*, long mhòr àluinn a dh' fhag Lunnainn luchdaichge ebathar luachmhor, arson, Shydney deireadh April, a long-bhriseadh air ceann-tìre creagach ris an abrar Sydney Heads. Bha corr a 's sea-fichead anam air bord oirre agus chaitleadh iad uile ach aon seòladair d' an ainm Johnson.

Bha oidhche anabarrach stoirmeil agus dorcha agus ged a rinn an Caiptean 's a' sgioba curanta na b' urrainn daibh a chum an long a theasairginn o bhi air a duadach air na creagaibh dh'fhairtlich orra sin a dhèanamh.

An *Champion*

Air a 21ad bhuaileadh an *Champion*, saothach smuid a bha seoladh eadar Melbourne agus Portland Bay, leis *Lady Bird*, bata-toit eile, dlù air Ceap Otway … d' rinn i toll mòr na cliathaich agus thaom an t-uisge a staigh cho dian 's gun do lionadh an saothach ann an tiota, agus mun deach' ach beagan mhionaidean seachad chaidh i fodha.

Thachair an sgiorradh seo, mar an ceudna, ann an dorchadas na h-oidhche, agus ged nach robh an t-sid fiadhaich bha cho gaothar … Thèaruinn an *Lady Bird* na b' urrainn di den luchd-turuis 's den sgioba a bha 'ir bord *Champion*, ach chaidh deich-thar-fhichead diubh a bàthadh. A-measg na chailleadh, bha teaghlach Gaidhealach, ro mheasail, de Chlann-Choinnich …

Terrible Disasters

A sad accident – It is a cause of grief for us to relate that in the month of July past two sad accidents happened on the coast of Australia.

The *Dunbar*

On the evening of the twentieth, the *Dunbar,* a beautiful large ship that left London with a cargo of merchandise for Sydney, at the end of April, shipwrecked on the rocky headland to the Sydney Heads. There were more than 120 souls on board her and they all perished except one sailor of the name of Johnson.

The night was exceedingly stormy and black and, although the Captain and the heroic crew worked to rescue the ship from being driven onto the rocks, they were defeated in trying to achieve that goal.

The *Champion*

On the 21st, a vessel, the *Champion,* sailing between Melbourne and Portland Bay, was smashed to pieces, with the *Lady Bird,* also a steam-ship, near to Cape Otway … she made a large hole in the side [and] water rushed in so violently filling the ship in a moment, and after only a few more minutes she sank.

This accident also happened in the dark of the night, and though the weather was not tempestuous, it was very blustery …. The *Lady Bird* rescued what she was able of the passengers and crew that were on board the *Champion*, but thirty of them drowned. Among the lost was a very respectable Highland family, belonging to Clan MacKenzie…

Section Three - Looking Back

Not without reason did homesickness give rise to the largest single output of Gaelic verse from Australia in the years immediately following the arrival of the Highland emigrants. Only a small fraction of that verse can be included here. Sitting down to weep, or at the very least, to remember, beside their own 'waters of Babylon', has been part of the experience of exiles throughout history – captives, economic exiles, forced and voluntary emigrants alike. When they came to give voice to their pining for what they had left, they were thus following the experiences of the Israelites after leaving Egypt, wandering in the wilderness complaining and longing for the world they had left behind, notwithstanding that that world included great hardship and poverty and a form of social and economic slavery.

If homesickness is the general lot of the emigrant, these homesick voices from Gaels in Australia show us a number of specific features about its nature. The child it seems is father to the man; several poets are conscious that their fond memories of 'home' are not just memories of place and kin – part of the nostalgia is for the vanished 'golden days' of childhood and youth even if, in truth, those days, for many, were not so 'golden'. Personal identity is to some extent rooted in our experiences in the distant past. Recalling the scenes and the pursuits associated with one's homeland affirms part of an emigrant's personal identity and so serves an important psychological purpose.

We see this in MacKinnon's *Fàilte Don Ghaidhealtachd.* Perhaps that is why so many persisted with it and why so many of these types of poems were written despite the pain that the very writing about one's homeland entailed. If hyperbole led some to extremes of grief and exaggerated loss, we nevertheless find in the body of these poems some clear-eyed reasons given for the sense of loss expressed in, say, Ewan Cameron's *Òran do Thìr M'Òige.* Emigration all-too-often meant separation from family and friends and it meant a loss of familiar rituals and pastimes and occupations. Of course, as time went by the experiences of many was that of 'getting on' and improving their circumstances and that too becomes part of the message to the homeland.

In a new land where the seasons were reversed, and the geography so different, and with the old social set-up all but gone, these things were almost impossible to recreate. Further, in most districts of Australia, Gaels were unable to form sufficiently close settlements which would provide the critical mass needed for the retention of Gaelic in day-to-day social and work environments. Adding piquancy to homesickness for landscapes, family, friends and culture was the awareness most Highland emigrants had that distance and cost meant that their separation from natal hearth and home was final and irrevocable, as we see in *Sa' Choill' fo Sgios* and *Òran do Thìr M' Òige*, among others.

With the long and arduous voyage behind them, and scattered wherever their jobs took them in their new land, the burden (nostalgia and home-sickness) which every exile carries, could be made more bearable through an indulgence in emotional outpourings of feelings. Some handled these emotional strains where, in fancy, they return home. In their dreams they recreate Highland life, idealized although it might be, and draw some comfort from such imaginings. *Am Bruadar, Òran Do Mo Dhachaidh* and *Na Tulaichean Boideach* illustrate the range of such dreams. Some comfort, perhaps, but pain too as in MacMillan's *Mo Mhàthair*

17 Mu She'oladh Thairis Air Crios-Mheadhoin na Talmhainn

[An unnamed eyewitness account from an unnamed passenger on board]

Tha mòran, a rèir coslais, de luchd-leughaidh a *Chuairteir* nach cual guth riamh mu na cleasaibh iongantach a ta 'gam gnàthachadh air longaibh, as uair a bhios iad a'seòladh null thar crios-meadhoin na talmhainn. Nithear dichioll, uime sin, an so, air cunntas goirid a thoirt mu na cleasaibh sin, do bhrìgh gum bheil iad air an gnàth-achadh gu ruig an là 'n diugh air mòran de na longaibh a ta 'seòladh thar a' chrios sin dh'ionnsuidh Innsean na h-Aird' an Ear, Australia, no àite air bith ann an cuantaibh na h-àirde deas.

Anns an rìoghachd so, chìthear a' ghrian deas oirnn aig meadhon-là; ach nam biomaid ann an Australia, chìtheamaid i mu mheadhon-latha tuath oirnn. Tha 'n talamh cruinn, agus leth-char air cumadh uibha. Tha, uime sin, àite sònraichte aig meadhon an astair, eadar ceann deas agus ceann tuath na talmhainn, far am bheil a' ghrian aig meadhon-là air amannaibh de 'n bhliadhna, dìreach os ar ceann; agus 'se sin an t-àite ris an abrar anns a' Bheurla an "Line," no "Equator" - 'se sin, an crios no an cearcall a ta 'cuairteachadh na talmhainn, o 'n àird-an-ear gus an àird'-an-iar, agus 'ga roinn na dhà leth.

Ach, chum ar sgeul a dheanamh so-thuigsinn, feumar a thoirt fa'near gun robh mòran de dhiathaibh-breige aig na cinnich o shean, anns an robh iad gu dall agus gu h-amaideach a' cur an uile dhòchais. Is gann nach robh dia no ban-dia aca airson nan uile nithe. Mar so, b' e Mars dia a' chogaidh - Bacchus, dia an fhiona - Pan, dia nan coilltean - Ceres, ban-dia an àrbhair - Minerva, ban-dia a' ghliocais - agus mar sin sìos.

Tha e cinnteach, air do na cinnich a bhi mar so a' dealbhadh diathan 'nan inntinn fein gu riaghladh thar gach nì, nach fàgadh iad an cuan mòr agus doinionnach gun a dhia fein mar an ceudna. B' e, uime sin, Neptun dia a' chuain, agus b' i Amphitrite ban-dia a' chuain. An uair nach robh eòlas sam bith aig na cinnich iodhal-aorach sin air an aon Dhia bheò agus fhìor a chruthaich nèamh agus talamh, bha iad gu diomhain an dùil gum b' e Neptun a b' aobhar do gach anradh agus doinionn air a' chuan mhòr, agus gun robh uile uisgeachan an domhain aige-san fo 'smachd fein!

Chum sùgradh agus cridhealas a chumail suas air na longaibh a ta seòladh do dhùthchannaibh an cein, tha na seòladairean a' leigeil orra fèin gum bheil Neptun ann, agus gum bheil àite-còmhnuidh anns a' chuan mhòr, dìreach aig crios-meadhoin na talmhainn; agus nach ceadaich e do luing sam bith a dhol seachad air a' chrios sin gun fhàilt' a chur oirre.

An uair a ruigeas long an t-àite sin den chuan, thèid seòldair suas gu mullach a' chroinn-mhòir, a ghabhail fradhairc air a' chuan ceithir-thimcheall air; agus chan fhad gus an glaodh e le uile neart.

"Tha mi faicinn ni-eigin cosmhuil ri sgoth air taobh an fhuaraidh!"

Ann an ùine ghoirid an deigh sin, cluinnear guth anns a' chuan, aig toiseach na luinge, dan toir oifigeach àraidh freagradh. Their an guth ris an oifigeach seo.

"Cuir an long air an luidh'-chuige, oir tha Neptun, dia a' chuan, a' teachd air bòrd."

Air ball cuirear suas an long, agus air a' cheart mhionaid sin leumaidh òganach sgiamhach suas air a' chlàr-uachdair, air a sgeudachadh gu riamhach le briogais ghoirid, le bucallaib h na bhrògaibh, agus leis gach nì eile a reir sin.

Grad chuiridh e mòran cheistean, ag iarraidh fios air ainm na loinge, cia as di, càit' am bheil i dol, agus ciod leis am bheil i air a luchdachadh.

An sin, their e gu modhail gur seirbhiseach esan do Neptun, agus gun do chuireadh e a dh'innseadh gum bheil a mhaighstir a' teachd gu grad air bòrd. An sin tha seòl mòr air a thilgeadh tarsuing air meadhon na luinge, leis am bheil a toiseach air fholuchadh o a deireadh.

Ann an ùine ghoirid, thig Neptun agus a luchd-frithealaidh a mach o chùl an t-siùil sin, agus nochdaidh iad iad fèin, nam buidhinn eagallaich, air a' chlàr-deiridh! Cumamaid nar cuimhne nach eil annta seo gu lèir ach na seòladairean fèin, air an sgeudachadh le culaidhibh iongantach, agus air an cur as aithne le dathaibh geala, dearg, agus dubh, agus le h-aghaidhibh coimheach.

Tha Neptun ga nochdadh fèin na shuidhe air carbad, a ta air a tharraing le seisear ghillibh treuna. Tha na gillean sin a' gluasad mar bheathaichibh ceithir-chosach, len corpaibh ach beag rùisgte, agus air an còmhdachadh le ballaibh dearg' agus geal, fa seach. Tha feamainn agus luibhean-mara, mar fholt, air an cinn; agus tha sligean araidh aca nan làmhaibh, leis an dean iad fuaim agus gleadhraich eagallach!

Tha Neptun na shuidhe gu h-àrd air a charbad fèin, le coron rìoghail air a cheann, agus le sleagh tri-mheurach na làimh-dheis. Fon choron seo, tha gruag mhòr air a cheann, air a dèanamh de chòreach-calcaidh; agus tha feusag uamhasach den stuth cheudna a' tuiteam sios air uchd! Aig uachdaran seo a' chuain tha mòran luchd-frithealaidh, a ta air an sgeudachadh le trusganaibh a thogras gàire na sgioba, agus leis gach nì eile a chuireas iad fo choslas fiadhaich agus gruamach!

Am measg chàich, chìtear leigh Neptuin, leis gach cungaidh leighis na làimh; agus mar an ceudna bearradair Neptuin, aig am bheil ealtuinn dà throidh air fad, eadhon mir de chearcall iaruinn air meirgeadh! Aig a' bhearradair seo tha gille mòr dubh, a ta giùlan cuinneig na làimh mar bhocsa-siabuinn, làn tearra agus nithe eile.

Ri taobh Neptuin chìthear Amphitrite, a bhan-righinn fèin, na suidhe air carbad eile, a ta air a tharraing le seisear ghillean làidir, borb, air an sgeudachadh cosmhuil ri luchd-tarruing carbaid a companaich. Chan eile ann an Amphitrite ach fear fo eudach boirionnaich. Tha sleagh aig a' bhan-righinn, mar an ceudna, na làimh; agus na h-uchd tha aon de bhalachanaibh na luinge, mar naoidhean.

Tha banaltrum aig an leanabh sin, a ta taomadh brochain le ladair iaruinn na bheul. A bhàrr air seo, tha mòran de luchd-frithealaidh aig Amphitrite - maighdeana-mara, le sgàthanaibh, ciribh, bruisibh, agus nithibh eile mar sin, air an siubhal.

An uair a bheirear na carbadan chum a'chaisteil-deiridh, thig caiptean na luinge a làthair, le fion agus deochaibh eile, chum beatha Neptuin altachadh air bòrd. Grad thilgidh uachdaran a' chuain agus a cheile an sleaghan air an làr, mar so a' toirt ùmlachd do phrìomh-fhear na luinge, agus do bhan-righinn na dùcha as an d' thàinig e.

"Thainig mise," their Neptun, "chum failt a chur ortsa, a dheagh Bhreatannaich, agus chum innseadh dhuit gum bheil mi toilichte t'fhaicinn an taobh a stigh de m' chrìochaibh. Seo agad Amphitrite, mo cheile-sa, agus seo agad mo leanabh. Ceadaich dhomh a-nis foighneachd airson mo bhan-charaid chòir, Bhictoria, ban-righinn Bhreatainn,- agus airson a companaich, Prionns' Ailbeirt,- agus airson an teaghlaich rìoghail gu lèir."

Caiptean.- "Dh'fhàg mise slàn, fallain, iad uile."

Neptun.- "Is taitneach, gun teagamh, an naigheachd sin leamsa, a chaiptean chòir; ach cionnas tha na naoidheana rìoghail, am Prionns' òg agus a phiuthar?"

Caiptean.- "Le 'r cead, chuala mi gum bheil na pàisdean a' tighinn air an aghart gu math agus gu ro mhath; ach ged a fhuair mi, a-nis, an t-urram agus an toil-inntinn mac rìgh a' chuain fhaicsinn a'm luing fèin, chan fhaca mi riamh ar leanabana rioghail fèin, am Prionns' òg agus a phiuthar; ach tha iad gun deireas sam bith - gu seasgair, sàmhach, anns an lùchairt rìoghail; agus, cosmhuil ris na craobhaibh, chan eil tuilleadh aca ri dhèanamh ach a bhi fàs suas."

Neptun.- "Is binn leam fèin do sgeul, a Bhreatannaich - is math leam a chluinntinn gum bheil na pàisdean a' soirbheachadh. Ach innis seo dhomh;- am bheil Ailbeart beag, Prionnsa na h-Adhailt* co tapaidh, tomadach, ris an leanabh-gille seo agamsa, nach eil fathast ach beagan mhios a dh'aois - a rugadh am measg nan tonn atmhor, geala, gàireach - agus aig nach eil pàilliun ach garbh-aigeal a' chuain ànradhaich?"

Caiptean.- "Chan eil e gu dearbh, agus cha bu dual màthar da a bhi mar sin, oir is boirionnach beag Bann-righinn Bhreatainn."

Neptun.- "Ciod sin a thubhairt thu, a chaiptein - Ban-righinn Bhreatainn na boirionnach beag! Am boirionnach is mò air an talamh, gidheadh a d' bharail-sa tha i beag! Smuainich car tiota co i, agus co iad na sinnseara mòra, gaisgeil, cruadalach, o 'n d'thàinig i. B'eòlach mise air righribh Shasainn agus Albainn re iomadh linn air ais, agus b'iad fèin an laochraidh threun agus chalma.

Smuainich air fad, agus leud, agus farsuingeachd nan rioghachdan, nan tìrean, agus nan eileanan, thairis air am bheil uachdaranachde an diugh aig Ban-righinn Bhictoria,- agus an abair thu an sin gum bheil i beag? Chan eil a' ghrian a' luidhe air na na tìribh thairis air am bheil i a' riaghladh. Tha i na farmad do chumhachdaibh an domhain, agus na cùis-eagail do gach rìoghachd nàimhdeil! N aon fhocal, tha i mòr, mòr!"

Caiptean.- "Tha fios agam gum bheil i mòr mar bhan-righinn, ach beag mar bhoirionnach - mòr a thaobh dreuchda, ach beag a thaobh pearsaidh."

Neptun.- "Ro cheart; ro cheart. Ach, a chaiptein, chan eile ùine ri chall. Seo, òlamaid deoch-slàinte deagh Bhan-righinn Bhreatainn, agus a deagh Chompanaich. Fàs agus gràs d'am dithis chloinne; agus gum b'ann a lionas sliochd nan daoine còire brògan an aithriche'. Do thaobh an Teaghlaich Rìoghail uile, guidheamaid,-

Beatha shona a's bhuan doibh,
Slàinte bhos agus shuas doibh;
Sliochd an sliochd, 's gach sliochd uatha-san,
Feadh gach linn gu robh sluaghmhor a's mòr."

Caiptean.- "Tha mi fad a' d' chomain, a righ nan tonn beucach, airson do dheagh rùin don rìoghachd sin dom buin mise, agus d'a riaghlairibh - do dheag rùin, a chuir thu an ceill co h-ullamh h-eallamh, deas-chainnteach."
Albert, Prince of Wales

Neptun.- "A-nis, a chaiptein, feumar a bhi a'dèanamh deas gu dealachadh. Is maiseach gu cinnteach an long seo, agus, a-rèir coslais, is gleusda agus is ealanta a sgioba; ach ar leam fèin gum bheil mi faicsinn mòrain sluaigh air bòrd nach robh riamh roimhe a' m' chrìochaibh-sa, agus saoilidh mi nach bu mhisd iad an aghaidhean a nigheadh, agus am feusagan a bhearradh, mun teid iad thar a' chrios mhòr."

Caiptean.- "Tha sin, a Rìgh Neptun, gu h-iomlan aig bhur toil-sa."

Neptun.- "Si mo thoil-sa, matà, gun deanar e, agus sin air ball."

Air do Neptun labhairt mar seo, buailidh e an clàr-uachdar leis an t-sleagh a bhios na làimh, a chuireas an long gu iomlan air chrith! An sin glaodhaidh e ri a luchd-frithealaidh, ag ràdh, "Thigibh an seo, mo ghillean tapaidh! Nighibh, glanaibh, agus bearraibh, gach mac màthar a ta nan coigrich; ach tha mi ai g àithneadh dhuibh a bhi bàigheil riu, agus na deanaibh dochann air uasal no iosal."

Cha mhothaichear a-nis ach cabhag, ùspairn, odhail, agus fleadhraich, thall agus a bhos! Cuid an seo a' call an treòir trid eagail, do bhrigh nach robh iad riamh roimhe nam fianuisibh air a leithid seo de shealladh; cuid eile an sud, a chunnaic a leithid roimhe, làn toil-inntinn leis an fhearas-chuideachd, air doibh a bhi gam faicinn fèin tèaruinte, agus saor o gach dolaidh!

Chìthear Neptun fèin, le sealladh àrd agus uaibhreach, na shuidhe air a charbad, ann am meadhon a luchd-frithealaidh. Ach ged is grinn an carbad sin ann an sùilibh uachdarain a' chuain agus a sheirbhiseach fèin, is suarach e an coimeas ri carbad-cogaidh Chuchullin, mhic Sheuma air am bheil;

"Oisean liath nan ceilearan" a' toirt a' chunntais a leanas:-
"Carbad! carbad garbh a' chòmhraig,
Gluasad thar chòmhnard le bàs;
Carbad cuimir luath Chuchullin,
Sàr-mhac Sheuma nan cruaidh-chàs.
Tha earr a' lùbadh sìos mar thonn,
No ceò mu thom nan carragh geur;
Solus chlocha-buadh mun cuairt,
Mar chum mu eathar san oidche.
Dh'iuthar faileasach an crann,-
Suidhear ann air cnàimhibh caoin.
'Se tuineas nan sleagh a t'ann,
Nan sgiath, nan lann, 's nan laoch."

Cha bhi ach a-mhàin aon de ghunnachaibh-mòra na luinge aig Neptun mar charbad; ach freagraidh sin fèin na bhios r' a' dhèanamh leis.

Air do Neptun a bhi nis air a chuairteachadh leòsan a bhios deas agus deònach air geill a thoirt d' a iarrtasaibh, cuirear sìos do bhroinn na luinge gach mac màthar nach robh riamh roimhe aig crios-meadhoin na talmhainn; agus suidhichear freiceadan laidir orra, gus an gairmear sìos iad aon an deigh aoin.

Thèid ballan mòr uidheamachadh, agus bithidh ochd no deich baraillean uisge air an taomadh ann. Thairis air beul a' bhallain seo cuirear sgealb fiodha, mar àite-suidhe dhoibh-san a tha gu bhi air an glanadh agus air am bearradh le seirbhisich Neptuin.

Air do gach ni mar seo a bhi air a dheasachadh, gairmear a-nìos as an luing a' cheud fhear a tha gu bhi air a laimhseachadh leis an luchd-frithealaidh aig rìgh a' chuain. Cuirear na shuidhe e os-ceann a' bhallain, le foluch air a shùilibh, chum nach faic e ciod a ta gu tachairt da. Cuirear a' cheisd seo air, "Càit' an d'rugadh e? agus co luath 's dh'fhosglas e a bheul chum sin innseadh, sparraidh am bearradair bruis làn tearra a stigh na bheul; agus comhdaichidh e a ghnùis gu lèir leis an teàrr sin, a ghnàthaicheas e an àite siabuinn! An sin glacaidh e an cearcall meirgeach na làimh mar ealtuinn, agus sgriobaidh e gnùis an duine a bhios fo làimh leis, co cruaidh agus co garbh 's gun sil a shùilean, agus gum bi a ghruaidh dearg le fhuil fèin.

Air am àm cheudna dlùthaichidh leigh Neptuin ris an duine seo, agus cumaidh e searrag-fàile ri shròin, de nach bi, gun teagamh, fàile ro chùbhraidh; agus, ciod is miosa na sin, bithidh an t-searrag làn de bhioraibh co geur ris na snàthadaibh, a bheir gu h-ealamh fuil an duine a mach! an uair a nìthear mar seo gach droch càramh air le luchd-dreuchda Neptuin, tilgear e an coinneamh a chinn sa bhallan-mhòr, chum faotuinn as air an dòigh is feàrr is urrainn e!

Nìthear an cleas ceudna air gach duine san luing nach robh riamh roimhe sa' cheàrnadh sin den chuan. Is iongantach an sgioba iad, an dèigh dhoibh a bhi mar seo air an tumadh agus air am beubanachadh. Chìtear iad bog, fliuch, salach, agus còmhdaichte le fuil, a' dèanamh spàirn a dh'fheuchainn co is luaithe a gheibh iad fèin a ghlanadh.

Is minig tha aimhreite agus tuasaid ag eiridh o na cleasaibh mi-thaitneach seo. Tha cuid ann nach striochd air chor sam bith don droch cleachdadh seo, gus an toirear a dh'aindeoin iad gu fulang mar a dh'ainmicheadh. Tha cuid eile a' ceannachadh saorsa dhoibh fèin le h-airgiod, agus le deoch a thoirt do cheirbhisich Neptuin - nithe air an dean iad greim len uile chridhe.

Air mòran de longaibh, chan eil na droch cleasan seo a-nis air an gnàthachadh idir; agus air longaibh eile, chan fheudar dol fad air an aghaidh leò. Chan eile iad air chor sam bith air an cead-achadh air longaibh-imrich - 'se sin, air longaibh a ta giùlan sluaigh gu ùr-threabhacas ann an tìr chein.

O cheann beagan bhliadhnachan air ais, bha duin-uasal araidh a' dol null air fairge, agus dhiùlt e a shaorsa a cheannachadh, agus mar an ceudna cha strìochdadh e don chleachdadh sin air an d'thug sinn cunntas. An uair a chunnaich cuideachd Neptuin seo, bhris iad a steach do sheòmar an duin'-uasal,-shlaoid iad leò e dh'ionnsuidh a' bhallain-mhòir, - bhearr agus bhog iad e,- agus an sin leig iad air cead a choise e.

Lionadh an duine le corruich, farran, agus tàmailt. Thog e fianuisean air a' chàramh a dh'fhuiling e; agus an uair a ràinig an long ceann a turuis, chaidh e gu lagh ris a' chaiptean, do bhrìgh gun do cheaduich e a leithid de ghiùlan mi-riaghailteach air a luing, agus thug e trì cheud punnd Sasunnach dheth!

Chan eil teagamh nach eil fearas-chuideachd na nì taitneach air cuan-thurus fada, an uair a bhios cuideachd mhòr air an druideadh suas ann an luing, agus nach faic iad re iomadh miosa ach na speuran os an ceann, agus an cuan mòr, farsuing, fosgailte, ceithir thimcheall orra; ach an dèigh sin uile, co aca tha daoine air muir no air tìr, bu chòir do gach sùgradh agus cridhealas a ghnàthaich-ear leò a bhi air gach seòl gun chron do dhuine sam bith, agus nan nithibh neo-lochdach annta fèin, do nach faighear coire le lagh Dhe no dhaoine.

Crossing the Equator

[An eyewitness account from an unnamed passenger on board]

There would not, in all likelihood, be many *Cuairtear** readers who would ever have heard of the extraordinary ritual that is the custom of ships crossing the equator. An attempt will be made here, therefore, to give a short account of the substance of that event that is the custom of the day on many ships as they sail across that line towards the East, to Australia or any place in the Southern Ocean.

In this country the sun from the south would shine on us at noon; but if we were in Australia it would shine on us about midday from the north. The world is round and, in some respects, egg shaped. Therefore, at a specific place in the middle of the journey, between the southern tip and the northern tip of the world, the sun at midday on a certain time of the year is directly above our head; and this place is called, in English, the 'Line' or 'Equator' - this is, the band or the circumference around the world, from east to west, and dividing it in two halves.

But, to keep our story easily understood, it needs to be understood that there were many lying gods of the heathens in whom they foolishly and blindly put their hopes. It was rare for them not to have a god or goddess for everything. In this manner, there was Mars, god of war - Bacchus, god of wine - Pan, god of the woods - Ceres, goddess of corn - Minerva, goddess of wisdom - and so on.

It is obvious that increasingly creating gods for everything in their own minds in this way, they would likewise create a god for the large and stormy oceans. This was Neptune, god of the seas, and Aphrodite goddess of the seas. When there was ignorance of the one true living God, creator of heaven and earth, there was an increase in idolatry, that vainly believed that it was he, Neptune, who was the cause of every storm and tempest on the large seas, and that all the world's waters were under his rule!

To maintain mirth and hilarity on any ship heading for foreign lands, the sailors pretend that Neptune exists and dwells in the huge ocean at the equator; and that he will not permit any ship to go past without his welcoming her.

When a ship reaches that place on the ocean, a sailor will go to the top of the main mast, looking out on all sides. It is not long before he cries with all his strength.

"I see something like a boat on the windward side!"

A short time after that, a voice will be heard from the sea from the prow of the ship, and a special officer answers. The voice will say to this officer:

"Heave-to the ship, because Neptune, god of the ocean, is coming on board."

Immediately the ship puts up, and at the same moment a handsome youth jumps up on the deck, in fancy clothes with short breeks, with buckles on his shoes, and with everything else after that fashion.

He quickly asks many questions, wanting information on the name of the ship, how many are aboard, where she is going, and what is her cargo.

Then he says politely that he was the servant of Neptune, and that he has invited his master to quickly come on board. Then as the big ship crosses the middle of the earth, they begin to hide themselves in the stern.

In a short time, Neptune then appears. His attendants, who come from behind the sail and show themselves, form a terrifying group on the stern deck! It is ignored that these were actually part of the ship's crew (i.e. sailors,), wearing wonderfully designed clothes, white, red, and black colours, and with foreign faces.

Neptune himself appeared sitting on a chariot that was drawn by six strong young men. The young men advanced like animals on all fours, with their bodies partly bare, but also with some clothing coloured with alternating red and white stripes. Seaweed and sea plants-like hair were on their heads, and with special shells in their hands, also making a terrifying, rattling noise!

Neptune sits high on his own chariot, with a royal crown on his head, and with a trident in his hand. Under this crown, a big wig of rope strands is on his head; and a beard of the same coarse material fell down across his breast! The ruler of the seas had many attendants, some with clothes that made the crew smile, and others with the appearance of fierce savages!

Among others, Neptune's physician can be seen, with every medicine in his hand; likewise Neptune's barber, with a razor two foot in length, (in reality, a bit of a rusting iron hoop!). With this barber is a little black boy, who is carrying a small pail in his hand like a soap box, but full of tar and other things.

Alongside Neptune can be seen Aphrodite, his queen, sitting on another chariot, drawn by six strong young men, outrageously dressed and resembling those drawing the chariot of her mate. Aphrodite was really a man dressed in woman's clothes. The Queen also had a spear in her hand; and on her breast one of the young boys (from the ship's crew) posing as an infant.

A nurse was beside the infant emptying porridge with a metal ladle into his mouth. At the end of this parade were many of Aphrodite's attendants - mermaids, - with mirror, comb, brush, and other things like that, at the time.

When the chariots were borne, in order, to the quarter-deck, the ship's captain came, with wine and other drinks, in order to welcome Neptune on board. The ruler of the seas suddenly threw both the spears on the ground, in this manner paying respect to the ship's chief, and to the queen, following proper protocol.

"I came," said Neptune, "in order to give a welcome to you, worthy British, and in order to tell you that I am happy seeing you within my territory. Here you have Aphrodite, my wife, and here you have my child. Permit me now to ask after my good kinswoman. Victoria, Queen of Britain - and of her companion, Prince Albert - and of the large royal family."

Captain. - "I left them all sound and healthy."

Neptune, - "Without doubt that is good news to me, good captain; but how are the royal infants, the young Prince and his sister?"

Captain.- "With your permission, I heard that the infants are coming on very well; but though I have the honour and pleasure of seeing, on my own ship, the son of the king of the seas, I will never see our own royal infants, the young Prince and his sister; but they are without any harm - at ease, comfortable, in the royal palace; and, like the trees, there is nothing more for them to do but to grow up."

Neptune,- "Your story is pleasing to me; Britisher - it is good to hear that the infants are prospering. But tell me this - is little Albert, Prince of Wales, as manly and as large as my own child, only a few months old - that was born among the white, roaring and swelling waves - and not in a palace, but in the deep stormy ocean?"

Captain.- "He certainly is not, and nor was his mother like that, because the British Queen is a small woman."

Neptune.- "What's that you said, captain - the British Queen is a small woman! She is the greatest woman in the world, yet your opinion is that she is small! Consider a little the large, heroic and hardy ancestors from which she came. I was acquainted with English and Scottish rulers over many past generations, and they themselves were brave, stout, and heroic.

Knowing the length, breadth and extent of their reigns, in their lands and islands, over which Queen Victoria today has dominion, - and you say then that she is small? Is not the sun on every corner of the land over which she rules? She is not envious of world powers nor fearful of any hostile kingdom! In one word, she is big! big!"

Captain,- "I know that she is big as a queen, but she is small as a woman - big in her office, small in her person."

Neptune,- "Very true; very true. But, captain, there is no time to lose. Here, drink my toast to the British Queen, and to her Companion, Albert Prince of Wales.

Prosperity and grace to the two children; may their offspring increase. To all the Royal Family, wishing,

Life, long and happy to them,
Health from here and above to them;
Generation to generation, and every generation from them,
Through every age, many and long."

Captain,- "I am much obliged to you, king of the roaring waves, for your excellent regard for the kingdom that I belong to, and to its ruler – and your toast that you put so readily, wonderfully and eloquently."

Neptune,- "Now, captain, there is need to do something apart from this. This is certainly a fair ship, and in all likelihood its crew are alert; but I will guess that there are many people on board who have never before been in my country, and I suppose they will be none the worse for having their faces washed and beards shaved, before they will go across the big line."

Captain,- "That is, King Neptune, altogether at your pleasure."

Neptune,- "It is my pleasure, then, to do it, and that immediately."
As Neptune was speaking like this, he struck the deck with the spear that was in his hand, that sent the whole ship trembling! Then, shouting to his attendants, he said, "Come here, my manly boys! Wash, clean, and shave, each person that is a stranger; but I am ordering mercy for them, and do not punish the noble or the humble."

There was nothing now but haste, struggle, bustle and entertainment, here and there! Some were weak through fear, by virtue of not having ever witnessed anything of the like before. Others were fully satisfied with the diversion seeing that each was free from any harm!

Neptune himself was seen, high and proud, sitting on his chariot in the midst of his attendants. But though the chariot of the ruler of the seas and his servants were an imposing sight, it was insignificant in comparison to Chùchulainn's war chariot.

"Ossian grey-haired of the songs" gives a description, as follows:

"Chariot! terrible chariot of war,
Moving across a field of death;
Chùchulainn's chariot well-proportioned, swift,
Worthy son Sheuma of the danger.
Its tail flowing down like a wave,
Or mist about a hill's sharp peak;

A gleam around a jewel,
As is kept about a boat in the evening.
The mast, polished yew,
Sitting in polished ivory.
A receptacle for the spears,
Of the shield, of the sword, and of the hero."

Neptune's chariot was one of the ship's big guns; but it was fitting for him.

As Neptune was now surrounded by all those who were ready and willing to obey his command, everyone who had never been to the equator was put in the belly of the ship; and a strong guard appointed over them, until they were called up one by one.

A large tub, with appropriate instruments, was overflowing with eight to ten barrels of water. Over the lip of the tub was a plank of wood for sitting those chosen to be clean-shaved by Neptune's servants.

As everything like this was in preparation, the first man who was to be handed to the attendants of the king of the seas was called from below. He was seated above the tub, blindfolded in order that he could not see what was to happen to him. This question was put to him, "Where were you born?", and as soon as he opened his mouth to tell, a shaving brush full of tar was put inside his mouth; and his face was covered with plenty of that tar in the place of soap! Then the rusty iron was wielded like a razor and the man's face was roughly scraped so that he sheds tears and his cheeks were red with blood.

Then Neptune's doctor approached this man, and put a bottle to his nose, which would not be, without doubt, a very fragrant bottle; and, what was worse, he was fed a full bottle of prickles sharp as a needle; that quickly drew blood out of the man! When every wicked treatment like this was done by Neptune's officers, the interview is ended by throwing him in the big tub.

The same game was carried out on every man in the boat that had never been in that region of the seas. And those following who were, in this manner, to be ducked and mangled, feared the crew. They could be seen drenched, dirty, and covered with blood, anxious to have it over with so they could get themselves cleaned.

Unpleasant quarrelling and brawling often arise from these games. Some do not, on any condition, submit to this bad practice until, despite their resistance, they are compelled to agree. Some purchase their freedom by giving drink and money to Neptune's servants - things they grasp eagerly.

On many ships, these wicked games are not now the custom at all; and on other ships, they are against them going so far. They are not permitted under any condition on immigrant ships - that is on ships carrying rural people to foreign lands.

A few years ago, a certain gentleman, that we were given an account of, was going across the ocean, and he refused to give a freedom payment, and he also would not yield to the custom. When Neptune also saw this, they smashed into the gentleman's room and dragged him with them towards the big tub, - shaved and dunked him, - and then permitted him to leave.

The man was filled with anger, offence, and shame. He collected witnesses of the abuse that he had suffered, and when the ship reached the end of its journey, he took the captain to law arguing that he permitted the likes of such behaviour on his ship, and the captain had to give him three hundred pounds!

There is no doubt that such a wild group of people is not a pleasant thing on a long sea journey, when they are shut up on the ship and see nothing for many months but the skies above, and the wide ocean all around. But after all that, whether men are at sea or on land, they ought to have some harmless amusements on every ship, harmless under the law of God or man.

18 Tuireadh a' Ghàidheal

[Neo-Ainmichte]

'S Mòr am mùgh th' air an dùthaich-
O 'n b' anns' leam bhi 'n tùs a' na còir;
'S lìonmhor dorus tha dùinte,
'S an robh mi gu sunntach àm òig;
Càirdean dìleas air sgaoileadh-
'S tearc nis luchd mo ghaoil mu na bhòrd-
Cuid diubh 'n tìr fad air astar,
'S cuid sinnte 'n taigh-tasgaidh fon fhòid.

'S ioma teaghlach ghrinn, chiatach,
Bu ghnà bhi air sliabh nam beann àrd,
Th' air an sguab as na crìochan,
A 's uachdrain sìor mhiadach am màil;
Luchd na dùthch' air an treigeadh,
A 's coigrich tric leumadh nan àit-
Cuid le maoraibh gan ruagadh,
'S cuid air faondra mar uain gun am màthair.

'S ioma taigh tha na Làrach,
A's gleannan na fhàsach neo-ghrinn;
Àite' beag gan cuir suarach,
'S àite mòr gan cuir suas air ar cinn;
Tha cuid eile fo chaoraich
Thug lòn dh'ioma teaghlach nar linn;
'S iad a fògradh thar chuantan
Nan Gaeil da 'm bu dual bhi sna glinn.

'S mòr am beud na Gaeil ghasta,
Bha fiùghantach, tlachd' or, grinn còir,
Bhi gan ruag as na bacaibh
Feadh an t-saoghal air an sgapadh cho mòr;
'S mòr am beud gum biodh daoine
Dhith fasgaidh dhith aodaich, no lòn,
'S caoraich 'g ionaltradh 's na h-àitean
'S an d' fhuair iad as àrach o'n òig.

Gaideadh, b' aithne dhomh uachdran,
Ri bochdan bha truacant thar chàch,
Toirt gu fialaidh do dheoraibh
Cuibhrinn deoch agus lòn ioma là-
Meag a's bainne gun phàidh-
'S taigh-còmhnuidh do dh'aireamh gun mhail;
'S mòr am beud nach robh phacaid
Deagh-lìonte le h-òr as an Spainn.

Sliochd nam fineachan Gàidhealach
Nan gaisgach, 's nan sar dhaoine còir!
'S mòr an t-urram a fhuair iad,
Le 'n dillseachd 's an cruadal thar slòigh.
Ge d' bhiodh feachd anns na blàraibh
Tri-fillte da 'n aireamh, a 's còrr,
'S minig chuir iad an ruaig air
Rag-nàimhdean bhiodh cruaidh air an toir.

Daoine furanach, fiachail,
'S mnaithean cinnedail, rianail do rèir;
Òigridh eireachdall, iùlor-
B' iad comann bhiodh sunntach air fèill;
Tìr nam beann 's nan gleann boidheach.
'S am b' anns' leò bhi chòmhnuidh gu lèir-
'S tur a tha i air caochladh-
'S tearc neach ann nì aoidheachd ri chèil.

Tha 'n dubh Gall tighin don dùthaich;
A 's cleachdana ùr tigh'nn ri linn:
Mar' aisg uil' air na Gallaibh,
A shanntaich cho ealamh na glinn;
O 'n a thriall iad don tìr seo,
Toirt fasana' mi-chiatach dhuinn,
Chan eil nì mar a b' àbhaist
'S na gleanntan san d' arraichear sinn.

Bha mi aon uair a saoilsinn-
Measg òigridh, luchd aoidheachd a's rann-
Ri! gum maireadh sud daonnan,
'S gum bith'maid cho aobhach sa b' anns;
'S ioma car thug an saogh'l as
Gach dream bha cuir faoin-dhochas ann,
'S char e mise air aon diubh,
Cuir smuaintean cho faoin ann am cheann.

Tha luchd Beurla cho lìonmhor,
'S an aireamh a miadach gach là,
Cuir na Gàelig a fasan,
'S toirt cànain lom Chrossuinn na h-àit-
Teangaidh fhuar a's làmh fhalamh,
Nach d' thoireadh, 's nach gabhadh, ma chàch
'S mòr an diùbhail a thachair,
Gun d' thàin iad o 'n mhachair gu bràth.

O 'n bu leò-san gnè eòlais,
Air talamh gu sònraicht' 's air bàthaich,
Fhuair sinn sud mar bu deòn leinn-
Measg fasana bronach gun stà:
Ach an eirig na fhuair sinn,
Bu mhiann leò ar gluasad a' 'r n' àit,
Mar chuir Breatun 's na Innsean*
Sluagh dligheach fo chìs anns na blàir.

Ach thig cumhachd o eòlas
Don àl tha teachd oirnne nar dèigh;
'S feàrr na treubhantas mòr-fheachd
A bhuaidh thig o' fhòghlum nach trèig,
Tha nis àrd-chlèir a's uailsean-
Mòr bheannachd a's buaidh leò le chèil'-
Togail lòchran 's gach garbh-chrìoch,
Feadh iomala' na h-Alba gu lèir.

O 'n tha sgoilean gam planntach
Feadh eileanan 's gleanntan na tìr,
Gheibh na Gaeil, mar as àill leò,
De 'n fhòghlum a b' àbhaist doibh bhi dhith-
Tuille eòlais air ceartas,
Air laghan a's reachdan na Sìth,
'S tuillidh tuigse chum reusan
A thoirt do luchd Beurl' ann an strì.

Ciod ach innleach 'o fhòghlum
Thog Gallaibh cho mòr o 'n lom làr:
Ann an gaisgeachd làmh làidir,
'S minig thug na treun Ghaeil orra bàrr;
Leamsa 's èibhinn an dòchas,
Nach gèill iad an eòlas do chàch,
'S nach bi iad tuile mar bha iad,
Aig Gallaibh nan traillean fon sàil.

O 'n a dh'fhalbh uainn thar sàile
Liuthad treun-laoch de Ghaeil as an tìr,
Buaidh a's tapadh 's gach càs leò,
Chuid nach faic sinn gu bràth 's chuid a chì:
Luchd a chridhe chaomh fhialaidh!
Be 'm beud gum biodh iadsan a dhith-
Mìle beannachd leò uile,
Gach cèarn de 'n chruinne am bi! 'R'

*Probably colonies, maybe the East Indies.

A Gael's Lament

[Anon]

The country has greatly changed
Since I went away;
And many a door is closed,
And I was happier in my youth.
But true friends are scattering -
Only a few are now about the table -
Some of them are in lands far away,
But some are dead and buried.

And many excellent, honest families,
Customarily settled around the high slopes,
Have been cleared out beyond the borders,
And the chief continually increases the rent;
The country people are leaving
Some with the bailiff pursuing them,
And some wandering like motherless lambs,
Strangers often jumping into their place.

And many homes are in ruins,
The glens are empty and neglected,
And small plots are despised.
It is now large areas that are praised and used.
Sheep are on some of these lands
Where many families used to be settled;
But they were exiled across the seas
From the glens - the Gaels' birthright.

It is a great loss of these excellent Gaels,
Who were generous, decent and honest.
They were harassed unceasingly
And scattered widely throughout the world;
And it is great shame that men
Need shelter, and clothes and food
In the north, where they were raised,
But where sheep now graze in their place.

I once was acquainted with a chief,
Incomparably compassionate to the poor,
Providing assistance to needy men
With food and water for a lengthy period-
Giving whey and milk without charge
And accommodation, without rent, to some;
And more's the pity that his wallet
Was not well-filled with Spanish gold.

Descendants of the Highland clans
Of heroes, and of worthy, pious men!
They were greatly respected,
Brave and faithful above other peoples.
Though an army on the battlefield
Was triple their number,
Often, they would put them to flight
And pursue the obstinate enemy.

Worthy, respectable men and women,
with families, likewise peaceable;
With children both handsome and sensible-
They were a cheerful community on market day;
In a land of high mountains and beautiful glens.
There they dwelt together -
This has now completely passed away -
And scarcely will one be hospitable to another.

The Foreigner has come to this country;
Bringing new customs
Such as greed
Which covets so quickly the glens.
Since travelling to this land
They have brought customs unseemly to us,
Nothing is as it was
In the glens where we were raised.

I was thinking once -
Among children, cheerful singing people-
That there is always tomorrow,
And let us be glad that it is so.
Yet, many twists brought this world about
People were foolish to trust in it,
Of whom I was one,
For having such naive thoughts in my head.

English people are so numerous,
And their number increases each day
Making Gaelic unfashionable,
Bringing a bleak tongue to you, Chrossuinn-
A cold tongue and an empty hand
That will not live and let live like the others.
And great destruction has resulted,
And cattle removed from the machair for ever.

They had a form of knowledge
Of the land particularly; and of the byre.
We got what was assigned to us-
Poor and useless land to cultivate:
But we received no recompense.
They chose to move us from our land,
As Britain did to its colonial peoples,*
People becoming tributaries on their own land.

But power comes from knowledge
For the generation coming after us;
It is preferable that victory comes from education
Rather than from the feats of a great army.
Many are now high clergymen and gentry-
Many blessings and success to them
Who carry the torch out of every rugged district
Throughout all the borders of Scotland.

From the schools to founding a colony
Throughout the islands and glens of the land,
The Gaels shall get what they desire,
The education that customarily was wanting-
More knowledge about justice,
Of statutes and of the Spirit of the law;
And more understanding in order to reason
And contend with the English people.

By what means, except through education,
Was the foreigner raised from his lowly position?
The strong hands and valiant deeds of the heroes
Often brought the Gaels superiority;
It is my hope
That they will not knowingly submit to others
And never return to what they were,
As slaves beneath the heel of the Foreigner.

Since they departed from us across the sea
Many brave Gaels from the land
Have successfully overcome every emergency.
Some we will never see again, others we will see:
Beloved, kind and hospitable people!
It is disgraceful if they should be in want-
A thousand blessings to them all,
Wherever in the world they may be.

*The colonies, maybe the East Indies.

19 Fàilte Don Ghaidhealtachd

[le Dòmhnall 'ic Ionmhainn senior]

Mise 'n diugh aig taobh a' chuain
Stoirm a' sèideadh 's frasan fuar,
Tonn air thonn a' ruith gu tràigh,
Gaoir 'n am chluais le cruas an gàir;
Thug e 'm chuimhne làithean m' òige
Nuair bha mi buachailleachd nam bò
An Cola creagach, tìr mo ghaoil,
'S na tuinn a beuchdaich air le gaoir.

Fad air falbh o thìr mo rùin
Thall an seo 'n taobh eile 'n t-saoghall,
Australia, ged 's mòr do mhaoin,
Gum b' annsa leamsa tìr an fhraoich,
Tìr mo chàirdean 's mo luchd-dàimh,
Tìr mo mhàthar 's m' athair chaoimh,
An tìr 's an d' fhuair mi m' àrach òg,
Tìr nan gleann 's nam beanntan mòr.

Bidh aoibhneas mòr 'n tìr mo shluaigh
Nuair thig an samhraidh ann mun cuairt,
Eòin ri ceòl 's a' dèanamh chuach,
'S an sprèidhh a' geumnaich suas gu buaile;
B' e mo mhiann bhi falbh nan raoin,
M' aghaidh suas gu beinn a' chùirn
Fàile cùbhraidh flùir mun cuairt dhomh,
Is sgiathan luath na circe-fraoich.

Smeòraichean air gheugan ùra
A' seinn le seirm an òrain ghaoil,
Uiseagan os ceann gach raoin,
Is cuthag shuas 's a' choille chaoil;
Torman ciùin aig eas an fhuarain,
Ruith gu luath gu bonn a' chùirn,
'S mìle seillean air gach taobh dhomh,
Tional mil a flùir an fhraoich.

Tha ormsa nàire 's rughadh gruaidh,
Tha mo Ghàidhlig tuilleadh 's fuar,
Mo theanga balbh cha dean i luaidh
Le ceartas còir air tìr mo shluaigh,
An tìr 's an cluinnt' a' Ghàidhlig bhlàth,
Cànain ghaoil nan sàr 's nam bàrd,

Cainnt nan Gàidheil ghaisgeil mhòir
Tha eòlach ainmeil 's an Roinn-Eòrp.

Chan eil gaisgich air an t-saoghal
Bheireadh buaidh air cloinn an fhraoich,
Fear ri fear le'm buillibh trom,
Gach nàmhaid chaisg iad, sàir nan sonn;
'An teas a' chath 's an tuasaid throm,
Gàidheil a' spealtadh chorp is cheann,
Sgal na pìob 'g an cur gu loinn,
Mire-chath' aig laoich nan gleann.

Ach se Clann Fhionghuin clann mo ghlòire-s',
Ceathairn àillidh, slàn gun ghò,
Daoine foghlaimte beachdmhor còir,
Modhail cluin 'n an cainnt 's 'n an dòigh;
Flathail, aoibheil, caoimhneil, mòr,
Daingean, seasmhach 'n ceart 's an còir,
Fuil rìoghail anns gach cuisle 's pòr,
A sruthadh sìos bho Ailpein mòr.

Rium-s' thuirt bodaich ghabach cham
Nach eil Clann Fhionghuin nise ann,
'N tìr nan gleann 's nam beann cho gann
'S nach cliù an ainmeach' measg nan clann;
Sin fhreagair mis' na fir air baill,
Tha mìltean chlachan anns gach gleann,
Ach clachan luachmhor daonnan gann,
Bidh daoimein priseil anns gach àm.

Ar n-eachdraidh re gach tim a bh' ann,
Ag innseadh dhuinn le cinnteas cainnt
Nach robh riamh, 's nach eil 's an linn seo,
Fear-brathaidh no mi-thapach ann;
'S chan eil àit' an dèan iad triall,
Soillseachail 'n an gnàth 's 'n an gnìomh.

'Ur mnathan gràdach is bhur clann,
Aoidheil blàth-chridheach 's gach àm,
Modhail, eòlach, socrach, sìobhalt',
Cha bhiodh moit no mi-mhodh ann;
Beannachd leibh, a Chlann mo ghràidh,
Is guidheam sith dhuibh as gach àl,

Saoibhreas, sìolas, 's cliù 's gach àite,
Deas no tuath 's an dèan sibh tàmh!

Rè mhìltibh bliadhn' ruith sìos na tìm
Bha sluagh gun àireamh anns na glinn,
Na maighdeannan 's na fleasgaich òga,
Dreachmhor, stòlda, òrdail, grinn;
Mo thruaighe 'n diugh tha 'n àireamh gann,
Chaidh am fuadach fada thall;
Fèidh is caoraich anns gach gleann,
Chan eil rùm do Ghàidheil ann.

Ach cuidheall an fhortain thig mun cuairt,
'S an là sin gheibh na Gàidheil buaidh;
Le saoibhreas thig an siol thar chuain,
'S bidh glinn a' crith le iolaich sluaigh;
Àrd-Rìgh an fhreasdail, greas an t-àm
'S an còrd na coigrich is na goill,
Is tìr nan gleann 's nam beann 'g a roinn
Le ceartas seasmhach sìor d' a cloinn.

Chan fhaic mise glòir nan gleann,
Mo leòn! chan fhaic, cha bhi mi ann,
Tha mi ro-shean, 's gur liath mo cheann,
Gu bràth mi dh'fhaicinn tìr nam beann;
Ach, 'fhir 'tha seòladh thar a' chuain,
A' dol don Ghàidhealtachd mu thuath,
Thoir mìle beannachd uamsa suas
Gu tìr mo mhàthar, tìr mo luaidh!

Greetings to the Highlands
[by Donald MacKinnon senior]

Today I am beside the sea;
A storm blowing and cold rain falling,
Wave upon wave rushing to shore.
The noise resounding in my ear
Recalling memories of my younger days
When I was herding cows
In rocky Coll, my beloved land,
With the roaring waves crying out.

I am far from the land I love-
And now on the other side of the world,
Australia - though great your wealth
It is the land of heather I love more,
Land of my friends and my kindred,
Land of my beloved mother and father,
The land of my early training,
Land of glens and of high mountains.

Great joy will be in the land of my people
When summer comes around,
With birds singing and nesting,
And cattle lowing in the fold;
I long to be in their field,
My face towards a mountain cairn
The fragrant scent of flowers around me
And the beating wings of the moor-hen.

Mavis, perched on new saplings,
Melodiously singing their love songs;
With larks hovering above each meadow,
And the shrill cry of the cuckoo from the woods;
The peaceful murmur of the waterfall pools,
Running quickly over the stony bottom,
And a thousand bees on each side of me,
Gathering honey from heather flowers.

My cheek blushes with shame,
My Gaelic is growing cold,
My tongue is silent, not using it
As people from my land should,

The land where pleasant Gaelic is heard,
Beloved language of the hero and the poet,
Speech of the great Gaelic warriors
Known and lauded throughout Europe.

There is no force in the world
That would overcome the children of the heather,
Man to man, swapping heavy blows,
They subdue every enemy, these matchless heroes;
In the heat of battle and wearying tumult,
Gael cleaving body and head,
The skirling pipes sounding joyously.
Inciting to battle the heroes of the glen.

But it is the children of Clan Mackinnon I praise,
Fair champions, wholly without deceit,
Learned men, just in their opinions,
Courtesy apparent in their speech and manner;
Noble, kind, friendly, renowned,
Strong, steadfast, true and just,
Royal blood in each vein and pore,
Flowing down from Ailpein mòr.*

A gossipy, deceitful old man said to me
That there was not now a Clan Mackinnon;
That it was scarce in the land of glen and mountain
And that the name was not famous among the clans;
I answered that man immediately
That there are thousands of stones in every glen
But valuable ones are always scarce;
And that a diamond is precious in every age.

Our record of every past age
Tells us in no uncertain terms
That there never was, in the past or present age,
Any betrayal or cowardice in them;
And there is not a place wherever they travelled
But that they shone in manner and deed.
*
Your loving women and your children,
Hospitable, tender-hearted, and always
Courteous, intelligent, quiet and civil,
Not being overproud or impolite;
Blessing to you, my beloved Clan,
I pray peace on them and on every generation,

Prosperity, fruitfulness, and fame everywhere,
South or north, and wherever you rest!

During thousands of years, down to this time,
There were people without number in the glens,
Maidens and young men
Graceful, composed, orderly, elegant.
My misery today is in their scarcity,
Evictions sent them far away;
Deer and sheep are now in every glen,
But there is no room for Highlanders.

However, the wheel of fortune will turn,
And on that day Highlanders will get victory;
Descendants, with their wealth, shall return from abroad,
And glens will shake with the people's triumphant shouts;
Wait upon God, speed the time
And let there be reconciliation and not grief,
In the land of glens, of mountains and of poetry;
Let justice be established forever in her children.

I will not see this glory of the glen,
Alas! I will not see it, I will not be there,
I am too old, and my head is grey.
Never will I again see the land of the mountain;
But, I would ask one across the seas,
Going northwards to the Highlands,
To give a thousand blessings from me
To my mother's land! My beloved land.

*A reference to Kenneth MacAlpine (810-858), purported King of the Picts and, later, of the united Scots and Picts.

20 Loch Laggain

(Neo-Ainmichte)

'S e èibhinn am sealla
Loch Laggain, mo rùn,
Ann 'n glacaibh nan àrd cheanna
Là sèimh agus ciùin,
Le ceò air gach mullach
Coille uain' air gach sliabh
Far 'n gloine a ruitheas
Pattach* soilleir mar ghrian.

'S mi 'g amharc mun cuairt
Dh'èirich fonn air mo chri
Bhi faicinn Airdmheirigie
Còmhdaichte le sgiamh,
Faicinn faileas gach cnoic
Fìor chumadh gach sliabh,
Ann 'n sgathan an fhuar uisg
A's neo-ghruamaiche fiamh.

Tha caisteal an t-eilean
'N robh lùchairt Righ Fearghais**
Air crìonadh gu buileach
'S air tuiteam na laraich
Tha 'n innis faith'st àillidh
Le bòichead a flurain,
'S beith' uain toirt deadh fhaile
Aig tra feasgair na driùchd.

Ach tha flùrain as maisaich,
'Na chinn riamh 'n taobh sruthain,
Fo dhubhair na dos choill
Aig aghaidh a bhruthaich;
Ged s' cuanar 'n laogh ballach
'N colman clisgeach ged 's caomh,
Mar blàth mhaighd'na mo ghaoil!

Gu robh 'n freasdal gan glèidheadh
Bho aimhreit is strì,
Frasadh nuas orr am pailteas
Beannachd sonuis is sìth
'S cuireadh torman sruth Phattach

Cagradh sàmhach nan cluas
Gu bheil mo ghaol sa gun mhearachd
Sìor mhairionn as buan!

*Pattach – A river flowing into the Loch.
**King Fergus (430-501) – Legendary first King of the Scots.

Loch Laggan, Scotland

Loch Laggan
(Anon)

It is a delightful spectacle
My beloved Loch Laggan,
In the hollow of the high peaks
On a quiet and placid day.
With mist about every summit,
A green wood on every moor,
And Pattach*, running like glass,
shining in the sun.

Looking around me
Desire awakened in my heart
Observing Airdmheirigie
Dressed in beauty,
Seeing the reflection of every hill,
Each peak perfectly formed,
The joyful hues
Mirrored in the cold water.

The island castle,
That was King Fergus'** court,
Is now completely weathered
And fallen into ruin,
On an island surrounded by beauty
With elegant blossom
And green birch providing a worthy wreath
In the early evening dew.

And beautiful flowers
Ever grow beside streams
Falling over the ruin
Under the shadow of forest bush
Against the hillside;
Here is the handsome spotted fawn,
The dove, timid and gentle,
As tender-hearted as my beloved.

May providence preserve them
From confusion and strife,
Showering abundance down on them,
Blessing, happiness and peace.
Sending the music of Pattach's ripple
Peacefully whispering in the ear;

That is my perfect love
For ever and ever

*Pattach River which runs into the Loch
**King Fergus (430-501) – Legendary first King of the Scots.

21 Mo Mhàthair

[le Seumas MacIllemhaoil, Melbourne]

O, beannachd leat, a mhathair,
'Us beannachd leat le mhùirn:
'S e dh'fhàg gut inn 's fo phràmh mi
Gun abhachd no gun sunnd
Nach faod mi fuireach làmh riut,
'S a mheudaich dealt mo shul.\,
Mo chridhe tha 'g a sgàineadh,
'S mo mhànran chaidh air chùl.

Gur cianail leam bhi d' fhàgail,
A mhathair ghràdhach ruin,
Gu tìr fad' as gun chàirdean,
Gun fhàrdach no gun smùid;
Ach dè ged thèid bho d' làthair
'S bho shealladh blàth do shul,
Cha di-chuimhnich mi gu bràth thu
Gus 'n càirichte mi 's an ùir.

Ged sgarar mi fo d' leirsinn,
'S a's fheudar toirt riut cùl,
Na smointich gun do thrèig mi
An spèis a thug air ghlùn-
Mo chridhe tha cho blàth dhuit
'S an uair a bha mu dlùth;
Chan fhuaraich, 'us cha traigh dhuit
An gràdh a thug air tùs.

Ged a tha mi aotrom,
'S m' a dh'fhaoidte air bheag tor,
A siubhal cian 's air faontraigh,
Taim daonan leat 'an smaoin,
Ag cuimhneachadh nuair bha mi
Fo sgiathan gràidh do ruin,
A mhathair no bi 'g ràdhuinn
Gun d' fhàg mi thu air chùl.

M' a labhras tu na briathran
Gun d'thriall mi bh' uat-gun saod,
Gur sgolb a thèid troimh' 'm chliabh e
'G a 'm phianadh air gach taobh;
Nan saoilinn fhin gur trian mi
Gu liathadh fuiltein caol
A' d' cheann a mhàthair, dh'fhiachainn
Am bliadhna bhi ri d' thaobh.

Nuair bhios mi ann am aonar
'S gun aon air bith mun cuairt
'S ann chaillear mi ri smaointinn
Mum mhàthair tha mi thuath,
Na suidhe aig a' ghealbhann
Bhios cnamh air falbh gu luath,
'Us ise 'cur ri càrdadh
'S ri clàdadh cloimh nan uan.

Ged shiubhlainn air feadh rìogh'chdan
'S gu tirean fad' air chuairt,
Chan fhaod gun tèid air di-chuimhn'
An t-aon nach dibir luaidh,
Urran thoirt 'g afr pàrantan
Chaidh àithne dhuinn bho shuas,
Chum bhi buan ar làithean
Air fearan Rìgh nam Buadh.

Tha gaol peathar aithnichte,
'S e seirceil ciùin 'us foil,
Tha gaol bràthar furana h,
'S e duineil air gach dòigh,
Tha gaol leannain deothasa h
Ach 's sleamhain deothasach
Ach gaol na m`their mairidh e
Gus 'n taisgear I fon fhòid.

My Mother
[by James MacMillan]

O, farewell, my mother
Farewell with my tender affection,
I left you sick and under grief
Without joy or cheerfulness,
I am unable to stay by your side,
And my eyes are full of tears
My heart is rending
And my song has left me.

That sadness will accompany me,
My beloved mother,
To a far land without friends,
To a hearth without a fire;
But although I will go from your presence
And from the warmth of your eyes,
I will never forget you
Until I am laid in my grave.

Though I am cut off from your sight,
I will return to you;
Do not think that I am forsaking you
Or that attachment that I got at your knee.
My heart is so warm toward you,
As when I was near,
It has not grown cold nor lessened towards you,
It is the same love that was there from the first.

Though I am light-headed
And, perhaps, lacking common-sense,
Travelling far and wide,
You were always in my thoughts,
Remembering when I was
Under the wings of your love.
Mother do not be saying
That I left you behind.

Speaking the words
That I was leaving you,
Was as a sharp splinter piercing my breast
With tormenting pain on every side.
Thinking when I am in your presence
That a single hair would be grey
On your head, your worthy head.
I will be by your side in a year.

When I am alone,
Without anyone else around,
It is then I get to remembering
About my mother in the north,
Sitting with me at a feeble fire
Which was quickly dying away,
And I carding wool
And combing it off the lamb.

Though travelling throughout the kingdom
And to lands far away,
May not that one be forgotten,
The one that will not be neglected;
Honour given to our parents
Raising us up in the knowledge,
Which will last all our days,
Of the king of Righteousness.

My sister's love is known,
It is affectionate, gentle and patient.
I have, too, a loving and caring brother,
He is manly in every way,
Fond and loving
But it is an idle kiss
But a mother's love, it endures,
Until she is laid under the earth.

22 Òran Do Mo Dhachaidh

[le Iain dubh MacDhomhnull 'ic Iain]

Nuair dhìreadh tu suas ri bruaich Creig Thollaidh,
'S tu 'g amharc mu'n cuairt bu chaomh an sealladh;
Loch Ma-rithe fo d' shùil gu lùbach, fonnaireach,
Sèimheil, somalta, còmhnard.

Sèisd: Ged tha mi gun sunnd 's e sùrd dhomh mulaid
Nach leig iad mu suas 'n taobh tuath air thurus;
Tha phasaids cho daor 's mi caol 'san sporran
'S gum faodar fuireach air fògar.

Beinn-eigh nan fiadh* an taobh siar a' bheallaich,
'S ma coinnimh Beinn-Slioch 's gur fiadhaich cas i;
Chearc-fhraoich le cuid eun san t-slèibh am falach,
'S gur liònmhor eilid 'na còsan.
Sèisd: Ged tha mi gun … etc.,

Gum faic thu Loch-eubh gu muirneil farsuinn,
Le acarsaid chiùin, gach lùb is camus;
Mu chuairt air gach taobh gu cùmhraidh fallain,
Tha 'n dùthaich eireachdail bhòidheach.
Sèisd: Ged tha mi gun … etc.,

Ionbhar-asdail mo ghaoil, le raointean maiseach,
'Na laighe gu caoin ri taobh a' chladaich;
Gach seòrsa de bhàrr a' fàs 'sa mhachair,
'S dealt mhin na madainn dha 'n comhdach.
Sèisd: Ged tha mi gun … etc.,

Bìdh an crodh air an àraidh am bràigh a' bhaile,
'S am buachaille bàn dha 'n tàladh dhachaidh;
Bidh bhanarach uallach, ghuineil, bhanail,
Toirt uatha bhainne gu h-òrdail.
Sèisd: Ged tha mi gun … etc.,

Mus èirich a' ghrian bidh an t-iasgair fearail
A' taruinn nan lion gu rianail geanail;
Bidh sgadan is iasg gu sgiathach, lannach,
Gach bliadhna sailleadh 'sa chlòsaid.
Sèisd: Ged tha mi gun … etc.,

Gur tric 's mi òg le cròcan camain
A ghord mi gun choir fo shròin a' chlachair;
Ag iomain air lòn 's e spòrs bu bhaith leam
Bhi an cùl ann thall an còmhnaidh.
Sèisd: Ged tha mi gun … etc.,

Nuair thig feasgar bliadhna ùir bidh surd air balaich,
Le rannan de dhuan mu'n cuairt air Challainn;
Nuair chluinneadh bean sgùideig fuain nan caman
Bhitheadh cruachag bhonnag air dòigh aice.
Sèisd: Ged tha mi gun … etc.,

Thoir beannachd an dràsda a Ghèarrioch dhachaidh,
'S mo dhurachd dha 'n t-sluagh tha shuas sna srathan;
Ged chaidh mi thar sàl 's e b' fheàrr leam fathast
Tìr àluinn channach nam mòr-bheann.
Sèisd: Ged tha mi gun … etc.,

Song to my Homeland
[by John MacLennan]

When you climb to the edge of Creig Thollaidh,
You are surrounded with beauty;
Loch Maree spreads out before your eyes,
Calm, placid and gentle.

Chorus: I am without health and sadness overwhelms me
As I am not permitted to journey to the northern hemisphere,
Costs are so dear and my pocket is so bare
And I must remain an exile.

Beinn-eigh* of the deer, with its glen to the west,
Faces Ben Slioch, deer are hunted at its foot
And moor-hen and other birds hide on the moor,
With numerous hind frequenting the little gorges.
Chorus: I am without … etc.,

You can see the wide, beloved Loch Eubh
With its calm harbour and each creek and bay;
Every spot fragrant and wholesome,
The countryside graceful and beautiful.
Chorus: I am without … etc.,

My beloved Inverasdail, with your beautiful plains,
Tender grass beside your shore;
Every kind of foliage grows on your machair,
Covered by the gentle morning dew.
Chorus: I am without … etc.,

The cattle will be feeding on fertile town braes,
With the shepherd safely guiding them home;
Where modest, cheerful milkmaids
Will be milking them as usual.
Chorus: I am without … etc .,

Before sunrise the fishermen
Are methodically drawing their nets
With gleaming, white-streaked herring,
And are salting the flesh for the year.
Chorus: I am without … etc.

Often, when young, with my shinty stick,
I would slip away under the stonemason's nose
To play shinty and sport on the meadow,
Generally, in the area behind the homes.
Chorus: I am without … etc.,

With hogmanay come the boisterous youths
Singing songs about the New Year;
And each housewife, hearing the sound of shinty sticks,
Will have her usual heap of bannocks ready.
Chorus: I am without … etc.,

Give my blessings now to my Gairloch home,
And my good wishes to it and the people of the valleys;
Though I migrated across the sea I would rather be back there,
In the land of beauty with its great mountains.
Chorus: I am without … etc.,

*Beinn Eighe is now part of a National Nature Reserve, Wester Ross, Scotland. The village of Kinlochew is nearby.

23 Camus Oinich - Cuimhneachain Ionmhainn

[le 'Abrach' Ailean Camshron, Melbourne]

Cia m' àite tàimh no 'm bi mi cuairt,
Mo smuaintean bi 'dh mun am a threig,
'S air tìr nam bean tha fada tuath,
Ged dual nach till gu bruaich mo cheum.

Tha cearnag choisrigte den fhionn,
Le baisteadh thonn Loch libhinn àigh,
Tha mosgladh aoibhneas m' òige 'm chom,
'S an aois a chrom cha chaisg mo bhàigh.

A 'm bruadar 's tric mi ann 's an àit',
Mar bha mi 's mi na m' bhalachan òg,
A' faicinn cruth gach ionnaidh gràidh,
Measg aidhear, faladhà, a's ceòl.

Bha 'n sgoil a sin, 's a nise tha,
'S na theagaisgeadh dhomh m' A B C,
A 'n cuileig tha cho tìorail tlàth,
'S a tha fo cheithir àird nan speur.

'N so leugh mi 'n leabhar tha toirt fios,
Na slighe dhuinn gu flaitheas shuas,
Le stoldachd inntinn, 's le mor mheas,
Mar fhacal naomh an De bhith-bhuan.

Bha taigh a mhinisteir aig laimh,
Gu seimh de 'n aird o 'n seidedh gaoth,
'S mar shailm na beatha, 's le mor mheas,
Bha anail bith na fardaich naoimh.

Air leam gu 'm faic mi broluinn gheas,
An eachrais chas nan sruth 's nan stuadh,
Shios mar tha 'n linne sgaoiladh' mach,
Gu fosgladh farsuinneachd a chuain.

Tha Beinn-a-bheithir* 's stàtail cruach,
Cuir fasgadh 's dion air tuar gach ni,
'S tha glean, a's srath, 's an luch ri bruaich
Ag aidmheil so gu suairce min.

Greis uaip' san car ag eiridh àrd,
Le 'm picibh beur a' bearnadh, shios,

Tha beanntaibh Chomhan, 's uaisle straic,
Is tric ni sgail do chith nan slan.

Air mhodh thug barrachd ann am miadh,
So gniomh an Ti as treine neart-
Na dathan soillse agus ciar,
'N comh-bhoinn cuir mais 'air nial gach feart.

Mo dhuthaich! Aros gin nan clear,
Ri m' bheo dhuit togam m' iarrtas suas;
'S biodh seinn guth t-aoibhneis dol a meud,
Nuair bhith's mi 'n caidreamh cian na h-uaigh.

Looking down from Righ Forest on Ballachulish village and across Onich Bay.

Looking over North Ballachulish and Onich Bay to Garbh Bheinn, under low cloud. This is the highest peak of the Hills of Ardgour.

Ounich Bay - Precious Remembrances
[by 'Abrach' Alan Cameron]

No matter where I go and stay,
My thoughts always return to what I left,
To the land of mountains of the far north,
Though I don't expect to set foot in it again.

This piece of land is consecrated,
Baptised with Loch Leven's sacred water,
And awakens in me that youthful pleasure
Which old age has not dimmed.

In my dreams I am often in that place,
As I was when still a young boy;
Seeing each beloved shape and form,
Among those scenes of happiness.

The school now, as then, still remains,
Where I was taught my A B C,
In a corner so warm and dry
As ever there was under the heavens.

It was here I learned to read the book of life,
The path for us to heaven above,
With prayerful thinking, and with great respect
For the sacred word of the eternal God.

The minister's home was near-by;
Peaceful, no matter how the wind was blowing,
And as a psalm of life, rising in the air,
So was this home a blessed breath of life.

The little waves due to the tidal agitation,
The sudden disturbance of the running billows,
Flow downwards in the pool,
And, opening out, down to the ocean.

And majestic soars lofty Beinn Bheithir,*
Giving shelter and protection to all below,
With the glen, and strath, and the loch and its bank
All acknowledging this kindness.

Meanwhile from it and rising high,
Pinnacles thrusting upwards,

Are Coma's peaks, with proud nobility,
Often wearing a covering of mist in bad weather.

To all of this more love was given,
For this is the powerful act of almighty God-
And the colours, light and dark,
Provide the cloud with a beautiful hue.

My country! Home of the brave,
I shall, in my life-time, raise my voice
And sing with gladness your greatness,
Even when I am long in my grave.

High in the Righ Forest looking over Onich Bay (Loch Linnhe) to the Ardgour Hills.

24 Sa' Choill Fo Sgìos

[le Seumas Mac 'Ille-Mhaoil]

Tha mi nochd sa' choill fo sgìos,
Tri cheud mil' is còrr bho'n chuan,
An àite loireachd, gun sòlas,
Fiadhaich, cròcach, borb, neo-stuam,
Gun aimhnichean, gun uillt, gun fhuaran,
Chuireadh dreach is snuadh air fonn:
Talamh acrach 's e saillte,
Uisge gann 's na gleanntean lom.

Tho mo chompanaich 'nan laidhe
Ann an cadal trom na suain,
Ma dh'fheudta bruad' rach air an dachaidh
Far 'n robh gràdh 's dàimh is luaidh,
Ach O! tha smaonintean air m'aire
Rinn an cadal a chur bhuam,
A bhi cuimhneach' tùs m' òige
Làithean solusach neo-bhuan.

'S e bhi cuimhneach' tùs m' òige
Dh'fhàg mi bronach anns an àm
Tha mo chridhe trom 's e cràiteach
Deòir gu frasach ruith nan deann
Tha mi smaointeachadh an dràsda
Air na càirdean gaolach bh' ann
Chaoidh nach coinnich sinn mar b'àbhaist
Cluich ri àbhacas feadh na' gleann.

Càit an diugh am bheil an òigridh
Cluich bha 'n còmhnuidh leam sa' ghleann
Tha iad sgapt' 's cha till iad còmhladh
Siubhal lòin, no dìrich bheann.
Tha iad sgaoilt': tha cuid air fògradh
Bhrist' iad còraichean an dàimh
'S o! nach truagh cha till gu sòlas
Mar bu chòir dhaibh anns a' ghleann.

Cha till cha till, tha cuid air fuadach,
'S gaoth bho 'n tuath gan iomain teann.
Chaidh cuid an ear 's an iar thar cuantan
Cuid mu dheas gun thriall neo-ghann.
Ach coma leat gu faic 'nam bruadar
Baothan suairc' fo shàth nam beann

Far an robh iad òg is uallach
Ruith mu'n cuairt 's a' cleasach ann.

Dh'fhalbh an aisling, sgaoil am bruadar,
Dhùisg bho'n suain 's b'e call san àm,
Fhuair iad sealladhan bha uasal,
Fraoch is cluain is streathan ghleann.
Bheir e furtachd dhaibh, creid uamsa,
Mhaireas buan 's chan fhàs e fann
Dh'èrich e a càil gu cruadal,
Sgaoil gach bruaillean bha 'na cheann.

Nuair a dh'fhàg mi ir mo dhùthachais
Bha mo dhùil ri tilleadh ann,
Ach thionndaidh 's dh'atharraich na cùisean
'S bha na lubhan carrach can
A threòraich mi gu mòran ùspairn
'N iomadh dùthaich bhos is thall.
Dh'fhalbh an tìm is chaochail ùine
'S chaidh 's na lubhhan mi air chall.

Weary in the Forest
[by James MacMillan]

Tonight, I am weary in the forest
Upwards of three hundred miles from the sea.
It is a dirty place, without comfort,
Without the proud, wild, antlered deer;
Without rivers, or mountain stream or spring
Giving any form and colour to the country:
It is a hungry soil full of salt,
With little water and bleak valleys.

My companion is stretched out
In a deep, heavy sleep;
Dreaming, perhaps, of being back home
Where there was love and beloved friends.
But O! my mind is reminiscing
Driving sleep far from me
As I remember my early youth,
Transitory days, full of joy.

I am remembering my youth,
Of the time when I sadly left.
My heart is heavy and tortured,
Tears are pouring down
As I consider just now
My dear friends back there;
We will never gather as usual
To play sport throughout the glen.

Where today are the young men
Who always played with me in the glens?
They are scattered, never will we be re-united
To cross the streams or to climb the mountains.
They are dispersed: some have been driven away
Breaking this honest friendship;
Alas! that happiness will never return
As it ought to be in the glen.

It will never ever return, some are expelled,
A wind from the north has firmly driven them away.
Some to the east, and some west across the seas,
And not a few went down south.
But don't attend to what you see in my dream,
See instead the young men below the mountains

Where, young and sportive,
They playfully run around.

The reverie left, the dream dispersed,
Roused from deep sleep, that time has now gone.
Those were precious views
With greenery fringing the glen.
But such memories, I believe, will bring comfort.
Lastingly durable, the dream will not grow faint,
It will rise above any difficulty,
Removing every disquiet from the mind.

When I left my homeland
My hope was to return
But to have changed and improved my circumstances
From that of a timid shoemaker.
I was led into many struggles
And many lands here and there.
Time and seasons passed by
And I went astray as a lost lamb.

25 Òran do Thìr m' òige

[le Seumas Mac 'Ille-Mhaoil]

Tha còrr is fichead bliadhna 's còig-deug
Bho a dh'fhàg mi 's a thriall mi air falbh
Bho luchd-dùthcha mo ghaoil,
Coireachdan cùirneach fraoich,
Is lodachd ghruamach 'nan caol 's nan cala;
Chaoidh cha till mi gu bràth
Do mo chàirdean 's luchd-gràidh,
Is, O mo dìobhail, gu bheil pàirt dhiubh marbh.

Thig 'n am chuimhne bhi òg
A bhi siubhal nan òb
'S a' dìreadh bhruthaichean nan sròintean garbh'
No bhi teàrnadh do'n ghleann,
Ruith 's a' leum 's mi 'n am dheann,
Is mi gun chùram 's an àm làn sòlais,
Treis a' dìreadh na stùic.

'S fliuch a còta fo'n drùchd,
Anns a' mhadainn chiùin ùir,
'S anns a' ghlòmaidh,
Grian ag èirigh bho bonn,
Snamh gu mullach nan tonn,
A' deoghal drùchd bhàrr gach fonn is mòinteich;
Eòin air dùsgadh à suain',
'S milis ceòlmhor an duain.

A' togail cliù bhàrr gach cluain is lònain:
Leam bu mhiann a bhi ann,
Bhi 'g an cluinntinn 's an àm,
'S e thogadh m' inntinn ri srann nan òran;
Ach, mo thruaigh! Gu sìor,
'S duilich leam gur a fìor,
Cha till mi tuilleadh do thìr nan crònan.

Song to the Land of my Youth
[by James MacMillan]

It is more than thirty-five years
Since I left and journeyed away
From my beloved fellow countrymen,
And from the heather-covered glens.
And gloom gathers over firth and shore
For I never will return
To my friends and beloved people;
And, O my loss, some now lie dead.

The recollections of youth come to me,
Crossing the harbour
Ascending the braes of the rugged headlands,
Descending into the glen.
Running and leaping with speed
Without a care, and full of joy
While climbing the mountain peak.

And the ground covered with dew
In the peaceful morning
And at twilight.
The sun rising from below
Swimming on top of the waves
And drinking the dew from the peat moss;
Birds awakening from sleep
With melodious song.

The nightingale's praise rising above every meadow;
And I long to be there, listening.
The sound of the song would cheer my mind.
But, my misery!
For ever.
Truly I am sorrowful,
For I will never return
to the land where the deer cry.

26 Gràdh Dùthcha

[le Alasdair Macdomhnuill]

Tha bliadhn' agus ràidhe
Bhon a thàinig mi'n taobh-s',
'S ged is toilicht' an t-àite
Gum bheil faillinn 's a' chùis:
Tha mi fhada bhom chàirdean
Air m'fhàgail air chùl
Far an robh mi'n àm ghille
Leam ri tilleadh gun dùil.

Aon an seirbhis na ban-rìgh
Ged a tha mi 's an tìr seo
A' teagasg a' ghrammair
Do pàistean na sgìre!
Ged nach obair ro-làidir,
Tha mi fàs dh' i car sgìth,
'S nach labhair rium Gàidhlig
Bhon là dh'fhàg mi Port-rìgh.

'S olc an obair do Shlèibhteach
Air an Fhèinn 'bhi 'cur call,
A 'ghàidhlig g'a trèigsinn
'Tabhairt Beurla do chlann:
Ach mar bitheadh an èiginn
Is mo sprèidh-sa 'bhi gann,
'S ann a chumainn sgaoil Ghàidhlig
Bhon 's i cànain a b' anns'.

Ged is uaine 'tha choille
'An Australia an òir,
'Adhar grianach gorm soilleir,
Gun smàl air is gun neòil,
Gur h-e dheanadh a-rithist
Mo chridhe-sa òg
A bhi 'm fasgadh a' chuilinn
Far am fuireachd an ceò.

Gur h-e thogadh dhìom easlaint
'S a lèighseadh mo thaobh
A bhi siubhad na slèibhtean
D' an aodach am fraoch;
A bhi cèilidh 's a' gheamradh
Ann an gleannan nan laoch,
Ged a bha iad gun oighreachd
Ach caoimhneas is gaol.

Beloved Homeland
[by Alexander MacDonald]

It is now the season
That I arrived here,
And though the place is pleasant
There is one thing lacking:
I am far from the friends
I left behind me
In my youth
Without any hope of my ever returning.

I was once in the service of the Queen,
Though, in this land,
I am teaching grammar
To the children of the parish!
Although it is not hard work
I am growing tired of it;
No one has spoken to me in Gaelic
Since the day I left Portree.

It is distasteful work for a Sleat man
And a great loss to a Fingalian
Leaving off Gaelic
To teach English to children:
But hardship makes it necessary
For my livestock are poor
And the Gaelic community is scattered
And my favouite language with it.

Though there are green woods
In golden Australia,
With sunny, clear blue sky,
Without mist and without clouds,
That which will again make
My heart young
Will be the shadow of the Cuilins
Where the mist lingers.

It lifts me out of my infirmity
And brings healing to my side
So that I am once again walking
The heather-clad mountains,
And going to the ceilidh in the winter
In the glens of the brave,
Though they possessed nothing
Except love and kindness.

27 Na Tulaichean Boideach

[le Seumas Mac 'Ille-Mhaoil]

Fàilte air na tulaichean bòidheach
'S iad uaine fon dreach,
Luibhean milis gun fhòtus
A' brùchdadh a mach,
Gu elùmhor is comh-naisgte,
Gu sòghail gun aire
Agus dealt orra 'drùghadh
'S ag ùrachadh 'n neart:
Agus dealt orra … etc.,

'S iad na tulaichean rìomhach
Le mìn-fheur gun chnap,
Agus neòineinean nòsail
'G an còmhdach mar bhrat:
Tha an t-seamrag 'n an aodainn,
Tha 'm braonan 'n an laig,
Agus sòbhraichean ruadh-bhuidhe
'Am bruachan nan stac:
Agus sòbhraichean … etc.

Sud na tulaichean àraidh
A 's àluinne dreach
Far'm bheil fasgadh ri fhaotainn
Do chaora 's do mhart,
Agus fuarain gu saorach
A' taosgadh a mach;
'S e sud ionad nan uchdaich
'S a' bhuaile bheann cheart:
'S e sud ionad … etc.

'S bòidheach lurach mu Bhealltuinn
Gach meall agus croit,
Cnoc-nan-long fo dheadh èideadh,
Sealbh èibhinn neo-ghoirt;
Tha fraoch meurach gu dlùth dha
'S e 'lùbadh le toic;
Coille-chnò air gach taobh dheth,
Gagain chaoin air gach ghlac:
Coille-chnò air gach … etc.,

Glac-nan-laogh tha fo dhuilleach
Air uilinn 'dà chnoic
Far an cluinnear an smeòrach
'Seinn ceòl ann gun sprochd;
Tha an uiseag air phreasan,
Tha nead aic' air ghlac,
A' chuthag 's gug-gùg aic'
A' lùbadh le moit:
A' chuthag 's gug-gug … etc.,

'S tric a dhìrich mi 'm bruthach
'S a mhàgair na cnoic
Mar-ri companaich m' òige,
'S sinn còmhla gun lochd.
A' cluich mar bu dù dhuinn
Feadh lùban is shlochd;
Bhi 'g a smuaintinn an dràsda
'S e chràidh mi 's a lot:
Bhi 'g s smuaintinn … etc.

Ach mur till mise tuilleadh
'S nach faic mi na conic
Far 'n do chaith mi na làithean
Bha gràdhach neo-olc,
Nì mi innseadh 'an Gàidhlig
Anns an àite so 'n nochd
Gum bi mo chridhe 'an tàmh ann
Gus an tràigh e gun phlosg;
Gum bi mo chridhe … etc.

The Beautiful Hills
[by James MacMillan]

Welcome to the beautiful hills
Under their flawless green cover
Of abundant sweet herbs
Bursting forth;
Sheltered and knit together
In a natural display,
With a covering of dew
Giving them new life
With a covering … etc.

And the elegant rises,
With their grass, smooth and plain,
Blanketed as usual
With a covering of daisies
And clover about their brow,
With brier buds in the hollow,
And auburn primroses
On the sides of the high cliffs
And auburn primroses … etc.

These hills are special
And a glorious image
Where sheep and cattle
Can find their protection.
And where springs
liberally gush forth;
And yonder is the steep brae*
With its cattle and sheep fold.
And yonder … etc.

It is especially beautiful about May-day
Each mound and croft,
Cnoc-nan-long** in excellent dress,
Harmonious, delightfully coloured;
With fingers of heather nearby
Profusely meandering across it;
Hazel wood on every side
In delightful clusters in every hollow:
Hazel wood on every … etc.

Glac-nam-laogh is under foliage
In the hollow of two hills
Where is heard the mavis
Singing its song without sadness;
The lark is in the bushes,
Her nest in the hollow,
And the cuckoo with her 'gug-gug'
Cocks her head with pride:
The cuckoo … etc.

And I often ascended the brae,
Crawling over the hills
With a companion of my youth,
And we, without mischief,
Played together our usual games
Along the length of the meandering pools;
But remembering those things now
Brings me pain.
But remembering … etc.

But I will never again return,
And I will not see the hills
Where I spent my days
With you in harmless pleasure.
I am relating this in Gaelic,
And tonight, in this place,
My heart will not be at rest
Until the waves stop beating.
My heart … etc

28 Comh-Chomunn Ri Eas Ridhe, am Bun Lochabar, ann am Bruadar

[le 'Abrach' Ailean Camshron, Melbourne]

Mi dearcadh mar 's an tim o chian
Ort fèin O Eas! as miadhail cruth:
Air garm mo dhleasnais 's fada a thriall
Mo chionn o chopadh dian do shruth.

'S na laithean an robh m' aigne maoth;
B' e m' annsachd suidhe taobh do bhruaich
Am fochair toirmrich neart do bhraoin,
A bhiodh mar òran gaoil a' m' chluais.

Tha t-uisgeachan, air leam, ag ràdh,
Am briathran bàigh fo shileadh dheur:
"Ciod e, fad bhlianaibh sgìth, an t-àit'
Air iomral cian 'n d' thar do cheum?"

Do chruth gun ionndrain mi o m' choir,
A's t-fhaileas òg 's an linne shìos,
Nuair chuireadh tu, le aithris boil,
Bladh mheaghair t-fhoghluim dhuit air rian.

"Gun aon dùil lamh ruit ach mi fèin
'S an Ti tha stiùireadh ceum ar ròid-
Lan bàigh don chruthachadh gu lèir,
Tha 'm boinn a' cur an cèill a ghlòir.

"Ach O! shearg blàth do bhuadhan as,
'S mar airgiod glas tha gruag do chin;
'S e 'n guth a mhain, bha aoibhneach àit
Tha cur do chleachdaidh ann am chuimhn';

"Tha gàirdeachas nan creag mun cuairt
Comh-fhreagairt ris le fuaimrich bhinn,
'S thèid seirm mo ghuth-sa leò a suas,
'S nì nàdur òran nuadh a sheinn.

"Na crainn tha crathadh shuas mu'm cheann
Le'n cuanail ghreannar 's annsa tèis
Le meoghail ghlòirbhinneach neo-ghann,
'Nì còmhla'n rann a choir air ghleus."

Shiubhail mi 'n ear, a's shiubhail mi 'n iar,
A's thùinich mi 'n tìr chian mu dheas,
Ach taisgt' am chom, mar chàirdeas fial,
Do bhorbhain tiamhaidh mhair gun cheist.

Mar airgiod loinnreach tha do chliabh,
'S 'n uair dhearsas grian air sgiath do chaoir,
Gum faicear bogha 's daithte neul
A' cluich ri ciabhan shian do spairn.

Thèid uachdaranachd mhòr air chùl,
'S thèid àl nan ioma gineal 'sìos,
Ach, mar o d' bhreith-sa, bithidh tu
Gun ni chuir ruit na thabhairt dhìot.

Mar ann 'n uair thaosgas tuillte 'nuas,
Cur at mu d' bhruaich le buathadh cas,
'S bhios mòralachd a's neart de bhuadh
Cuir t-inbhe 'suas gu h-uaibhreach bras.

Tha briathran coimeis bacach, mal,
Aig meud am puirp an ranntachd bhàrd,
'S tha ealdhain lag-chùiseach a's gann
Chuir modh do ghreadnachais air àird.

Gu mosgail guth nan uisgean garbh
Comh-sheirm mhictalla anns a' chom,
Gu smaointean air an Ti a dhealbh
Na neimhne àrd, an fhairge, 's fonn.

A's mar tha tim do shìorruidheachd, tha
Do chor, trid Òrdugh Dhia nam feart,
Am measg nam beò, bho àl gu àl,
'Nì aoradh maille ruit gu ceart.

Am shuidhe 'so, an laithean m' òig',
Gur tric a shil mo dheòir gu geur,
'S mo smuainte orra-san fon fhòid,
Bha roimhe 'n cleachdadh dòigh rium fèin.

Ach 'nis an t-àm a ta ri teachd
Sgaoil fhaileas ciar thar dreach gach àigh

Toirt sanais dhomh, rèir chor gach neach-
Gun tig a chrioch – 's nach fhada 'n dail.

Tha cuimhneach an nam bliadhn' a thrèigh,
Rinn còmhnuidh so le chèile a' d' chòir,
Ri gean rium, ged tha blàth nan deur
Ri fhaicinn air eudainn fòil.

Tùs dòchais le chuid smuaintean àrd,
A's tograidh anama 's gràsmhor stuaim,
Tha so an dlùth's mu chàraidh thràth,
Comh-mheasgnachadh an gàirich t-fhuaim.

Near the top of the Abhainn Righ Gorge (King's River Gorge) looking down on one of the first of the eight natural 'steps' making up the Righ Waterfall. The Righ River tumbles almost 1,000 feet in a series of eight steps (waterfalls) into the Righ River Gorge.

A lower 'step' of the Righ Falls.

Ree Waterfall in a Dream
[by 'Abrach' Alan Cameron, Melbourne]

I look, as I did long ago,
On you, oh Waterfall! Your esteemed sight;
My obligations caused me to travel far
From your foaming torrent.

In past days, when I was young,
It was my delight to sit beside your bank
Near to your powerful flow,
Its noise like a favourite song to my ear.

I imagined the waters asking me,
The affectionate words dripping with tears,
"What places, in these long tiring years
Have your footsteps crossed?"

"I miss your face near to me,
And your youthful reflection in the pool
When you would rehearse out loud
The lessons you regularly learned."

"With no one beside you but me,
Except God who guides our steps.
He is full of love towards his creation
Which unites together in giving Him praise."

"But oh! Your excellence has faded,
And how silver-grey is your hair;
It is your voice alone that is cheerful
As I remember it."

"Gladness is in the hills around
Resounding with sweet echoes,
And my voice will rise up with them
And will sing nature's new song."

The trees are swaying above my head
With a lively chorus of beloved music,
With numerous, sweet-sounding melodies,
Each with its prepared part.

"I have travelled East and West
And dwelt in the far distant South,
But the precious memory, still deep within me,
Was of that low, affecting sound of you."

"Your breast is like gleaming silver
And when the sunlight reflects from it
A many-coloured bow can be seen
Sporting with the tresses of your flow."

"Great empires will pass away
And many generations come and go,
But you will be as from birth
Without any change in you."

"Except when the flood tumbles down,
Swelling, with headlong fury, about your bank,
Then power and majesty
Shall increase your dignity and pride."

"Words of comparison are inadequate
And are beyond the greatest poet's verse;
Art is impotent and can scarce
Portray your magnificence and honour."

"The voice of the rough water awakens
Redolent echoes in my breast;
And reflections on the form of the One
Whose splendour is greater than land or sea."

"As time is to eternity
You are to be, by God's command,
From generation to generation, among the living
Who, along with you, give due worship."

"Sitting here in days of my youth
I often shed plentiful, painful, tears,
Thinking of those, now in the grave,
Who were, like me, acquainted with you."

"But now the future approaches,
Its dark shadow spreading across this joyful scene,
Bringing to me that knowledge, common to man,
That death will come – and soon."

"My memories during my years of absence,
That have made their home near you here,
Are cheerful to me, though seeing your tranquil face
Brings warm tears to my eyes."

"The beginning of hope, with other exalted thoughts,
And a desire for a gracious and modest spirit,
Here join together in my final state,
Blending with the echo of your roaring sound."

Another 'step' of the Righ Falls.

29 Am Bruadar

[le Dòmhnall 'ic Ionmhainn senior]

An raoir am Bruadar bha mise thall
Taobh eile an tadhail e an tìr nan gleann
Tìr mo Mhàthair mo ruin 's mo chàirdean
Luchd-gaoil a b'àbhaist bha uile ann.

B' e 'n t-aobhar gàire bhi measg nan Gaeil.
An crathadh làimhe dhomh le fàilt' is fonn
Pìobmhòr a rànaich 's clanna bheaga gairich
'S gaol chainnt ar Mhàthair cur blàth nam chom.

Air gaol an dùthcha bha Gaeil cliùteach
Cha bhiodh an dùrachd ri dùthcha thall,
'S chan fhacas Nàmhaid chuireadh geilt astair os,
'S e buaidh bhiodh aig Laoch nan Gleann.

Lean siubhal dubhailt 's le' m claidhean rùisgte
Cò churaidh cùis orra an iomairt labhar,
Bu no mhi-nàdur dhoibh bhi nan tràilleas
'Se buaidh no bàs* bhiodh aig Laoich nan Gleann.

Ach mar bu gnàth dhomh bha math air Bàrdachd
Le tugadh Gàileig gun diomhair luaidh
Air na mnathan ghràdach mhàthair n' àrach
Tha togail àrach an tìr mo shluaigh.

Gach nighean uasal ribhinn 's ghruagach
Gun anns do dh'fharranachd nan Cridhean Gaoil
Chan fhaighear suarachas faoin nan gluasad.
Tha nàdur uasal anns na h-uile aon.

O 's lurach fàs iad na h-òighean bhlàth shùil
Tha cliù 's gach àite orra 's chan iongnadh leam
Na Flùirein àillidh dhìolas chàirdeil
A fhuair an àrach fo sgail nam Beann.

Bha maise as ciatachd ra fhaicinn riabh ann
Bithidh cliù gu siorruidh air tìr nan Gleann
Tìr mo shinnsir 's mo chàirdean dìleas,
Gur mar an dìleab a bhith cànain ann.

Tha sealladh Riaghail an tìr an thall
Tha as seallaidh rìomhach an tìr nan Gall;

Ach uireadh dhomhse feàrr shaillach ghlòmhor
Nuair bha mi 's òg ann an Tìr nan Gleann.

Bu shealladh mear fhàilte gu fìor b' ann
Moch, madainn shamhradh 's mi suas nan gleann,
Bha na h-eòin le aibhneas a' seinn sna coilltean,
'S ghrian a' boillsgeadh thar tìr nam Beinn.

Bha neòil nan cruachan sneachd gheal suas air
An cùrsa tuathach san gluasad shèimhic,
An sin grad bhuail mu an smuaintinn luachmhor
Gun robh mi suas faisg air a geata Nèamh.

Ach dhealbh an là shud tha mise trath so
A chaoidh gu cràiteach an dùthaich chèin
Phaisg an chlarsach 's cha leibh na dana
Tha mo shùilean rùisgte a shileadh dheòir.

Alba bàn ghràdhach mòr thìr nan Gaeil
Ag rinn mi fàgail sgur mòr na chall;
Cha chrìon gu bràth as cainnt bhinn mo Mhàthair
'S latha Bràtha bithidh Sàbaid ann.

Ach molladh dhàsan tha riumsa lathail
Ar th' uair mi am fàbhar nam fàs mi fan,
Na 'm trèig mo chàil mi 's mun glac ann
Bàs mo chuir mi thaigh fàilte gu tìr nam Beinn.

*Motto of the MacDougall clan.

The Dream
[by Donald MacKinnon senior]

Last night I dreamed I was, again,
Back visiting the land of glens,
Beloved land of my mother; my family;
And all my loved ones were there as usual.

It was a cause of celebration among the Gael
Of hand-waving with music aplenty,
Bagpipes roaring, children shouting for joy,
And our mother's beloved tongue warming our breasts.

The Gael is renowned for love of his country
Which cannot be given to a foreign land,
No enemy has been seen that could put them to flight,
And victory would be to the hero of the glens.

Follow the dark journey and, with sword unsheathed,
As a champion, enforce an end to the conflict.
It was against their nature to be slaves;
It is 'conquest or death'* that motivates the hero of the glens.

It was my habit, from suitable Gaelic verse,
To give praise, alone, with genuine affection,
To the loving women, and to a beloved mother
Who raised me in the land of my people.

Every gentle maid and beautiful young lady are there
With no room for vanity in their loving hearts,
No contempt or foolishness is found in their conduct
In each one of them lies a gentle nature.

O, the sight of the maidens grows lovelier
Their fame everywhere is no surprise to me
As truly resplendent flowers, beloved, tender,
And reared under the shadow of the mountains.

Such beauty and grace as ever were seen
Will be remembered for ever in the land of the glens,
Land of my forefathers and my true friends
Your precious tongue will be your legacy.

The country abroad is a Regal sight,

And though the Lowlands are elegant
My preference is for that glorious spectacle,
When I was young, of the land of glens.

It was a joyful sight indeed to see it
Early on a summer morning, and I up the glens;
Or with the birds, joyfully singing in the woods,
And the sun breaking over the Mountain tops.

Clouds were about the white, snow-clad peaks,
Moving calmly towards the north,
When I was struck with the precious thought
That I was near the gate of Heaven.

And the image of yonder day is with me still,
Causing my misery in this foreign land;
Put down the clarsach, you dare not play it,
Tears, as can be seen, are pouring from my eyes.

Greatly beloved Scotland, land of the Gael
Sore was my loss when I left you;
Where my mother's sweet tongue will never fade
And where every day will be as a Sabbath.

I daily praise him who made me
My growing weakness a sign of my age;
I feel my strength about to leave me
And death welcoming me home to the Land of the Mountains.

*Motto of the MacDougall clan.

30 Beannachd do *Tiom an Obain*

[le Alasdair Macdomhnuill]

Beannachd buaidh le Tiom an Obain
'S i bhi sgaoileadh feadh gach àite
Giùlan naigheachdan bhios cùirteil
Air an dùthaich 's an d'fhuair mi m'àrach;
Tìr an robh mi òg is sunndach
Siubhal lùghmhor feadh na fàsaich.
Tìr a-chaoidh nach tèid a'm chuimhne
Gus an claoidhear leis a' bhàs mi.

Tìr nan sruithean, tìr nam fuaran,
Agus àitean uaine nan sgàirneach,
Tìr an fhraoich 's e' ghaoth 'g a ghluasad,
Sealladh uasal nach gabh àichead;
Tìr na canaich, 's geal an cuailean
Sìoda dualach gruag fo bhlàth oirr',
'S fàilte cùbhraidh tighinn bho ghucag
Cuiridh neart an uchd nam gailleann.

Chan eil gleann no meall no sìthean,
Lianag uaine no aonach ròmach,
Glach no loch, gach cnoc is iosal,
Nach tig 'n am chuimhn' le *Tiom an Obain*;
Ged 's ro-fhada bhon a dh'fhàg mi
Tìr nam beann, an dachaidh gràdhach,
Faic an-diugh mi mar a b'àbhaist
Labhairt cainnt le srann na Gàidhlig.

Air chinnt gur toigh leam *Tiom an Obain*,
'S cuiridh coinneamh oirr' le fàilte,
Nuair a nì sinn suidhe còmhradh
Bheir i solas dhomh bhios làidir:
Tha iomadh naigheachd innt' tha prìseil
Ged nach d'innis i bheag 's a Ghàidhlig;
Gabh mo leisgeul chur 'n ad chuimhne
Tha ghabhail suim do chainnt ar màthar!

Compliments to the *Oban Times**
[by Aleander MacDonald]

Compliments and success to the *Oban Times*
It is spreading everywhere
Bringing worthwhile news
Of my homeland;
The land of my youth and happiness,
Where depopulation took place very quickly.
Eternal land that will never leave my memory
Until death overtakes me.

Land of rivers, land of springs,
And of green places among the rocks,
Land of the heather rustled by the wind,
A noble sight that cannot be denied;
Land of the cotton-sedge, and white blossoms,
Silk braided hair under her bloom,
And fragrant scent coming from the bell flower
Growing strongly in the heart of the storm.

There is not a glen or hill or knoll
Green meadow or shaggy heath,
Valley or loch, or humble hillock,
That will not be mentioned by the *Oban Times*;
Though it is long since I left
I can still see, as usual,
The land of the mountains, my beloved home,
And I still converse in Gaelic.

In truth I like the *Oban Times*,
Receiving it with a welcome,
When we are sitting in conversation.
It deepens my understanding;
And though it contains much precious news,
It tells little of it in Gaelic;
Excuse me for reminding you
To take account of our mother tongue!

* The *Oban Times* was a newspaper partly English and partly Gaelic which was popular among Gaels in Australia. It carried much Gaelic verse including contributions from Australia.

31 An Moladh gu 'Thair an t-Sàl' Gu Kate M. Powrie

[le Seumas Mac 'Ille-Mhaoil]

Gum bu slàn don mhaighdein bhòidheich,
Tha i 'm Faisgeadal an còmhnuidh,
A sheinn cho binn mun t-samhradh nòsail,
Anns an t-òran "By The Sea,
Anns an t-òran "By the Sea."

Chuir i sios gu measail briathrach
Ann an cainnt bha taghta riaraicht'
'S chòmhdaich i gach glean is sliabh
'An èideadh sgiamhach "By the Sea,"
An èideadh sgìamhach, etc …

Chuir i sios mu ghaol na h-òige
Làmh air làimh a' siubhal còmhla
Suairceas 's mùirn a' gabhail còmhnuidh
'S a' bhothan bhòidheach "By the Sea,"
'S a' bhothan bhòidheach, etc …

Iad ag iomramh air a' bhàta,
Gluasad aotrom air uchd sàile;
Nuair a bhios iad sgìth ri àbhachd,
Bheir gu tràigh i "By the Sea";
Bheir gu tràigh i, etc …

Rinn i innseadh dhuinn mun chaorrunn
Daithte dearg an sgànrach aonaich
Agus cuairt air feadh an fhraoich
Mun tèid gu faoileach "By the Sea";
Mun tèid, etc …

Nuair a leugh mi-fhèin an t-òran
Las mo chridhe suas le solas,
'S thug e 'm chuimhne làithean m' òige
'G èisdeachd onfhaidh "By the Sea";
'G èisdeachd onfhaidh etc …

Tha mo dhùrachd fhèin gu sìorruidh
Leis a' mhaighdein chaoimhneil rianaich,
'S i 'bhi fada beò gun iargain
'Am bothan grianach "By the Sea":
'Am bothan grianach, etc …

'Nuair thig feasgar fuar na h-aois oirr',
Ceann air 'ghlasadh, ceann neo-aotrom,
I 'bhi 'm fasgadh càirdeas gaoile
'Am bothan aoidheil, "By the Sea."
'Am bothan aoidheil, etc …

An O'er the Sea Compliment to Kate Powrie
[by James MacMillan]

To your health, my beautiful lady,
Where you live in Faisgeadal*
Singing so sweetly about summer
In your song "By the Sea,"
In the song "By the Sea."

Her composition was so eloquent
And in words so carefully chosen,
And she dressed each glen and moor
In graceful clothing, "By the Sea,"
In graceful clothing, etc ...

She wrote about youthful lovers
Hand in hand, walking together
And passing by her home,
That beautiful cottage, "By the Sea,"
That beautiful cottage, etc...

And rowing together in the boat
Moving lightly on the breast of the sea;
And when they tire of that sport,
He will bear her to the shore, "By the Sea,"
He will bear her, etc ...

Her song told us about the rowan
Tinting red the spreading heath
Around and throughout the heather,
And there will be a ready welcome, "By the sea,"
And there will be, etc ...

When I first read the song
My heart lit up,
And I remembered the days of my youth
Listening to the waves, "Beside the Sea,'
Listening to the waves, etc ...

My own eternal good wishes
To the kind and courteous lady,
May she live long and healthily
In the sunny cottage, "By the Sea,"
In the sunny cottage, etc ...

When the cold night of age comes upon her,
With greying head, and heavy step,
May she have the protection of family
In that cheerful cottage, "By the Sea,"
In the cheerful cottage, etc …

Section Four - The New Homeland - First, and Later, Impressions.

Much of the content of first impression letters dealt with descriptions of the land. None of the emigrants was spared the normal fears and uncertainties of stepping off their ship and into a new world whose size, flora, fauna and inhabitants were as different as anything could be to that which they had left several months before. Although they had physically left their homeland, their mental, religious and emotional attitudes formed part of the 'invisible baggage' which all emigrants carried with them wherever they travelled.

There was a variety of 'First Impression' accounts which ranged from presenting negative opinions to those which were highly positive. Nostalgia and homesickness, or bitterness at having been driven from their traditional homeland, did not consume all correspondents. There were some, *Tha an fhàilte chridheil*, *Luchd-Imric Ghaidhealach* and *Litir bho Donnchaidh Camshron*, for example, whose authors were overwhelmed by what they saw, and whose first impressions were akin to those of the Children of Israel as they gazed on the promised land, and who believed that, in bringing them to this new world, they could see the very hand of God at work. Experiences of the new life and the search for a living, or a quick fortune in 'tìr nan oir' - the land of gold. - also provided many of the emigrants with inspiration for their verse.

Rev Dr A. MacIntosh MacKay's first impressions of Melbourne, which he praised highly in a private letter to an unnamed friend in Scotland, were starkly candid.

He was less complimentary, for example, about some country areas which he saw as lawless and dangerous; a fact which he illustrated by recounting his own experience of being shot at and nearly killed!

A long letter giving a settler's impressions of Van Diemen's Land (Tasmania), appeared in *Cuirtear nan Gleann*, and had little to say that was positive or uplifting. Similarly, Angus Beaton's experience of loneliness and his fear of aborigines and wild dogs, Tha mi seo aig loch-Elisa (from his longer poem *Oran an Eilthirich*), presents his terrified account of his new homeland.

But many of the new settlers in the Australian colonies were anxious to reassure family and friends, still in the homeland, that they had arrived safely and were prospering. Their 'First Impressions', therefore, could be highly coloured in a positive fashion so as to allay fears and to encourage others to follow their example. Iain McLeòid's letter, '*An Sgiathanach Ann An Astraillia*', and that of 'W.K'. are examples of this. Their positive messages present a less descriptive picture of the land and, instead, concentrate positively on the life, work and opportunities in the new colony. Further examples can be found in *Litir bho Donnchaidh Camshron* and *Thàinig Calum a's mise.* Rob MacDougall's descriptive piece was also meant to reassure readers that Australia was not a wild and savage land.

In the end, perhaps, it was forces outside of their control which determined the emigrant's success or failure. Hard work and sober and frugal living were no match, on occasions, for the vagaries of the Australian climate or economic downturns. God's providence - many times his inscruitable providence - some wrote, had to be acknowledged in all things.

32 A Chuairtair mo rùm,

[Unnamed correspondent to *Cuairtear nan Gleann*]

A' bharrachd airson, tha an t-uisge 's an t-samhradh anabarrach gann, agus duilich r' a fhaotainn; - seadh na h-aimhnichan a bha 's a gheamhradh ag doirteadh sios an tur-làn mar mhaoime sleibhe, is ainmic a gheibhar uirad annta 's an t-samhradh 's a chasgadh padhadh astaraich. Math dh'fhaodteadh gum faighar beagan ann an lag an so agus an toll an sin, ach bùrn glan nan chaochan chan 'eil ann. Mar meallta mi b' eigin do gach aon de mhuinntir Baile Oatlands an aimsir tioram togsaid a chur gach latha air càrnn, agus uisge a ghiulan a sluic amhainn a bha tri mìl air falbh.

Dh'oidhirpaich iad sin a leasachadh le tobair a chladhachadh gu doimhneachd mun cuairt de dha cheud troidh; agus 'n a chladhachadh b' eigin dhoibh gearradh no snaidhadh troimh craig gharail gu doimhuachd tri fichead troidh. Ged fhuair iad mu dheiradh deich troidh thar fhicheadh a dh'uisge, cha b' urrainn doibh feum a dheanadh dheth anns a' mheud 's gun robh e làn meirge iaruinn, agus uaithe sin bha an t-anart a chaidh a nighadh ann, iar a dheargachadh 's iar a mhilladh.

Bho so chìthear nach fiù na tobraichan tochailte no Artesian mar a theirar riu anns a bheurla. Ge neònach, is firinnach e, gu bheil na lochan iad fein air crìonadh 's air tiormachadh suas. Bha Loch Fhederic an còmhnuidh làn dh'fhearthuin no dh'uisge nan speur, agus air uairibh bha e aig aon cheann ag ruith thairis air rathad mhòir a bha 'n a ghar.

Chaidh bruach a dheanadh dha gus a chas-cheum a thearnadh.

Bhon àm sin thiormaichadh e, gan ro-fhios cimar, a tha nis air a thomhas agus ullamh r' a reic. Agus de bhrigh gur gairal bunaitas an eilain agus gum bheil na sreathan trian-fhiarte, is e ar barail gun d' fhuair e trompa doigh druidhaidh dh' a' fein.

Dear Cuairtear,
[Unnamed correspondent to *Cuairtear nan Gleann*]

… the water in summer is excessively scarce, and hard to get;- indeed the rivers, that in winter were rushing down like a mountain torrent, in summer will rarely have as much in them as to quench a thirsty traveller. This treasure can be found a little in a hollow here and in a pit there, but there is no clean water in the streamlets. Unless I am mistaken, it was a necessity for every one of the people in the town of Oatlands*, in the warm weather, to use a hogshead** each day, and to carry the water from a river pool that was three miles away.

The people there attempted to improve things by digging a well of about two hundred feet; they firstly had to cut or hew through neighbouring rock sixty feet deep. Although at last getting thirty feet of water, they could not use it in any amount as it seemed like it was full of iron rust, and linen that was washed in it afterwards reddened and spoiled.

From this it will be seen that it is not worth digging wells, or Artesian as they say in English. It is true, though strange, that the small lochs themselves had shrunk and dried up. Loch Federic was always full of water, or rain from the heavens, and sometimes it was overflowing over the large road that was near. Edging would be made for it to protect the footpath.

From that time, however, it dried up, and it has now been surveyed and is ready for sale. Because of the hardstone inflexibility of the island, and without a bottom layer of rock, it is our opinion that it seeped through and just drained itself away.

*A town in Tasmania.

**This could be anywhere between 63 to 140 gallons.

33 *Cuairtear nan* Gleann

Mothaichadh iadsan

Mothaichadh iadsan tha cleachdadh an Cuairtear a leughadh, mùthadh eadar dòigh sgrìobhaidh a' chùnntais so agus a' chuid eile don leabhar; ach b' e iarrtus an duin'-uasaid a chuir gar n-ionnsuidh e, gun rachadh a chlò bhualadh dìreach mar a sgrìobh esan e; agus rinneadh sin.

A Chuairtair mo rùm,

Tha thusa gan agadh dèidheil agus ullamh air gach fios a thoirt dar luchd-dùtcha, aig am bheil earbsa an staid a leasachadh le imrich gu tìr chein, ciod an turus bu choir dhoibh a roghnachadh. Ceadach dhomhsa mo pheighinn, ge beag i, ìocadh as an leth, agus m' eòlas a dhèanadh aithnichte dhoibh; oir thachair dhòmhsa gum faca mi le mo shùilibh fèin na tha ag cuir an ceill.

Aithriseadh mi 's a chiad àite sgeul firinneach agus so-fhìosrach mu thimchioll eilean Mhan Deimein. Guidheam ort, èisd gu foill ris na their mi, agus is cinnteach mi, 'n a dheigh sin, nach can thusa no neach 's am bith eile, gur àite e gus an comhairleachadh sinne iad a dhol mar bitheadh miann againn mòr-chron a dhèanadh dhoibh.

Agus ma ni na Gàidhail droch roghainn 'na dheigh sin, orra fèin bitheadh a choire, agus an dragh agus an dolaidh a thachras. Ach mun tèid sinn na 's fhaide, is còir dhuinn fios a thoirt mu dheidhinn na tìre-sa, ciod an ìre 's an robh i raighe, agus ciod an ìre 's am beil i an trà-sa.

Tha an t-eilean-sa eadar an 40dh agus 50dh ceum ri deas air leug an t-saoghail, eadar an 145dh agus 150dh ceum ri soir air sgrìob. ... Tha an aimsir aca-sa ach ro-bheag gu bhith calg-dhìrach an aghaidh an aimsir againn. Tha dearbh mheadhan an t-samhraidh aca mu nollaig, agus àirde a' gheamhraidh beagan an deigh Bhealltainn. Tha a' ghrian ri tuath orra, agus uime sin tha fuachd a' teachd as an taobh deas, agus teas bhon taobh tuath. Tha iomadh diùbhras eile nach ruigar leas aithris 's an àm.

......

Bha uair ann, gun robh na h-uile ag ruith d' a h-ionnsuidh, ach chaidh an àm sin seachad. Fhuair an ciad luchd-imrich còir air fearainn airson ro-bheag ach a shaothrachadh agus mòran cogh-naidh gu sin a dhèanadh. Ach thàinag atharrachadh mòr bhon àm sin. Chaidh taghadh an fhearainn a shealbhachadh, agus air an aobhar sin rinn cuid-eigin de mhuinntir saibhreas a chruinneachadh.

Ged tha am fearann a dh'fhàgteadh mòran na 's measa, tha e mòran na 's daoire. Is tearc, ro-theirc e is fhiach na 's mò na crùn gach acair, ach is e dà thasdan-deug a chuid is lugha air an cuirteadh suas e r' a reic, agus ma dh'fhaodteadh gun èirich a' phrìs gu trì no ceithir uirad 's bu choìr dh' ì.

……………………..

... is duilich r' a ràdh, nach 'eil am fiodh ion-luaidhadh. Tha an t-eilean làn choilltean, ach is e buinteanas do na craoibh, agus a chuid is mò, is bigh-chranna iad, nach urra-innar an sùgh a thiormachadh asda. Air an aobhar sin, tha am fiodh air bheag stà ach airson losgaidh, agus gach uair a thèid a snaidhadh no a locradh, ci b' e ùine a bhitheas 's an eadraiginn crionaidh agus seargaidh e air fad 's air leud.

Chunnaic mi tigh 's an deach ùrlar a dhèanadh dheth, dh'fhosgail na bùird uiread bho chèile, gun robh a' ghaoth ag sèidadh trompa co fhuar ri toll tora, agus b' èiginn slatan no bùird amhleathan de fhiodh a spàrradh eatorra. Airson àirneis agus a leithid, tha fiodh aca r' a fhaotainn a Canada 's America thuathach.

A-nis abramaid facal m' an timchiol-san a thèid air imrich, agus gan teagamh is muinntir iad aig am bheil sporan làn no sporan falamh. Dhiù-san aig am bheil airgiod fimridh iad tuathanachd no cìobairachd a chleachdadh, agus dhiù-san aig nach eil airgiod is luchd cèaird no luchd cosnaidh iad. Air an dòigh sin, tha iad iar an roinn fa cheithir, gabhamaid gach aon dhiù fa seach.

Air tùs theirinn nach bu chòir do thuathanach a dhol idir don duthaich ud. Chan fhaigh e ach ro-bheag fhearainn a ghiulanas cruithnachd no leithid sin de bhàrr. Chan eil 'san eilan uile gleann tarbhach cosmhuil ri Srath-Chluaidh no ri cursaibh us comhnardibh na h-Eaglais bhrice agus Ghabhraidh. Chan fhaighar ach mìr fhearainn in seo agus mìr in sud, agus chan urrainnar na tha ann a shaothrachadh ach a-mhàin dlùth ri traigh na mara, no in gleanntibh nach eil fada uaipe.

Tha eadarmheodhan an ealain ro-fhuair, far am bheil fasgadh nam beann 's nan cnoc ag dunadh mach blàthas uisge na fairge. Air uairibh eile, tha iad iar an sgìursadh le gaoth loisgach as an taobh tuath, no as an àirde sin tha eadar an àirde tuath us àirde an iar.

Tha iomadh cruadhas eile ann in lorg suidheachaidh in seo, is eigin a chomhlachadh agus a chothachadh. A 'bharrachd air teircais an t-uisge, tha aca ri gleachd in aghaidh olcais is gann is aithne dhuinn aig a' bhaile, agus is e sin an reothadh samhraidh.

Is minic an uair a bhithas a' chruithnachd no an eorna fo bhlàth, no fagus air abachadh gun tig a' phlàigh mhilltail seo agus in aon oidhche sgriosar uile shaothar an tuathanaich. Bithidh mar gun b' ann air ball gach duillag iar marbhadh 's iar fàs dubh, gan shùigh 's gan fheum; bithidh eodhan am meas, na siristean na peitsean 's na h-ubhlain iar seirgadh mar gun tilgteadh uisge goil orra.

Agus ma thachras gum faigh an tuathunach am bàrr air deagh uidham 'n a shabhal, bithidh a duilich a thoirt gu feill no margadh, - duilich a reic agus airgiod fhaotuinn air a shon. Chan eil Glaschadh na Grianag aca no Dun-eidin no Londhuinn far an faighar ceannaichean air ball, agus cead pilleadh dachaidh gan mhaille le sporan iar a lionadh.

Chan eil deagh ròidean aca no goiras ceart cheum a ghiulan bhon bhaile. In aon fhacal theirinn nach tig tuathanachd gu mhaoin a dhioladh dha airson a shaothair, 's an t-eilan chian ud.

Ma cha comas soirbhachadh in gnothaich 's am bith, is ann ann an àrach chaorach gu h-airidh agus fheudail air uairibh, ach tha iomad duilgheadas 's an rathad mun urra dhoibh am fearann fhaotainn. Cha ruig e leas smuainachadh gum faigh e gabhaltas fearainn dh' a fèin ann na 's lugha dh'ùine na bliadhna gu leth. Ach bho nach urrainn e a bhith beò mar an arc no an dearc gainminach* le deoghaladh an adhair, is èiginn d' a cur suas in tigh osda, far am pàigh e rèir mo bharail airson na thèid 's a ghoile na 's daoire no in tigh-osda bith ann in Glaschadh.

Early Impressions

["Those in the habit of reading the *Cuairtear* will notice a different style of writing between this article and other material in this journal; but this is due to a request by the gentleman who wrote it that it be printed as it was originally written."]

Dear *Cuairtear*,

"You are, without doubt, desirous and ready for any information to give to our countrymen, who trust their condition will improve by emigrating to a foreign land, and where that might be. Permit me my penny-worth, though it is small, rendered on their behalf, making known to them that which I know; because everything which I declare I saw with my own eyes.

I am providing a true, well-informed and first-hand account about Van Diemen's Island*. Let me appeal to you to listen thoughtfully to what I will say, and I am certain, after that, that neither you nor anyone else will mention this place again unless they announce that they intend coming here, though we are sure that they would be making a great mistake.

And if the Highlanders still make the decision to come, they will have chosen badly and if, after that, hardship and trouble and loss occur, then they will have only themselves to blame. But before we will go on about it at length, we ought to give news concerning the land, the condition in the first quarter, and the progress of it for the season.

The season is a very short one, being directly opposite what they [i.e.the settlers] are used to. Truly, the middle of summer here is about Christmas-time back home, and the height of winter falls shortly after May-day. The sun is to their north and therefore cold comes from the south side, and heat from the north side. There are many other differences but this is not the time to go into them.

. . .

There was a time when everyone was flocking to this place, but that time has passed. The first emigrants got the land cheaply and, through labour and much assistance, it was cultivated. But a big change came after that time. The land was acquired through selection, and for that reason some persons of wealth acquired much of it.

Notwithstanding that the land that is left is a great deal worse, it is, nevertheless, a great deal dearer. It is scarce, very scarce, and it is priced more than five shillings an acre, but it is twelve shillings at least on being put up for auction, and that price may rise to three or four times as much as it ought.

[I am] sorry to say, that the timber is unsuitable. The island is full of forests, but trees are uprooted, and the greater part are decaying, the sap not able to dry out of them. For that reason, the wood is of little use but for burning, and all the time chopping and planting are going on, time itself is intervening, scorching and drying its length and breadth.

I saw a house with the floor that had been constructed, the planks were so broken that the wind was blowing through them as cold as a wimble-hole, and there were some rods or broad planks of nailed timber between them. For furniture and the like, timber has to be obtained from Canada and North America.

Now let us say a word about those that have emigrated and who, without doubt, form two major groups; those with money and those without it. Of those with money they become farmers or become accustomed to shepherding; and of those that do not have money they make up the tradespeople and the labourers. In that manner, they are divided into four groups; let us take each one alternately.

At the beginning, farmers ought not to come at all to this country. It has got very little land that will support wheat or any grain crop like that. There is not in the whole island a profitable glen that resembles Strath-Clyde or a flat plain to put up our new brick Church.

You will only get a piece of land here and there, that is able to be worked, except near the seashore, nor has it a valley of any length. The middle of the island is very cold, where shelter is provided by mountains and the hills shutting out heat, rain and sea. At other times, there are lashing westerly winds burning out the north side, or out of that place between the north and the west.

There are many other trials for those colonizing here, and meetings and discussions are necessary. Furthermore, there is scarceness of water and they have to struggle against sickness and the lack of knowledge that exists in the town, and there is the freezing month of May.

There is many a time the wheat or the barley will be in blossom, or near to ripening, when some pestilence will come spoiling this and in one evening all the farmer's work will be destroyed, immediately! It is as though every leaf is killed and blackened, without sap and useless; namely the fruit, the cherries, the peaches and the apples, withered as though boiling water had been thrown over them.

And if it happens that the farmer has had a good harvest stored in the barn, taking it to the market is a hardship, - with further difficulty in selling it and getting money for it. They have no Glasgow or Greenock or Edinburgh or London, where buyers will immediately be found, and then returning home without delay with a full purse.

They do not have good roads nor proximity to a proper path to the town. In a few words I would say that a farmer of substance having to pay for his pains will not want to come to this far-distant island.

If it is not possible to prosper in business, sometimes there is profit in the raising of sheep, but there is many a difficulty for someone on the road to obtaining land. He need not think that he will get tenancy of land for himself in less than a year and a half.

But he will not be able to live as the lizard or the chameleon by sucking the air. It is necessary to put up at an hotel, where the cost of satisfying the appetite, in my opinion, is dearer than a hotel in Glasgow.

*This was the name originally given to Tasmania. It was first visited by the Dutch explorer, Abel Tasman, in 1642. He named it Van Diemen's Land after the Governor-General of the Dutch East Indies, Anthony van Diemen, who had commissioned Tasman's voyage. It was re-named Tasmania in 1856.

34 Fhir mo Gràidh

A-nis, - tha an tìr gun teagamh 's am bith 'n dùthaich tha làn do mhaoin, gu nàdurra – 'n an tìr reamhar shultmhor mhèidh. Chan e gum bheil i uile mar sin, agus gum faodadh a' mhòr-roinn so Victoria, sluagh na h-Alba a ghabhail a steach, agus deadh ghabhail do fearann bhi aig na h-uile teaghlach sin, agus gidheadh 's e Victoria a-mhòr-roinn a's lugha farsuingeachd do'n triùir New South Wales, Victoria agus South Australia.

Rinn mi aon turas an àraidh, an so, gu ruig criàchan South Australia – mharcachd mi air an turas sin! Tuilleadh 's ochd ceud mile a dh'astair, air chùl dol air muir, gu ruig Portland Bay, tuilleadh 's dà cheud mile. Chaidh mi troimh dhùthaich a's farsuing na Alba gu leir "a mhaidne kirk gu John o' Groats." – Agus chan eil 'san fharsuingeachd sin uile, ach 'grid no oisinn bheag do mhòr-roinn Victoria! – 'S i mu bheachd gum bheil Victoria ni 's farsuing na Alba, Eirinn, a Sassann an ceann a chèile – mòran ni 's farsuing.

Agus chunnaic mi ruith dhùthchan – ceàrna fa leth – is bòidhche 's reamhra, 's a 's àillidhe, na ni 's am bith idir an do buidhe riamh ma shùil – do uile sibh cruthachaidh. O'. dhuine! – ar leam nam faigheamaid so air a shuidheachadh – le teachlaichibh Gaidhealach, agus sileadh an t-soisgeil bhi pailt, glan, fallain 'n am measg – cha robh tìr a' gheallaidh innte fèin mar thìr, idir cosmhail ris an tìr sin.

Chan eil o 'n fhìon gur a' bhainne, aon ni air an cuireadh an creatair feum, nach cinneadh an so, gu rèidh, sultmhor pailte am fonn a' feitheamh gu bhi air àiteachadh.

Chan ann mar so tha Australia uile, air chor 's am bith – a' ghabhail seallaidh air an dùthaich mar thìr, 's na iomlan 's ann a tha an tìr – dìreach – 'n a stiallaidh – an dara stiall mar a chèarna ad làn do chalt – an ath stiall, tioram, greannach, cruaidh, gun fheum – shaoileadh bu gur e am fraọch fèin a th' ann!

Monaidhean fada, farsuining tioram, gun dreach – gun mhaise – agus a ris, tha an deadh fhearainn a' tighinn 's an t-sealladh agus mar sin air agaidh, ach, thigeadh na Gàidheal bhochd, air tìr an so – agus càite an teid aca air dol. Chan fhaigh iad am fearann, 's cha mhò is urrainn doibh 's a chur air a' bheag dheth a cheannach ged thaingteadh dhoibh e.

Feumaidh iad an cosnadh a thoirt orra – far am faigh iad e. Tha iad air an sgapaidh thall 'g a bhos – agus gun fhios aig an dara fear, càit an deachaidh am fear eile. Agus mar so, tha na creatairean air an call. 'S chan iad fèin a-mhain, ach an duine da ruidh iad sin suas gun fhòghlum gun eòlas agus ciod a dh'uireas doibh! Chan e na ma biodh iad fèin smiorail, cneasda, stòlda, agus comhairle 'n an ceann …

My dear friend,

Now, this land is, without any doubt, a country full of natural resources with extensive ground, fertile and rich. It is not like this from end to end. However, there is so much of it like this, and this province of Victoria can take in the people of Scotland with all of the families being able to have land; and yet the province of Victoria is the least extensive of the three Provinces - New South Wales, Victoria and South Australia.

I did one trip especially, here, reaching as far as the border of South Australia. I was on horseback on that trip of more than eight hundred miles, returning by sea, reaching Portland Bay, another two hundred miles. I went all over the country which is far larger than the whole of Scotland altogether "from Maidenkirk to John O' Groats", and not in all that area is there the quality of a small corner of the province of Victoria! And the opinion is that Victoria is as large as Scotland, Ireland and England together, many say even larger.

And I saw rolling countryside, all as separate districts – fair and fertile and resplendent, not a thing more gratifying has my eye ever seen in all your creation, O, man! I think if we can get this settled by Highland families, the gospel dispensation will be abundant, pure and wholesome in their midst. The promised land itself could not be likened to that land.

The needy people, in good health, and having no kindred here, should be sent, free, to settle the fertile, extensive land waiting to be cultivated.

This is not the same in all of Australia by any means, taking a view of the country as a whole, it is not all exactly the same - it is in sections. One section will be fully fertile - the next, dry, of little worth, difficult and useless. Imagine ground without even heather itself in it! Long moors, wide and dry, without form, without beauty and then, excellent land again coming into view, and so on progressively.

But, should the poor Gael come, after landing here where will they go on arrival? They will not get the land, and neither have they the ability, or ways and means, available to them to buy even a little of it.

They must obtain a wage where they can get it and be thankful. They are scattered hither and thither – and one man does not know where the other has gone. And in this way the people get lost. And not only they themselves, but those who follow them - without education, and without skill of what was required of them!"

35 Lìtir bho Rob MacDhùghail [Extracts only]

Tha na srathan, dà thaobh nam beann seo, anabarrach àillidh mar an ceudna. That iad in tràsa còmhdaichte le feur agus luibhean, fo "mhìle blàth 'us suaicheantas." Gach gnè fheòir - chan e fhraoich, thoiribh fainear - a tha tarbhach agus feumail a thoirt piseach, fàis, agus saille air feudail, co aca crodh, caoraich, eich, no gobhair.

Agus bha aon duin'-uasal, ma dh'fhaodas mi an t-ainm sin a thoirt do fhear a nòis, a thug trì cheud muc don nàbuidheachd seo, an làn dùil gun d'rinn Nàdar gach ullachadh agus solaradh a bha freagarrach don càil. Ach ged a rinn Nàdar, a bhen-uasal, an t-àite seo freagarrach airson nam muc, cha d' rinn i na mucan freagarrach airson an àite seo, anns an staid sam beil e fathast; agus is soirbh ri thuigsinn gun deachaidh na mucan agus a dhòchas bun-os-ceann ceart còmhladh.

Shuidhich mi mo chùrsa deas 's a bhi 'n iar, gus an d' thàinig mi mu dheireadh don àite roimh-ainmichte - a tha mu thuaiream sia-fichead mìle a Melbourne, agus trì-fichead a Geelong. Chunnaic mi iomadh gleann, coire, agus aonach, ri linn an turuis seo, a chaidh thar cainnt ann an àilleachd* ... Is dìomhain domh oidheirp a thoirt air aogas innseadh dhuibh - chan urradh ann mi. ... 'Se dh'fheumadh e rogha filidh!"

Tha na mulain uaine, àghmhor so, air am breacadh, an sud 's an so, le cora chraoibh bhig, dhosanaich, dhòmhail, a tha'n còmhnuidh a'beò-chrathadh le "eòin bhuchallach, bhreac na coille," a bhìos a' feadarsaich "air bhogadan, 's 'a togairt dol a dhannsadh" air bhachd gach geige.

An uair a sheallas mi ris an àird-an-iar, chì mi sreath bheanna ag eiridh gun athadh, agus a' sgoltadh nan neul - na Pyrenees, agus mullach na Garbh Bheinn. Cha tholmain beaga iad seo idir, ach cruachan gualuinneach, dòmhail a tha chòig uiread deug ri Beinn-a-ghlogha, a h-ogha, 's a h-iar-ogh!

Ach a leantuinn mo sgeòil: tha lochain-uisge, mu leud seòl luinge - cuid ni's mò, agus cuid ni's lugha - thall 's a bhos feadh an àite seo. Tha cuid diubh seo co domhainn, a's nach eil fios agam am faighear ìochdar aca. Gheibhear iad an àiteachan mar dheich mìle, an àiteachan mar chòig, agus an àiteachan mar thrì mìle d' a cheile. De gach sonas a chì an coigreach 'san àite, tha iad seo nan taisbean co miorbhuilleach 's a th' ann air gliocas agus maitheas Dè. [An tìr seo] a dh' uidheamaich agus a shocraich iad an seo, gu beachaidh, airson feum' a' ghinealaich seo, agus gach ginealach eile a shealbhaicheas am fearann mar oighreachd.

Rob MacDhùghaill
Boningong, Geelong, Australia Felix

Letter from Rob MacDougall (Extracts only)

"There are plains, both sides of this mountain, each exceedingly beautiful. In September they are covered with grass and small plants, under "a thousand blooms and colours." Every kind of grass – note, not heather – captures the attention; it is productive and useful for fattening cattle, sheep, horses, or goats, which people here possess.

However, one gentleman, if I may so name a man who brought three hundred pigs to this neighbourhood, was in full expectation that Nature would provide that which was suitable to their needs. But though Nature, being a lady, made this place suitable for pigs, she did not make the pigs suitable for this place in the existing conditions; and it is easy to understand that the pigs wandered off and sent the owner's expectations altogether topsy turvy.

I settled my course south westerly until I reached the neighbourhood forementioned - that is about twenty-six miles from Melbourne, and sixty miles from Geelong. I saw many glens, hollows, and hills, during the course of this journey, that went beyond language in their beauty; ... It is idle for me to attempt to give a description to you - I have not the ability* ... it would require the best poet!

There is this pleasant little green field, dotted here and there with the most fitting small trees, bushy and dense; it is a habitat lively with "birds nestling, dotting the trees, whistling, bobbing, and keenly hopping", and filling every branch.

When I look to the west, I can see a series of mountains boldly rising, and splitting the clouds - the Pyrenees, and the summit of Ben Garbh. These are not little hills, but mountains, fifteen of a size equal to Beinn-a-0ghlogha, a h-ogha, 's a h-iar-ogh'.

But continuing my tale: there are little pools of water, about the breadth of a ship's sail - some big and some smaller - hither and thither the length of this place. Some of them are deep but I do not know how deep. They are to be found at intervals in places some ten miles, some five, some three miles from each other. Every success that the stranger sees in this place reveals the miraculous power; the wisdom and goodness of God. [The land] is well equipped and suited, most assuredly, for this generation's need, and every other generation that will receive the land as a heritage.

Rob MacDougall
Buninyong, Geelong, Australia Felix

*MacDougall is being extremely modest here. He had, in fact, travelled widely overseas and had spent several years trapping in outback Canada and was an accomplished Gaelic writer and poet. He was also a man of great commercial ability and became one of the two leading cattle breeders in Victoria and a member of the Victorian parliament.

36 Do Na Gaeil An Albainn

[By 'Caraid nan Gaidheal', Ballarat,

A Theachdaire Ionmhuinn

Thàinig mi don dùthchaich seo fo cheann Ceithir bliadhna agus gun mhòra dàil thog mi orm gu talamh an oir 's le gliocas, cùram, a 's dìchioll leanail teach chruinnich mi na chumas gu math ri 'm bheò mi agus beagan ri sheachnadh. 'S aithne dhomh iomadh aon eile as a' Ghaeltachd aig an robh an soirbheachadh ceadna, ach air a' shon sin bha 'n pailteas ann nach d'rinn dad deth; cuid dìchiollach gu lèoir ach mòran diubh amaideach.

Tha mi cinnteach gu 'm bi an Teachdaire dol don Ghaeltachd, agus leis a sin ma bheir sibh àite don litir seo uam theirinn ris na Gaeil an Albainn, gur mòr a b' fhearr dhaibh a bhi seo na bhi dol bàs far a bheil iad.

Na d' thigeadh Gaidheil, air bith an seo ann am beachd gu 'n dèan iad stòras 's gu 'm bi iad nan daoine uaisle ann am bliadhna na dhà;—chaidh na tìmean sin seachad; ach thigeadh iad ann an dùil beolaint mhath a bhi aca, agus beagain a chuir mu seach an dràsda 'sa rithis, agus cha bhi iad air am mealladh.

Duine air bith as urrainn obair gu math a tha glic 's a chumas fo 'n deach ni e feum; agus mar seo faodaidh e eiridh ri tìm gu bhi cho math air a chasan ri pairt de na tighearnan beaga.

Lìtir bho 'Caraid nan Gaidheal', Ballarat,

To Gaels in Scotland,
[signed 'Friend of the Gael', Ballarat]

I came to this country just under four years ago and I soon dug some gold from the ground and with care and diligence I have managed to obtain a piece of land and a house for myself and I live well with a little to spare. And many others, from the Highlands, known to me, have achieved similar success through diligence but nevertheless there were many who could not make anything of it; some were very industrious but many of them were foolish.

I am certain that the Messenger will be going to the Highlands and because of that if you will give space to this letter from me I would say to the Gaels in Scotland, that it would be better for them to be here than to die where they are.

Those Highlanders who come here will, in my judgment, so succeed that they will be gentlemen in two years time. It will take time, but they should come in the lively expectation that they will do well, and putting a little by now and then, they will not be disappointed.

Men who are able-bodied, hard working and not under the power of, nor in need of, drink; will, in time, in this manner raise themselves to live like little Highland lords.

Letter from 'Friend of the Gael', Ballarat.

37 Tha an fhàilte chridheil

[*An Teachdaire Gaidhealach*]

Tha an fhàilte chridheil a fhuair a cheud àireamh de'n Teachdaire ann an tìr a' dhùthchais – Gaeltachd na h-Alba, a' toirt deadh mhisneach dhuinn anns an obair air an do thoisich sinn, a-chum leas ar luchd-dùtcha gràdhaich, anns na h-Eileanna seo, agus, mar an ceudna, a' nochdadh, gu soilleir, nach cuir astar na ùine smàl air aonachd inntinneil nan Gaidheal. Cha chuir gu bràth!

Tha iadsan a fhuair an àrach ann an dùtchaich na fraoch-bheann, nan sluagh air leth. Ged a sgapar iad, mar na h-Iudhaich o shean, a measg chèarnaibh iomallach an domhain gheibhar iad a "Leanntuinn gu dlù cliù an sinnsear", a-thaobh a'n dàimh ris a Ghaeltachd gun lagachadh air bith.

Nach cruaidh, matà, gum biodh sluagh aig a bheil uiread spèis da'n dùtchaich air am fògradh air falbh o fhearann an athaireichean, le uachdrain an-iochdmhor, seadh gu cinnteach; ach tha a'm Freasdal gu minic, a tionndadh ain-tighearnas nan daoine ud gu mòr-bhuanachd don t-sluagh bhochd a tha iad a fuadach as an dùtchaich.

Tha mìltean, aig an àm seo, ann an Astraillia, a chaidh, chan e mhàin a bharlinneachdh, ach a' chuir a-mach as an taighean, le maoir, anns a' Ghaeltachd, a tha mòran n' is fèarr dheth na iadsan a thug a leithid do dhroch-àbhaisteachadh dhaibh.

'Se ar dùrachdna gun èirich gu maith do gach Gael a chuireas a chas air tìr anns na cèarnaibh seo; agus chan eil teagamh againn nach èirich, ma bhitheas iad fèin dìchiollach bunailteach-mar a tha sinn toillicht' fhaicinn, a tha iad an coitchionntas. Bithidh sinne 'g oidhearpachadh, o àm gu àm, n' is urrainn duinn a dhèanamh airson sonas aimsireil agus spioradail nan Gael àrdachadh.

The kind welcome …
[Editorial *The Gaelic Messenger*]

The kind response we received to the first number of the Messenger in our native-land – the Highlands of Scotland - has encouraged us in the work we have begun for the benefit of our fellow countrymen in this Island, and also shows, clearly, that neither distance nor time will ever extinguish the sincere unity of the Gael. Not ever!

The Gaels were reared in the country of the heather-covered mountains; a separate people. Though they are scattered as the Jews of old among the uttermost regions of the world, they "Follow the fame of their fathers," without, at all, weakening their connection to the Highlands.

Is it not distressing that a people as much attached to their country as they are, are expelled from the land of their ancestors, by merciless rulers? Indeed, it is! But Providence frequently turns the oppression of a people to great advantage to the poor who were driven out of the country.

Thousands, who are at this time in Australia, came, not only after being given a warning to quit, but by actually being physically evicted from their homes in the Highlands by the bailiff, but they are now better off than those who behaved viciously towards them.

We wish every Highlander well that puts foot in this region; and we have no doubt that they will succeed if they are diligent and sober and part of a community as we are pleased to see they are. We will be endeavouring, from time to time, to do what we can to ensure the temporal and spiritual prosperity of the praiseworthy Highlanders.

38 A Theachdaire Rùnaich

[Lìtir bho Iain Mac-Leòid]

Tha sibh toilteach air mòr-chliù agus mile taing fhaotinn 'a gach chan e mhàin ann an Astraillia, ach ann an Gaeltachd na h-Alba, airson bhur caoimhneis blàth cuir theach a thaobh ar luchd-dutcha, le bhi, aig ceann gach mios, a tabhairt dhuinn, anns an fhior spiorad fhialuidh. . . .

Nuair a dh'fhàg mi an t-Eilein Sgitheanach 's beag fiuthair a bh' agam ri Teachdaire Gaidhealach, fhaotinn ann an Astraillia, agus faodaidh sibh a bhreritheachadh an t-ioghnadh a chuir e orm aireach den Teachdaire fhaotinn ann an aon de thaigheann osda Mhelbourne. Air dhomh a' leughadh le mòr-dhùrachd smaointich mi, aig a cheart an gum faodadh an Teachdaire, a bhi air a dhèanamh na mheadhon fior fheumail a chum fiosrachaidh a thabhairt dar cairdean anns a Ghaeltachd a thaobh 'ar cèarn anns an dùtchaich fharsuing …

Dh'fhàg mi talamh Mhic-Leoid anns an t- Eilein Sgitheanach, focheann trì bliadhna, le teaghlach mòr – triùr mhac agus cuid nigheanan. Nuair thàinig do Mhelbourne, cha robh agam de dh'airgiod, ach ceithir puinnd shasannach suim nach cumadh mo theaghlach os cionn seachdain anns a bhaile; ach mar a bham freasdal fab h-àrach dhomh fhuair mi tairgas dhuin uasal Sasannach gu dol am againn da' ionnsuidh air a tha ort latha a' thàinig mi air tìr.

Cha robh an tuarasdal a dhublachadh an deigh dhomh a bhi bliadhna na sheirbhis. Aig ceann bliadhna eile amaointich mi gun deanain na bearr air mo chuid fèin na bhi ceangailte ri maighistir, aig an àm seo bha corr a's fichead punnd Sasunnach agam seachad. Leig mi ris don t-shasannach gun robh e 'm bheachd fhàgail agus acair na dhà fhearainn a cheannach 's aiteach; thug an duine cneasda gu h-ealamh, a chomhairle aorm sin a dhèanamh gun dail.

Cheannaich mi, an ùine goirid fhearainn, agus tha e na aobhar toileachais dhomh a bhi agam ri innseadh gu bheil e coltach nach fhada gus am bi mi cho maith dheath ris a mhaighistir chruaidh chrisheach a' bha mi seirbheiseachadh, anns an t-Eilein Sgitheanach fo mhoch gu dubh, airson sgillin-shasannach 's an latha. 'S i seo dùthaich a phailteas, anns am faod gach neach a bhios dichiollach, bunailteach, a dhèanamh anns a Ghaeltachd far nach eil meas nan con aig mòran de na h-uachdrain leibideach air an iochdrain …

Ann an comhdhùnadh, chomhairleachinn dom an t-Eilein Sgitheanach ach ann an cèarnaibh h-eile den Ghaeltachd, iad a thiginn don tìr seo – far am faigh iad fearann gu leòir, air shaor chunnradh; agus nach cuir bairlinnen na' Cuingeis na màil na Fèill-Martuinn* iomaguin orra.

Slàn leibh.

Lìtir bho Iain Mac-Leòid
Port Phillip, an Seachdamh Mìos, 1857

A Skyeman in Australia
[John MacLeod]

Dear Messenger,

You deserve praise and a thousand thanks for showing each Gael, not only in Australia but also those in the Scottish Highlands, your warm kindness on behalf of your countrymen ... there will be at the beginning of each month, in the true, generous Highland spirit, news, stories and everything substantial, in our own sweet tongue. I am not sure how Teachdaire Gaidhealach, with such a large work-load and expense, is able to publish in my region, for this reason it is very proper for every gael to help.

After I left Skye a small surprise awaited me on finding *An Teachdaire Gaidhealach* in Australia. Imagine my astonishment finding An Teachdaire in one of the hotels in Melbourne. On reading it carefully, I think that An Teachdaire is timely in providing genuine information for our friends in the Highlands as well as for those in our corner of this wide land.

I left the land of Macleod on Skye three years ago, with a large family – three sons and some daughters. When I came to Melbourne I only had four English pounds, a sum not able to support my family in town for more than a few days but, as usual, Providence was looking after me. That day an Englishman offered me work on his land.

The wage he offered was small but he promised that if I pleased him he would double my wages at the end of a year of service. At the end of another year I thought of doing shearing on my own and not be bound to any master. At this time, I had a surplus of twenty English pounds saved. I explained to the Englishman that it was my intention to leave, and I bought an acre or two of agricultural land; and the man gave me expert advice straight away.

Within a short time, I bought a piece of land and began, with myself and a lad, to clear it and it was a source of contentment to me that I will be the equal of him who was my hard-hearted master whom I served on Skye from dawn to dusk for an English shilling per day. This is a country of plenty, and every person who is industrious and steadfast will do well, a thing which is impossible to poor men working in the Highlands where many of the chiefs have no respect for their people.

In conclusion, advise my countrymen who patiently bear oppression and poverty, that it is not good to remain on Skye; in other regions of the Highlands, families are coming to this land – where they get plenty of land on cheap bargain terms and not have the worry hanging over them of a summons to quit at Whitsun or Martinmas.*

Yours

Letter from John MacLeod
Port Phillip, August, 1857

39 Am Bhliadhna

[le Dòmhnal Mac Ionmhainn senior]

Tha Bhliadhna nis air teachd gu a ceann thall 's bliadhn' ùr a toiseachadh am màireach.

Dh'fhàg i bhliadhna so dithis don teaghlach nan Sgiobairean soithichean smùid an triùir eile nan luchd-deanamh siucair, an triùir nighean singlete maille nam mathair, mise am Ghibeonach a toirt dhachaidh connaidh 's air uairean uisge airson an teaghlaich.

Dh'fhàg i an citsean gun mhullach ged tha chuid iosal air a cur suas o cheann leth bhliadhna.

Dh'fhàg i am buntata againn nam plaoisg air grodadh anns an talamh le romheud air teas 's na tiormachd.

Dh'fhàg i an abhainn an seilbh air cuig soithichean smùid gu bhi tarruing amach agus a steach soithichean seolaidh don abhainn

Dh'fhàg i an tuathcheathairn an iomagain mu 'n chòrn nach gabh e toradh aig smùid na tiormachd

Dh'fhàg Tearlach na Mharsanta aibheis chearc, buntata, 's corn is oranges etc.

Dh'fhàg i lethdusan muilean-siucair air an abhainn … 's loisg i ormsa na camain airson n h-iomanach, och on, och on.

Dh'fhàg i talamh an seo air sgàineadh leis an tiormachd … dh'fhàg i an abhainn leth shaillte ionnus fad dà fhichead mile dhi nach feudar a h-uisge òl ….

Dh'fhàg i 'n crodhlaoigh air bheag bainne le cion an fheòir 's na uisge , tha mairt is mucan a bàsachadh, tha feoil daor …

Dh'fhàg I againne dà cheud phluir, glè bheagan tea, ach paitleas siucair 's sallain, ach gun dad feola and feumalachd an teaghlaich de ìm 's baine is buntata 's call ceitherleach 's càl eile, siucar-cèan cuideachd cearcan is tunnagain ach air glè bheag feuma, aon each mareachd, dà each threabhaidh, is bullock oga air nach deachaidh cuing fhathast.

Dh'fhàg I sinn mar an ceudna domhàin am an ainfhiach, chan eil fhios agam ciod cho domhain.

The Year

[Donald MacKinnon-Diary]

The year is now coming to its end, a new year begins tomorrow. This year left burned two of the family of the Captains of destroyed boats, three sugar workers, and three single daughters, along with their mother. I in the Ghibeonach brought home firewood and, at times water, for the family.

It left the kitchen without a roof, though a part was put up half a year ago.

It left our potatoes in their skins rotting in the ground by the excessive greatness of the heat and dryness.

It left the property on five vessels on the river destroyed, that is ferries floating on the river.

It left the common people who were on the land anxious about corn and that the harvest will be greatly reduced because of the dryness.

It left Charles the Merchant with hens, potatoes, corn and oranges etc.

It left half a dozen sugar mills on the river … it left burned my caman for the shinty. Ochone! Ochone!

It left the ground here parched and cracked open and the river half salty for a distance of almost forty miles and it cannot be used for drinking water.

It left milch cows with little milk and with a lack of grazing and water, cattle and pigs perished and meat is dear …

It left us with some flour, very little tea, but plenty of sugar and salt, but without any meat and necessitating the family to utilize butter and milk, potatoes and catfish and other kale, sugar cane, also hens and ducks but with a very small grazing area; one riding horse, two plough horses and a young bullock not yet on the yoke.

It left us, likewise, deep in debt, but ignorant of just how deep.

40 'Uasail Ionmhuinn

[Donnachaidh Camshron]

Ann an dearbh chinnte gur a math leat cluinntinn bho sheana charaid as minis a' chuir seachad feasgar nad chomann le sòlus, nuair a b' àbhaist dhomh bhi eadar Thirie agus Glaschu, suidheam sìos gu sgrìobhadh chugad.

Dh'fhàg mi Tobar Mhoire le long Dr Boyter, bho chionn a-nis ceithir bliadhna, le aon phunnd Sasunnach nam phòca: chan e sin, ach bha mi an ainfhiach; oir b' èiginn do chàirdean a bha air bòrd dà-phunnd-deug Shasunnach a phàigheadh airson m' fharaidh, mun leigeadh an sgiobair mo shròn air bòrd.

Ràinig sinn Sydney gu sàbhailt ann an seachd-seachduinean-deug agus trì laithean. Nuair chaidh mi air tìr, se na bh'agam d' an t-saoghal seachd sgillean ruadh Albannach! Their thu nach robh seo mòr air traigh choimhich; ach ciod e air nach toir Gael buaidh, le beannachadh Dhia, an cois measarachd agus dìchill! Cha b' fhada bha gus na choinnich mi seana charaid, fear a mhuinntir Lochabar, a thairg dhomh a thiota fichead punnd Sasunnach! Thug mi taing dha, agus thuirt mi gunn gabhainn da-phunnd-deug, a phàigheadh a' charaid a phàigh m' fharadh.

Cha robh mi bheag 'us seachde uairean an uaireadair air tìr nuair rinn mi fasdadh ri fear-ghabhalach, mar àrd-chìobair chaorach, airson ceithir fichead punnd Sasunnach sa' bhliadhna! Ar leam nach robh seo gu h-olc! Dh'fhalbh mi le m' dhithis chìobairean sèa ceud mìle mu iar-thuath air Sydney, far am faod neach deich mìle caor' a chumail air deich puinnd Shasunnach sa' bhliadhna de mhal! 'Se cron as mò th' air an àite, gu bheil ar beatha an cunnart bho na nàistinean fiadhaich. Mhort iad dithis de m' chìobairean-sa, agus ceithir no cùig de m' choimhearsnaich; ach a-nis tha iad an sìth ruinn.

'Si seo tìr is àille chunnaic sùil! - aon samhradh fada fallain! Bheir am fearann dà bhàrr sa' bhliadhna gun leasachadh,- cruineachd agus coirce. Chan eil rud as urrainn duine smaoineachadh nach fàs agus nach cìnn, agus sin ann am mòr phailteas. Tha sgalagan a' faotainn bho £30 gu £40 de thuarasdal, a bharrachd air min chruithneachd, feòil, tea, agus tombaca, gun sòradh!

'Si mo bharail gur h-e'n Dia uile-thròcaireach fèin a dh-ullaich an dùthaich àghmhor seo airson dhaoine bochda Bhreatunn; agus mur gabh iad an cothrom tighin a nall, sann aca fèin tha choire.

Tha mo thuarasdal air a thogail am bliadhna gu seachd fichead punnd 's a deich (£150), agus mo bhòrd! agus an ath-bhliadhna, tha fiughair agam ri dà cheud! (£200)
Tha mi dol a cur na litreach seo gu Sydney le fear-cinnidh dhuit fèin, a mhuinntir

In'ernathrainn (Aye) - fear nach b' fhiach, ochd bliadhna roimhe seo, £60, ach is fhiach an diugh £10,000!

Sgrìobh chugam, air chùram mo bhràthar; agus gum beannaicheadh Dia thu.

Slàn leibh

Litir bho Donnchaidh Camshron
Ohoi, New England, New South Wales, 19th June 1841

Dear Friend,
[Duncan Cameron]

In the certainty that you will be pleased to hear from an old friend who frequently, with pleasure, spent an evening in your company when I customarily travelled between Tiree and Glasgow, I am sitting down to write to you.

I left Tobermory, by the ship Dr Boyter, over four years ago now, with one pound English in my pocket: not only that, I was in debt, because there were some friends on board who had to pay twelve pounds English for my passage before the skipper would allow as much as my nose on board.

We reached Sydney safely in seventeen weeks and three days. When I went ashore, all that I had in the world was seven Scottish pennies! You will say this was not much on a foreign shore; but what Highlander will not succeed, with God's blessing, and by perseverance! It was not long until I met old friends, natives of Lochaber, who immediately offered to lend me twenty pounds English! I thanked them for it, but I said that I would only borrow twelve pounds, to repay the friend who paid my passage.

I was hardly seven hours ashore when I was hired by a tacksman as head shepherd for twenty-five pounds English a year! I thought to myself that this was not so bad! I left with two other shepherds for a place six hundred miles north west of Sydney where a person may keep ten thousand sheep on a rent of ten pounds English! A great drawback of this place is that your life is in danger from the savage tribes. They killed two of my keepers, and four or five of my neighbours; but now they are peaceful towards us.

This land is as beautiful as the eye saw! - one long healthy summer! The ground will, without manuring, yield two harvests a year - wheat and oats. There is nothing that a man can think of that will not grow, and that in great abundance. Farm workers get from £30 to £40 for wages, in addition to wheat, meat, tea, and tobacco unstintingly!

It is my opinion that it is the all-merciful God himself who prepared this magnificent land for poor British men; and unless they take the opportunity to come here, they only have themselves to blame.

My wage for the year is £150, and my keep! and the second year, my expectation is £200! What is more, my friend, I have already £200 in the Bank. In short, I am beginning to buy a beast now and again; and if I live long enough, I will not envy a Highland lord!

I am sending this letter to Sydney by a kinsman of yours, a native of In'ernathrainn (Aye) - a man not worth £60 eight years ago, but who is today worth £10,000.

Write to me, care of my brother; and God bless you.

Yours truly,

[Duncan Cameron, Ohoi, New England,
New South Wales, 16th June, 1841]

41 Lìtir gu *An Teachdaire Gaidhealach*

[Calum a's mise]

Thàinig Calum a's mise don dùthaich seo gun aon sgillinn ruadh nar pòcaid, ach an diugh, ged a thàinig calldach mòr, air cuid againn le 'r gòraich fhèin, chan eil, sinn, taing do Dhia, gun bheagan cul ar laimhe, agus dòigh mhath air tuille a' dhèanamh.

Tha agamsa seachd acraichean fo bhuntàta, trì fo chruithneachd, agus dà acair mar lios, làn chraobhan ubhall, ghròiseid, dhearcan, a's iomadh seòrs' eile air nach cuala tu mòran iomraidh an Albainn, a bharrachd air ceud stuth-gàraidh, nach ruig mi leas ainmeachadh.

Tha ceithir mairt bhainne agam, a's sia mucan an dràsda a-mach feadh na coille, gus an toir mi iad g'an reamhrachadh, mìos no dhà mu'n reic mi iad. ... Chan eile am màl oirnn a chan eil Factor na duin eile aig a bheil a chridhe a bhus fhàsgadh rinn.

Ach na smaointich aon uair gun d' thàinig mise gus a staid seo gun mhòran saoithir a's dìchill – 's iumadh boinne trom fallais a shruth air mo ghruaidh a' chuir nam fuirbinnean mòra duilleagach thar am buinn. A sin a sàthadh sa sgoltadh an fhiodha, s' ga reic cho fhad 's bha am buntàta 's rudan eile cinntinn 's an àite bha cheana air a ghlanadh 's air a' rèiteachadh.

Nuair a tha duine gun airgiod a tighinn don dùthaich seo, feumaidh e cuir ri dh-sùil dol gu seirbhisd fad bliadhna no dhà, a bhi glic grunndail, cùramach, as fuireach air a h-uile cor fon uòl, - ged nach robh mise air mo thoirt a suas da rinn e coire mhòr dhomh uair no dhà - agus an ceann bliadhna no dhà eile cha ruig leas farmad a bhi agam ri duine air bith.

Tha seirbheisich de gach seòrsa air am brod bhiadhach nan tìr seo, tì, aran as feòil, trì uairean nan latha. Am fear nach cuir seo ri shùil, b' fhèarr dha bhi "dèanamh bolg ri grèin" air Dun-Mac-Snitheachain, no air mullach Dun-Chonuill.

Letter to the *Gaelic Messenger*
[Calum and I]

Calum and I came to this country without one penny in our pocket, but today, though we suffered some great losses due to our foolishness, we, thanks to God, without many other setbacks, but with good circumstances, prospered.

I have seven acres under potatoes, three under wheat, and two acres as a garden, full of apple trees, gooseberries, grapes, and many other kinds that you would not have heard of in Scotland, besides a hundred garden varieties that I need not name.

I have four milch-cows, six pigs just now out in the woods fattening, I will sell them in a month or two ... We have no rent, nor factor, nor any other man daring to meddle with us.

But don't think for one moment that I arrived at this state without much hard work and the utmost endeavour – and many large drops of sweat running down my face from felling the great leafy trees at their base. Then pushing and splitting the timber, and selling the lengths, and growing potatoes and other things in the prepared clearing.

When a man without money comes to this country, he must determine to go to work for as long as a year or two, be prudent, frugal, careful, abstaining by all means from drink. Though I did not take it up I did offend once or twice – but, at the end of another year or two, I will not need to envy any other man's success.

There is work of every kind on the choicest land here with rations provided; tea, bread, meat, three times a day. If a man can't see the opportunity that all of this presents, it will be better for him to be sunning himself on Dun Mac Snitheachain, or on the summit of Dunconnel."

42 Òran an Eilthirich

[le Aonghas Peutan]

Tha mi seo aig loch-Elisa, ceud mìle bho shagairt,
Na bho mhinisteir dìleas a dhèanamh fìrinn a labhairt,
'S ged tha biadh agus aodach ri fhaotinn 's ri ghabhail,
Tha mi 'g ionndraichinn daonan nach eil daoine dhomh 'm fagus.

'S olc na coimhearsnach tha agam o 'n a thàinig mi 'n àite,
Daoine dubha 's coin-fhiadhaich gur e 'n gnìomh bhi ri mèirle,
'S tric a dheasaich mi suipeir gun chupan gun spàinean,
'S ged a gheibheadh iad tuilleadh cha bhiodh fuigheall a màireach.

Tha mi mach gach aon la ri frasan 's ri gaodhaibh
'S gun agam do chuideachd ach an cuilein ra fhaotainn,
'S ged a bhitheadh mo nàmhaid ri 'm bhàs thoirt gun aobhar,
Cho b' urrainn mi seasamh mun teicheadh na caorich.

'S fhad mu faic sinn a cheille ged a b' èibhinn leinn tachairt,
Là Dònuich na fèille na cuir èideadh an clachan,
Ach daoine dubha gun èideadh, gun leine, gun chasbheirt,
Ach luideag m' an leisean a' cumail an leasaibh a falach.

Song of the Exile
[by Angus Beaton]

I am now here at loch Elisa, a hundred miles from a priest
Or from a faithful minister proclaiming the truth.
Though food and clothes are there for the taking,
I long for human company as no one is near me.

Wicked neighbours are around me since I came to this place.
Black men and wild dogs continue to thieve.
Often, I take supper without cups or spoons,
And though I replaced them, none would remain by morning.

I am out each day hunting in showers and in wind,
Without any company except the pup I found,
And though the natives seek my death without reason,
I am not capable of standing and letting my sheep be driven off.

It is long since we saw anyone, though it is a delight meeting with friends
on the Lord's Day or market day, wearing our town clothes,
But the aborigines are without clothing, without shirt, without footwear,
Except for a little rag about their thighs keeping the loins covered.

43 'Theab Peilear Burraidh'

[An t-Urramach Dr A. Mac an Tòisich Mac Aoidh]

Theab burraidh do shaighdear righ peilear na measg a chur tromhain aon oidch', 's mi air Balarat ri àm a' chogaidh a bha aca an sin – ach coma "Cha deach theab riamh a mharbhadh!

Bha ò an àm an riaghailt ris an abair na beus dan ('Martial Law'*), air a chuir cha do ghabh mise cùram no aire mun cuid leam – 's thàinig mi tuilleadh 's dlùth air a' chumha gun fhios, gun fhaireachadh, 's an oidhche dhubh dhorcha ann.

Ghlaodh e rium – cha tug mi spèis d' a ghlaodh - tuit no loisgidh mi ort, ars esan! Thuit mi an sin creid. 'S mar b' fheàrr an dara cas na chas eile, chan i bu mheasa – an ceann mionaid a dèigh as, thàinig fear eile air a' chum cheadna loisg an saighear air – agus ged nach do mharbh e am fear an do loisg e, mharbh e fear eile, chan abair e ghabh, gu nì gnothaich ris.

"Almost Shot."
[Rev Dr A. MacIntosh MacKay – to a friend in Scotland]

A ball from a foolish soldier of the king almost went through me one evening. I was at Ballarat at the time there was fighting there – but, however, I had not gone so close to almost being killed before.

It was from the time that the government directly imposed their ruling authority – and, as the saying is, "martial law" was imposed.

I did not take care to have my permit with me and, moreover, I came close to a guard's position without informing him, without warning, and on a pitch-black night.

He again shouted to me – I initially ignored his first cry – "fall or I will shoot you." I fell then, totally convinced, accepting that if his first order had been no better than his second, it could not be worse. After a minute went by, another man came and the soldier, likewise, shot at him, and though he did not kill the man he shot at, he killed another man, so that he would not tell a thing about the matter.

Section Five - New Life and Old - Life and Death and Relationships

For many of the Gaels, love, joy, sadness and lament were experiences which were all played on the same strings of the clarsach. Each had its own strain but for the Highlanders little there was to distinguish them as they all played out in life and death and relationships.

Some settlers could not avoid regarding the customs and lifestyle of his birthplace as the normative ones. Thus, Donald MacKinnon, while recording in his diary the outline of his daily life in Australia did so in Gaelic and frequently put alongside these daily entries, a record, in verse, of what would be happening at the same times of the year on his native island of Coll (e.g. *An Latha an Diugh* and *Ag Iasgach*).

Allan Cameron ('Abrach') seeks to give a reasoned explanation of why and how his youth at Ounich Bay exerted a formative influence on his life. Others, such as James MacMillan with his *Bliadhna Mhath Ùr* and *An Moladh*, attempt, too, to celebrate seasons and traditional events as though they were still in the Highlands and still very much part of the scene and the company where these events were occurring.

Perhaps it was a manifestation of the tension that all emigrants carry within themselves or perhaps it was a way of coming to terms with their new environment, but whatever the reason, many Australian Gaelic poems and prose pieces tended to juxtapose the 'here and now' with the 'there and then' as is clear, for example, in MacKinnon's *An Latha an Diugh.*

The usual cycle of birth, marriage and death was marked appropriately with tender memorials. Personal relationships are feelingly and emotionally expressed, too, in many of the contributions in this Section. These encompass the sad recognition of the ageing of a once vigorous, young and famous huntsman in *Òran do Aonghas Brocair* by Alexander MacDonald.

Other expressions of the whole range of human emotions is demonstrated in such examples as *Di-Luain an t-Sainnseal, Fàth mo Liunnduith, Alastair an Gaol* and *Marbhrann do Alastair MacPhilip a Chaochail air Latha Caingeis* and the pithy *Air a' Chèilidh* and *Chan eil Sùil.* And who would not be cheered by the brightness of *Òran Do Fhloraidh Bheag*?

44 An Latha an Diugh (coig dànain)

[le Domhnull Mac Ionmhuinn senior]

An Latha an Diugh

An latha an diugh maiseach
'S gach duine na chabhaig
A deas-ach an fhearainn
Arson cur an t-sìl. An Astràilia.

Ach s-an t- eilean Chollach,
Gach gille agus bodach-
is eadhon na mnai-
Na an fallas a buain!!! An Caledonia.

Tha Bhuain-eòrna

Tha bhuain-eòrna seachad an Colla,
'S an coirce mòr ag abachadh.
Na cruacha monadh 's na daisean feòir
Gu h-òrdail air an deas-achadh, 's.

Latha Lùnasdal ùr

Latha Lùnasdal ùr
An tìr mo dhùchais 's mo bhreith,
Bhiodh aran is buntàta ùr,
Iasg, is ìm, 's càise is gruthim
Don teaghlach uile na mnathan.

An Latha Ma Dheireadh

[le Dòmhnall MacIonmhainn, senior]

An latha ma dheireadh don mhios
teas is toradh an Colla.
Fuachd reòthadh' is seargadh an tìr 's.
Aca-san, ìm, is càise gun ghainne.
'S bidh 'n aig an ti na mnathan
Solagan, cnodainn is sgaddan ùr,
Creagagan mòra ruadh cuideachd.

Cruinneachadh na meala seileana ruadh,
'S a chònsbeach a cur ruaig air na h-aighean.
Na nighean le 'n cumman 's le 'm buarich
aig na faing-buaile feithibh.

Ag iasgach

[le Dòmhnall MacIonmhainn, senior]

Na gillean òga mach
ag iasgach le slatan iasgaich 's dubhanaibh,
A ghlacadh piocaich 's cudinan
Is bodach ruadha is liuchan,
A mach air suinn na saoithean
Gan toirt dhachaidh ann an cliabh,
le mòran, mòran subhachais.

Today (Five poems)
[by Donald MacKinnon, senior]

Today is a beautiful day
And everyone is in a hurry
Preparing their land
For sowing the seed. in Australia.

But on the Isle of Coll,
Every boy and man-
And even the women-
Are sweating at the harvest!!! in Scotland.

The Barley Harvest

The barley-harvest is finished on Coll,
And the many oats are ripening.
The peat stacks and the stooks of grass
Have been neatly prepared.

The First Day of August

On the first day of August
In my homeland, the land of my birth,
There will be bread and new potatoes,
Fish, butter, cheese and crowdie
For all the women's families.

The Last Day …

The last day of the month of warmth
And fertility in Coll:
Cold, frost and withering are over the land.
But they have butter and cheese aplenty,
And the women have food and tea,
Shellfish, linn and fresh herring
And large red perch as well.

Honey is being gathered from the red bees
And wasps put young cows to flight,
While lassies, with milking pails and cow fetters,
Wait patiently at the cow stalls.

Fishing

[by Donald MacKinnon, senior]

The young boys are out
Fishing with rods and hooks,
Catching coal-fish and cuddy
And cod-fish and lythe,
Sharing them out on the land bank
And carrying them home in their creel
With much, much happiness.

45 Gearr-Chunntas Air Trathan Araid Dhe 'M Shaoghal Aig An Taigh agus Anns An Dùthaich Seo

[le Alasdair MacDhomhnuill, Geelong, Bhictoria]

Mac Aula:- "Thug mi sgrìob air feadh a' bhaile
'S thàinig mi dhachaidh 'n am ònar:
Dè bha romham air stairsneach
Ach ainm Alexander 'ic Dhòmhnuill!
'S e thug togail mhòr dh' am aigne,
Ged bha mi lag-choiseach Breòite,
Sgrìobhadh a bhi 'n cainnt nan seanair
Sheasadh daingeann 'n cùis na còrach."

Mi-fhèin:- "Bha mi 'm lùireach, crùbach lapach
Air mo leabaidh ann am sheòmar,
Mar shaighdear an dèigh a' bhatail
Gun lùths gun tapadh 's e leòinte;
Nuair a chuala mi Mac Aula
Thilg mi phlangaid dhìom le solas
'S mi ri smaointinn air a' bhreacan
Bha mi cleachdadh 'n làithean m' òige.

Ged a thilg mi dhìom a' phlaide
Chum an laigse mi 'n am shìneadh
Ged bu togarrach bha m' aigne
'S ged bha mo mhaide dhomh dìleas;
Cha robh mi ach gliogach glagach,
'N am chulaidh mhagaidh aig mhìltean,
Peanas freagarrach do shlaightear
'S math a thoill mi leth-chead fillte!

'S fad is cian tha leth-cheud bliadhna
Bhon a chuir mi dhìom am fèileadh;
Chumainn astar ris na mìol-choin
Eadar Liondal agus Gesto;
Abhainn Snisort ag iasgach,
Cho beò ri liathaig a' leumraich;
'N diugh tha mi mar cheò no failleas,
Gun treòir is ni' anail 'g am thrèigsinn.

Thug mi ceithir bliadhna 'n Glascho
Measg nam marsantan a b' uaisle,
Bùthan làn air sràidean farsuinn,
'S bu neo-airtnealach mo ghluasad,
Dol a mach 's a' tilleadh dhachaidh
Sunndach, astrach, sgairteil, uallach,

Ged a tha mi 'n diugh 'n am chailleach
Aig a' phairilis 'am buaraich.

Bha mi ochd is fichead bliadhna
'N am fhear-riaghlaidh air sgoil Bheurla,
Teagasg ùmhlachd chlann an dìorrais
Dha mo riaghailtean nach gèilleadh;
Gum b' i sud an obair shunndach
Teagasg cunntais agus leudhadh,
Sgrìobhad, is eòlas na cruinne
Cur char mu choinneamh na grèine.

Bha mi iomadh bliadhna 'bùrach
Air mo ghlùinean fad fon talamh,
Poll is uisge bras a' brùchdadh
'Cumail an smùraich* am falach,
'S ged a fhuair mi tric dhe ùnnsa
Gum b' e sud an sùgradh salach:
'S mairg do Mhammon riamh 'rinn ùmhlachd
'S nach 'eil sailm 'n a chùirt, ach talach.

'S iomadh latha 's oidhche thoilicht'
Chaidh mi thairis air a' Bharwon
Gus an d' thàinig an dubh Nollaig,
Rinn an dolaidh air mo shlàinte,
An Gàidhlig a' seinn mo chiùil
Am measg nam flùr bu chùbhraidh fàileadh
Ged a tha mi 'n diugh cho diblidh
Ann am phrìosanach 'am thàmh-àit.

Cliù don Tì a shin ar làithean
'S a thug sinn bho 'n bhàs le chèile,
Mac sìorruidh na Muire-màthair
Le chumhachd o 'n bhàs a dh'èirich;
Thug E Làsarus gu beatha,
'N ceathramh latha thog bhon eug e;
Thug E mac air ais don bhantraich,
'S do na daoine dall an lèirsinn.

Ach tha m' earbsa 'n Righ-na-tròcair,
Ged a chaidh ar leòin 's a' chruadal
Buaidh gu faigh sinn air ar naimhdean
'S air gach eucoir ruinn tha fuaighte;
'N creideamh 's an dòchas làidir
Gun gabh an Slàouighear truas ruinn
Mar a ghabh e ris a' mhèirleach
'S gun dean Pàrras a' bhuannachd.

A Reply to Mr Samuel MacAulay

(A short account of God's blessings in my Life at home and in this Country)
[by Alexander MacDonald, Geelong, Victoria, Australia]

MacAulay wrote: "I took a trip through town
and I came home alone:
What was on my doorstep in front of me
But the name Alexander MacDonald!
And it lifted my spirits,
Though I was infirm,
Written as it was in the language of our forefathers
Which has always championed justice."

MacDonald's reply:- I was in harness, a lame cripple
On my bed in my room,
Like a soldier after the battle
Without power of movement without alertness and in pain;
When I heard MacAulay
With joy I threw off the blanket covering me
And got to thinking of the plaid
I was accustomed to in the days of my youth.

Though I threw the blanket off me
I remained helplessly lying.
Though my spirit was willing,
And though I had my faithful stick;
I could only clumsily totter,
An object of mockery to thousands,
Punishment fit for a rogue
It is just; I deserved such fifty-fold.

It is fifty years ago
Since I put off the kilt,
Keeping up with the greyhounds
Between Liondal and Gesto;
Fishing at Snizort River,
So lively with leaping salmon;
Today I am as a mist or shadow,
Without strength or breath.

I went to Glasgow for four years
Among the gentlemen merchants,
Full shops in wide streets,
And my movement was untroubled,
Going out and returning home
Joyful, speedy, energetic, cheerful,

Though, today, I am as an old woman
Shackled with palsy.

I was twenty-eight years old
The master at an English school,
Teaching obedience to enthusiastic children,
My rules were diligently applied.
It was joyful work
Teaching arithmetic, reading and writing,
And general knowledge,
During daylight hours.

Then I was many years digging
On my knees far under-ground,
Mud and water suddenly rushing in
Keeping the gold dust hidden,
And though I frequently got ounces of it
It was a dirty sport.
It is foolish to ever submit to Mammon
There are no psalms, only censure, in his court.

And many a contented evening
I went across the Barwon river
Until that dark Christmas time
When my health was damaged.
I used to sing my Gaelic music
Among the scented air of flowers,
Though I am today as a poor wretch
A prisoner in my home.

Praise to the God who prolongs our days
And who saves us from death altogether.
Eternal Son of Mary
With power to raise from the dead.
He brought Lazarus to life
Raised him up from death on the fourth day;
He gave back the widow's son,
And to the blind men their sight.

The King of Mercy is my only hope,
Through his affliction and distress
We obtained victory over our enemies
And on him is pinned our every wrong;
Our faith and strong hope
Is in the Saviour who pitied our wretchedness
As he did to the thief
Who gained Paradise.

46 Bliadhna Mhath Ùr

[le Seumas Mac 'Ille-Mhaoil]

Bliadhna mhath ùr dhuibh, bliadhna mhath ùr dhuibh,
Bliadhna mhath ùr dhuibh uile gu lèir!
Bliadhna mhath ùr dhuibh, dh'òlainn gu sunndach,
Slàinte na dùthcha 's an d' rugadh mi-ein!

Deoch-slàinte so b' fhearr leam, 's traodhainn gu màs i,
Lùdag mo làimh fo ghloine ri 'm bheul,
Chan fhàg mi 's an t-soitheach na dhalladh do fhradharc
'N am iarraidh gun faighainn de rogha nan deur.

Deoch-slàinte nan Gàidheal dh'òlainn gu h-àraidh,
A' guidhe gu bràth àdh bhi nan dèidh;
Tha Freasdal 'g an rianadh 's le Mhaitheas 'g an lìonadh
Gun droch-bheairt no iargain bhi 'g iadhadh 'n an-dèidh.

Deoch-slàinte nan Gilleran 's nan Caileagan grinne
Gun òlainn gu seirceil aig tional gach fèisd;
Cuir thairis trom-lìon i, chan fhaod i bhi spìocach,
'S mi 'g òl mar bu mhiann leam do shiol nam fear treun.

Deoch-slàinte nam Bodach is Chailleach* nan crògan,
Gu'n òlainn le sogan aig Nolleig nan fèisd;
A' guidhe le dùrachd deadh bhliadhna mhath ùr dhoibh
'S an teann-shàth bhi dùnadh gach mùig agus creuchd.

Deoch-slàinte mo Chàirdean dh'òlainn gu gràdhach,
Cridheachan blàth a dh'fhàg mi 'n àm dhèigh;
Chan fhàg mi 's an t-slige na fhliuchadh a' bhileag,
'S ged loisgteadh mo bhilean cha tillinn an deur.

Deoch-slàinte mo Nàimhdean dh'òlainn gun ghamhlas,
Ma tha a' bheag ann dhiùbh cluinneadh iad sgeul;
Cha d' rinn iad dhomh coire le mi-rùn no oilbheum,
'S mar ghogail a' choileich, tha goirsinn am bheul.

Happy New Year
[by James MacMillan]

Happy new year to you, happy new year to you,
Happy new year to everyone!
Happy new year to you, I drink to your health,
Health to the homeland, the place of my birth!

This is the toast I prefer, and drink it dry
Raising the glass to my mouth;
I stayed at the ship-rail until out of your sight
All the time wanting to shed tears.

I especially drink a toast to the Gael,
Praying for everlasting joy and prosperity.
May Providence direct you and fill you with Goodness,
And may no evil or sorrow ever overtake you.

A toast to the lads and the beautiful girls
To whom I lovingly drink at every gathering;
It is done in full measure, it will not be stinting,
And I will drink, too, to the descendants of the heroes.

A toast to the venerable old Man and Woman,*
That I drink to at the Christmas feast;
Sincerely wishing them a happy new year
And that abundance will cover their every worry.

A toast, I drink to my beloved friends
Warm hearts that I left behind me;
I haven't left the path of sobriety
Though my lips be parched I will not take another drop.

Here's health to my enemies, drunk without malice.
Even if some would listen to lies about me
Their spite or scandal doesn't offend me;
For, "as the crowing of the cock so is the prattle of the mouth."

*Old Man and Old Woman – used generally or possibly a reference to the poet's parents.

47 Di-Luain an t-Sainnseal

[le Dòmhnall 'ic Ionmhainn senior]

Air Di-luain an t-sainnseal
Bìobull brèagha Gàidhlig
O Iain Arnot Neacalch
Do bhean an taighe-
Isabal Fhoirbeisach
A h-ainm roimhesa, ach-
A chaochail i 's a bliadhana 1834
'S gabh i ainm ùr eadhon-
Bean òg i Dhomhnuill 'ic Ionainn.

48 Fàth mo Liunnduith

[le Dòmhnall 'ic Ionmhainn senior]

Agus O! Fàth mo liunnduith
Fàth mo liunnduith thu bho m' dhìth
Isabeal a spioraid chiùin
Chan fhaic mi thu nis mo a chaoi'.

Ochòin a righ, Ochòin a righ,
'S mi tha leam fhèin o thrèig thu mi;
Tha t-àite 's falamh ann mo chri'
'S cha lìon na tha fon ghrèin seo e.

'S mi chaill an seud luachmhor
A fhuair mi an Glenelg.
Isabeal nan gruaidhean
Air nach fhacas riamh fearg.

Bu chaoimhneil, taitneach sìobhalt
An rìbhinn i a choidhche.
O fhuaras leam dhomh fhìon i
Ann comann dìleas dlùth.

Beannachd leat
gu ruig
An lath mòr, tha tighinn.
'S coinnichear leinn a rìs.

Handsel Monday*
[by Donald MacKinnon senior]

On Handsel Monday
A beautiful Gaelic Bible
From John Arnot Nicholson
To a house-wife.
Isobel Forbes was
Her previous name,
But in 1834 she changed that
And took a new one,
As Donald MacKinnon's young wife.

*Handsel Monday - In Scotland, the first Monday after New Year's Day is, traditionally, known as Handsel Monday. Gifts (Scottish-Handsels), are usually given out at this time.

The Cause of my Tears
[by Donald MacKinnon senior]

Oh! Cause of my tears
You, the reason for my sadness, my need,
Isobel of the gentle spirit
I will not see you again, oh my sadness.

Oh, my dearest, oh, my dearest,
I am alone since you left me;
My heart is an empty void
With no one under this sun to fill it.

And I lost my precious darling
Whom I found in Glenelg,
Isobel, on whose brow
Anger was never seen.

She was ever beautiful,
Beloved, pleasant and peaceful,
Since I found her she was true to me,
A faithful and close companion.

Blessing be with you
until
The last day comes
And we meet again.

49 Alastair an Gaol

[le An t-Urramach Ailean MacDhomhnuill Mac Philip]

Alastair an gaol
'S toigh leam fhin e,
Alastair an gaol
'S toigh leam fhin e:
Alastair an gaol,
An gaolach e 's an gaol,
Alastair an gaol,
'S toigh leam fhin e.

Marbhrann do Alastair MacPhilip

[le An t-Urramach Ailean MacDhomnuill Mac Philip]

Thàinig e Chaingeis gruamach, goirt
Geur, guineach, greannach cruaidh;
'S fhuair Alastair am bàirlinn teann
Dh'islich a cheann san uaigh.
Dh'fhàg siod mi nochd gu tùrsach bochd,
Is m' aigne tinn le bròn,
Oir ormsa thuit a bhuille throm
A rinn mo chridhe leòn.

Thug Dia mo mhac gu h-obann bhuam,
Chuir sin mi sìos gun treòir,
Gur tric a chluinnear m' osna chùirt
'S mo Shùilean làn do dheòir.
Oir 's mòr an dochas dh'altrum mi,
A Ghaoil, bho laithean d' oig,
Gu faiceadh thusa mi fon ùir
'S thu fèin gu mùirneach beò.

'S e Dia a dh'atharraich ar cruinn;
Dh'fhan mis', 's be thùs' a dh'fhalbh;
'S an eug gun dhuinn mi fèin do shùil
'S mo spiorad brùite balbh.
Nuair dh'aithnich mi gun chaochall thu,
Chaochall mo chridh' am chliabh,
Oir leithid eile seo do luchd
Cha d' leagadh ormsa riamh.

Cha sinne mhàin a tha ri caoidh
Bhon sgaradh bhuain thu, Luaidh,
Dhuit thaisbeanadh fior spèis is thlachd
Gu coitchean measg an t-Sluaigh.
Tha iomadh fleasgach agus òigh
An tràth seo tur fo sprochd,
Gun sgaoil an Comann aighearach,
Nuair ghairmeadh thus' an nochd.

Ach buidheachas do Dhia nan dùl
Chan eil mo dhachaidh fàs;
San dh'fhàg E agam teaghlach caomh,
Ged dh'aom E aon fon bhàs.
De ainm ro uasal bheireamaid
Mòr mholadh feagh gach àl:
Oir ged tha speuran dorch' an-duigh,
Dealraidh a ghrian gun dàil.

A Bhràthair, Ghràidh, mo bheannach leat,
'S thu nis san dachaidh bhuan;
Le foighid fannaidh mis' an seo,
Strìochte ri taobh a chuain.
A feitheamh aisig Fhath - Innis,
Gam' threòrachadh ad choir,
Far mealar linn gu suthainn sìor
Làthaireachd Righ na glòir.

Alastair's Birth - (A piece of mouth music)
[by Rev. Allan MacDonald MacKillop, Alastair's father]

Alastair the dear one
how I love him,
Alastair the beloved,
How I love him;
Alastair the dear one,
The darling and dear one
Alastair, the dear one
How I love him.

An Elegy
To Alastair MacKillop
Who 'changed' on Whitsunday, 1936
[Written by his father, Rev Allan MacDonald MacKillop.
And rendered freely into English Prose.]

Whitsunday came, frowning, sore,
Sharp, piercing, threatening, cruel;
And Alastair got the sharp notice-to-quit
Which humbled his head in the grave.
That left me tonight sorrowful, poor,
With my mind sick with grief,
For on me fell the heavy blow
Which wounded my heart.

God took my son suddenly from me,
This bowed me down without strength.
Often may my painful sighing be heard
And my eyes filled with tears.
For great was the hope cherished by me,
My Darling, from your childhood days
That you would see me under the sod
With yourself held in high regard and living.

It is God Who changed our lots:
I remained; it was you who went;
In death I myself closed your eye,
My spirit being bruised and dumb.
When I realised that you had 'changed',
Changed was my heart in my bosom,
For such another load as this
Was never laid on me before.

It is not only we who are sorrowing
Since you were separated from us, chosen one,
To you was manifested much regard and affection
In general, among the people.
Many a youth and maiden
Are at present greatly sorrow-laden
For the joyous company was dispersed
When you obeyed the Call tonight.

But thanks be to the God of Hosts,
My home is not desolate;
For He has left with me an affectionate family
Although He inclined one in death.
To His excellent name let us give
Much praise in all generations:
For, although His skies are dark today
Soon shall the sun shine forth.

"Brother" beloved, my blessing with you,
As you are in your everlasting home;
With patience I shall stay here,
Submissive by the side of the Ocean,
Awaiting the ferry to Heaven,
Conducting me to your company
Where we shall enjoy for ever and aye
The presence of the King of Glory.

50 Marbhrann

[le caraid, 'Creagan-an-Fhithich']

'S bochd an sgeula ud a fhuair sinn,
Air Di-luain 'an àm èiridh,
E Taigh-eiridinn Mairi-
'S e chràidh-lot gu lèir sinn:
Smior a' Ghàidheil, daonn', cuanna,
Inich, fuasgailteach, truebhach,
A bhi 'n tasgadh gu sìorruidh!
'S truagh nach briag bha mi 'g èisdeachd.

'S truagh nach briag bha mi 'g èisdeachd,
'S thigeadh fèath air art ùrsadh;
Sguireadh caoidhràn mo dhuanachd,
'S b' àrd ar luath-ghàir 's ars ùgradh.
Ach na meall mi, mo mhiann-smoin,
Tuille 's fior a tha 'n sgeula:-
'S cianail basgair' nan òg bhean,
'S trom na deòir air an lèirsinn.

'S trom na deòir air an lèirsinn
'Caoidh an treun-thir nach maireann;
Bu mhòr 'uaill as ùr bàigh ris,
'S cruaidh an gabhadh nach d' fhan e,
Nis mar ùr-ròs a bhuaileadh,
'S a thuit luath anns an Earrach,
Dh'fhalbh thu 'n àilleachd do Chèitean,
Òig-fhear èibhinn na meall-shùil l'.

Òig-fhear èibhinn na meall-shùil',
'S goirt ar sgarradh, 's cha leigh'sear.
Fàth mo bhròin anns an uair seo;
Cridh' an t-suairceis fo [nèamh];
Cridh' a thaomadh le solas
Dùsgadh òigridh gu èibhneas,
Sud 's a thaice ri taobh e,
'N glaic an aoig anns a' chrè-thaigh.

'N glaic an aoig anns a' chrè-thaigh.
Cridhe spèiseil nam mòr-bhuaidh;
'N trom 'na shuain e 'san fhuar-thaigh,
Chaoidh cha ghluaisear le ceò! E,
B' e shìor 'àbhaist, bhi, èatrom.
Aig bord fèile nan coisir;

'S Beulan-iùil nan tlàth fhinne,
Bu rèidh fileanta chomhradh.

Gu rèidh fileanta ceòl-bhinn
Seinn nan òran le caithream,
B' e sid àros na mùirne!
Boisgeadh sunntach 's gach anam!
Ach Dan fhuar-chridh' na dosguinn,
'S cruaidh àm pòsdadh a rinn i,
Bhris i beulach 's na Gaeil.
'S cha chairear am feasd e.

Truaigh' air thruaigh' ort a thàinig
Gun do chàirdean bhi dlùth ort;
'S och nan och gun do mhàthair,
Roimh an bhàs teachd a' dh'ionnsuidh.
B' i sud cridhe na bàighe
Anns gach càs agus tionndadh,
'Na caomh-shùil dhuit bhiodh slàint'
Aiseag càileachd a's lùthais.

Creagan-an-Fhithich

Lament
[by Creagan-an-Fhithich - the Raven's Rock]

We got the sad news,
When rising on Monday,
From St Mary's Hospital –
We were altogether wounded by the pain:
A courageous Gael, humane, handsome,
Strong, active, heroic,
Will be buried forever!
It is a pity that it was not a lie I heard.

It is a pity that it was not a lie I heard,
Let peace come on our sorrow;
Let my moaning and wailing cease,
And lift high our joy and our mirth,
But my senses are not deceived,
The news is altogether real:-
Sad and melancholy is the young widow's mourning,
The heavy tears blinding her vision.

The heavy tears blinding her vision
Mourning the strong man no longer living;
Great was the love so recently expressed for him,
It is distressing that he was taken and could not stay
Like a fresh rose that was struck
And fell quickly in the Spring,
You left in the beauty of Spring,
A delightful young man with the twinkling eye.

A delightful young man with the twinkling eye.
And sore is our sorrow, that will not heal
It is the cause of my grief even now;
The gentlest heart under [heaven];
A heart overflowing with comfort
Awakening young people to joy.
There in comparison he lies
In the embrace of death in the grave.

In the embrace of death in the grave.
Esteemed for courage and bravery;
Sadly, he sleeps deeply in the grave,
No mourning will move its mist,
It was long the custom to be cheerful
At the liberal table of the wake;

And to direct attention to the tender maids,
With eloquent, uninterrupted conversation.

Relaxing, tuneful, melodious
Singing the song with joyful noise,
It was in yonder cheerful house
That every spirit was bright and lively!
But the cruel face of misfortune
Is a painful time for she who married him.
She expressed praises of that Gael
But he will never rise.

Woe upon woe on you who came
Without your friends near you;
And sadness upon sadness that your mother
Died on her coming to you.
It was she whose heart was tender
In every emergency and set-back;
In her kindly look there was healing for you
And restoration of your natural state and strength.

Creagan-an-Fhithich (The Raven's Rock),

51 Air a' Chèilidh
[le Dòmhnall 'ic Ionmhainn senior]

Iain Mac Imhir-Caimbealach
Aig dinnear an diugh maille rium
O 'n bha 'n latha fliuch, is fuar
Bha fois is ceilidh freagarrach.

Chan eil Sùil
[le Dòmhnall 'ic Ionmhainn senior]

Chan eil sùil ri beannachadh
Fhaighinn o 'n co-laibhairtean
Ach faoineis agus amaideachd
Is magaireachd an còmhnuidh.

On a Visit
[by Donald MacKinnon senior]

John MacIver-Campbell
At dinner today with me.
Since is was a cold, wet day
Rest and fellowship took place.

Do not Expect
[by Donald MacKinnon senior]

Do not expect to get a blessing
From conversations,
Only vanity and foolishness
And continual jesting.

52 Òran do Thormod Mac Neachdail

[le leannain do Thormod Mac Neachdail]]

Sèist: Tha mi fo chùram
'S fo mhòran curaim,
'S mo ghaol air cùairtear 'bhroillich ghlè-ghil,
Tha mi fo chùram i-u-ro-eile.

Tha mi fo mhi-ghean,
'S mi 'n iomail sgìre,
'S mi nach feud mi sgrìobhadh
A dh'ionnsuidh m' fheudail
Sèist: Tha mi fo chùram ... etc., ...

'S ma gheibh mi ùine,
Gum fàg mi 'n dùthaich,
'S gun lean mi 'n cùmhnant'
A rinn thu fèin rium.
Sèist: Tha mi fo chùram ... etc., ...

'S ma gheibh mi airgiod,
A bheir air falbh mi,
Gun lean mi Tormad
'S cha dhealaich mi ceum ris.
Sèist: Tha mi fo chùram ... etc., ...

'S mo ghaol an t-àrmunn,
Bu mhaith gu mànran,
'S tu le do laimhe,
Air bharr 'nan geugan.
Sèist: Tha mi fo chùram ... etc., ...

'S ged thig an geamhradh,
Is m' nam bainnsean,
Chan fhan mi ann sin
Gun m' annsachd fèin ann.
Sèist: Tha mi fo chùrm ... etc., ...

Mo ghaol an t-òig-fhear,
A 's gile, bhòidh'che,
'S e 'n diugh a' seòladh
'Null thar a' mhòr-chuain.
Sèist: Tha mi fo chùram ... etc., ...

'S ged thig fear-fuadain
Cha thaobh mi uair ris,
Oir 's fada uam-sa
Air chuan na thrèig mi.
Sèist: Tha mi fo chùram … etc

Song

[Composed by the wife of Norman Nicholson, Scorrybreac, Skye. He had sailed as a brave, vigorous young man, from Skye to Australia. He never returned to the island of his birth because, sadly, he drowned in his prime and at the beginning of his prosperity, when he went to bathe in the sea one warm morning.]

Sèist: I am troubled
and deeply anxious,
For my absent beloved's breast is very white,*
I am greatly worried, i-u-ro-eile.

I am sad
Here on the outskirts of the parish,
And unable to write
To you, my darling.
Sèist: I am anxious … etc.,

If I am spared
I will leave the country
And I will continue the covenant
That you made with me.
Sèist: I am anxious … etc.,

If I can obtain money
I will use it
To follow my Norman
And not be parted from him.
Sèist: I am anxious … etc.,

And you my beloved hero
You were good at music,
And your accomplishments
Raised you high.
Sèist: I am anxious … etc.,

And though winter comes,
The time of the wedding feasts,
I cannot endure that
Without my own beloved there.
Sèist: I am anxious … etc.,

My beloved, the young man,
Fair and handsome,
Today is now crossing
The great ocean.
Sèist: I am anxious … etc

He has become an exile
And I cannot be beside him,
Because he is far from me
On the ocean, O! forsake me not.
Sèist: I am anxious etc …

Cliff Falls, Isle of Skye

53 Cumha Airson Anabla

[le Seann Leannan]

Sèist: Bu gheanail sìobhalt Anabla,
Gu ceanalt, maiseach, suairce,
Is lìonmhor òigfhear ghlaihte
Leis a bhòidhichead bha na gruaidhean.

Thug Tim-an-Oban** teachdaireachd
Ga m' ionnsuidh nall thar chuantan;
Gun d' chaochail a bhean eireachdail
Bhiodh tric a tigh'n fo m' smuaintean.
Sèist: Bu gheanail … etc.,

Dh'athnuadhaich sud seann chuimhne dhomh
'S gaoil sgleothan air mo lèirsinn
Nach fhaicinn sealladh tuilleadh
Air an ainir rinn mo lèireadh.
Sèist: Bu gheanail … etc.,

Air raointean teth na h-àirde deas*
'S am chòmhnuich mis' an uair sid,
'N trath chàireadh fo na clairibh thu
Fo sgail nan àrd bheann fuara.
Sèist: Bu gheanail … etc.,

'N uair chuir mi fhèin ceud eolas ort,
Sinn faoin baoth òg le cheile,
Chaidh gath do ghaoil grad shàitht am thaobh
'S gu h-aontach, aotrom ghèill mi.
Sèist: Bu gheanail … etc.,

Ceann tacan 's maith a dh'fhaithnich mi
Ged thug mo leannan spèis dhomh,
Nach robh e anns an lùdhaigadh
Gu faighinn thu mar chèile.
Sèist: Bu gheanail … etc.,

Tha leth-cheud bliadhn' bhon phosadh thu,
Ri fleasgach gasda gleusda,
'S e crìoch gach comunn dealachadh,
'S rinn sinne sin le rèite.
Sèist: Bu gheanail … etc.,

Thug mise bòid an dìomhaireachd
Gu siubhlinn fad air fuadachd
'S nach fhantain far am faicinn thu
'S fear eile ri do ghuallainn.
Sèist: Bu gheanail … etc.,

Chaidh nis dà fhichead samhradh triall,
Bhon d' fhàgadh ghrian fo thuath leam
Ach 's tric am smuain dh'iath m' anam 'n Iar
Gu brìodal riut am bruadar.
Sèist: Bu gheanail … etc.,

Feuch fhuair mi gràdh is baigh is mùirn
As fàilte san dùthaich chèin seo;
Cha d' bhts mi sud riamh gu tur an rùn
Thug mi air tùs dom cheud-ghaol.
Sèist: Bu gheanail … etc.,

[Tri nithean a thig gan iarraidh eagal is eudach is gaol.]

Elegy for Anabella
[by An Old Sweetheart*]

Chorus: Anabella was cheerful and fair,
Kindly, handsome and meek,
And many young men were captivated
With the beauty of her countenance.

The *Oban Times* brought news
Across the seas to me
That that fair woman had died
And my thoughts quickly raced back.
Chorus: Anabella was cheerful … etc.,

Old memories returned to me
Of a vision of my beloved;
A sight that I would not see again
Of the young woman, and my painful love.
Chorus: Anabella was cheerful … etc.,

It was in the sultry plains of the South**
That I resided
When you were laid in your coffin
Under the shadow of the cold high mountain.
Chorus: Anabella was cheerful … etc.,

When I first knew you
We were both young and foolish,
The dart of love pierced my side
And I giddily yielded to it.
Chorus: Anabella was cheerful … etc.,

In a short time I knew you well
And you showed me much affection,
But it was not permitted
For you to marry me.
Chorus: Anabella was cheerful … etc.,

It is fifty years since you married
A clever, industrious young man.
Every friendship has its end
And ours did so in harmony.
Chorus: Anabella was cheerful … etc.,

I took an oath of secrecy
To go far into exile
And not stay where I would see you
With another man at your side.
Chorus: Anabella was cheerful … etc.,

Forty years have now passed
Since I left a northern sun
But, even here, it often dominates my mind
Courting you in my dreams.
Chorus: Anabella was cheerful … etc.

Though I got love, and affection, and tenderness
And a welcome in this far-off country;
I never ever broke the secret
I gave at the beginning to my first love.
Chorus: Anabella was cheerful … etc.,

[Three things that come without asking; fear and jealousy and love.]

*This was Rev Allan MacDonald MacKillop.

**That is, the Southern Hemisphere.

54 Lìtir Thun Caraid

[le Seumas Mac 'Ille-Mhaoil]

Ceud fàilte dhuit, Iain!
Am bheil thu gu slàn?
No 'm bheil thu ad chabhaig
Feadh chladaich 's muir-làin?
An d' fhuair thu mo lìtir?
No 'n deachaidh i ceàrr?
Ma diùlt thu a freagairt,
Dhiòt chreisinn na b' fheàrr.

Tha 'n t-saoghal na chabhaig
Cur char dheth o thùs,
Le ùpraid 's le glagais,
Gach maide 's gach sùist,
A' bualadh 's a' slachdadh
Gach cleachdainn 's gach ùis;
Chaidh càirdeas is dìlseachd
A shìneadh 's an ùir.

Ach cluinn mi, leig t-anail,
Aom tamull do chluas,
Na dùin i cho ealamh,
Eisd eagar thar chuan;
Do ghealltanas daingean
Nach teannadh tu bhuam,
Ach dìleas mar charaid
Gum maireadh tu buan.

Tha mùthadh is caochladh
Air daoine 's an àm,
Chan eil iad mar b' àbhaist
Nuair bha mi 's a' ghleann,
Gum faighte ann càirdeas,
Is bàigh nach bu ghann;
Bha caoimhneas is fialachd
A' riaghladh na bh' ann.

'Se their thu. "is faoin thu,
Tha ao-dìon 'n ad cheann,
Nuair tha thu a' saoilsinn
Gun d' chaochail an glean;
Tha dàimh ann is fialachd
Mar riamh anns gach àm,
Is nàrach do bhriathran,
'S neo-chiallach do rann."

Ma bheir thu dhomh dearbhadh
Nach dearmadach thu,
'S gur mise th' air seachran
Am bheachdannan ùr;
Fair do làmh; tha mi aithreach
Gun d' choirich mi thu;
Thoir a-nis dhomh do sgiala,
Ged lìonadh e 'n t-sùil.

Letter to a Friend
[by James MacMillan]

A hundred welcomes to you, Iain!
Are you well
Or are you hurrying along the shore at high tide?
Did you get my letter?
Or did it go astray?
I prefer not to believe of you
That you would not answer.

The world has been in a rush
and turmoil since the beginning,
With confusion and prattle,
Each flail and staff,
Beating and threshing
Every custom and hospitality;
Friends and relations gone
Lying in the grave.

But, listen to me, take your breath,
Incline your ear for a while,
Don't shut it so quickly,
Listen to the whisper across the sea;
Remember, the strong pledge
Not to part from me,
But that you would be as a faithful friend
To me for ever.

Change and decay
Affect man and time.
They are not the same
As when I was in the glen.
I received friendship,
And love was not scarce;
Kindness and bravery
Ruled those who were there.

And you will say, "You are foolish
That you have a hole in the head,
When you are thinking
That the glen has changed;
Friendship and courage are in them
As ever they were,
Your words are shameful,
And your verse foolish."

If you prove to me
You are not forgetful,
And that I am astray
In my new opinions
Give me your hand; I am sorry
That I reprimanded you;
Give me your news now
Though it brings tears to the eye.

55 Òran do Aonghas Brocair

[le Alasdair MacDhomhnuill, Geelong.]

Deoch-slainte' Aonghais Bhrocair,
Cuir am nochd i mun cuairt,
Agus òl i le socair
Gun sprochd no gun ghruaim;
Sàr shealgair an t-sionnaich
'Ga chumail bhon uan,
Bhiodh fùdar ri theine
Agus peileir tro' chluais.

Mo sheann Aonghais Bhrocair,
Nì mi nochda dhuit duan,
Ged is duilich leam aithris
Laidh smal air do shnuadh;
Thug an aois bhuaith do mhaise,
Tha claisean 'n ad ghruaidh,
Tha do cheum dol na 's maille,
'S na 's taine do ghruag.

'S e bhi t-fhaicin 'san fhàsach
'An àite nan gleann
Gun abhag gun mhiol-chù
Dh'fhàg cianail mo rann;
Thu bhi gualainn do ghunna
'S an sionnach air chall,
'S cha bu diù leat bhi froiseadh
Nan 'Possum thar chrann.

Cha bu diù leat mo riar,
Cha b' e riaraicheadh d' fheòil,
'S ann a chleachd thu 'bhi fiadhach
'An coire riabhach a' cheò;
A bhi 'cosd do chuid fùdair
Ri udlaich 's ri geòidh,
A bhi marbhadh nam fìor-eun
'S iad mìle 's na neòil.

Ged a tha thu 's a' choille,
'S e bu toigh leat a's fearr,
Far an cluinneadh tu 'n coileach
'S an doire bheag ghorm,
Agus deileann do chuileanan
Guinideach borb
As a' chàrn 'cur na bèist
Air an èireadh an colg.

Cha bu ghealtair 's an oidhch' thu,
Ach saighdear gu leòir,
Ged a chruinnicheadh do nàimhdean
Le foill aig an Stòr
Ann an riochd nan cat fiadhaich
Le diabhuil aig mòd,
Cha robh bana-bhuidseach riamh dhiù,
'Chuir fiacail air t-fheòil.

Eadar Rudha Aird-'ic-Eòlain
Agus sgòrnan a' Chaoil,
'S ann a fearann nan Leòdach
Thug gach seòrsa dhuit gaol;
Chuireadh furan is fàilt' ort
'S gach àite le aoidh,
Anns a' chaisteal a b' àirde
'N taigh àiridh an fhraoich.

Ged a thilleadh tu dhachaidh
Gu d' aitreabh 's gu d' thìr,
'S ann 'bu chianail leat tachairt
'An clachan no 'n cill;
Cha chluinneadh tu Gàilig
An sraid 'am Portrigh,
Ceòl cruinneag 'am buaile,
No nuallan na pìob.

Song to Angus Brocair
[by Alexander MacDonald, Geelong]

Good health to you, Angus Brocair,
Take advantage of the encroaching night,
And drink at your ease
Without sadness or gloom;
You excellent hunter
Who kept the foxes from the lambs,
With gunpowder to fire
A ball through their ear.

My old Angus Brocair,
I will tonight make a song to you,
Though I am sorry to relate
That infirmity shows on your face.
Old age has taken the bloom from you,
Your brow is furrowed
And your step has become slower,
And the hair of your head is thinner.

Seeing you in your solitude,
Instead of your place in the glen,
Without terrier or hound,
Has left my verse melancholy.
You have shouldered your gun
And deprived now of your fox hunting;
But you will soon be scattering
The Possums across the trees.

But that was not good enough for you
Nor was the flesh satisfying to you,
Accustomed as you were to an abundance of deer
In the grey-misted corrie,
Where you would expend your gunpowder
On stag and on geese
And in the death of an eagle
Though a mile in the clouds.

Though you are out of the forest
It is what you liked best,
Where you would hear the game
In the small green grove,
The young dogs savagely barking,
Fiercely inflamed,
Chasing the beast out from the rocks
With rising fury.

You were not afraid of the night,
But possessed much courage,
Though your enemies gathered
With treachery at the Stor
In the likeness of the wildcat;
With the devil at court
There was never a witch as bad
As could lay a tooth on your flesh.

Between Point Aird-'ic-Eòlain
And the narrows of the Kyle,
And in the land of the Macleods*
You are shown every kind of affection;
A welcome invitation is given you
With hospitality shown wherever you go,
From the castle on high
To the shieling among the heather.

But now, if you returned home
To dwell in your own land,
You would find it lonely
In village or in churchyard;
You would not hear Gaelic
In the streets of Portree,
Or the music of the lass in the dairy
Or the skirl of the pipes.

*Isle of Skye

56 Òran Do Fhloraidh Bheag [Priomh Ranntachd]
[le Seumas Mac 'Ille-Mhaoil]

Sèist: Gur i' chaileag shunndach,
Gur I' chaileag lurach laghach,
Flòraidh bheag an t-sùgraidh!

O, gur i mo leannan Flìoraidh
'S bòidhche tha 's an dùthaich!
Dhùraichdinn gu saor do phòsadh
Nam biodh m' òige dùbladh.
Sèist: Gur i' chaileag etc …

Nuair a thigeadh tu le t-àbhachd
'Suidhe blàth gu dlùth rium,
'S tric a bhuanaich thu mo ghàire
Gus 'm biodh àirnean brùite.
Sèist: Gur i' chaileag etc …

'S ann dheanadh tu rium seanachas
Mar bhean thàrmaich shùghail,
Leam bu mhiann a bhi 'g ad èisdeachd
'G innseadh sgeul le mùirn dhomh.
Sèist: Gur i' chaileag etc …

Nuair a sguireadh gluasad sheisreach,
'S am feasgar air dùbhradh,
'S tu gum fuadaicheadh gach leisg bhuam,
Breisleach agus stùrrtan.
Sèist: Gur i' chaileag etc …

Do dhà ghruaidh mar chaorunn coille
Dearg 's an doire lùbach,
Solus gruaidh a' tighinn bho d' shealladh,
Lasadh ann ad shùilean.
Sèist: Gur i' chaileag etc …

'S gur a faillein thu chloinn Eanruig,
Freumhach nach gabh mùchadh,
Tha iad cliùiteach 'n tìr na h-Alba,
Ainmeil anns gach dùthaich.
Sèist: Gur i' chaileag etc …

Bhon a chaidh thu bhuam do Shanna,
Thar a' bhealaich stùchdaich,
Tha mi 'g ad ionndrain gach latha,
'S leanabh thu bha ùiseil.
Sèist: Gur i' chaileag etc …

Ach nuair chinneas suas mo Fhlòraidh,
Faillein 'og nan ùr-dhos,
'S cinnteach mi gum faigh i leannan
Ma bhios fear 's an dùthaich.
Sèist: Gur i' chaileag etc …

'Se mo mhiann gun cinn thu sàbhailt',
Aillidh agus mùirneach,
'S gum bi thu mar chraoibh nan ròsan,
'N dealt a' dòrtadh ùr oirr'.
Sèist: Gur i' chaileag etc …

Gur h-ghuidhinn dhuit, an t-slàinte,
Beairt a 's fèarr tha 'in dhùrachd,
Agus sonas bhi cur sgàil ort,
Àdh a bhi cur sunnd ort.
Sèist: Gur i' chaileag etc …

Mo rùn 's mo bheannachd leat, a ghràidh,
Air sàile no air dùthaich
Agus maitheas cur ort fàilte
'S gach àite 'n dean thu dùsgadh!
Sèist: Gur i' chaileag etc …

Song to Little Florrie [First Part]
[by James MacMillan]

Chorus She is a kind and pretty lassie
She is a cheerful girl,
She is a lovely, lively maid,
Playful little Florrie!

Oh, Florrie my darling
As beautiful as the countryside!
I would willingly marry you
If I were young again.
Chorus: She is a kind … etc.

When you would come with your joy
And sit snugly close to me,
Often I laughed so long
That my side hurt.
Chorus: She is a kind … etc.

And you made conversation with me
Like a sensible, mature woman,
And I enjoyed listening to you
Joyfully telling me a story.
Chorus: She is a kind … etc.

When the ploughing stopped
In the shadows of evening,
You drove away all my weariness
Confusion and sullenness.
Chorus: She is a kind … etc.

Your cheeks were like rowan berries
Red and chubby
Your face gleaming
By the light of your eyes.
Chorus: She is a kind … etc.

You are descended from the Eanruig's children,
A line that has not died out,
Famous throughout Scotland,
Renowned in every land.
Chorus: She is a kind … etc.

You left me to go to Shanna,
Across the craggy glen,
You were a loving child
And I miss you every day.
Chorus: She is a kind … etc.

But when my Florrie will grow up,
A young bud on a new bush,
I am certain she will get her sweetheart
If there is a man in the land.
Chorus: She is a kind … etc.

It is my desire that you grow up safely,
Bright and beloved,
And that you will be like the rose bush,
Fresh with dew on it.
Chorus: She is a kind … etc.

My prayer for you
Is for health and best wishes
And that good fortune, happiness and joy
May shine upon you.
Chorus: She is a kind … etc.

My love and blessing be with you, my dear,
On sea and on land,
And may goodness bid you welcome
In every place that you awaken.
Chorus: She is a kind … etc.

57 Beannachdan Chum Dhòmhnull

[le Seumas Mac 'Ille-Mhaoil]

Thoir mo bheannachd gu Dòmhnull
A nì na h-òrain a 's grinne
Ann an rogha na Gàidhlig
Briathran gràidh agus milis
'Chuiredh sunnd air gach Gàidheal!
Bho thìr àrd nam bean binneach,
Bhi 'g an leughadh 's mi 'm aonar
Bheir e sòlas g' am chridhe,
    Mo Ghille Math, mo Ghille Math!

Gum a fad thu ri òrain
Is ceòl bòidheach fo d' bhilibh,
Do theanga g' an gleusadh
Agus t-inntinn g' am filleadh,
Le deadh thuigse 'g an àireamh
'S iad a' fàs dhuit gun inneadh,
Air am figheadh ri chèile,
Naigheachd shlèibh agus ghlinne,
    Na bruachan cas, na bruachan cas!

Tha mi 'd chomain, a Dhòmhnuill,
Tha gu mòr anns an àm so,
Chuir g' am ionnsuidh na h-òrain,
Briathran còir agus bàigheach
Thug toil inntinn is sòlas
Air gach dòigh mar a b' annsa,
'S thug thu comhairle shònraicht'
Ann an òrdugh 's an ran sin,
    Ma 's math mo bheachd, ma 's math mo bheachd!

Dè do bharail, a Dhòmhnuill,
Ma fhuar e còmhmnadh 'n ad chridhe,
Gu bheil dàn dhuinn 'an òrdugh
'S e 'n ar còdhail a' tighinn?
'Se mo bheachd-sa gu sònraicht'
Ged is gòrach a bhruidhinn,
Gun d' rugadh leinn sgrìobhta
Dealbh's innleachd ar siubhail,
    Ma 's math no olc, ma 's math no olc!

……………………

Leig mi seachad an samhradh,
Is tha geamhradh dhomh dlùth
Nì mo chiabhan a ghlasadh,
Dh'fhàgar small air mo shùil;
No mar chraoibh anns an earrach
'S cairt a snodhaich gun lùths,
Ged tha 'barr tighinn fo dhuilleach
Freumh a bun tha gun sùgh,
    'S i seargadh as, 's i seargadh as!

Greetings to Donald
[by James MacMillan]

Give my compliments to Donald
Who composed an excellent song
In the choicest of Gaelic.
Expressive, melodious words
Bringing cheer to every Gael
From the land of high-peaked mountains.
I intend reading it now all alone,
It will give comfort to my heart,
    My good lad, My good lad.

Though your songs are far away
The music is beautiful from your lips
Your language is deft
And your mind that of a poet
With good understanding of metre;
And with words, growing effortlessly,
Combining and weaving together
To bring news of mountain and glen,
    The steep bank, the steep bank.

I am greatly obliged to you, Donald,
At this time,
Sending me the song,
With its worthy and loving words,
That brought me satisfaction and comfort,
In every way more acceptable,
With its particular advice
In the arrangement of that verse,
    If I remember rightly, if I remember rightly!

What do you think, Donald?
And how does your heart incline?
Is your song to us an instructive message?
Is our reproach yet to come?
In the early days of my youth,
I had hoped to travel
For the restlessness of my mind
There was mental stimulation to be had.
    If for good or evil, if for good or evil

....

My life's 'summer' has now passed
And winter is close to me;
My hair is greying,
My eyes grow dim;
I am no longer like a tree in spring
My body is without energy,
Though the top is inclined to bushiness
Its root is dried up.
    It is withering away, it is withering away!

Section Six - The Gael and His Religion

All emigrants bring with them to their new homeland certain attitudes towards life – a philosophy or a credo perhaps, although few would have expressed it in these terms. Attitudes to life and death and to the influences which guided them in those great experiences were a strong part of the Highlanders' 'invisible baggage' and this came in the form of religion, mostly Presbyterianism. Gaelic was an important part of the mind-set which accompanied Highlanders to Australia, and there was a strong desire to maintain their worship in their own tongue. Gaelic-speaking ministers were often difficult to obtain from Scotland and this was, on occasions, to lead to tensions within and between church congregations. A Gaelic-speaking Roman Catholic priest, Ranald Rankin, followed out his congregation from Moidart to continue to minister to them and other Gaelic-speaking Roman Catholics.

Many Gaels took their religion seriously and were shocked by the different mores and attitudes which they found upon their arrival in Australia as expressed, for example, in *Deoch Làidir* and *Mi-Naomhachadh na Sàbaid*. The scattered nature of these emigrants often made it impossible to establish formal churches and come together for worship as they had done back in their homeland. Those who did live in lonely places without benefit of company or access to formal church life were, nevertheless, enjoined not to let that be an excuse for forgetting family worship or for failing to recognise God's holy day. (*Litir Aodhaireil*). Where there were sufficient numbers for a congregation, public appeals were made for funds for such buildings (*Litir a Chum nan Gaidheal a tha Chòmhnuidh*). A constant lament was the lack of ministers and the shortage of Gaelic worship to which the emigrants were accustomed (*Litir bho Iain MacLeoid*). Establishing Gaelic pulpits required much hard work, but keeping them filled proved to be an even harder task, for few Gaelic-speaking ministers in Scotland could be spared to sail to churches in the colonies. The inexorable progression toward worship in English split a number of congregations and caused much heartache.

The Australian Gaelic language paper, *An Teachdaire Gaidhealach*, understanding the lack of Gaelic ministers in Australia, and the situation in which many of the Highlanders and their families were placed, lacking the benefit of church or minister, sought to redress this a little by providing sermons and other suitable Christian reading in the Gaelic language, in its pages. (See, for example, *An Dìbleach Bochd*, *Aran na Beatha* and *Fath Ioghnaidh*).

Australia, for a variety of reasons, not least its vast distances and scattered populations and the scarcity of ministers, was often considered an unpromising field for evangelism or religious life in general. Donald MacKinnon, however, sounds a note of expectation in *Tha Mill do Neoil.*

Large centres of population, however, were better placed in terms of church buildings and settled ministers, as Rob MacDougall identified in his *Litir Don Chuairtear à Astràilia*.

58 Tha Mill do Neoil

[le Dòmhnall Mac Ionmhainn senior]

Tha mill do neòil gheal thioram
A snàmh air aghaidh an speur
Ach chan eil ann t'ach ceò
Air an iomainn leis a ghaoith
Thiormaich iad uile air falbh
'S tha aghaidh an speur glan.

Le teas is tiormachd ro mhòra
seargadh feòir is lus.
Mur tig na frasan a nuas
A thaiseachdadh an fhuinn
Bidh an fheudail caol
'S cha bhi barr 's na glinn
ach tha gu leòr an stòr
fo laimh Righ nam feart.

Ionmhasan araon
an uisge 's an t-sneachd
'S nuar bheir e àithne dhaibh
thig iad gu luath mach
bith athbheothachadh ann
'S moladh do Thriath nam feart.

Clouds
[by Donald MacKinnon senior]

Clusters of dry, white clouds
Swim across the face of the sky
With nothing in them but mist.
They are driven by the wind
And the moisture evaporates
Leaving the face of the sky clear again.

Heat and great drought
Have withered the grass and flowers,
And if showers do not come
To soften the earth
The cattle will be lean
And there will be no harvest in the glens.
But the storehouse is full
By the bounty of the Lord of miracles.

Both treasures,
The rain and the frost,
Will quickly come
When He commands them to-
And there will be revival.
Praise the Lord.

59 Lìtir a Chum nan Gaidheal a tha Chòmhnuidh san Tìr Seo,- A Chuid Diù gu h-Àraidh d' an Thug an Tighearna Saibhreas

[le an t-Urramach Uilleam Mac-an-t-Shaoir]

A Chlann Nan Gaidheal-

Bha Gàidheil riabh ainmeal air son gràidh d' an dùthaich is do mhuinntir an dùthcha. To riaghladh a ghràidh seo b' e an cleachdadh riabh, ('s e seo co dhiù an cliù) a chèile a chòmhnadh ann an tìrean coimheach a chum nach fuilgeadh am fann foirmeart nam bochd uireasbhuidh - a bhi, mar a their iad, "an guailibh a chèile." Chan eil teagamh agam nach eil an gràdh seo air a chaidreabh leibhsa, agus nach bi e a-rèir feum a chuspairean air a chleachdadh.

Ceudaichibh dhomh, ma ta, bhur n-aire a ghairm a chum suidheachaidh nan Gàidheal a th' anns a bhaile seo a-thaobh nan nithe a bhuineas d' an sìth shìorruidh. Tha mòran diù nach tuig facal Beurla, and mòran tuille nach tuig a bheag: air an aobhar sin feumaidh orduighean an Tighearna a bhi air am frithealadh dhoibh 'n cainnt fèin; ach cha ghabh seo a bhi air a' dhèanamh gan eaglais Ghàidhealach a bhi air a togail. 'S ann a dh'iarraidh bhur còmhnaidh-sa chum seo a ghabh mi fos làimh sgrìobhadh d' ur n-ionnsaidh an cainnt bhur aithriche.

Tha na Gaill a togail eaglaisean air gach laimh; agus tha seo na aobhar bròin agus na mhasladh nam bitheadh na Gaidheal, aig a cheart àm, cho beag fialuidheachd, cho beag gràidh do Dhia agus do dhaoine, agus nach togadh iad a h-aon. Ach cha tachair seo; thàinig cuid a cheana air an aghaidh, agus tha mi cinnteach gun d-thig càch, eadhon tuille agus a dh'fheumar.

Cuimhnichibh, mo chàirdean, bhur dùthaich; cuimhnichibh bhur "luchd-dàimh a thaobh na feòla," – abraibh mu'n dèibhinn ann an cainnt an abstoil (agus bitheadh bhur cleachdadh a-rèir bhur cainnt), "is e dùrachd mo chridhe, agus m' urnuidh ri Dia, gum biodh iad air an tearnadh"; cuimhnichibh nach urrainn d' ur anama fèin a bhi air an soillseachadh le solus slàinteal gun sibh a chomhpàrtachadh an t-soluis sin ri muinntir eile, nach urrainn e bhi gun d' thàinig Criosd do bhur n-ionnsaidh gun sibh, mar gum b' eadh, 'ga thoirt air aghaidh air a shlighe.

Deanaibh seo a-nis. Na measaibh beagan airgid ni 's luachmhoire na anamanna neo-bhàsmhor. Aidichibh gur le Dia na h-uile ni a th' agaibh le roinn d' ur saibhreas a thiodhlachdadh dha.

Gabhaibh leithsgeul an dànadais seo, agus creidibh gur h-e m' earbsa 'n ur fialuidheachd agus mo dheadh rùn do Ghàidheal a bhrosnaich mi gu sgrìobhadh d' ur ionnsuidh.

A Letter to the Highlanders Residing in this Country, to Those of Them Particularly to Whom the Lord has Given Riches

[by Rev. William MacIntyre]

Highlanders

Gaels have always been renowned for love to their country and their countrymen. It has ever been their practice, under the influence of this love (this, at least, is the character they bear), to assist each other when in distant lands, that the weak might not suffer oppression, nor the poor experience want - to be, according to their motto, "shoulder to shoulder." I have no doubt that this sentiment of patriotism and clanship is cherished by you, and will be exhibited practically as its objects may require.

Permit me, then, to call your attention to the spiritual wants of the Highlanders resident in this town. Many of them scarcely understand a word of English, and many more understand but very little: the ordinances of religion, therefore, must be dispensed to them in their own language, if dispensed at all; but this cannot be done, except at such a time as renders attendance less convenient to all and impossible to many, unless a Church be built for their own special use. It is for the purpose, accordingly, of soliciting your assistance for the accomplishment of this object, that I have taken the liberty of writing to you in the language of your fathers.

Churches are being built on every hand for the English-speaking population; and for this we have reason to rejoice; but it would surely be a cause of the deepest shame and sorrow if Highlanders should, at the same time, be so destitute of liberality, so destitute of love to God and to man, as not to build one Church. But they will build it: some have already come forward, and I feel certain the rest will follow their example, and that even more will be subscribed than the object requires.

Remember, my friends, your country; remember your "kinsmen according to the flesh',:- adopt in regard to them the language of the apostle, (and let your deeds correspond with your words), "my heart's desire and prayer to God for them is that they may be saved." Remember that if your own souls are enlightened with saving knowledge you cannot but desire to give this knowledge to others, and that Christ, therefore, has not at all come to you unless you are inclined, as it were, to make Him known.

Excuse this liberty. My only apology is that I have strong confidence in your liberality, and feel a deep interest in the welfare of the Highlanders.

Contribute now, then, to the advancement of His cause. Do not regard a little silver or gold of more value than an immortal soul. Acknowledge that God is the proprietor of all you possess by consecrating to his service a portion of your substance.

Excuse this liberty, and I have strong confidence in your liberality, and feel a deep interest in the welfare of the Gael and I write for your benefit.

60 Naigheachdan

A Theachdaire Rùnaich

[Litir bho Iain Macleoid]

"Tha aon nì, co dhiù a tha mi ag ionndrainn gu mòr anns an tìr seo — agus 's e sin nach eil cothrom agam air an t-soisgeul a chluinntinn air a shearmanachadh anns a'ghàilig. Cha'n eil uireasbhuidh air bith eile orm fèin na air theaghlach."

[Iain Macleoid, Port Phillip (A Skyeman in Australia)]

Na Gaidheil an Astràillia

A Theachdaire Rùnaich Highlanders in Australasia (1857).

"Tha aireamh nan Gaidheal ann an Astraillia, a-nis a ruigheachd dlù air ficheal mìle. Tha an roinn mhòr dhiù seo sgaoillte air feadh Phort Phillip, New South Wales, Tasmania, a's South Australia. Chan eil ach fior bheagan diu an Western Astraillia a's New Zealand.

Don aireamh mhòr Ghaidheil seo tha ochd Ministeirean - an comh-chomunn ri Eaglais-Shaorsa h-Alba, a searmanachadh an t-soisgeuil, na Cànain bhlasda fèin.

Tha ceithir do no Ministeirean seo 'n New South Wales, triùir 'an Port Phillip agus a g-aon 'an Tasmania.

Chan eil Eaglais air bith uile a cuir luchd-teasaig spioradail Ghaelach, a chum nan Gaidheal anns na cèarna seo."

[*An Teachdaire Gaidhealach*]

61 Lìtir - Aodhaireil O Sheanadh

Agus fhad 's a tha sinn a' dèanamh bròin os ceann bhur n-ionadaibh aonaranach, agus bhur cuibhrinn aonaranaich, agus os ceann bhur sàbaidibh tosdach; tha sinn aig an àm cheudna a' guidheadh oirbh, a Bhràithre Gràdach,- eadhon anns n h-ionadaibh sin- "Cuimhnichibh là na Sàbaid, a choimhead naomh."

Cruinnichibh bhur teaghlaichean fèin, eadhon an sin, 'n ur ionadaibh còmhnuidh fèin fa leth, air là naomh an Tighearn. Leughaibh na Sgrìobtuirean dhoibh, agus maille riutha. "Togaibh bhur clann ann an oilean agus ann an teagasg an

Tichearn;" a' toirt orra, gun aithnich, agus gun cuimhnich iad, agus gu 'n toirear urram leò don t-Sàbaid naomh. Bithibh foighidneach: Irioslaichibh sibh fèin fo làimh chumhachdaich Dhè, chum 's gun àrdaichear leis-san sibh ann an àm iomchuidh.

Fear-riaghlaidh, Sheanadh na h-Eaglais Saoire ann am Bhictoria, 1855

News Items

Dear Messenger

"There is one thing which I long for greatly in this land which is lacking and it is that there is not the opportunity for me of hearing the Gospel in Gaelic. There are plenty of English Ministers near me but there is a lack of the other for myself and my family."

Iain MacLeod, Port Phillip (A Skyeman in Australia)

Highlanders in Australasia (1857).

"The number of Highlanders in Australia now is reaching near to twenty thousand. The large part of these is split throughout Port Phillip, New South Wales, Tasmania and South Australia.

There is only a small number split between Western Australia and New Zealand.

For this large number of Highlanders there are eight Ministers - connected to the Free Church of Scotland - preaching the gospel in their own language.

Four of these Ministers are in New South Wales, three in Port Phillip, and one in Tasmania.

There is no other church in this country with pastors able to provide for the spiritual needs of these people.

Call to Worship - From the Synod of the Free Church in Victoria

"And for long we have been sad about your loneliness, your isolation and about your lack of Sabbath meetings; we at the same time beseech you, Loving Brothers - even in that situation, "Remember the Sabbath day to keep it holy."

Gather the individuals in your own family, in your own dwelling place, on the Lord's sacred day. Read the scriptures to them, and together with them."

"Raise your children in the nurture and the teaching of the Lord." Give to them, that knowledge, and that memory, and give them reverence for the holy Sabbath. Be patient; humble yourself under the mighty hand of God, in order that you will be exalted at the proper time."

62 Litir Don Chuairtear à Australia' in Cuairtear nan Gleann [Extract only]
[Rob MacDoughall]
Boningong Geelong, Australia Felix

Ghabh sinn suas an abhuinn Yarra Yarra, gu ruig Melbourne; agus 'nuair a chunnaic mi am baile sin o cheann gu ceann, bha mi gu cinnteach air mo dhaigneachadh sa' bharail a leig mi roimh thugaibh air thuaiream - 'se sin, nach robh bail' aoise riamh 'san t-saoghal a ghabhadh coimeas ris.

Tha Melbourne air a leigeadh mach - no, mar a dh'fhaodas mi a ràdh, air a thoirt a steach - le suas agus eireachdas a tha 'nan urram don dream a steidhich e. Tha mòran de dh'aitreabh ghasda ann, agus bùthan a dh'fhaodadh nàir a chuir air iomadh tigh-ceannachd, an dà chuid, 'an Albainn agus 'an Sasunn.

Tha iomadh tigh-aoraidh flathail ann; ach tha tri sònruichte ann, a chosd mòran airgid agus saothrach 'gan togail - an Eaglais Shasunnach, an te Albannach, agus an te Phàpanach. Tha 'n te Phàpanach - mar is tric leis an t-seorsa bhi - fathasd gun chriochnachadh; ach chan iongantach sin - tha obair an Uile-Chumhachdaich anabarrach duilich a riocachadh 'san dùthaich so.

Tha an te Albannach - mar a chunnaic mi anns gach àit ùr i riamh - air thoiseach; agus, moladh don Fhreasdal! tha sinn a nis a' cur cheann cuideachd a dh'fhaotuinn te Ghàelich suas. Tha ministear Gàelach againn a cheana, a' searmonachadh an t-soisgeil 'an cainnt liobhaidh nam beann, na h-uile Sàbaid; agus tha a cho'-thional, mar is taitneach ri aithris, a' dol am meud gach seachdain.

Tha tigh-sgoile anns a' bhaile, a-rèir gach eaglais; agus tha dà òganach uasal, shuairce, Ghàelach, a' teagasg anns an sgoil Albannaich. Tha an clagh air a dhùnadh a steach, mu thuaiream leth-mhile o 'n bhaile; agus uime-san dh'fhaodta da rìreadh a ràdh:-

'N seo gheibhear as gach fine iad-
Treubh, cinneach, agus sluagh,
A thug am bàs an ciomachas,
'S a dh'iomain e do'n uaigh.

Letter to Cuairtear nan Gleann
[Robert MacDougall]

We went up the River Yarra Yarra, as far as Melbourne, and when I saw that town from end to end, I was now sure about that which I had previously guessed;- which was, that there was not a town of its age ever in the world to equal it.

Melbourne is laid out or, as I might say, taken in [i.e. enclosed, demarcated] with a swagger and a good appearance that brings honour to the people that established it. Many dwellings are excellent, and shops that put many commercial establishments, both in Scotland and England, to shame.

There are many elegant houses of worship, but three are notable, that cost much money and labour to construct – the English Church, the Scottish one, and the Popish one. The Popish one – as a rule with that kind, - is yet unfinished; but that is not surprising – the Almighty's work is exceedingly difficult to represent in this country.

The Scottish one – as I have seen in every new place – is in the forefront; and, praise to the Lord, we are now putting up a Gaelic one. There is a Gaelic minister over us, preaching the gospel every Sabbath in the beautiful language of the mountains, and his congregation, it is pleasing to relate, increases every week.

Each church has its own schoolhouse in the town; and there are two fine affable young men, Highlanders, teaching in the Scottish school. There is a cemetery, enclosed, around about half a mile from town; and about it, it must truly be said:-

Here will be found those out of each clan-
Tribe, nation and people
That death brought into captivity,
And drove to the grave.

63 Mi-Naomhachadh Na Sàbaid

[Neo-ainmichte]

Tha dùil agam nach eil ni air thalamh is mo chuireas do dhoilgheas air a' Ghael chràbhaidh an dèigh a dhùtchaich fhàgail, na bhi faicinn latha an Tighearna ga bhristeadh, anns gach dòigh as comasach do phacaich neo-iompaichte a dhèanamh. Thachair e gur ann air latha na sàbaid a thàinig mi air tìr, a Albainn, anns a bhaile seo, agus chòir e uamhas mòr orm mar a bha an latha naomh sin air a dhearmad leis an luch-àiteachaidh. Cha robh sràid troimh an deachadh mi nach robh gràinealachd a pheacaidh air fhoillseachadh ann an iomadh dòigh — misg, mionnan, caonnagan, 's mar sin sìos.

Dh'fheòraich mi do fhear tigh-osda anns an robh mu fhicead fear ag òl dlù air taobh a staigh an doruis, an robh an t' shàbaid ga cuir buileach air cul anns an dùtchaich seo. Fhreagair e gun robh chan eil sàbaid idir an Astralia'. Is muladach an cùnntas seo air Dùtchaich a tha aig aidmheil a chreideamh chrìosduidh, agus anns a' bheil an soisgeal air a shearmonachadh gu pailt.

Cha deachaidh mi ach goirid air m aghart fon taigh-osda nuair a thachair sean duine còir orm, a b' aithne dhomh ann an Arasaid, agus an dèigh dhuinn fàilte a 's furan a chuir air a chèile, dh'innis mi dha am freagradh a thug fear an, taigh-osda do 'm cheist ris, a-thaobh na Sàbaid.

"Chan eile sin a cuir dad ioghnaidh orm," arsa easan, "oir gu cinnteach tha bhriathran fìor."

Dh'fheòraich mi dom chàraid Gaidhealach an robh fios aige a na Infidel a bha anns an Osdair?

"Chan e" arsa easan, "buinidh a don Chreideamh ath-leasaichte, agus a bharrachd air a sin tha e suidhe aig bòrd a chomunachaidh ann an aon do dh'Eaglaisean a bhaile tha a chuid mhòr do mhinisteirean na dùthcha seo caoin-shuarach mu staid anaman an t-sluaigh agus an air aobhar sin tha cuid de na daoine is an-diadhaidh ga an gabhail a staigh aig suipeir an Tighearna."

Tha e a' toirt mor-aoibhnais dhomh a chluintinn gu bheil na Teachdairean-spioradail Gaidhealach anns na h-eileanabh seo a dearbh-adh atharaich, agus a leigeil ris nan teagasg 's nan caithe-beatha, gur seirbhisich Chrìosd iad.

Tha dochas agam nach bi iad mall ann an togeil an guth an aghaidh luchd mi-naomhachaidh na sàbaid, agus gun comh-oibrich na gaeil, mar aon duine leò a chum a pheacaidh oillteil sin a sguabadh as an tìr. Cluinnidh sibh uam a rithist an ath-ghearr.

S.T. Melbourne
(Lìtir bho 'S.T.' (Melbourne, Victoria)

Dear Messenger

Desecration of the Sabbath

I will be grieved if the Highlander's devotion to the Sabbath, which he held to in the land that he has left, is broken here and if, in every way, he behaves like the unconverted. On one Sabbath, in this town that I came to from Scotland, I was horror struck regarding the neglectfulness of the inhabitants. There was not a street from one end to the other that was not filled with every manner of sin, drunkenness, cursing and fighting.

I enquired at the door of an inn, in which about twenty men were drinking incessantly and who were fighting, whether the Sabbath had completely perished in this land. I was answered that there was no Sabbath in Australia. This is sad given the number in this country who profess the Christian faith, and in a town where gospel preaching is plentiful.

I had scarcely left the hotel when I happened upon an old pious man whom I knew in Arisaig, and after our joyous welcome of each other I told him the answer the innkeeper had given to me to the question about the sabbath.

"He has not told you anything misleading", he said, "because in that regard his words are true."

I asked my Highland friend about the infidel who was in the hotel.

"He is not," he said, "a member of the reformed faith and besides that, he sits at the table in celebration of the Lord's supper in one of the other Churches in town. A large number of the ministers of this country are indifferent to the conditions of the souls of the people and of the new arrivals, and of the moral state of the godly, who are inside partaking at the Lord's supper."

It is important and welcome and glad news to me to hear evidence of the Highland spiritual teachers in this island, who are prepared to teach and who spend their lives in Christ's service.

It is my hope that they will not be slow in lifting their voice against the people desecrating the Sabbath, and that they will have the cooperation of the Highlanders as a whole against that dreadful sin which should be swept away out of the land.

You will shortly hear again from me.

Letter Signed 'S.T., Melbourne)

64 Litir gu a' charaid

[An t-Urramach Dr A. Mac an Tòisich Mac Aoidh]

[C]han eile son teaghlach dhaibh, nach feudadh uread a chosnadh, ann am bliadhna – no dhà, no thrì, 's a dh'fhàgadh comasach ni 's leòir iad, air feuram a cheannach, agus e sin bhi aca saor, saor, 's aig an chean 'n an diugh. Ach mo thruaighe, 's iad a' chuid a's ainneamh dhiubh a ni dad idir d' a bithidh.

Fàsaidh iad coma co dhuibh! Faigheadh iad feòil is dibhe – 's gheibh iad an sàth – 's a tha iad a' tuiteam siòs gu bhi 'n an anablach sibh truagha gun fheum;- dìomhuin – mo thruaighe mar cleachd iad – a' chìamhaireachd ni iad sin a mach - 's beag taing dhoibh – chan eil i so thaom orra – fàsaidh iad borb - "Stupid" – agus theid as daibh.

Chan eil ach na h-uile eisimpleir a 's measa na chèile timchioll orra, 's mu an coinneamh air son nam bailtean mòra, 's cruaidh leam a ràdh, is droch sgoilean iad do rìreadh do na Gàidheil. Tha iad air am measgadh leis na cinneach, - agus foghlumidh iad an dòighean. 'S mi bha thall 's a chunnaic!

Ochain! agus ochain nan och! – tha dhiubh 's a' cheart bhaile so fèin, na ceudna agus na ceudna, nach dorchaich dorus taigh arraidh 's nach robh riamh an taobh – stigh d' a bithidh a chuir an cas air tìr an Astralia!

Seadh agus cuid dhuibh sud a bha ag aideachadh – aig a' bhaile! Tha agus is aithne cuid dhiubh sud a bha 'n an luchd-dreuchd 's an Eaglais-Shaoir aig a' bhaile! – agus air son na cèirde truaighe sin bhi ri cledhach an air; 's i direach bruaich na h-ìfrinn a càird sin do na mìltibh

Letter to a friend in Scotland
[Rev Dr A. MacIntosh MacKay]

There is not one family of them that couldn't earn enough in a year, or two or three, which would enable them to leave in a prosperous state. They could do so with enough, at the end of the day. But, unfortunately, there are some of them that would be without anything at all.

They become quite indifferent, content to eat worthless food - miserable, useless, lazy – alas they are inured to loneliness - shepherding outside – and little thanks to them, it is not a burden to them. [T]hey live like savages - "Stupid" – and associate with them.

But that is not the whole story, it is worse. None of their spouses are around, just the opposite in fact, in many of the larger towns. I am distressed relating this evil news; it is hard for me saying this, that the Gaels are indeed learning evil. They mix with the heathen – and are learning their habits. And I was there and witnessed it!

Alas! Alas! for them and for the town itself - hundreds and hundreds had never darkened the door of the wicked house at home, and were never inside such a place before setting foot in Australia!

Truly, some of them were communicants at home! - and I know some were actually office-bearers in the Free Church there! - and for that evil their 'occupation' will be to dig directly down to the borders of hell, that 'occupation' of the millions!

65 Aran na Beatha

[Anonymous –*An Teachdaire Gaidhealach*)

Thàinig bean bhochd a bha air chuairt ag iarruidh na deirce, agus leanabh beag aig aice, far an robh Mr Lachuin Mac Coinnich, am ministeir ainmeil a bha a sgìreachd Loch-Carruinn.

Thairg Mr Lachuin mir arain don leanabh; ach air don leanabh dorlach shligean a bhi aige na dhorn beag, cha b' urrainn da an da chuid a chumail, no greimeachadh riutha le cheile.

Mu dheireadh thilg e uaithe na sligean, agus ghreimich e ris an aran.

"Ma ta" arsa Mr Lachuin, "a leinibh bhig, 's mi a tha toilleichte leat, — chan ionann thu agus muinntir Loch Carruinn.

Is tric a tha mise a' tairgsinn an arain dhalbh ach is e an cleachdadhsan na sligean a chumail agus an t-aran a dhiultadh. Is duillich ri smaointeachadh nach ann an Loch Carruinn a-mhàin a tha an sluagh a diultadh aran na beatha mairionnaich, ach anns gach cearna den t-saoghal."

Bread of Life – A Preaching Illustration
[The Gaelic Messenger]

A poor wandering woman asked for charity for herself and her little child from Mr Lachlan McKenzie, the famous Minister of the Loch Carron parish.

Mr Lachlan offered a piece of bread to the child, but the child had a handful of little shells in its fist and was not able to grasp both of them.

At last he threw the shells from him and grasped the bread."

"Truly, said Mr Lauchie, the little child and I were happy - it is not the same with you and the people of Loch Carron.

Often, I offer the bread to them but holding the shells they refuse the bread of life as in every region of the world."

66 An Dìbleach Bochd

[le Eoghan Mac-an-t-Shaoir]

Ge dìblidh bochd, O Thruigh, do shluagh,
Gun mheas a measg luchd spòrs as uails,
Ged ‘s iongantach e ‘n sealladh dhaoine
Chan eil am farmad ris an t-saogh’l.

Nan dìblidh bhochd tha iad gu beachd,
Fo bhròn, fo churam, ‘s iad gun neart;
Ach bheir an Tì dhòirt fhuil ‘nan àit.
Dhaibh saors as ùr ‘s na h-uile cas.

Nan dìblich bhochd tha iad gu dearbh,
Gidheadh na cluinnear gearan searbh,
Cha mhath thig dhaibh bhi diùlt’ le ‘tair
Na cuibhrinn bheir e dhaibh na ghràdh.

Gu dìblidh bochd gidheadh gan ghò
Le cridhe brùite nì iad ceòl,
Don Tì a bhàsaich ‘s a tha beò
‘S a tha comh-fhaireachdainn le ‘m bròn.

Ge dìblidh bochd iad ‘s geàrr an dàil
Gun saltair iad gach nàmh fon sail,
‘S an d’ thig an triobhlaidean gu crìch
‘S am faigh iad fois bho ’n uile sgìos.

‘S ag imeachd dhaibh tre ‘n fhàsach chruaidh
Is tric an gearan a’ dol suas
“Thig fèin a-nis, O Shlanuigh fhear ghraidh,
‘S thoir sinne leat don taigh as àird.

Oir tha sinn air fàs sgìth don t-saogh’l,
Da shòlasan, ‘s da shonais bhaoth,
‘S a-nis ‘s e b’ fhèarr leinn bhi dol suas
Gu seinn gu ceòlmhor glòir an Uain.”

The Wretched Ones
[by Ewan McIntyre]

Though abjectly poor, O Wretched, you people,
Disrespected among the proud scorners,
Though wonderful in the peoples' sight
The world does not envy them.

They are clearly poor and wretched,
Under grief and anxiety, they are without strength,
But God has shed his blood in their place
To free them and for all to walk afresh.

They are indeed of the wretched poor,
Yet their earnest supplication shall be heard,
No good will come to those who contemptuously spurn
Those to whom grace will be given.

To the one reviled, though without blemish,*
With a broken heart, they will sing
To the God who died and who is alive
And who it is that watches with sadness.

Though they are wretchedly poor, it is but a short while
Before every enemy is trampled under the heel,
And their tribulations come to an end
And they receive rest from all their labour.

They have travelled through the wilderness
With supplications often being offered up,
"Come now, you, loving Saviour of man,
And take us with you to your home on High.

Because we grow tired of the world,
With its solace, its giddy joy,
We would now prefer to ascend
To sing melodious praises to the Lamb".

*A reference to the sinless Jesus Christ.

67 Deoch Làidir

[le Dòmhnall Mac Ionmhainn junior]

Cha toil leam fèin deoch làidir tha deoch làidir, cronail don mhuintir a bheir deidh oire, tha i cronail don chaluinn, agus, don Anam, bheir an deoch làidir sgrìos shìorruidh air a mhuintir a bheir deidh oire. Se 'n deoch làidir a thal cuail a chreidimh Chrìosdaidh, o, bhi air a sgaoileadh, feadh Rìgheachdan a T-saoighail.

Se mo bharail fèin, gu bitheadh an creideamh Crìosdaidh anns a chuile cearna don t'saoghal roimhe seo, mar a bhitheadh na crìosdion na misgeirean.

Cha chreid na Cinnich gur e creideamh math a tha ann nuair chi iad na Crìosduidhean a' dèanamh Bruidean dhiubh fèin leis an deoch agus chan eil ionguntas ann gu dearbh, chan eil. Mort, na strìopachas, na meirle, na t-sabaid, na bochduinn, na aon de na peacachadh graineil nach fhaodar a chur as leth na deoch làidir. Chuir gaol na deoch làidir ann an cridhe nan crìosduidhean. Their iad si "Ni Math a chuir thugainn an deoch òlaidh sinn beagan dìth air math ar cuirp, ach cha rig sinn a leas a bhi air mhisg", oh, nach e Satan a tha gan dalladh.

Bu choir dhaibh cuimhne a chumail air t-sean fhàcal, mar an t-athair is amhluidh am Mac agus mar a Mhàthair is amhluidh an Nighean. S' peacach an eisimpleir do na Pàrantan a bhidh ag òl deoch làidir fo choineamh an cloinne ged nach bitheadh na Pàrantan fèin nam misgearn, tha an droch eisimpleir, a' dèanamh glè bhitheanta cron mòr dan clan a' dèanamh drongairean dhuibh, glè bhitheanta ma 'n ruig iad aois fearachais.

'S eagalch an ni re smaoineachadh air gum bheil tuilleadh agus muillean, anamanan a tuiteam ron am don uaidh, leis a mhisg anns na Rìghachd Neamh, agus s' eagalch an ni gu bheil muilleanan air mhuilleanan, air an rathad a chum Bàs Sìorruidh tre an deoch làidir agus a choid mhòr dhiubh, aobhar aca am Pàrantan a mhallachadh air leabaidh am bàis air son an deoch a thort dhaibh nan òige, aig Pàrantan dall bidhsidh clan dall.

Strong Drink

[by Donald MacKinnon junior]

I dislike strong drink. Strong drink is harmful to the people who acquire a desire for it. It is harmful to the body and to the Soul and it will bring eternal ruin on those addicted to it. It is strong drink that is hampering the Christian faith from spreading throughout the nations of the world.

It is my own opinion that the Christian faith would have reached every corner of the world before this but for Christians drinking.

Disbelief in the true faith increases when it is seen that Christians make Beasts of themselves with drink and, indeed, it is not to be wondered at. Murder, fornication, laziness, theft, Sabbath breaking, extreme poverty: there is not one of these abominable sins that may not be laid to the charge of strong drink. Satan has put a love of strong drink in the hearts of Christians. They will say, "God instructed us to take a drink for the good of our body, but we will not be needing that if drunk." Oh, is not Satan misleading them!

They ought to remember the old saying, "Like Father like Son, like Mother, like Daughter." The parents set a sinful example by drinking strong drink in front of the children. Though the parents themselves are not drunkards, it is a bad example. It very frequently does great harm to the children, making drunks of them, quite often by the time they reach adulthood.

It is a dreadful thing to contemplate, too, in Christian countries, the millions of dear souls that fall, strong-bodied, into the grave through drunkenness, and the Lord himself has said that drunkards will not inherit the Kingdom of Heaven. It is a terrible thing that millions upon millions are on the road to Everlasting Death through strong drink, and many of them have cause, when upon their death-bed, to curse the parents who gave them drink when they were young. Children of blind parents will themselves be blind.

68 Cuairt ann an Àit'-Adhlacaidh

[le Seumas Mac 'Ille-Mhaoil]

Cun air t-ais! Càite am bheil thu?
Leig do cheileiridh air chùl:
Feuch air uaigh tha thu 'n ad sheasamh,
Nach tig preasadh ann ad ghnùis?
Iadsan tha còmhnuidh fodhad,
Bha iad roimhe 'n tìr na daonnachd
Chridheil, dh'fhaoidte, mar tha thu.

Seall mun cuairt ort feadh na leacain,
'S dèan orra beachdachadh gu dlùth,
Sean is òg gu foil'n an laidhe
'S iad 'n an cadal as nach dùisg
Gus an seid an trombaid sgalant'
Fo àrd chathair Righ-nan-dùl'.
Nì an gairm gu tìr nam flaitheas
No gu peanas dol air chùl.

O! mo charaid, thoir fainear e,
Ma 's òg no seann duine thu,
Thig am bàs, an sàr-fhear gnothaich,
Cha dean comhairl' chur air chùl;
Buainidh e gach stoc is faillean,
Bochd is beartach ni dha lùb,
Chan eil anam aige do phearsa
Seirbhis gach fo Righ-nan-dùl.

Around the Cemetery
[by James MacMillan]

Stop! Do you know where you are?
Let your singing cease:
See on whose grave you are standing.
Will you not pause and consider?
They who are lying beneath you,
They who were once in the land of the living,
Hearty, perhaps, as you are now.

See around you how far they extend,
And consider them closely,
Old and young rotting under the grass.
In a sleep from which they will not awaken
Until the trumpet sounds
From the throne of the God of creation
Who will call to eternal life
Or to punishment.

O! my friend, take heed,
Whether you are young or old
Death will come, on its appointed business
Do not ignore wise counsel:
Every tree and branch will be cut down,
Poor and rich both shall be humbled.
No one is unknown to him
But each will submit to the God of creation.

Section Seven - Folklore Tales and Songs

Many Highlanders who migrated to Australia carried with them a personal repository of stories, beliefs, charms, poems, songs, lore of places and whimsical explanations for everyday phenomena. The degree to which such lore was transmitted by word of mouth has not been well charted in Australia

We do know that some immigrant bearers of a significant body of oral folk material (such as Donald Beaton) felt despairing about the prospect of its survival (along with that of Gaelic itself) in Australia. They took steps to write down (and sometimes forward to Scottish journals for publication) their personal stock of folkloric prose and poetry as well as that which they transcribed from other emigrants. The bearers chose to commit a hitherto largely oral body of lore to writing in order to ensure its immediate survival.

The poems, songs and stories collected here were all gathered in the form in which they were originally related by the emigrants and some differ from those found in major collections such as that of J.F. Campbell. Some have remained in the diaries and papers of those who kept such things in Gaelic and have not, before this, been brought to light in a published form. Donald MacKinnon's short verses, *Cù Aig Tighearna Dhiùra*, display a trait that is also evident in certain poems and stories elsewhere in this anthology. This constitutes a tendency to invoke aspects of the old heroic legends in order to explain and deal with present events or memories. Sometimes, too, emotions and nostalgia associated with legendary events such as MacCrimmon going into exile are useful to echo the contemporary emigrant's own sense of loss.

The editor of the Gaelic paper, *An Teachdaire Gaidhealach*, which was published in Australia in 1857, makes quite plain the tensions these amateur folklorists experienced in offering items for publication. The theme of many of the paper's editorials was the need for education and the benefits which this would bring to the individual and to society as a whole. In carrying this theme into the realm of the store of "superstition" which was brought out with emigrants, the Editor of *An Teachdaire Gaidhealach* sought to apply reason and the cold light of day to such beliefs in order to show that those things belonged to a more distant and darker past, when the mind was not so illuminated as it was now. Despite a long editorial, *Linntean Dorcha an t-Shaobh-Chràbhaidh*, seeking to dispel the notion of witches, second sight, fairies and the like, the Editor's own views are somewhat ambivalent in some areas. For all his apparent attempt to rid the Highland emigrants of these beliefs, he opened up the pages of his paper to contributions which related such stories as he would have his readers believe were based upon ignorance and superstition!

The printing of such contributions as the Raonull stories and the re-telling of traditional tales such as *Sgeulachd Na Trì Saighdearan* and traditional sports such as *Crom-an-Fhàsaich* (*Cluich Lùth-chleasan*), suggest that the Editor was, perhaps, not so convinced himself of the message of his own editorials on the subject!

69 Linntean Dorcha an t-Shaobh-Chràbhaidh

[*An Teachdaire Gaidhealach*]

Deasachaidh

Anns na tìmean sin, bha saobh-chràbhadh ann an làn sheilbh air innteinnean nan Gaidheal, agus a' riaghladh an gnìomharan uile. Bha iad air an tiugh chòmhdach' le daibhre nuarrannt' an ain-eolais, mar loingeis air chuan ann an ceò, gun chairt gun chombaist, ach a' sìor stiùradh air lunn aimlisgeach neo-chinnteach beul-aithris, gus an do thòisich grian ghlòirmhor Reusain air a gathan …

… neartmhor neo-mhearachdach a bhualadh air na neòil dhuaichnidh ud, agus an sin theann iad ri gluasad, a' siòladh as gu h-aithiseach, cinteach, gus nach eil ach sgaile glè thana de shaobh-chreideamh na liuaidhe air "tìr nam beann," agus bithidh an t-iarmad seo fhèin gun teagamh, ann an ùine ghoirid, air a chuir gu buileach as. Faodaidh sinn a-nis beagan de na dòighean anns an robh e ga nochdadh fèin ainmeachadh.

Droch shùil.- Ma bha duine air bith a' fàs gu tinn agus a' caitheadh as gach latha, gun fhios ciod a b' anshocair dha, bha e air a ràdh anns a' mhionaid, gun robh e fullang fo bheum-sula, agus rachadh grad fhios a chuir air neach aig an robh eolas-a-chronach-aidh a chum a leigheas. A bheil e comasach gun deanadh aon duine coire do dhuine eile le coimhead gruamach air, na 's lugha na bhiodh an duine seo cho neo-steidheil agus gun cuireadh e inntinn fhèin troimh-a-chèile le bhi toir gèill d' a leithid? Tha làn chinnt againn gu bheil cumhachd mòr aig an inntinn thairis air a' chorp; agus ma tha ni air bith a' tachairt do dhuine a tha ghnàth cuir bruaillein air, snaidhidh e sìos e a an an ùine glè ghoirid mur a d' rinn sùil duine coire d' a chomh-chreutair anns an dòigh seo cha d' rinn riabh ann an aon dòigh eile.

An Dà-shealladh.- Chìteadh na daoine sin aig an robh an dà shealladh fo chomh-àir an sùil gu – riochdail, nitheannan a bha ri tachairt, theagamh greis mhath na dhèigh sin ged nach fhaiceadh an fheadhain a dh'fhaodadh a bhi ri'n guallainn iad gus an cuireadh fear na tè an dà-sheallaidh cas air an cois-san, - chìteadh iad an sin gu soilleir iad. Tha iomadh aon a tha fhathasd a creidsinn anns an ni seo. Beachd-aicheamaid air, matà, le 'r tuigse nàdurra fhèin car mionaid na dhà, agus leigea'maid dhinn a bhi a' toirt creideis do ni nach seas ri reusan.

Tha cuspair so-fhaicinn air bith a tha a' tighinn an taobh a staigh de chearcall ar seallaidh, a' tilgeil iomhaigh air ar sùil ged nach biodh ann ach am faileas, agus ma tha sinn a' toirt aire dha tha sinn fiosrach nar n-inntinn, aig an àm, gu bheil sinn ga fhaicinn, agus ma tha ni sam bith a' tighinn air ar sùilean, no a' tighinn eadar sinn 's an cuspair sin a tha ga ghearradh fo 'r sealladh tha sinn fiosrach air an ni sin mar an ceudna.

Bha da dhuine a gabhail an rathaid mhòir còmhla, oidhche àraidh, bha sealladh an dara fir cho math ri sealladh an fhir eile, gu nitheannan fhaicinn, mòr na beag, fad air falbh na dlùth laimh, ach gu robh e air a ràdh gun robh an dà-shealladh aig fear dhinn.

Air ball chunnaic am fear seo coslas eich air an rathad, dìreach air thoiseach orra bheil thu faicinn sud ars' e ris an fhear eile?

"Chan eil" ars' esan, "gu de th' ann?"

Tha each bàn na sheasamh air meadhon an rathaid, fichead slat romhainn – cha b' urrainn dà fhaicinn; ach nuair a chuir am fear eile a chas air a chois-san, chunnaic e 'n sin e.

A-nis nach eile sin calg-dhìreach an aghaidh reusain: nam biodh an cuspair sin ann, nach tilgeadh e iomhaigh air sùilean an fhir eile mar an ceudna, nuair nach robh dad eadar e 's an t- àite san robh e? – gun teagamh. Bha baothaireachd, agus gu minic, lag-inntinneachd ri gnothuichean den t-sheòrsa seo.

Daoine-sìthe, na Daoine-beaga. – Bha iad seo a chòmhnuidh 's na creagan, 'an taighean ris an abrar bruithean, ach ge b' e de thàinig orra, chan eil gin diu r' a fhaicinn fo cheann beagan bhlidhnachan. Bha iad, air uairean, fior chaoimhneil ri daoine den t-sheòrsa againne. Bha dà dhuine choir a chaidh roimhe seo a dh'iarruidh uisge-beatha na Nollaig, agus air dhaibh a bhi tilleadh dhachaidh feadh na h-oidhche le buideal làn, am fear, chunnaic iad bruth fosgailte; a's ceol a's dannsadh a dol air aghaidh ann; chaidh fear dhiubh staigh, a's thòisich e air dannsadh comhla ri càch, agus bha iad cho math dha 's gun do smaointich e fuireach tacain den oi'che leò.

Nuair a shaoil e gun robh an t-àm aige falbh, leig iad a mach e. Thog e 'm buideal air a ghuallainn 's dh'fhalbh e. Nuair a ràinig e dhachaidh 's gann a b' urrainn d' a bhean a's don duine choir a bha leis a thoirt air a chreidsinn gun robh a bliadhna air falbh; oir cha do shaoil fhèin ach mar aon oidhch' e. Chan eil fhios a bheil gin an-diugh de shliochd Adhaimh a b' urrainn seasamh fad bliadhna a dannsadh gun chadal! Bha e na chleachdadh aig na sìthichean mar an ceudna, a bhi toirt mhnathan as an laidhe shiùbhladh na a' giulan air falbh an leanabanan fon taobh agus a' fagail sheann bhodach liath nan riochd.

Tairbh-Uisge.- Cha robh lochan nach robh làn de na tairbh seo, agus chìteadh iad air uairean a dol a-measg a' chruidh, 's ag ionaltradh còmhla riù. Cha robh gaol sam bith aig tuathanaich air sliochd nam beathaichean leibideach seo, ach bha e ro chunnartach oidheirpeachadh air an loch anns am bitheadh iad a thraoghadh. An oidhche a chaidh an Lochan Tuimhneach a thraoghadh cha robh sgian na forc ann an taigh a Chlachain-Shaolich nach b' fheudar a chuir 's gach uinneig a's dorus a chumail a mach nan tarbh-uisge. Tha e coltach nach b' urrainn do dhroch ni air bith tighinn an goireadh do dh'iarunn. Chan eil oscionn bliadhna fon a fhuair duine foghainteach laidir a shàruchadh gu fuasach, le each-uisge ann an t-eilein Uidhist.

Buidseach.- An robh buidsichean ann roimhe seo? Bha, agus tha, air an latha 'm diugh, seana mhnathan ann a fhuair ainm a bhi nam buidsichean. B'ainmeil r' an linn am boireannach a bha 'n Endor, Cailleach gharbh Nic-an-Uidhair, Cas-a-mhogain, Nic Ille Dhuidh, agus mòran eile.

Gun robh iad seo a gnàthachadh ghisreasgan a-chum an ni bu mhiann leò, a thoirt gu crìch, tha làn chinnt againn, ach gun d' thug iad an rùn gu bheil tre na meadhonan seo, cha chreid neach air bith ach iadsan nach eil a' dèanamh feum den reusan agus a tha fhathast fo dhoilleireachd an t-shaobh-chreidimh:- dh'fhaodadh iad gun teagamh, oibreachadh a-chum dolaidh, air inntinn na feadhmach seo, mar a dh'ainmich sinn cheana.

Nuair a dh'iarr Saul air a bhoireannach a bhan, Endor, Samuel a thogail, thuirt e rithe,

"Ciod e a Choslas?"

Agus thuirt ise, "Tha seann duine air teachd a nìos agus e còmhdaichte le falluinn, agus dh'aithnich, na thuig, Saul gum b' e Samuel a bh' ann."

A bheil coltach gun ceadaicheadh an t-Uilechumhachdach Samuel a dhol air falbh fo shuaimhneas sìorruidh aig iartas Shauil agus a bhoireannaich seo? Chan eil idir, agus se barail dhiadhairean ainmeil, nach fhaca Saul Samuel aig an àm sin,- chan eil e soilleir o 'n Bhìobull gun faca.

Cha bu toigh leis a bhoireannach Saul a-thaobh gun robh e cuir as d' a seòrsa, agus bha fhios aice fhèin 's aig a leannan-sìth gun creideadh e na reachadh ceudna, air Cùisean na rìoghachd. Chreid Saul gun robh e ri bàs fhaotuinn, air an latha màireach, agus nuair a chaidh an ruaig air, seach gun tuiteadh e le laimh a nàimhdean, thug e a bheatha air falbh le làimh fhèin.

Chaidh long Chaptein Forest a chuir fodha ann an Caol-Muile, ann an dòigh ro iongantach. Chuir tè de bhuidsichean ainmeil an t-eilein sin ropa thar a h-aon de spàrran an taighe anns an robh i chòmhnuidh, agus cheangail i an dara ceann ri bile cuaich a bha air snàmh ann an tuba làn uisge, agus bha i toirt spadhadh air a cheann eile an drast 's a-rithist, gus an do lìon a chuach agus aig a cheart mhionaid Chaidh an long fotha!

'S tric a chaidh an tè seo ann an riochd maighich 's a thig i 'm bàin fo chrodh a coimhearsnaich - 's truagh nach robh an Doideag chumhachdach seo 's a Chrimea, 's bheireadh i 'n t-arm Breatunnach mar sgaoth chuileag a-staigh do Shebastopol, gun urchair a losgadh.

Tha làn fhios a's cinnt againn gu bheil cuid de na leughas an Teachdaire a' toirt gèill do phàirt de na gisreagan air a bheil sinn a labhairt aig an àm, agus 's ann air an aobhar sin a chuir sinn sìos na h-uidhir mun timcheall.

Mun reachadh neach ann an coltas maighich, na creutair air bith eile dh'fheumadh aon de thrì nitheanan tachairt:-

1ud - Dh'fheumadh sealladh na feadhnach a dh'fhaodadh a bhi coimhead 's an am a bhi air mhilleadh cho mòr 's gun tilgeadh cruth boireannaich dealbh maighich air an sùilean. Nam b' ann mar seo a bhoidh' chìteadh iad iad fhèin a's càch a cheile' nam maighichean aig a cheart àm.

2ra - Dh'fheumadh an neach a bhi air a dhinneadh a sìos gu nàdurra, gun dochann, gu meudachd a bheathaich agus air a chòmhdach gu h-innealta, le a craicionn.

3ra - Dh'fheumadh spiorad an neach seo an corp fhàgail, mar a nì am muirsgein air a shlige, agus dol a-staigh ann an dearbh chorp na maighich; ach chan eil sinn a smaointeachadh gun teannadh Cailleach Gharbh Nic-an-Uidheir fhèin ris a seo, oir bha tuille na sin de spèis aice d' a seana chreubhaig, gu fhàgail air faontraidh 's an dòigh sin, 's gun fhios an amaiseadh i tuillidh air.

Bha, fo cheann chuig na sèa bhliadhnachan, duine a bha na fhear-frithealaidh ann an eaglais àraidh nach eil ro fhada fo Liabasd (Lybster) an Gall-thaobh, a thog garbh chasaid an aghaidh boireannaich a bha lamh ris airson a bhi toirt an toraidh a bainne na bò aige.

Bha o chionn ghoirid seann duine den fhine Stiubhartach anns an Apuinn a bhiodh a' dèanamh shoisgeul, (Spells) airson leigheis thinneasan de na h-uile seòrsa. Bha an soisgeul seo ri bhi air a ghiùlan leis an duine thinn na fhochar gus am biodh a shlàinte air a h-aiseag dha. Bhan Stiubhartach a' dèanamh beò-shlàinte mhath air an dòigh seo. Cha mhòr dar luchd-dùthcha nach cuala iomradh air Màiri mhòr Nic-an-t-Shaoir, buidseach a Ghearasdain' "ann Lochabar.

Chaidh a h-ainm fad' as goirid a's bha daoine tighinn d' a h-ionnsuidh as gach ceàrn, a dh'iarruidh ni sam bith a bhiodh a dhìth orra a shaoileadh iad a b' urrainn an dreuchd aice-sa fhaotuinn daibh. Dh'iarradh i a duais mar fhear-lagha air bith, agus diùltadh chan fhaigheadh i aon uair, oir bha earbsa mhòr aca as a cumhachd, agus cha robh iad ga fhaicinn sàbhailte dhaibh, air chor sam bith, mìothlachd a chuir oirre.

Bha sinn a rùnachadh iomradh a thoirt air taibhsean ach cha cheadaich rùm dhuinn. Ann an comh-dhùnadh, theirea'maid, a chàirde, mar a biodh dearbh-chinnt gu bheil iomadh fhathast 's sa ghaeltachd, seadh 's ann an Astraillia cuideachd, a tha creidsinn na nithean seo, cha chuirea'maid aon uair peann air peipeir gu sgrìobhadh mu a leithid de dh'fhaoineis.

Glanadh iad seo an inntinnean, mata, fo cheò an dorchadais mhuladaich leis an robh iad cho fada air am mealladh, agus na biodh iad tuillidh nan culaidh àbhacdais aig an coimheasnaich a tha dèanamh an fheum sin den tuigse airson an deachaidh a bhuileachadh orra.

The Dark, Superstitious Generations

[The Gaelic Messenger Editorial]

In times past superstition was in full possession of the minds of the Gaels, and ruled all behaviour. They were greatly afflicted with woeful poverty and ignorance. Like a ship at sea without chart or compass, they were continually driven along on a heavy wave of doubtful oral tradition causing confusion, until the light of the glorious sun of Reason began to shine ....

[Those] powerful and unerring rays of light struck the ugly clouds, and then began to move and disperse this affront so completely that not even a thin presence of superstition is now mentioned in the "land of the mountain". There is little doubt that this race itself will shortly be free of it. We can now mention a few of the forms in which it revealed itself.

Evil Eye:- If a man was sickening and wasting away each day without understanding what sickness he had, he would straight away say that he was suffering from the evil eye, and would hastily seek out any one who had the knowledge to effect a cure. Can a man, by a forbidding look, harm another man? Do not believe it.

We are fully convinced of the power of the mind over the body; and if something is happening to a man troubling him and he is wasting away in a short time, the look of a good man could no more make his fellow creature well any more than any other man could do the opposite.

Second Sight:- Those people with this could see with their eyes with certainty things that were yet to happen though other people who may have been standing right next to them could not see these same things until invited to by the man or woman with second sight – they might then be clearly seen. Many still believe in this thing. Let us observe, then, with our natural reason for a minute or two, and let us let go of belief in this thing that will not stand up to reason.

A conspicuous object approaching may lie outside our circle of sight casting an impression on our eye though it may not be but a shadow, and if we are paying attention to it we are conscious in our mind at the time, that is we 'see' it, and if there is anything on our eyes or between us and the object which blocks our view of it, we are convinced, nevertheless, of it 'being there'.

Two men were going along a large road one particular evening. The second man's sight was better than the other man's at seeing things, large or small, from a far distance or from nearby, but it was said that he had second sight. Immediately this man saw the likeness of a horse on the road first.

"Do you see that?" he said to the other man.

"I cannot", he said, "what is it?"

"It is a white horse standing in the centre of the road, twenty yards in front of us."

But the second man was not able to see it, but when the other man drew him close to himself he was then able to see it. Now, that does not contradict reason; is it not the case that that object would likewise cast an image on the eyes of the other man if there was not anything between it and the place from where he was standing? – without doubt. Foolishness and, frequently, conceitedness, were much involved in matters of this kind.

Fairy Folk and Little People:- These live in rocky places, and in houses according to some reports, but whatever became of them not a single one has been sighted for a few years. They were, at times, truly kind to men. Two decent men wanted whisky for Christmas, and were returning home with a full cask when one man saw an open fairy mound; music and dancing were going on inside. One of them went in and began dancing along with the others and they were good to him and, without thinking, he stayed a short part of the evening in their company.

When he thought it was time for him to leave they let him out. He lifted the cask on to his shoulders and left. When he reached his house, he was hardly able to believe his wife or his companion that he had been away for a year, because he himself thought that it was only one evening. There is not one of Adam's descendants today that could stand dancing for a year without sleep! It was the custom as well for the fairies to take away the women's loved ones, carrying away the little children from their side and leaving the likeness of an old grey-haired man in their place.

Water-Bulls:- There were no lochs but that they were full of these bulls, and they could be seen at times going among the cattle, and grazing along with them. There was no love among the farmers for these long-legged, avaricious animals, but it was a very dangerous endeavour to drain the loch. One evening a farmer went to Loch Tuimhneach to drain it. Every knife and fork in the house at Chlachain-Shaolich was put on every window and door to restrain the water bull. It is believed that it is not able to do evil on coming into contact with iron. It is not more than a year ago that a brave, strong man was horribly overcome by a water-horse in the Island of Uist.

Witches:- Were there witches formerly? There were, and are; in my day, old women who got the name of being witches. There was the famous woman of her race that was at Endor, as well as Cailleach gharbh Nic-an-Uidhair, Cas-a-mhogain, Nic-Ille Dhuidh, and many others.

That they used superstitions in order to bring about the thing desired by them we do not doubt, but no one, unless they were still under the darkness of superstition, and not making right use of his reason, would believe that they were able to reveal secrets by means of this medium:- they may, without doubt, work some harm to the detriment of others for, as we have already mentioned, the mind is a powerful thing.

When Saul asked the old woman that was in Endor, when Samuel was raised, he said to her,

"What is this appearance?"

And she said, "An old man is rising up from below and he is dressed in a robe."
Saul did not perceive that it was Samuel.

Is it likely that the Almighty permitted Samuel, who has gone away to his eternal rest, to appear at the request of Saul and this old woman? Not at all, and it is the opinion of a famous theologian that Saul was not looking at Samuel at that time,- it is not clear from the word of the Bible.
The old woman was not pleased with Saul as it was he who had exterminated her kind, and she knew that he would behave in the same way again in matters of the kingdom. Saul believed that he was going to his death the next day when he went to battle, and rather than fall at the hand of his enemies, he took his own life with his own hand.

Captain Forest's ship hit a sunken rock in Caol-Muile in an extraordinary way. A woman who was a witch renowned on that island put a rope across one of the joists of the house in which she was dwelling, and she tied the other end to the rim of a bowl that was floating in a full tub of water, and she was giving tugs on the other end now and again and the bowl filled and at the same minute the boat sank!

This woman often went about in the likeness of a hare and she would take the milk from under the neighbour's cattle - it is a pity that the Doigeag* was not as powerful at Crimea where she could have carried the whole of the British army like a swarm of flies into Sebastopol, without a shot being fired.

[* the Doigeag was a famous Mull witch., eds]

We are sure that some readers of Teachdaire would have given homage to some of the superstitions about which we have been talking here, and it is for this reason that we have included them.

For a person to take the likeness of a hare or some other creature would require three things to take place:-

1. It would require that, throughout the whole time, the hare have that appearance to the eye but not, at the same time, shed the personality of the woman. In this manner they would see themselves as hares and other hares would see them as hares at the right time.
2. It would require that the person would shrink naturally without damage to the body of the beast or to its neat covering of skin.
3. It would require that the person's spirit leave the body, in the same way a razor-fish leaves its shell, and go about in the likeness of a hare; but we do not think that Cailleach Garbh Nic-an-Uidheir herself was able to do this, because there would not be enough of herself left for her to know how to return to her normal self.

About five or six years ago a man, who was an attendant in a certain church that is not far below Lybster in Caithness, raised a complaint against a woman who was in his hire for drying up his cow.

A short time ago an old man of the Stewart clan in Appin was having a spell made for the cure of all kinds of diseases he had. This 'spell' was that the sick man was to be brought into the witch's presence until he was healed. The Stewart man was brought to good health in this way.

There will not be many of our fellow countrymen who have not heard of Màiri mhòr Nic-an-t-Shaor, witch of Fort William in Lochaber. Her name was spread far and wide and soon men were coming to her from every quarter, desiring that something be done for their ailment, thinking that there was, in her, the means of their alleviation. She wanted payment as a lawyer does, and refusal meant that she could not be got. Because of the great trust in her power those needing help on any account bore no resentment towards her.

We were intending mentioning ghosts also but space will not allow us. To conclude, we would say, friend, that it is certainly still the case for many in the Highlands, and, furthermore, it is also the case in Australia, that these things are believed; not that we would give time putting pen to paper writing about such foolishness.

Clearing the mind, then, of the sad fog of darkness under which Highlanders were for so long deceived, let them not ridicule their neighbour who, from want of understanding, returns to them.

70 MacCruimein, - Na Cumhadh an Fhògaraich

['Mactalla' an t-Urramach Donnahadh MacCalman]

Bratach-bhuadhail Mhic-leòid o'n mhòr lasadh,
'S luchd-iomraidh nan ràmh greased bhàrc tha ghlas chuan;
Bogha, sgiath' 's claidheamh mòr 's tuagh gu leòn airm nam fleasgach,
'S Mac Cruimein cluich cuairt soraidh-bhuam le Dunbheagain.

Slàn leis gach creig àrd ris 'm bheil gairich àrd thonnan,
Slàn leis gach glean fàs san dean cràic dhaimh an langan-
Eilein Sgiathanaich aidh! Slàn le 'd bheanntaibh 's guirm fireach;
Tillidh dh'fhaoilte Macleòid ach cha bheò Macruimein.

Soraidh bhuam don gheal-cheò tha còmhdachadh Cuillein
Slàn leis gach blàth shùil th' air an Dùn, 's iad a tuireadh,
Soraidh bhuam don luchd ciùil 's tric chuir sunnd orm a's tioma;
Sheòl Macruimein thar sàil 's gu bràth cha phill tuilleadh.

Nuallan allt' Pìob-mhoir, cluich marbh rann an fhilidh,
Agus dearbh bhrat a bhàis mar fhalluing aig uime;
Ach cha mheataich mo chridhe 's cha ragaich mo chuislean,
Ged dh' fhalbhan le'm dheòir – 's fios nach till mi chaoidh tuilleadh.

'S tric a chluinnear fuaim bhinn caoidh thiom-chridh, Mhicruimein,
'N uair bhios Gaidheil a'falbh thair an fhairge ga'n iomain;
O chaomh thìr ar gràidh O do thràigh 's rag ar 'n imeachd,
Och cha till – cha till – Och, cha till sinn tuilleadh.

Macrimmon - The Exile's Lament
[by 'Mactalla', Rev. Duncan MacCalman]

Macleod's victorious banner, proudly shining,
People famed as oarsmen on the pale sea;
Bow, shield, great claymore and axe, a young man's arms,
And Macrimmon* playing a lasting salutation to Dunvegan.**

Farewell each high crag and loud roaring waves,
Farewell each desolate glen and the lowing of the stag-
Skye! Farewell mountains and green moor;
Joyfully, Macleod has returned, but Macrimmon has departed.

Farewell from me to the mist covered Cuillins
Farewell each affectionate, weeping eye,
Farewell the musicians who often cheered and warmed my heart;
Macrimmon sails across the sea, never to return.

The wild sound of the great pipes plays the dead poet's song,
And death's shroud is a mantle about him;
But my heart is not daunted, nor my chanter still,
Though it is in tears I leave, knowing I will never return.

And often shall be heard the tender lament, "Macrimmon",
When Gaels leave to cross the driving sea;
Alas, to journey, unwillingly, from our beloved land and shore,
Oh, not to return, not to return – Oh, we will never return.

71 Cù aig Tighearna Dhiùra

[le Dòmhnall Mac Ionmhainn senior]

Am moil chù aig Tighearna Dhiùra,
Chan fhaic a leithid riamh 's an tìr
Ach Bran a bh' aig Rìgh na Fiann.

"Ciod a bhuaidh a bhiodh air Bran?"
Arsa Conan uaibhreach mear:
"A cheud leigeadh a fhuair Bran"
"Air druim Coille Coire ruadh"
"Naonar do gach fiadh air bith"
"Leagadh Bran air a cheud ruith."

72 A Chrìthionn Seo

[le Dòmhnall Beaton]

A chrìthionn seo, 'se an crìthionn crìon
Air 'n do chrochadh mo Rìgh,
Mallachd air an t-sùil a chì
'S nach cronaich an crìthionn crìon.

Lord Jura's Hound
[by Donald MacKinnon senior]

Praise to Lord Jura's hound,
Its equal has never been seen in the land;
Except for Fingal's Bran!*

"What could overcome Bran?"
Proud Conan said sportingly,
"The first outing that Bran got
On the ridge of the red Corrie Forest
He felled on his first run
As many deer as nine others.

This Aspen Tree
(by Donald Beaton)

This is an aspen tree, it is a little aspen tree
On you hung my King,
And cursed is the eye that will look and see,
And not rebuke the little aspen tree.

73 Fath Ioghnaidh a' Choigrich air Talamh

[Seann Sgeulachd]

Anns na linntean a dh'fhalbh, nuair a bha sgeulachdan a' faotainn tuille creideis na tha iad a-nis, bha e air aithris gum facas coigreach àraidh a' sràid imeachd troimh aon de bhailtean mòra na h-Àird-an-ear, agus e beachdachadh le àrd ionghnadh air gach uile nì mun cuairt da.

Air do shluagh cruinneachadh m' a thimcheall dh'fheòraich iad dheth mu dhèighinn a dhùthcha, agus mu fhàth a thairis. Ach ghrad thuig iad gun robh e aineolach air an cainnt, agus chunnaic esan gun robh e fèin aineolach air an cainnt 's air an cleachduidhean-san. Ach chunnaic iad gu soilleir bho choltas 's bho ghiùlan a bha flathail, uasal, an àite gum bu duine cuthaich no amhlara e, mar a bha feadhain an toiseach ag ràdh gum bu duine àrd-inbheach, urramach e.

Nuair a thuig esan fa dheireadh leis an smèideadh, 's na comharan a bha iad a' dèanamh gun robh iad a' feòraich cia as a thàinig e, sheàll e le mòr dhùrachd a suas ris na speuran. Air don t-shluagh seo a thoirt fainear, gabh iad 'n am beachd gum b' aon de na de aca bhi ann, agus chrom iad sìos gu aoradh a thoirt dha. Cha luaithe chunnaic e seo na sheall e le mòr uamhann air an oidheirp, agus thilg se e fèin air a ghlùinean 'u-thog e làmhan ri nèamh a leigeil ris gu soilleir gun robh esan e fèin a' deanamh aoraidh do na h-Àrd chumhachadan.

Bha aon 'us aon de na bha làthair a nochd mòr chaoimhneas dha a-nis agus a dh'iarr a tharruing chum an tighean gu aoidheachd a thoirt do neach co sònruichte. Chaidh e le fear de dh'uaislean an àite, agus 'n chuideachd san thàinig e air aghaidh ann an ionnsachadh cànain na dùthcha co ealamh 'us an ùine fior ghoirid gun rachadh aig air còmhradh rèidh ghlèidheil ris gach aon a thachair na chuideachd.

Bha mòr dhèigh aig fear an tighe air cunntas cinnteach fhaghuinn mu dhùthaich, 's mu inbh a' choighrich ro iongantaich, agus fa dheireadh shocraich iad air feasgar àraidh 's an robh an diomhaireachd seo r' a leigeil ris. Nuair a thàinig am feasgar dhìrich iad a suas gu aon de àrd shràidean a bhaile tharsuing, shaibhir agus mhòr-shluaghrich seo.

Agus b' àillidh an sealladh a bha f'an comhair. Bha na mìltean lòchran a' dealradh am measg nan sràidean greadhnach sin. Bha na ceudan lùchairt rìomhach, agus mhaiseach o 'n uinneagan àrda taomadh soillse air an abhain mhòir a bha siubhal gu ciùin, sàmhach troimh an bhaile, agus a giùlan air a h-uchd nan luingeis mhòra luchdaichte le bathar luachmhor – le rìomhadh 's le àilleachd as gach cèarna de 'n t-shaoghal.

Bha tois na clarsaich', agus binn fhuaim na cruit-chiùil ri'n cluintinn air gach làimh. Bha caithream ait an fhir nuadh-phòsda, agus guth binn, tlàth na mnà nuadh-phòsda r'an cluintinn mar an ceudna. Bha ceol, 'us aighear, 'us aoibhneas, ga 'n cuartachadh air gach taobh. Sheall an coigreach car tamuill air na bha f' a chomhair, agus dh'èisd e ri torman, ri fuaim 's ri farum a' bhaile-mhòir. Ach gu h-obann thog e aghaidh ris na speuran rionnagach, agus shocraich e shùil gu ro dhlùth air reul àillidh an fheasgair.

"Na gabh ionghnadh," thuirt e ris an dion' uasal, "mise bhi dearcadh le urrad dheòthais air an reull ghloin, dhealraich ud. B' i sud mo dhùthaich 'us mo dhachaidh. Oh! b' i. Bho cheann beagan ùine bha mo chòmhnuidh anns an rionnaig àillidh ud gus an do tharruing an t-annas, 's an neònachas mi gu tighin an seo air astar 's air allaban. Is tric a sheall mi le mòr ionghnadh air an t-shaoghal seo a bha ri fhaicinn mar neamhnuid ro dhèarsaich 'n ar n-iarmailtene, agus bha mhiann ro làidir agam air fiosrachadh fhaghuinn mu thimcheall. Fhuair mi mo mhiann.

Thug an t-Àrd-chumhachd làn chead, agus comas dhomh imeachd troimh fharsuingeachd an athair thun an ionaid chèin seo; ach bha aon chùmhnant ceangailte ris a' chead seo – gum feumainn dachaidh o sin suas a' dhèanamh de 'n ionad seo, agus cur a suas le cor a luchdaitich', socair, no docair ga 'm bitheadh e. Dh'aontaich mi leis a chùmhnant seo. Tha mi a-nis fon aona chor ri clanna nan daoine, agus soilleirich dhomh nas mine na rinn thu fathasd, tha mi guidhe ort, seadh 'us brìgh gach nì tha mi faicinn 's a cluinntinn mun cuairt domh."

"Gu deimhin a Shàir," fhreagair an duin'-uasal" ged tha mi aineolach air nòs, 's air sochairean na dùthch' a dh'fhàg thu, tha mi ro thoilichte gun d' rinn thu roghainn co tuigseach 's a rinn thu, 's tha mòr aobhar gàirdeachais agad arson gun robh thu co sealbhach agus tachairt air cèarnaidh de 'n t-shaoghal 's am bheil urrad shubhachais, 'us shonais ri 'm mealtuinn 's a tha ri 'm faotuinn 's a' bhaile shaibhir, shòghmhor, ghreadhnach seo. Agus bi cinnteach gun toir e fìor tho! inn'inn dhomhsa do sheòladh gus gach nì taitneach, agus luachmhor a tha 's taobh a stigh de bhallachan."

An cois na tairgse shuairce so bhan Coigreach air a thoirt gus gach fleagh, 'us cuirm – a choimhead gach cluich' 'us coinnimh àbhaich – air a dha anemh eòlach air gach aoibhneas, gach riòmhadh 's gach àilghios o 'n robh muinntir an àite 'g iarraidh an àrd shonais; agus bha e ann an tomhas mòr air e fèin a dhèanamh ri an cleachdaidhean, 's ri 'n dòighean 'n uair a thachair ri àraidh a thug atharrachadh buileach air inntinn, 's air a bheachdan.

Air dha bhi co seachid am fionn-fhuaireachd an là mu oir-iomall a' bhaile thug e fainear àite farsuing air a chuartachadh le balla àrd, dorcha. Dh'fheòraich e:

"Carson a bha 'n t-àite seo air a dhrùideadh a suas?"

"S e sin" fhreagair an duin'-uasal, "an t-àit adhlacaidh."

"Chan eil mi ga d' thuigsinn gu ro mhaith" ars' an coigreach, "ainmich a rithist an t-àite?"

"Tha àite tiodh-lacaidh, no tòrraidh na clagh, ionad tasgaidh nan corp," thuirt an duin-uasal.

"Gabh mo leth sgeul" ars a chombanach, s e fo bheagan ioghnaidh," bi co maith 's a' chùis a' dhèanamh nis soilleire dhomh fathasd. Chan eil fhios agamsa co iad na h-àitheachan tiodhlacadh."

Mhìnich am fear eile a' chùis dha mar a bearr a b' urrainn da. Fhreagair an coigreach 's e mùthadh neòil le mòr ioghnadh air; "seo nì nach robh fios, no smuain agam a bhi 's an t-saoghal, agus ma tha mi tuigsin a' bheag no mhòr idir mun ghnoth-ch eagailach agus iongantach – is cùis e nas cudthromaiche mil' uair na aon nì eile air an d' rinn thu fathasd iomradh. Innis dhomh matà gun dàil, guidheam ort gach nì 's aithne dhuit mun nì bhrònach, agus uamhasach seo am bàs."

"Gu cinnteach tha thu d' Choigreach da rinadh" ars an duin' uasal; "nuair nach eil fios agad guin feum sinn uile, luath, no mall, strìochdadh don bhàs. Agus ged nach eil e cur urrad uamh-ainn oirne 's a tha e ortsa, 's e 'm bàs gun teagamh, crois is mo 'n ar slighe, agus an nì is seirbhe 's muladaiche 'n ar crannchur; uime sin is nì e nach eile ach ro ainmic air iomradh ann an cuideachd uasail, no mhodhail air bith. 'S ann mar so thachair e nach cual thu fathasd ùine 'n ar measg. Ach mar eil muinntir do dhùthcha-sa buailteach don bhàs chomhair-lichinn duit tilleadh rithe co luath 's a tha 'd chomas – oir bi cinnteach nach eil dol as dhuit an seo; agus a dh'innseadh na fìrinn' chan urrainn dhomh-sa, no do dhuin' eil dol an urras gun tèaruinn thu car latha, no uaire."

"Mo thruaighe! 's mo chreach lèir!" thuirt an coigreach, "feumaidh mi strìochdadh don bhinn eagalaich; oir chuir mi mi fèin don aon chor ri clana nan daoine 's gun fhios agam ciod a bha mi gabhail orm fèin. Tha mi naisgte, ceangailte. Chan urrainn mi dol air m' ais; ach Oh! soilleirich dhomh nas mìne mun chaochladh uamhasach seo, agus innis dhomh, guidheam ort, gach uile nì a tha tighinn na lorg." Thuirt e seo le guth air chrith – neul na crèadha tighinn air a ghnùis agus fallas fuar na bhoinneachan mòr air clàr-eudainn.

Air d' a chompanach fhaireachduinn gun robh an còmhradh a' fàs mòran na bu tuirsiche, 's na b' eagalaiche na bha idir taitneach leis, thuirt e gum feumadh am fear eile dol thun nan Sagartan arson an eòlais a bha ga dhith – nach buineadh mineachadh na cùise d' a dhreuchd'ann.

"Cionnas! Ciod!" thuirt an Coigreach, "chan urrainn gun do thuig mi gu ceart thu. Am bheil ri bàsachadh ach na Sagartan? Nach eil thusa ri bàsachadh mar an ceudna?"

Sheachainn am fear eile freagairt do na ceisdean seo; agus co luath 'sa b' urrainn e threòraich se e gu aon de na Teampuill sgiamhach a bha 's a' bhaile, agus dh'fhàg e ann sin e fo theagasg nan Sagartan.

Chual e uathasan mu neo-bhàsmhorachd an anama, agus gum biodh gach aon ann an sonas àghmhor, àrd, no ann an truaighe, 's am pian-dhòruinn re uile linntean na sìorruidheachd – gu cian nan cian. Rinn seo gach aigne na chridhe ioma-ghluasad bhon ghrunnd, agus bha e fo imcheist thruagh. Ach thionndaidh a theinnchràdh gu àrd-aoibhneas co luath 's a chual e gum feudadh e coir fhaghuinn air an t-sonas shuthainn, shìor le coilionadh chùmhnantan àraidh roimh àm a' bhàis. Nochd e a' leithid de dhian dheigh air mion-eòlas fhaghuinn air gach focal 'us lide de na cùmhnantan seo 's gun do chuir e ionghnadh 'us f' a dheireadh diomb air a luchd-teagaisg; oir cha robh iad arson a bhi air an ceasnachadh co dlùth, 's co teann.

Dh-iarr iad air a bhi toilichte leis na chual e aig an àm, agus e a' chur dàil an tuille còmhraidh gus an là màireach.

"Ciamar a nì mi sin?" ghlaodh an t-ùr-chreidmheach, "nach eil sibh ag innseadh dhomh gum feud àm bàs tighinn roimh an là màireach – gum feud e tighin air an uair seo fèin – Oh! ma thig e mun urrainn mi cùmhnantan na beatha shìorruidh a choi-lionadh ciod a nì mi? Na cumaibh uam an t-eòlas ro phriseil car aon mhionaid."

Chaidh na Sagartan air an aghaidh a mhinca-chadh am poncan creidimh dha agus b' ann thar tomhais a bha aoibhneas nuair a chual e gun robh na cùmhnantan a bha ga 'n iarraidh air, am bitheanta, furasda agus taitneach; agus nam biodh e dìleas gun tugadh am bàs dha làn fhuasgladh bho gach cunnart gach deuchainn, 's gach truaighe.

Bhon àm sin a mach thug an Coigreach air thalamh e fèin a suas le uile chridhe 's le uile neart do choilionadh nan cùmhnantan ri 'n robh a chor sìorruidh an earbsa. Ma bha e uair air bith air a bhuaireadh gu aon diubh a dhi-chuimhneachadh bha e gu grad air a lìonadh le mòr àmhghar, 'us aithreachas arson a bhi co cuthaichte; agus an uair a a bha càch ga tharruing gu amaideachd, no gu dearmad air a dhleasnas, cha robh ach an aon fhreagairt aige dhoibh a ghnàth –

"Tha mi ri bàsachadh! Tha mi ri bàsachadh!"

Am fad seo an sgeulachd bhrìghmhor. A luchd-leughaidh feuchaibh an toir sibh brigh as, agus an dean sibh buil dheth. Is àithne dhuibh-se uile "gum bheil e air òrduchadh do chaoine am bàs fhaotainn aon uair" – chan eil ach an aon uair – chan urrainn thu tighinn air t-ais gus a' chùis ath-dheanamh, no leasachadh; agus is àithne dhuibh nì is eagalaiche, "an dèigh a bhàis gun tig breitheanas." Eabh. Ix 27. Is àithne dhuibh gur e "tuarasdal a pheacaidh am bàs, ach gur e saor thiodhlac Dhe a' bheatha mhaireann ach trid Iosa Criosd ar Tighearna." Rom. V1 23. Is àithne dhuibh nach eil nì fon ghrein gu lèir co neo-chinnteach ri 'r beatha bhos.

"Oh! gun robh sibh glic, gun tuigeadh sibh seo, gun tugadh sibh fa' near ùr crìoch dheireannach!" Deut. xxxii 29. Deanaibh greim air a' bheatha mhaireannaich. Teichibh o 'n dara bàs.

" 'Se nis an t-àm bhi rèidh ri Dia
'Se nis an t àm thoirt gèill don Triath;
Am feadh a mhaireas là nan gràs
Feudaidh gach neach dol as o 'n bhàs.

'S nì seo an uair a sheachna' truaigh'
'S a thabhairt nèimh a mach le buaidh;
Seo cothrom àigh, ta dian dhol seach,
Deanar deagh bhuil dheth leis gach neach."

(Seann Sgeulachd)

A Cause of Wonder
[An Old Tale]

In the past, when storytellers received more esteem than they do now, it was related that a particular stranger was seen walking through one of the many towns in the east, and displaying great astonishment about everything round about him.

All the people gathered around him asking him where he was from and the reason for his journey. But they suddenly understood that he was ignorant of their language, and he himself was aware that he was ignorant of their language and their customs. But they saw evidence from his appearance and from his bearing that he was princely and noble; likewise, others were saying from the beginning that he was a man of high noble rank.

When he understood at last by means of the signs and gestures they were making that they were enquiring how he came to be there, he inclined his gaze up to the heavens. At this the people attending took particular notice that he was not one of them, and they bowed down as to worship him. He no sooner saw this than he beheld their attempt with great horror, and he threw himself on his knees and raised his hands toward Heaven making it clear that he was himself worshipping the Almighty.

Every one of them present that night now showed him great kindness and they invited him, pulling him towards their houses, persuading him to be their special guest. He went with a man of nobility to his home and in his company he quickly progressed in learning the national language and in a very short time he polished his conversation, attending to every one that he met in the company.

Long after, the head of the house, obtaining an account about the stranger's status and native-land, was very astonished, and at last the stranger decided on a certain evening to reveal the mystery to him. When the evening came they climbed up to one of the high streets across this wealthy and populous town.

It was a resplendent sight that was below them. Thousands of lanterns were shining among those cheerful streets. Hundreds of fine courts, and high ornamental windows were pouring out light on the great river that was gently moving quietly along through the whole length of the town, and bearing on its breast great ships laden with precious cargo – with elegance and beauty from every quarter of the world.

The clarsach began, and sweet sounds of the violin were heard on every hand. There was the joyful shout of the newly married men, and the sweet tender voice of the newly married women were likewise heard. There was music, and happiness, and pleasure around on every side. The stranger looked for a while on what was below him, and he listened to the music, to the noise and the bustle of the large town. But suddenly he lifted his face to the starry heavens, and he fixed his eye on the resplendent evening star.

"Do not be surprised" he said to the gentlemen, "that I am looking with so much longing on the glitter of the star on that window glass. Yonder was my home and my dwelling place. Alas! It was! Up to a short time ago my home was in that beautiful star until, enticed by the rarity and the wonder, and by curiosity, I came here on a journey from afar. Frequently I looked with great astonishment on this world that appeared like a gleaming pearl in the firmament, and my desire was so strong concerning it that I got my wish.

The Almighty gave full permission and liberty to me to journey across the wide heavens to this far-off place; but there was one stipulation attached to this freedom – that henceforth I must make this place my home, and put up with the condition of the inhabitants whether they be easy or hard for me. I agreed with this condition. I am now under the same circumstance as the children of men, but explain to me, as minutely as you can, I beseech you, the meaning and substance of everything I see and hear around about me."

"Certainly, O excellent Sir" answered the gentleman, "though I am ignorant of the customs and blessings of the country that you left, I am so happy that you did choose as wisely as you did, and there is great reason for you rejoicing, for you were very fortunate finding a corner of the world with as much joy and happiness as is found in this prosperous and happy town. And be assured that it is my intention to guide you into every pleasant and excellent thing that is within these walls."

Accompanying this kind offer the Stranger was taken to every feast and entertainment, watched every sport and merry assembly, became acquainted with every joy, every fondness and every pleasure of the people of that place who wished him good luck; he was in great measure himself adjusting to the customs, and to their ways when he found that certain changes were completely altering his mind and feelings.

As he passed the cool of the day about the edge of the town, he observed a wide area with a surrounding high dark wall. He asked.

"Why is this place shut up?"

"This is" answered the gentleman, "the place of burial."

"I do not understand you very well" said the stranger, "what is the name of this place?"

"The place of burial, or the place of interment, the place where the body is deposited," said the gentleman.

"Excuse me" said his companion, a little puzzled, "be so good as to make this matter clear to me. I don't understand whose places of burial. I don't understand who they are that are buried? I don't understand what these burial places are."

The other man explained the matter to him as well as he was able. The stranger's complexion changed to one of great astonishment as he replied, "this thing is unknown to me or my imagination or in my world, if I am understanding anything at all about this fearful business. Tell me then, without delay, let me beseech you, everything you know about this sad and terrible thing, death."

"Indeed, you truly are a Stranger," said the gentleman, "when you do not know that we must all, sooner or later, surrender to death. And though it does not have the same dread for us as it has for you, it is death nevertheless. It is, unfortunately, our way, and it is a bitter and sorrowful thing that is our fate; and as regards it, it is a thing rarely mentioned in polite company, not being mannerly. This is why you have not yet heard about it in your time among us. But as your countrymen are not subject to death I advise you to return quickly to your society – because it is certain you will not escape it here; and I have told you the truth and neither I, nor any other man, is capable of guaranteeing your life for a day, or an hour."

"My woe! It is my complete ruin!" said the Stranger, "I must submit to this terrible sentence because I have put myself under the same condition as the children of men without understanding what I was committing myself to. I am bound, obligated. I am not able to go back; but oh! explain to me in detail about this terrible death, and tell me, I beg you, the consequences of every thing that is coming." He said this with a trembling voice – a grave cloud coming over his face and large cold drops of sweat on his forehead.

Perceiving that his companion's speech was becoming increasingly sad and fearful and not at all pleasant, he said that the other man needed to go to the Priests for the information that he was lacking – as explaining the matter did not belong to his office.

"How! What!" said the stranger, "I am not able to understand you correctly. Are you all dying except the Priests? Are they not all likewise perishing?"

The other man avoided replying to this question, and as fast as he was able, he directed him to one of the handsome Temples that were in the town, and he left him under the instruction of the Priests.

He heard from them about the immortality of the soul and that everyone will be supremely happy, or in misery and torment for all eternity. This caused much agitation from the bottom of his heart, and he was under wretched anxiety. But his agony was quickly turned to joy as he heard that he might obtain a state of eternal, everlasting happiness by fulfilling certain conditions before the time of his death. He revealed his strong longing to become thoroughly acquainted with each word and syllable of these conditions and he astonished them and towards the end his teachers were resentful towards him as they were not used to being questioned so closely and incessantly.

They asked him to be satisfied with what he heard at the time, and he postponed further conversation until the next day.

"How can I do that?" cried the new believer, "have you not just told me that death might come before another day – that it may come this very hour – Oh! if it shall come about what shall I do to fulfil the conditions of eternal life? Do not keep this very precious knowledge from me for one minute."

The Ministers went on explaining the details of the faith to him and his joy was beyond measure when he heard that the numerous conditions that were demanded of him were pleasant and easy; and if he were faithful unto death full deliverance from every danger, every distress, and every misery would be his.

From that time on the stranger from above gave all his heart and all his strength to fulfilling the stipulations which were the conditions for eternal hope. If he was at any time tempted to neglect any of them he was soon filled with great sorrow and repentance for being so foolish; and when others were pulling him towards folly, there was only one answer he always had for them – "I am dying! I am dying!"

This is a long, meaningful legend. Readers, heed its meaning, and make use of it. It is a commandment for you all "that it is appointed unto men once to die" – there is only one time – you are not able to come back to do it all again, nor to improve; and it is a commandment, a fearful thing for you that, "after death comes judgment." (Heb. 9.27).

It is known to you that "the wages of sin is death, but that the gift of God is eternal life through Jesus Christ our Lord." (Rom. 6 v.23). And you know that there is nothing under the sun altogether as uncertain as our life here.

"Oh! that you were wise, that you understand this, that you would consider your latter end." (Deut. 32 v.29).

Take hold of eternal life. Flee from the second death.
Now is the time to be reconciled to God
Now is the time to submit yourself to the Lord.
While the days of grace last
Everyone may escape from death.
In this time of misery
Heaven is given to those who overcome;
This glorious opportunity, is fast going past
Every one should make good use of it.

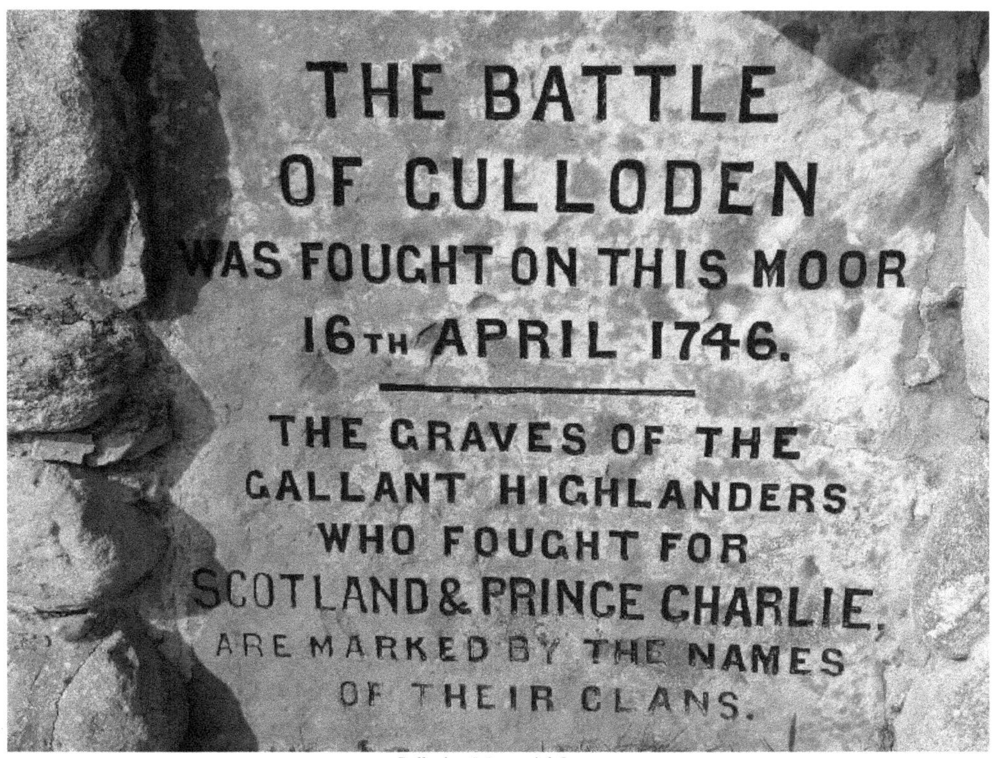

Culloden Memorial Stone

74 Raonull agus Collunn Gun Cheann

[Sean Sgeulachd le 'Fior Gaidheal', Geelong]

Tha ann am Morair mhic 'ic Dhughail baile ris an abrar an Traigh, ri taobh Chros. Anns a bhaile sin tha uamh Cholluinn gun Cheann.

Bha 'n uamh seo 'o chian air a tathaich i riochd neach gun cheann, ach ciod bu ghin den riochd a bha 'n sin bu dàna leinn a luaidh.

Aig àm àraidh chaidh doine' chloinn llios' a thoirt cuiridh chum bainnse d' a bhrathair altruim, da'm b' ainm Raonull Do'nullach, mac Ailein oig 'ic – Dhughail Mhorair. Bha slighe mhic Illios am fagus don uaimh anns an robh Collunn gun Cheann a' tàmh, ach, mo thruaighe; cha b' i 'n fhailte, a fhuair e anns an dol seachadh, ach cò'ail fhuilleachdach 'o nach do thill e riamh a dh'innseadh sgeoil. Fhuaireadh e an sin, air an ath là, na ablach gun deò, agus a ghunna snìomhte mar ghad spairte na mhuineal.

Chuir an gnìomh gàbhaidh seo mòr dhoil 'ios ai Raonall. Rùnaich e air ball comhail a thabhairt don cholluinn, agus fuil a dhàimhich a dhìoladh. Bu churaidh calma Raonull: b' fhaoin leis comhairle nan càirde' sin a dh'asluich air gun trèigeadh e a rùn misneachail. Cha chuireadh seud impidh air. Dh'falbh e air an ath oiche. Ràinig e 'n t-àite 's an robh an Fuathas. Thar iad an carramh a chèile.

"Gu cruaidh, cuideach, do-bheumach."

Theirinn lann Raonuill air "Cruth èiti" na Colluinn mar dhèann sitheadh na Beithir milltich, ach b' fhaoin 's bu shuarach an t-aithear. Dhlùthaich iad ann an gleachd agus bhuathaich Raonull 's an strì.

'S truime leam do ghlùn air mo mhaothan a Raonuill mhòir ars' a chollunn, na mile sice 'o d' lainn sgaitich.
Bu mhàth a chomhraig mac Illios rium mun do ribeadh a chasan na bhreachdan, ach shaor sin mise.

Bha luchd farclais ann a' dèanamh falach talamhuin air Raonull agus ge nach fac iad neach, do bhrìgh doirchead na h-oiche, chual iad na dh'airis sin 'n den chòmhra, ach bha mòran tuillidh sin de sheanachas eadar Raonull agus a Chollunn as nach tug iadsan oigheam.

Mu dheire, cheadaich Raonull don cholluinn a' bhi triall, agus cha bu luaithe a thog e' ghlun deth na dh'èirich e air cirein guanach na h-oiteig a seinn a phuirt a leanas:-

" 'S fada bhuam fhèin beinn 'o h-eadaruin,
'S fada bhuam fhèin bealach a bhorbhain,
'S fada bhuam fhèin beinn 'o h-eadaruin;
'S fada gun teagamh 'uam bealach a bhorbhain.
Cul nan mulaichean – bràigh nam bealaichean-
Cul nam mulaichean – bealach a bhorbhain."

Bu mhìnic an dèidh sin a chlùinnteadh Raonull a' cluich a' phuirt sin air a phìob-mhòir.

Raonull and the Headless Monster
[An Old Tale retold by a 'True Gael']

In Morar there is a MacDonal town called, Traigh, near Cross. In that town is Cholluinn gun Cheann's cave. In olden times frequenting this cave was the ghost of a being without a head, but it was a ghost celebrated in song.

At a certain time, a man's son, Illios, gave a wedding feast for his foster brother, who was called Raonull Do'nullach, mac Ailein oig 'ic-Dhughail Morair. Illios was approaching near the cave and was resting, but alas; it was not a welcome he got passing by, but a bloody meeting from which he never returned to tell the story. He was found then the next day a lifeless mangled carcase, with a gunshot wound as though an iron bar had been thrust through his jaws.

The great tragedy to Illios stirred up Raonull's district. He immediately proposed to speak to the Cholluinn and revenge his family's blood. Raonull was a brave hero; he foolishly ignored the counsel of his friends who implored him to quit his brave intention, urging him that it was not worth it. He left the next night and arrived at the place where the Spectre was. They came in contact with each other.
"Gu cruaidh, cuidreach, do-bheumach."

I would say Raonull's sword fell on the "Dreadful Form" of the Colluinn, the destructive Beast, like an impetuous force, but it was unavailing and ineffective. They joined in battle and Raonull was furious in the struggle.

"There is sorrow in my breast for your family, great Raonull", said the Chollunn, of the Smooth Mile, from under the sharp sword. "Your son Illios fought well against me until his feet were entangled in his plaid, but I freed that."

People were hiding on the ground eavesdropping on Raonull and although they never saw anyone, because of the darkness of the night, they heard the report of that conversation, but there was much more of the conversation between Raonull and the Chollunn that they did not get.

At last Raonull allowed the Cholluinn to depart, but no sooner had he lifted his knee from off him that the Cholluinn, trembling and unsteady in the gusty wind, sang the following tune:-

Far am I from my own Ben Hederin;
Far am I from the "Defile of murmuring".
Far am I from my own Ben Hederin;
Far am I, without doubt, from the "Defile of Murmuring".

Murmur of the pass/mountain pass

[And often after that Raonull could be heard playing that tune on his pipes]

75 Raonull agus an Sgiobair

[Sean Sgeulachd le 'Fior Gaidheal', Geelong Bhictoria]

B' e Iain Garbh Mac Ile Challunn Raasai bràthair màthar Raonull seo. Thàinig long eilthire gu cala ann an Raasa agus thug Ian Garbh cuireadh don Sgiobair a dh'ionnsuidh a chaisteil.

Ri linn daibh bhi fearas-chuideachd chuir an sgiobair a long an geall nach togradh duine, san eilein bha a chaithreach e; mu choinneamh sin, chuir Iain Garbh oigreachd an geall. Chuir Iain Garbh fios a dh'ionnsuidh Raonull agus thàinig e.

B' e Iain Garbh fèin a thug a chead ionnsuidh air an sgiobair. Thug e sgrothadh neo-dheis-thineach air a bhodach ach an àite thogail o 'n chathair s' ann a sgiol e 'n t-aodach dheth!

Chuir sin mi-thapadh air Iain Garbh oir shaoil e gum bu bhuidseach a bha e cràgairt.

An sin tharruin Raonull 'n charramh. Ghlac e air gach taobh crios-meadhoin an sgiobair agus le aon tulgadh sgiobiaich e leis na bha os cionn nan cruachann, a fàgail na bha fodha sin na shuidhe mar a bha e.

Mar sin choisinn aonuil long a choigrich, agus ghlèidh, e 'n oighreachd do bhràthair a mhàthair.

Sin agaibh sgeula Iain 'Ic Raonuill, agus ma 's breug bhuam i 's breug dam 'n ionnsuidh i.

[Seann Sgeulachd le 'Fior Gaidheal', Geelong]

Raonull and the Captain
[An Old Tale retold by 'True Gael', Geelong Victoria]

Raonull Do'nullach, mac Ailein oig 'ic-Dhughail Morair was Iain Garbh Mac 'lle Challunn Raasay's maternal uncle. A ship came to a harbour at Raasay and Iain Garbh invited the Captain to the castle.

During their raillery the Captain wagered his ship that there was not a man on the island who could lift him from his chair; against that Iain Garbh put his inheritance. Iain Garbh sent word to Raonull and he came.

Iain Garbh himself made the first attempt on the Captain. He gave a tug on the otherwise ugly old man but the part that was lifted from the chair was the clothes from off him. Iain Garbh was dismayed at this because he thought that it was a wizard that he had handled indelicately.

Then Raonull took his turn. He grabbed each side of the Captain's waist and with one toss he raised him above his hip leaving the chair behind.

In that manner he won a marauder's ship, and he retained the estate for his maternal uncle.

That is the story of Iain 'Ic Raonull, and if it has amused you then I am pleased.

[An old tale told by 'True Gael', Geelong]

76 Cù A' Chuain Ghuirm

[Sean sgeulachd le Dòmhnall Peutan]

Anns na linntibh fon eug, air oirthir na Mara Guirme bha iasgair a chòmhnuidh. Bha e daonnan ag iasgach ach cha robh a mhòr thoradh na lorg. Bha e fàs glè aosmhor agus bha eagal air gum bitheadh e ann an teanntachd (sa bhean maille ris) mun tigeadh a chrìoch. Là de na làithibh, air feasgar ciùin ciutharach chunnaic e meall ceò dorcha, dùmhail agus thàinig Guth a mach as a' mheall.

"Cò sid?" ars' an t-iasgair.

"Mise, Cu-dubh a' Chuain Ghuirm."

"De tha dhith ort? ars' an t-iasgair.

"Tha dhith orm do chuideachadh," ars' an Guth. "Tha thu nise ioma bliadhna ri iasgach agus tha thu fhathast bochd. De bheir thu dhomhsa mu sheolas mi dòigh dhuit air am faigh thu daonnan làn a' bhàta de dh'iasg?"

"Nì sam bith is urrainn mi," ars' an t-iasgair.

"Thoir dhomh a chiad mhac a bhios agad," ars' 'n Guth.

Smaointich an t-iasgair car ghreise - tha mi fhèin ceithear fichead bliadhna agus a bhean agam trì fichead sa deich, 's cha dù dhi clann bhi aice, 's leis a sin faodaidh mi gabhail ris.

Thuirt e ris a' Ghuth; "Bheir mi dhuit e."

"Glè mhath," ars' an Guth, "cuir a mach do lìon." Rinn an t-iasgair sid.

"Slaod a steach e," ars' an Guth.

Thòisich an t-iasgair air slaodadh 's b' e sid an slaodadh bha gramail. Cha d' fhuair an t-iasgair truadh riamh a leithid do throm-obair, ach lìon e am bàta gus an robh i 'n impis dol fodha.

"Gheibh thu 'n urrad sin a h-uile uair a chuireas tu do lìon," ars' an Guth.

"Slan leat, thig mi dh'iarraidh do mhic nuair a bhios e seachd bliadhn' diag a dh'aois."

Chaidh an t-iasgair dhachaidh gu cridheal èibhinn, reic e 'n t-iasg agus dh'fhàs e beairteach, agus naoi mìosan an dèigh na h-oidhche chual e 'n Guth, rugadh mac dha. Shoirbhich gu math leis an t-seann iasgair.

Thug e deagh sgoil agus ionnsachadh da mhac, gus an robh a mhac seachd bliadhna diag a dh'aois. An sin ghairm e air a mhac 's thuirt e ris; "a mhic tha thu nis a dh'aois seachd bliadhna diag, agus a nochd thig Cù dubh a' Chuain Ghuirm air do thòir agus bheir e leis thu, chan urrainn mise do shàbhaladh. Tog ort, thoir an saoghal fo 'd cheann, theagamh nach beir e ort."

Dh'fhalbh an t-òganach. Thug e 'n saoghal fo cheann, choisich e gu dian rè an latha gu dorcha nan trath nuair ràinig e taigh tuathanach. Dh'iarr e lòn agus cuid oidhche air an tuathanach.

"Gheibh thu sin'," ars' an tuathanach. Nuair bham biadh seachad thuirt an tuathanach ris - "Feumaidh tu an oidche chuir seachd san t-sabhal agus seo cù gu d' dhìon."

"C'ainm tha air a' chù?" ars' an Gille.

"Cluas-ri-Claistneachd" arsa an tuathanach, "cluinnidh e m feur a tighinn troi 'n talamh."

Chaidh e le chù don t-sabhal ach cha bu chadal da, a' feitheamh, gun fhios nach tigeadh Cù dubh a' Chuain Ghuirm.

Bha Cluas-ri-Claistneachd a giùigeadh sa liùigeadh a chluasan. Ma dheareadh thuirt e, "Cluinneam,"

"De chluinneas tu laochain?" ars' an Gille.

"Cu-dubh a' Chuain Ghuirm tighinn air do thòir, arsa Cluas-ri-Claistneachd.

"O, de nì mi?" ars' an Gille.

"Leig dhòmhsa choinneachadh," arsa Cluas-ri-Claistneachd, "is se mo bharail gun cuir mi moille air."

"Dean sin ma tha," ars' an Gille.

Nuair thàinig Cluas-ri-Claistneachd air ais thuirt e ris a' Ghille, "Caidil gu là cha tig an Cu-dubh a chur dragh ort a nochd."

Moch sa mhaduinn, 's am biadh maduinn gu sùmhail air ùrlar a ghoille chuir is chum e cas an t-siubhail air thoiseach, agus an dorcha nan tràth ràinig e taigh tuathanach. Dh'iarr e lòn 's cuid oidche.

"Gheibh thu sin," ars' an tuathanach. Nuair bham biadh seachad thuirt an tuathanach ris,

"Feumaidh tu an oidhche chur seachad san t-sabhal agus seo cù gu d' dhìon."

"C'ainm tha air a chù?" ars' an Gille.

"Luaths," ars' an tuathanach. "Bheireadh e air a ghaoth luath Mhàirt a bha roimhe 's cha bheireadh a ghaoth luath Mhàirt a bhios na dhèigh airsan."

Chaidh e le choin don t-sabhal. Air dhoibh a bhi ann, bha Cluas-ri-Claistneachde.

Bha Cluas-ri-Claistneachd a giùigeadh sa liùigeadh a chluasan. Ma dheareadh thuirt e,

"Cluinneam,"

"De chluinneas tu laochain?" ars' an Gille.

"Cu-dubh a' Chuain Ghuirm tighinn air do thòir, arsa Cluas-ri-Claistneachd.

"O, de nì mi?" ars' an Gille.

"Cha bhi mise fada beirsinn air", arsa Luaths?

"Cum e gus an ruig mise air," arsa Cluas-ri-Claistneachd, "ma fhuair Cù dubh a' Chuain Ghuirm a ghiollachd an raoir gheibh e thrì giolladh an oidhche seo.

Nuair thàinig na coin air ais thuirt iad ris a' Ghille, "caidil gu latha, thug sinne a dheagh liodairt da; cha chuir e dragh ort a nochd."

Moch sa mhaduinn sam biadh maidne gu sùmhail air ùrlar a ghoille chuir, 's chum e cas-an-t-siùbhail air thoiseach agus an dorcha nan tràth ràinig e taigh tuathanach. Dh'iarr e lòn 's cuid oidhche.

"Gheibh thu sin," ars' an tuathanach.

Nuair a bham biadh seachad thuirt an tuathanach ris- "Feumaidh tu an oidhche chuir seachad san t-sabhal agus seo cù gu d' dhìon."

"C'ainm tha air a' chù?" ars' an Gille.

"Tha Neart," ars' an tuathanach.

Chaidh e le choin don t-sabhal air dhaibh a bhi ann bha Cluas-ri-Claistneachd ri giùigeadh 's a liuigeadh a chluasan. Ma dheireadh thuirt e "Cluinneam."

"De chluinneas tu laochain?" ars' an gille!

"Cù dubh-a-Chuain Ghuirm tighinn air do thoir," arsa Cluas-ri-Claistneachd.

"O, de nì mi?" ars' an Gille.

"O," arsa Neart, "Nam beireadh cuidigin air sa chumail gus an ruigeadh mise air, bheirinn dha a dheagh ghiollachd."

"Cha bhi mise fada beirsinn air," arsa Luaths. A-mach gabh "Luaths" agus air a shàil "Cluas-ri-Claistneachd" agus nan dèigh gu toirteil mar b' iomchuidh bha an laoch, "Neart."

Bha trì duirn na oidhche thairis mun tàinig iad air an ais. "Thug sinn dà do ghiollachd a nochd agus nach cuir e dragh tuillidh oirnn," arsa Cluas-ri-Claistneachd.

Moch sa mhaduinn 's am biadh maduinn gu sùmhail air ùrlar a bhoille chuir is chum e cas-an-t-siubhail air thoiseach bho là gu là gus an d' thuirt Cluas-ri-Claistneachd, "Cluinneam."

"De chluinneas tu laochain" ars' an Gille.

"Leigemid air n-anail," arsa Cluas-ri-Claistneachd rinn iad sin agus an sin thuirt Cluas-ri-Claistneachd, "ann an ceann thrì laithean thig sin gu baile mòr, agus tha Banrigh a riaghladh ann, agus thu i a mionnan sa bòid nach pòsadh i ach fear a thigeadh a marcachd air tarbh. Nis tha tarbh air an rathad, beiridh sin air agus marcaich e don bhaile agus pòs a' Bhanrigh."

"Ach," arsa easan, "na dealaich ruinne."

" 'S mi nach dealaich gu brath." arsa 'n Gille.

Rug iad air an tarbh agus mharcaich e don bhaile agus phòs e Bhanrigh. Cha dealaicheadh e ris na coin, cha robh sid a còrdadh ris a' Bhanrigh. Là do na laithean, thuirt Cluas-ri-Claistneachd, "Cluinneam."

"De chluinneas tu laochain?" ars' an Gille.

"Tha do bhean agus Cù dubh a' Chuain Ghuirm gu dìomhair san taigh-chùil a' dèannamh suas do mharbhadh; gu sin a' dhèannamh tha a' Bhanrigh a' dol a ghairm faoghaid trèigidh iad thu gu lèir is thig an sin an Cù Dubh gu d' mharbhadh. Tha Bhanrigh san cu airson sinne a ghlasadh a suas ann an seòmar làidir, ach na leig thusa sin a' dhèanamh."

" 'S mi nach leig," ars' an Gille. Chaidh an fhaoghaid a ghairm, thàinig latha na faoghaid agus chaidh na coin a ghlasadh suas. Ann an teas na faoghaid fhuair an gille e fèin na aonar agus chunnaic e Cù dubh-a' Chuain Ghuirm tighinn aige los a mharbhadh. B' aithreach leis na coin a bhi glaiste.

Bho na glasaibh thuirt Cluas-ri-Claistneachd "Cluinneam."

"De chluinneas tu?" arsa Luaths.

"Tha mac an iasgair ann an teanntachd chruaidh. Tha e na aonar 's tha Cù dubh-a'-Chuain-Ghuirm greasadh aige," arsa Cluas-ri-Claistneachd.

"Nam faighinn-sa mach," arsa Luaths "dheanainn cobhair air mun ruig an cù air".

"A mach theirig," arsa Neart, is le spòg thòisich bhuail e 'n dorus agus chaidh an dorus na spealgan. A bha Cù-dubh-a'-Chuain-Ghuirm a sìneadh a làmh gu graim fhaodainn air a ghille, bha Luaths na ugan 's chum e grèim air gus an tàinig Cluas-ri-Claistneachd agus Neart agus liodair is liodair iad e gus nach b' urrainn e gluasad. Dh'fhàg iad sinnte air an raon e.

Bha gach ni gu math gus aon là an d' thuirt Cluas-ri-Claistneachd, "Cluinneam."

"De chluinneas tu 'laochain?"

"Cù-dubh-a-Chuain-Ghuirm agus do bhean a' dèanamh suas do mharbhadh," arsa Cluas-ri-Claistneachd.

"Cia mar a nì iad e?" ars' an Gille.

"Tha Cù-dubh-a'-Chuain-Ghuirm a creidsinn nach urrain e de mharbhadh se toilched inntinn, agus leis a sin chuir e fo bhoidean do bhean gu marbhadh i e fèin agus gun gearradh i suas e agus gun deanadh i pìthean deth. Gun gairmeadh i fèisd agus gun toireadh iad ort cuid den na phìthean itheadh, agus an uair a dh'itheadh tu dheth mharbhadh e thu," arsa Cluas-ri-Claistneach, "ach na ith thusa dheth agus na leig leò sinne ghlasadh a suas."

" 'S mi nach leig," ars' an Gille. Chaidh an fhèisd a ghairm. Cha stadadh a Bhanrigh gus an glaiste na coin. Bhagair i, chaoin agus bhuralaich i, gus ma dheireadh chaidh na coin a ghlasadh a suas ann an seòmar nì bu laidire na bha iad riamh. Chaidh an fhèisd air aghaidh gu cridheil.

Choitich agus choitich iad deoch làidir air a Ghille gus ma dheireadh nach robh fhios aige de a bha e deanamh agus thug iad uige a mhias phìthean, agus dhith e dheth agus thuit e marbh fon bhòrd.

Bha na coin glaiste suas ann an seòmar làidir, an dorus do dharach 's do dh'iarrunn, agus thuirt Cluas-ri-Claistneachd "Cluinneam."

"De chluinneas tu?" arsa Luaths.

"Mac an iasgair marbh fon bhòrd," arsa Cluis-ri-Claistneachd.

"A! na'm faighinn-sa mach as a seo," arsa Luaths, "leighisinn 's e fhathast."

"Cia mar a rachadh agad air sin a' dhèannamh?" arsa Neart.

"Rinn am puinnsean ball dubh anns a chridh' aige, dh'fhosglainn e 's ghearrainn am ball dubh as a chridhe, dheoghlainn e agus chuirinn a rithistann e, agus dh'èireadh mac an iasgair cho clàn sa bha e riamh," arsa Luaths.

"Mu nì thu sin," arsa Neart, "seo fosgladh dhuit."

Ghabh e roid bho thaobh cùil an t-seomair agus chaidh e direach le ghnos troimh an dorus, agus Luaths agus Cluas-ri-Claistneachd as an dhèigh. Ruith Luaths air thoiseach s cha b' fhada gus an robh e steach san t-seòmar. Dh'fhosgail e 'n Gille, gheàrr e 'm ball-dubh as a chridhe dheoghail e e, chuir e rithist ann e, agus leum an gille suas beò slàn mar a bha e roimhe.

"Falbhmaid, chan eile math dhuinn fuireach nis faide," arsa Luaths. Dh'fhalbh iad; shiubhail iad gus an d' ràinig iad dealachadh thrì rathaid, stad iad.

"Nis," arsa Cluas-ri-Claistneachd, "a mhic an iasgair tha sinne 's tusa ri dealachadh an seo."

"Cha dean mi dealachadh ruibh idir," ars' an Gille.

Chruinnich iad ma dheibhinn ach cha dealaicheadh e-asan riu. Mu dheireadh thuirt Luaths "cò sid a tighinn ad' dhèigh?"

Sheall an gille, chan fhaca e duine, ach nuair thionndaidh e ris na coin cha robh cù ri fhaicinn. Bha e duilich gun chaill e na coin agus bha e fo mhòr iomagain. Cha robh fhios aige de an taobh a thionndadh e. Mu dheireadh thall ghabh e air adhart air aon do na rathaidean, gu ciaradh an fheasgair nuair ràinig e tigh mòr briagh ann am badan coille agus duine spaisdearachd aig a cheann.

Bheannaich e don duine 's bheannaich an duine dha agus thuirt e- " 'Se do bheatha, mhic an iasgair. 'S fhada bha mi feitheamh riut."

"Tha 'm barrachd eolais agaibh," ars' an Gille, "chan fhiosrach dhomh gu faca mi riabh sibh."

"Chunnaic thu iomadh uair mi," ars' an t-uasal, "nach cuimhneach leat an cù bha agad, Cluas-ri-Claistneachd. Is mise Cluas-ri-Claistneachd, ach thig a' staigh, bidh an t-acras ort."

Chaidh iad a staigh. Bham bòrd làn do gach ni feumail agus grinn, agus theann iad ris agus thòisich Cluas-ri-Claistneachd agus thuirt e- "Tha sinn a seo triùir bhràithrean agus tha astar là eadar gach taighe againn chaidh air cur fo geasaibh gus an saoradh sinn thusa bho Chù-dubh a' Chuain Ghuirm."

Thug iad mìos a fèisteadh agus thug iad mìos eile 'n tigh Luaths, san treas mìos an tigh Neart an duine toirteil treun, 's chuir iad a sin dachaidh e gu sona beairteach gus dhealaich mise ris. Ma's briad uam e 's briad ugam e.

Blood-Hound of the Green-Blue Ocean

[An old tale recollected by Donald Beaton]

Long, long ago there was a ghost and on the coast of the bluest sea was a fisherman's house. He was always fishing but was not very successful in his search. He was becoming very old and was afraid he, together with his wife, would end their days in poverty. One day on a calm evening he saw a patch of mist in the dusk, and a voice came out of the mist.

"Who is there?" said the fisherman.

"It is I, Blood-Hound of the Green-Blue Ocean."

"What are you?" said the fisherman."

"I want to help you." said the Voice. "You have been fishing for many years and you are still poor. What will you give me for clearing a channel for you in such a way for you always to get a boat load of fish?"

"I will do anything I can," said the fisherman.

"Promise to give me your first son," said the Voice. The fisherman thought for a while - I am myself eighty years and my wife is seventy, and children cannot be expected of her, so in that case I will accept the deal.

"I will give him to you." he said to the Voice;

"Very good" said the Voice, "put out your net."

And that's what the fisherman did.

"Pull it in." said the Voice. The fisherman began to pull and the resistance was strong. The poor fisherman had never worked so hard, but he filled the boat until it was almost sinking.

"You will get as many every time" said the Voice; "Farewell, I will come to ask for your son when he is seventeen years of age."

The fisherman went home cheerful, he sold the fish and he soon became rich, and nine months after he heard the Voice, a son was born to him. The old fisherman prospered.

He gave a good education to his son, until he was seventeen years of age. Then he called on his son and he said to him; “My son you are now seventeen years of age, and tonight Cù Dubh a’ Chuain Ghuirm searches for you to take you away with him. I have not the power to save you. Rise up and find your way in the world and perhaps he will not catch you.”

The youth left and took his chance in the world. He quickly walked during the day until dark when he reached a farmer’s house where he asked for food and a night’s lodging.

“You shall get that,” said the farmer. When the meal was over the farmer said to him, “You must spend the evening in the barn and this dog will protect you.”

“What is its name?” said the boy.

“Listener”, said the farmer, “he can hear the grass growing.”

He went with the dog to the barn but he could not sleep, fearing, but not knowing if Cù Dubh a’ Chuain Ghuirm would come.

Listener was pricking up its ears. At last it said, “Listen”.

“What do you hear my little champion?” said the lad.

“Cù Dubh a’ Chuain Ghuirm coming in pursuit”, said Listener.

“O, what will I do?” said the lad.”

“Let me meet him,” said Listener, “I believe that I can delay him.”

“Do that then,” said the lad.

When Listener returned he said to the lad, “Sleep now until day, Cù Dubh will not come to trouble you tonight.

Early in the morning, he breakfasted quietly on the floor and set out to travel on foot, and by dark he reached another farmer’s house. He asked for provisions and a night’s lodging.

“You will get that,” said the farmer. When the meal was finished the farmer said to him,

“You must spend the night in the barn with this dog to protect you.”

“What is the dog’s name?”, said the Lad.

"Swift," said the farmer. "He could catch a swift March wind that was before him, but a swift March wind could not catch him. He went with the dogs to the barn where they were to lodge.

Listener was pricking up its ears? At last it said "Listen."

"What do you hear", said the lad.

"Cù Dubh a' Chuain Ghuirm coming in pursuit." Said Listener.

"O,' what will I do?" said the lad.

"I will not be long catching him," said Swift.

"Hold him until reach I him," said Listener. "If Cù Dubh a' Chuain Ghuirm got a serving last night he shall get three servings this night." When the dogs came back they said to the Lad,

"Sleep till day, we severely maimed him today; he will not trouble you tonight."

Early in the morning he breakfasted quietly on the floor and immediately set out to travel on foot, and by dark he reached a farmer's house. He asked for provisions and for a night's lodging. "You shall get that," said the farmer.

When the supper was finished the farmer said to him- "You must spend the evening in the barn and this dog will protect you."

"What is the dog's name?" said the Lad.

"It is Strength," said the farmer.

He went with the dogs to the barn in which they were to stay. Listener was pricking up his ears. At last it said, "Listen".

"What do you hear my little champion?" said the lad.

"Cù Dubh a' Chuain Ghuirm coming in pursuit", said Listener.

"O, what will I do?" said the lad."

"O," said Strength, "If someone will catch him and restrain him until I reach him, I would give him a severe serving."

"I will not be long catching him," said Swift. He took off and on his heel Listener and after them, as was fitting, was the hero Strength. The evening was three quarters over before they came back.

"We gave it two serves tonight and it will not give us any more trouble," said Listener.

Early in the morning the young man breakfasted quietly on the floor and immediately set out on foot day after day until Listener said to him, "Listen."

"What do you hear little hero?" said the lad.

"Let us have a rest," said Listener. They did that and then Listener said, "At the end of three days we come to a large town, and a Queen reigns there, and she has sworn an oath not to marry until a man comes to town riding on a bull.

"Now, said Listener, a bull is on the road, catch it and ride it to the town and marry the Queen."

"But," he added, "we must part."

"I will never part from you." said the Lad.

They caught the bull and the lad rode it into the town and he married the Queen. He would not part from the dogs; however, they were not on good terms with the Queen.

One day Listener said, "Listen."

"What do you hear little hero?" said the Lad.

"Your wife and Cù Dubh a' Chuain Ghuirm are in the back house secretly planning your death; the Queen is arranging a hunt, and when her signal comes they will abandon you altogether and then the Cù Dubh will come to kill you. The Queen is going to lock us up in this strong room but you must not allow that."

"I will not allow that," said the Lad.

The day of the hunt arrived and the dogs were locked up. In the heat of the pursuit the boy found himself alone and he saw Cù Dubh a' Chuain Ghuirm coming at him intending to kill him.

The dogs fretted that they were locked up and from the lock-up Listener said, "Listen."

"What do you hear?" said Swift.

"The son of the fisherman is in danger. He is alone and Cù Dubh a' Chuain Ghuirm is hastening at him," said Listener.

"If I could get out," said Swift, "I could rescue him from that dog."

"Go out," said Strength, and by clawing he began to strike at the door and it splintered. Out they got, Swift first. When Cù Dubh a' Chuain Ghuirm was stretching his hand to lay his might on the boy, Swift held him by the throat until Listener and Strength arrived and they were tearing and mangling him until he could not move. They left him stretched on the field.

Every thing was well until one day Listener said "Listen."

"What do you hear little hero?" said the lad.

"Cù Dubh a' Chuain Ghuirm and your wife getting ready to kill you." said Listener.

"How will they do it?" asked the Lad.

"Cù Dubh a' Chuain Ghuirm believes that he is not able to kill you as long as we are with you, but he desires your death, and with that he put your wife under a vow to kill him herself and to cut him up in order to make a pie out of him. Then, calling a feast she will give you a piece of the pie to eat, and when you have eaten it, it will kill you." said Listener. "But do not eat of it and do not let them lock us up."

"I will not allow that," said the Lad.

The feast was called. The Queen was not satisfied until the dogs were locked up. She threatened, and she wept and wailed, until at last the dogs were locked up in a room that they had made even stronger. The feast went forward cheerfully. Again, and again, they gave the lad intoxicating liquor to drink until at last he did not know what he was doing, and they brought to him a platter of pie and he ate some and fell dead under the table.

The dogs were locked up in the strong room, the door made of oak and iron, and Listener said "Listen."

"What do you hear?" said Swift.

"The fisherman's son is dead under the table," said Listener.

"Ah! if we could get out of here," said Swift, "we could still heal him."

"How would you do that?" said Strength.

"The poison made a black spot on his heart, it can be sucked out again, and the fisherman's son can be revived." said Swift.

"Do that then," said Strength, "this opening is for you." He chose a spot at the back of the room and with a bound he went straight through the door, with Swift and Listener after him. Swift ran ahead and it was not long until he was in the room. He opened up the lad, and sucked the black spot from his heart and then put it back in him, and the boy sprung up fully alive as he was before.

"Leave, it is not good for us to stay longer now," said Swift. They departed and they travelled until they reached a place where three roads diverged, where they stopped.

"Now," said Listener, "fisherman's son, we and you part here."

"I will not part from you at all," said the lad.

They gathered concerning the issue but he did not leave them. At last Swift said "Who is it that is coming after us?"

The boy looked around but he did not see anyone, but when he turned back to the dogs, not a dog was to be seen. He was sorry to lose them and he was greatly worried. He did not know what way to turn. At last he chose a direction and went forward on one of the roads.

It was in the evening and towards dark when he reached a fine big house in the small wood and a man was strolling at its edge. He greeted the man and the man greeted him and he said-

"You are welcome, fisherman's son. And long have I waited for you."

"You have the advantage of me," said the lad, "you are not known to me, I have never seen you before."

"You saw me many times," said the other. "Don't you recollect Listener the dog you had. I am Listener, but come in and satisfy your hunger." They went inside. The table was full of every good thing and well presented. Listener began to speak and he said, "We are three brothers and a day's distance is between each of our houses. We were put under a spell until we had freed you from Cù Dubh a' Chuain Ghuirm."

They spent a month of feasting and they took another month in Swift's house, and the third month in Strength's house, the strong, brave man, and they sent the lad home happy and rich, and parted from him.

Sunset over the Firth of Lorne, Oban, Argyll, Scotland

77 Chrom-an-Fhàsaich (Cluich Lùth-chleasan)

[le Dòmhnall Beaton]

Chruinnichmid air raon, no ann an taigh; shuidhemid an uchd a chèile, am fear bu mhomha 's bu chomasaiche na cheann, 's càch uile nan sreath na uchd.

Steach thigeadh Crom-an-fhàsaich, "Dideaga, Dideaga, Dia an seo."

An Ceann-suidhe:- "Fàilte ort fhèin a Chrom-an-fhàsaich, cia as an-diugh a thàinig thu?

Crom-an-fhàsaich:- "A m' fhonn, 's a m' fhearunn, 's a m' fhàsach fhèin."

An Ceann-suidhe:- "De chuir fonn is fearrann is fàsach agadsa, is mise gun fhonn gun fhearann gun fhàsach idir?

Crom-an-fhàsaich- "Mo chruas, mo luath, 's mo làidireachd fhèin. Fiach a bheil aon gearran bàn bacach agadsa a dh'fhiachas mi?"

Iarruidh an sin an ceannsuidhe air an fhear a's faigse don Chrom, èiridh. Ni e sin, agus tòisichidh a ghleachd, gach fear mar a chiosnichear e suidhe e 'n leth-taobh.

Mu bheir aon air bith buaidh air Crom-an-fhàsaich an-dèidh sin, agus mar sin sìos gu crìoch na cluiche.

Sid a' dh'ionnsaichemid gleachd, nar balaich o chionn trì fichead bliadhna.

[Fìos freagairt do Dhòmhnuill

A-thaobh seann chleachdainnean agus chleasan a bha cumanta ri linn Dhòmhuill an Dearbhaig shearg is chrìon iad.

Air an latha diugh chan eil cliamh mònadh, no srathair no sumag, no corain-shachdaich ri fhaichinn 's a' sgireachd. Chan eil sniomhadh no càradh, chan fhaicear brat no plaide air leaba. Na h-uile snathain aodaich Gallda. Chan eil figheadair, no tàillear san àite; chan eil caman ri fhaicinn aig Nollaig no aig Caisg. Chan eil àtha no muilleann; an còrr nach do shearg, chaidh am fuadach. Chan eil a h-aon do na seann eich Mhuileach seann no òg, san dùthaich. Tha pòrr ùr do gach ni againn a-nis. Caoraich an àite nan daoine sa Chillmhòir ann an Atha-an-tuim, sa Choireachan san Druim-na-croise.

Chan eile gearadh feumhann ga dheanadh, chan eil bàta an Dearbhaig an-diugh ach a h-aon. Nach b' e an dà latha e seach na làithean o chian! Chan eil Beurla shìos is shuas, air a measgadh le Fraingish. Chan eil cuinneag, cuach, measair, meadar, no nogainn ri fhaicinn ann an taigh an-diugh, chan fhaicear coran air an achadh-bhuana, gach dias air a ghearadh le speal, chan eil fraoch siomain a dol ni 's mò. Chan eil tubha chamhlaich air taigh an Dearbhaig an-diugh, seo còr an àite.]

A Sport played on the Island of Mull
[by Donald Beaton]

We would gather in a field, or in the house; sitting in separate rows, the biggest and strongest male at the top, and all the rest in separate rows.

Then out comes Crom-an-fhàsaich, "See! See! A god is here."

Chairman:- "Welcome to you Crom-an-fhàsaich, from whence did you come today?"

Crom-an-fhàsaich:- "From my land, and my country, and my own desolate Wilderness."

Chairman:- "How do you have land and country and wilderness and I am without land, without country and without any wilderness at all?"

Crom-an-fhàsaich:- "By my strength, my speed, and my own power. Is it worth one lame white horse to you to challenge me?"

The Chairman then asks the person nearest to the Crom-an-fhàsaich to rise. He does so, and begins to wrestle with Crom-an-fhàsaich, and every man sits aside if he is defeated.

If one is victorious over Crom-an-fhàsaich, then he becomes the new Crom-an-fhàsaich, and so on down to the end of the game.

That is how wrestling was taught to our boys sixty years ago.

[The author, Donald Beaton who was a native of Mull, but now a long-time resident of Australia, enquired of the Editor regarding the survival of the traditions of his youth on Mull.]

The Editor Replies to Donald,

Regarding old customs and games that were common to your generation, they have withered and died along with the town of Dervaig itself.

Today there is not a moor hurdle, or cart-saddle or saddle cloth, or harvest load to be seen in the parish. There is no spinning or mending done and there is not to be seen a sheet or blanket on a bed that was woven locally. Every thread is of Lowland cloth.

Not a weaver, nor tailor is in the place and shinty is not now to be seen at Christmas or Easter.

Not a kiln or mill; the best [people] not the worst were driven away. There is not one of the ancient Mull horses, young or old, in the district.

We have every kind of new crop now. Sheep in place of men are at Killiemore in Atha-an-tuim, in Choireachan and Druim-na-croise.

There is no need for seaweed cutting and there is only one boat today at Dervaig. What a change since the days of long ago. There is only English spoken everywhere, mixed with French.

There is not a milk pail, drinking cup, churn, bucket, or cup to be seen in the house today.

There is not to be seen a sickle in the reaper's field, each ear of corn is now cut by scythe, and heather cord is no longer made.

There is not a straw thatch on a house in Dervaig today, nor is there any music in the place.]

78 Na Trì Saighdearan

[Sean sgeulachd le Dòmhnall Beaton]

Anns an arm bha na saighdearan air bheag lòin agus air bheag pàigheadh. Chuir fear dhiubh roimhe gun teicheadh e. Thog e air nuair fhuair e 'n cothrom. Cha robh e fad air astar nuair chunnaic e fear eile tighinn as an dhèigh. Dh'fheuch e ri car-mu-chnoc a chur; ach bham fear eile dlùthachadh dhà. Stad e agus tharainn e sreing a bhogha ri chluais.

"Na tig na 's fhaide, neo cha bheò dhuit" ars esan.

"O, na tilg," ars am fear eile; "chan eile mise ach a' teicheadh mar thu fèin."

"Ma 's ann mar sin a tha" ars a' cheud fhear, "is compaich sinn."

Dh'fhalbh iad còmhla. An ceann treise, chunnaic iad fear eile tighinn as an dèigh. B' e seo fear eile theich mar iad fèin; agus ghabh iad ris, agus bha iad a-nis nan trì compaich; agus mhionnaich iad: biodh e math no dona na thachradh riù, nach dealaicheadh iad am feasda.

Bha iad a' siubhal gus an robh iad sgìth, claoidhte, acrach, an impis toirt thairis nuair chunnaic iad tigh brèagha geal am badan coille. Ràinig iad an tigh. Bha an seo tigh mòr, fialaidh, 's a dhorsan fosgailte. Chaidh iad a stigh. Cha robh duine ri fhaicinn. Shuidh iad. Chunnaic iad am bòrd a bha air an ùrlar agus còmhdach geal a' dol air, agus biadh de gach seòrsa; ach duine cha robh ri fhaicinn. Chaidh teine brèagha chur air; ach duine cha robh ri fhaicinn.

Ghabh iad an suipeir, is nuair a chrìochnaich iad shuidh iad aig an teine. Chaidh gach ni a thoirt bhàrr a' bhùird ach cha robh duine ri fhaicinn. Bha na seòid an dèigh an acras agus an sgìos a chur seachad, aig an teine 's an t-àm ri dol a chadal a' dlùthachadh, nuair thubhairt iad gun robh iad a-nis cho sona 's a b' urrainn daibh a bhi nam bitheadh bean am fear aca. Cha ghann bham facal as am beul na bha triùir bhan a stigh agus shuidh an te bu shine làimh ris an fhear bu shine, agus an te b' òige làimh ris an fhear a b' òige. Thubhairt an te bu shine: "Thàinig sinn a-rèir ur guidhe; agus fanaidh sinn leibh gus an abair sibh droch fhacal. An toir sibh dhuinn ur gealladh?" Rinn iad sud gu toileach is bha gach ni dol air aghart gu math, agus bha iad sona.

Là de na làithean chaidh an dithis a b' òige de nar fir am mach a shealg. Chuir iad faghaid; leòn iad am fiadh; ach thug e 'n abhainn air is fhuair e thairis as an t-sealladh. Bham fear bu shine an dorus an tighe nuair chunnaic e 'm fiadh a' dol as. Bhreab e an stairsneach agus thug e ruith mhionn as.

Thàinig na fir dhachaidh. Cha robh bean ri fhaicinn. Chaidh am biadh air a' bhòrd, ach cha robh bean ri fhaicinn. Thàinig àm a' chadail, chnàmh an oidhche agus chaidh am biadh maidne itheadh, 's cha robh bean ri fhaicinn.

An dèigh am bòrd a ghlanadh, thàinig na mnathan am follais. Thòisich na fir air cur iomchoir 's air foighneachd de chuir an naigneas an raoir iad.

An àite freagairt thubhairt an te bu shine: "Thàinig sinn a dh'fhàgail beannachd leibh, chionn bhris sibh ur gealladh."

"Cha do bhris mise." arsa gach fear.

"Bhris thusa e" ars ise ris an fhear bu shine, nuair a bhreabh thu an stairsneach an de nuair a chaidh am fiadh as; ach seo chuimhneachan a bheir mi dhuit, an sporan seo; agus fhad 's a chrathas tu e cha stad e shileadh òir."

"Ma ta," ars an te mheadhonach ris an fhear mheadhonach, "chan eil agamsa sporan òir, ach seo dhuit am bogsa beag seo. Cuir a 'd phòc e. Ma thig naimhdean ort, fosgail e 's dean fead is thig armailt as a chìosnaicheadh an saoghal. Dèan fead eile agus tillidh iad a steach ann."

"Ma ta" ars an te a b' òige ris an fhear a b' òige, "chan eil agamsa sporan òir no bogsa le armailt; ach seo dhuit am brat seo. Ma shuaineas tu thu fèin, no na bhuineas duit, ann agus gun òrduich thu thu fèin ann an àite sam bith, bithidh tu ann"; is chaidh na mnathan as an t-sealladh.

Dh'imich na fir 's cha b' ann le deadhghean; ach cha robh atharrachadh air: dh'fheumadh iad siubhal. Thriall iad fo sprochd gus an robh iad sgìth, claideardach nuair thubhairt am fear a b'òige:

"O nach sinn na h-amadain; feuchamaid am bheil a' chumhachd anns a' bhrat a thuirt an nighean bha ann." Sgaoil e 'm brat air an làr. Laigh iad sa bhrat agus tharuinn iad a bheanna m' an timcheall.

"Nis" ars am fear a b' òige, "Càit an orduich sinn a bhi?"

"Ma tà" ars am fear bu shine, "chuala mi gur h-i nighean righ na Spainne an t-aon is beairtiche air an t-saoghal; agus b' e mo mhiann a dhol chuice feuch co aige am bheil a' bharrachd òir, ise no mise, bonn air bhonn."

"Mu choinneamh tigh Righ na Spàinne bitheadhmaid" ars am fear a b' òige, agus bha iad ann.

Rinn iad an sin campa fagus don lùchairt agus chuir e 'n ceill fàth a thuruis. Chaidh a leigeil a stigh. Mar a chuireadh nighean an rìgh a sios bonn òir, chrathadh esan an sporan, agus chuireadh e bonn ris gach bonn a chuireadh ise mach. Theirig a buinn-se, ach ged bhiteadh a' crathadh an sporan gus a seo cha sguireadh e shildeadh òir.

Ghabh nighean an rìgh cneachdal agus dorran mòr gun do chaill i a h-ionmhas, agus bhoidich i na h-inntinn gun tugadh i 'n sporan uaithe air chòir no air eucoir. Mu dheireadh thall thoilich i gun laigheadh i maille ris an oidhche ud. Nuair thàinig àm dol a laighe thubhairt i ris a dhol an leabaidh an toiseach. Rinn e sin; agus chuir e 'n sporan fon chluasaig fo cheann. Nuair chaidh ise dhol an leabaidh, thuislich i air-san agus spìol i 'n sporan fo cheann. Bha i gu clis air an ùrlar; bhuail i bàs agus dh'eubh i 'n geard. Dh'òrduich i esan a chur am mach gun chron a dhèanamh air.

Chaidh esan, an duine truagh, air ais gu chompaich agus e fo mhòr smalan. Dh'innis e dhroch rath dhaibh. Cha robh comas air. An là màireach thuirt e ris an fhear mheadhonach:

"An toir thusa dhomh am bogsa?"

"Bheir, ma ni e feum sam bith dhuit", ars am fear meadhonach.

Dh'fhalbh e 's ràinig e tigh an rìgh. Dh'iarr nighean an rìgh a leigeil a stigh, chionn shaoil i dh'fhaodteadh gun robh sporan eile aige.

Nuair fhuair e stigh dh'iarr e gu ladarna oirre a sporan aiseag air ais dha.

"S i nach tugadh. Ghlaodh i 'n geàrd. Thàinig iad a stigh.

Thug esan am bogsa as a phòca. Dh'fhosgail e e 's rinn e fead. Thàinig an armailt am mach; Sgudadh na cinn bho cholainn a' gheàird nighean an rìgh uamhas.

Chaidh i sìos air a dà ghlùin is ghuidh gus ghuidh i air a' chasgairt a chriochnachadh. Dheanadh i ni sam bith a dh'iarradh e oirre, ach a chur stad air a' chasgairt.

Rinn e fead is chaidh an armailt a stigh don bhogsa.

Thòisich ise air a bhreugadh, agus bha i cho miodalach agus gun d' thug i air a chreidsinn gun laigheadh i leis an oidhche so da-rìreadh. Ach an duine truagh, fhuair e e fèin air taobh muigh an doruis, mar air an oidhche roimhe. Bha e nis gun sporan, gun bhogsa.

Chaidh e gu chompaich gu dubhach, brònach. Thug e làithean an trom bhruaillean. Mu dheireadh, thuirt e ris an fhear a b'òige: "An toir thu dhomh am brat?"

"Ma ni e feum sam bith dhuit, seo dhuit e," ars am fear òg.

Dh'fhalbh e. Ràinig e 's chaidh a leigeil a stigh. Bha nighean an rìgh na seasamh air meadhon an ùrlar a' cur fàilt air. Chaidh e chuice agus chuir e cirb de an bhrat mun cuairt dith, agus ghuidh e iad a bhi le cheile an eilean uaignech am meadhon a' chuain; 's an sin bha iad. Bha a-nis cothrom Lachainn air an reithe aige oirre. Thog iad bothan agus bha iad a' còmhnuidh ann.

Latha bòidheach, grianach agus iad nan suidhe air cnoc, thuit esan an cadal trom. Bha ise coimhead air agus ag ràdh rithe fèin: "Ciamar thàinig mi 'n seo? A' cheud uair a chunnaic mi e bha sporan aige nach sguireadh a shileadh òir. An ath uair bha bogsa aige as an tigeadh armailt a chiosnaicheadh an saoghal. Theagamh gum bheil rudeigin sa bhrat. Thog i oirre cho luath 's a b' urrainn i don bhothan 's lùb i 'm brat uimpe. Dh'òrduich i i fèin bhi na seòmar fèin an tigh a h-athar; 's an sin bha i.

Nuair dhùisg an laoch fhuair e e fèin na aonar. Thug e gu luath air don bhothan; ach bha nighean an rìgh air falbh leis a' bhrat. Thug i car as a-rithist. Bha e nis na aonaranach truagh air an eilean uaigneach gun dòigh air dol as. Cha robh de bhiadh aige ach tighinn beò air ùbhlan fiadhain bha fàs air an t-eilean.

Thug e san eilean mìos no dhà mun d' thàinig cobhair air. Chunnaic e long a' dol seachad. Rinn e comharradh smèididh rithe. Chuireadh bàta gu tìr agus chaidh e air bòrd. Thug e leis dà chliabh ùbhlan; aon chliabh de dh'ùbhlan beaga. Thug e leis an cliabh de dh'ùbhlan beaga sìos far an robh e ri còmhnuidh san luing, agus dh'fhàg e na h-ùbhlan mòra air uachdar na luinge.

Nuair thionndaidh e chùl, cha d' fhuair na seòldairean cùis a b' fheàrr na bhi goid nan ùbhlan mòra; agus air chor 's nach faicteadh gan itheadh iad, chuir iad an cinn am mach troimh bheairt nan crann. Cha luaithe dh'ith na seòladairean na h-ùbhlan na dh'fhàs cròicean fhiadh am mach as an cinn. Thàinig an t-àm don luing gu tighinn mun cuairt, ach cha b'urrainn na seòladairean tighinn a' beairt nan crann.

Cha leigeadh na cròicean leò. Chuir an sgiobair fios air fear nan ùbhlan, 's nuair thàinig e thuirt e ris, "Feumaidh gun d' rinn thusa cionta mhòr nuair a thàinig a leithid seo de bhreitheanas air mo sgioba."

Cha d'rinn mise cionta mhòr; ach rinn iadsan. Thug mise ùine mhòr air an t-eilean nam aonar, agus cha robh meadhon eile agam gu beò-shlaint fhaotainn nuair ruiginn far an robh sluagh ach am beagan ùbhlan ud a ghoid iad. Sin an ni thug breitheanas orra."

"Le ùrnuigh no le ni sam bith eile, dean an leigheas, oir thèid an long air a' chladach is cha tèid thusa no sinne as."

"Ma leighiseas mi iad, an cuir thu air tìr mi san Spàinn?"

"Ni mi sin," ars an sgiobair.

Chaidh e sìos agus gheàrr e ùbhlan beaga nan ceathramhan, agus nuair dh'ith iad, thuit na cròicean diubh anns a' mhuir. Chuir an sgiobair air tìr e san Spàinn."

Shiubhail e troimh 'n tìr sin; ach cha robh duine beartach gu leòir ann a cheannaicheadh na h-ùbhlan mòra bu bhreagha chunnacas riabh. A' dol seachad air tigh an rìgh, bha nighean an rìgh 's a ceann am mach air an uinneig. Cheannaich i iad agus thòisich i air an itheadh far an robh i. Dh'fhàs cròic mhòr as a claigeann. Sin far an robh an othail 's an ùpraid a' feuchainn ri a toirt a stigh. Le mòr strìth fhuair iad a stigh i le a smigead a chur an oisinn agus bàrr na cròice san oisinn fa chomhair. Bha i 'n sin na gugarlach na suidhe air leabaidh agus cròic an fheidh oirre. Cha an sin gairm a chur am mach gu uile chrìochan na Spàinne: neach air bith a leighiseadh nighean an rìgh, gum faigheadh e i ri phòsadh 's gum bitheadh e na àrd-cheannard air an arm. Nuair reic esan na h-ùbhlan ri nighean an righ cha d'aithnich i e, oir bha e na luid làn feusaig.

Chaidh e d' a àite còmhnuidh agus phronn e aon de na h-ùbhlan beaga agus chur e am bogsa beag e agus dh'fheith e. Nuair a chaidh a' ghairm am mach, dh'ullaich e e fèin an trusgan leigh - bha trusgan àraidh aig na leigh san àm ud anns an Spàinn. Thàinig e gu tigh an rìgh is chaidh a leigeil a stigh gu nighean an rìgh.

Nuair chaidh e na làthair cha d' aitnich i idir e. Sheall e na gnùis gu dùrachdach agus thubhairt e: "Feumaidh gun d' rinn thusa cionta mhòr."

"Cha d' rinn mise cionta air bith," ars ise.

"Cha leig thu leas sin ìnnseadh dhòmhsa; chionn mur bitheadh tu air cionta mhòr a' dhèanamh, cha tigeadh am breitheanas seo ort."

"Cha d' rinn mise cionta air bith," ars ise.

"Ma tha thu air son mise do leigheas, feumaidh tu aideachadh no falbhaidh ise; chionn chan eil thu toileach air thu bhi air do leigheas"; agus chuir e air mar gum bitheadh e falbh.

"Ma tà," ars ise, "cha d' rinn mise de chionta riamh ach duine iongantach a thàinig an seo le sporan òir aige, is fhad 's a chrathadh e an sporan cha sguireadh e a shileadh òir, agus thug mi uaith e."

Chrath e cheann. "Chan e sin uile e," ars esan.

Mu dheireadh dh'innis i mun bhogsa 's mun bhrat, is mar a dh'fhàg i air an t-eilean e.

"A bheil na rudan sin agad fhathast?" ars esan.

"Tha," ars ise.

"Ma tà," ars esan, "feumaidh tu an toirt dhòmhsa."

" 'S mi nach toir" ars ise.

"Mur a toir," ars esan, "gleidh do chròic maille riu; oir chan eil dòigh air do leigheas ach gun toir thu suas iad," agus chuir e air a bhi falbh. Ghlaoidh i air air e, agus thug is suas iad dhà. Thug e an sin dith an ubhal phronnte is dh'ith i, is thuit a' chròic dhith. Bha toil-inntinn an lùchairt an rìgh nuair a leighiseadh nighean an rìgh, is rinn an rìgh àrd-cheannard air an arm dheth.

Thug e òrdugh seachad gun rachadh an t-arm seachad fa chomhair air, là àraidh.

Chruinnicheadh an t-arm fa chomhair, chunnaic e fear de chompaich, is thug e òrdugh a chur am prìosan. Chunnaic e fear eile, is dh'òrduich e, esan cuideache don phrìosan. Chaidh an sealladh thairis. Mhol e 'n t-arm agus leig e fa sgaoil iad.

Bha a dhà chompaich sa phrìosan. Cha robh fhios aca de rinn iad air an àrd-cheannard ùr nuair a chuir e sa phrìosan iad. Bha iomaguin mhòr orra.

Thàinig an t-àrd-cheannard far an robh iad agus thuirt e ri fear dhiubh, "is tusa a leithid seo dh'fhear."

"Is mi," ars esan. Agus ris an fhear eile, "is tusa a leithid seo dh'fhear."

"Is mi," ars esan.

"Am bheil sibh 'gam aithneachadh?" ars an t-àrd-cheannard.

"Chan eil," ars iadsan.

"Is mise," ars esan, "bhur compach a bha sibh cho coibhneil ris. Thigibh am mach gus bitheadh sibh nur dithis is fhaisge bhios dhomh anns an arm." Agus bha toileachas mòr orra.

Phòs an t-àrd-cheannard agus nighean an rìgh; agus mhair a' bhanais latha is bliadhna; is chuir iad mise dhachaidh am brògan paipeir air cabhsair gloineachan.

The Three Soldiers – A Story
[An old tale recollected by Donald Beaton]

In the army the soldiers were on a scanty diet and were poorly paid. One of the men decided that he would escape and he left when he got the opportunity. He had not gone far when he saw another man coming after him. He tried to get behind a hill but the other man was approaching him. He stopped and he drew his bow-string to his ear.

"Do not come any closer else you will be killed." he said.

"O, don't shoot," said the other man; "I am only escaping, like yourself."

"If that is the case" said the first man "we can be companions," and they departed together.

A while later, they saw another man coming after them. This man had also deserted and they joined him. They now comprised three companions, and they made an oath that whatever happened to them, good or bad, they would never split up.

They travelled until they were tired, exhausted, hungry and at the point of giving up, when they saw a beautiful white house in a small wood. They reached the house which was big and hospitable with its doors open, and they went inside. No one was to be seen so they sat down. They saw the table that stood on the floor with a white covering, and with food of every kind, but no one was to be seen. A fine fire was burning but there was still no sign of anyone.

They took the supper, and when they had finished they sat at the fire. Every thing disappeared from off the table but no one was to be seen. With their hunger satisfied, weariness overcame them and at the fire they were becoming sleepy, when they said that they would be so happy if female companions could be with them. Scarcely was the word uttered and three women were there and the oldest woman sat by the oldest man, and the youngest woman by the youngest man. The oldest woman said: "We came according to your wish; and we will stay with you as long as you do not utter a curse. Will you give us your promise?" They did that willingly and everything continued well and they were happy.

One day the two youngest of our men went out to hunt. During the hunt they wounded a deer; but it went to the river and it got across and out of sight. The older man was at the door of the house when he saw the deer escaping. His foot knocked against the doorstep causing him to run out cursing.

When the men came home not a woman was to be seen. The food was ready on the table, but still there was no woman to be seen. Time came to sleep, the night passed and breakfast was prepared and eaten and none of the woman was to be seen.

After the table was cleaned, the women appeared. The men began reflecting and enquiring in secret about the previous night.

In the place of an explanation the oldest woman said: "We come to leave you our best wishes, because you broke your promise."

"I did not break it," said each man.

"You broke it," she said to the oldest man, "when you cursed the threshold yesterday when the deer escaped; but I will give this sporan to you as a keepsake; and for as long as you shake it it will not stop issuing gold."

"Well then," said the middle woman to the middle man, "not for you a purse of gold, but for you this little box. Put it in your pocket. If enemies confront you, open it and whistle and there will come out of it an army of great warriors. Whistle again and they will return into it."

"Well then" said the youngest woman to the youngest man, "not for you a gold purse nor a box with an army; but for you this cloak. If you wrap it around yourself, or touch it to you, and command yourself to be anywhere, you will instantly be there." The women then disappeared.

The men departed in other than a good frame of mind; but there was no help for it; they needed to move on. They journeyed dispirited until they were tired, when the youngest man wearily said:

"O are we not idiots; test the power that the woman said was in the cloak. Spread the cloak on the floor". They lay on the cloak and they drew the corners around them.

"Now," said the youngest man, "where will we order us to be?"

"Well," said the oldest man, "I heard that the king of Spain's daughter is one of the wealthiest in the world; and it would be my desire to go to her to see who has the most gold, she or I, coin for coin."

"Let us be opposite the King of Spain's house," said the youngest man, and immediately they were there.

They then made camp near to the palace and hid the means of their journey. They were allowed inside. As the king's daughter placed down a gold coin, he shook the sporan, and he placed a coin for every coin that she put down. Her supply of coins became exhausted, but so long as he shook the sporan the shower of gold coins did not stop.

The king's daughter moaned and was greatly angered that she forfeited the treasure to him, and vowed in her mind that she would get the sporan from him by hook or by crook. Finally, she wished that they would go to bed together that evening. When the time came for them to lie down she said to him to go to bed first. He did that; and he put the sporan under the pillow which was below his head. When she herself went to go to bed, she stumbled on him and she pulled the sporan from under his head. She was nimble on the ground and she clapped and shouted for the guard and ordered that he be put out but that he not be harmed.

The miserable man went back to his companions and was under great sorrow. He related the deceit done to him. But he was powerless to do anything. The following day he said to the middle man:

"Please let me borrow the little box."

"Take it if it will be of any use to you," said the middle man.
The tricked man then left and returned to the king's house. The king's daughter asked him inside, thinking that he may have another sporan.

When he got inside he asked her boldly to return his sporan. She would not give it and she shouted for the guard who came to her.

Taking the box from his pocket the man unlocked it and whistled. The warriors immediately came out and lopped off the heads of the guards.

The king's daughter took fright and she went down on her two knees and begged that the slaughter should end. She did everything he asked of her, in order to put a stop to the killing.

He whistled and the warriors returned inside the box.

She then began her flattery, and she was so smooth-lipped that she appeared believable and she actually went to bed with him that night. But the poor man, he found himself on the outside of the door like the evening before. He was now without the sporran and without the box.

Sadly, and full of sorrow, he returned to his companions. He grieved heavily for days. At last he said to the youngest man: "Will you give me the cloak?"

"If it can be of use to you, it is yours," said the youngest man.

The oldest man again arrived at the castle and with permission went inside. The king's daughter was standing in the middle of the floor and welcomed him. He went towards her and he put the edge of the cloak around her and he wished they were together on a lonely island in the middle of the sea; and straight away they were there. Now he had the opportunity of laughing at her. They built a hut and they lived in it.

They were sitting on a hill on a beautiful, sunny day, when he fell into a deep sleep. She continued to ask herself: "How came I here?" The first time I saw him he had sporan which would not stop showering gold. The second time he had a box that a world conquering army came out of. Perhaps it is something in the cloak. She set off as soon as she was able to the hut and she draped the cloak about her. She ordered herself to be in her room in her father's house; and immediately she was there.

When the hero awoke he found he was alone. He went quickly to the hut; but the king's daughter was away with the cloak. She had cheated him again. He was now forsaken and miserable on the island, alone and without any means of getting off it. He had no food except for wild apples which were growing on the island and which kept him alive.

He was on the island for a month or two before assistance reached him. He saw a ship going past and he made a signal by waving to it. The boat landed and he went on board. He took with him two baskets of apples, one basket being full of little apples. He took the basket of little apples down where he was to bunk in the ship, and he left the bigger apples up on the deck.

When his back was turned the sailors saw their opportunity to steal the large apples but so as not to be seen eating them, they put their heads through the rigging of the mast. No sooner had the sailors eaten the apples than deer antlers grew out of their heads. The time came for the ship to come about, but the sailors were not able to come out of the mast rigging. Their deer antlers prevented them. The skipper learned of the man with the apples, and when he came to him he said:

"You did a great wrong when you enacted the likes of this judgment on my crew."

"It was not I who did the great wrong but it was they who brought it upon themselves. I spent a long time on the island on my own without hope of ever finding civilization again, and I was without any means of staying alive except for the few apples over there that they stole. That is the thing that brought the curse on them."

"With prayer and with nothing else, will a cure be effected, because the ship will run aground and neither you nor we will go out of it."

"If I cure them, will you land me at Spain?"

"I will do that," answered the captain.

The man went below and he cut the little apples into quarters, and when the crew ate them, the deer antlers fell off them into the sea. The captain then put him ashore at Spain.

He travelled through that land; but there was not a man rich enough to buy the large apples which were as beautiful as ever was seen. Going past the king's house, the king's daughter's head was out of the window. She bought them and she began to eat them there and then and large deer antlers grew out of her scalp. There was hurry and confusion trying to get her inside. With a great struggle they managed it by turning her chin in one corner and the top of the deer antler in the other corner. She was then petulantly sitting on a bed with the deer antlers on her. A call was then put out throughout Spain that anyone able to cure the king's daughter, would get to marry her and be appointed the head of the army. When the man sold the apples to the king's daughter she did not recognise him, because he was in rags and with a full beard.

He went to his dwelling place and he mashed one of the little apples and he put it in a little box and he waited. When the call went out, he prepared himself in medical clothes - these were special clothes for doctors at that time in Spain. He came to the king's house and he was allowed inside to see the king's daughter.

When he was presented she did not recognise him at all. He looked on her face and fervently he said: "This must be due to your great sin."

"I did not sin," she said

"You will not get the benefit of the cure. If I am to cure you, you must confess to me; unless you do, the deer antlers will remain on you and the curse will not be removed."

"I did not transgress," she persisted.

"If you want me to cure you, you must confess or you will perish; because unless you do so willingly you will not be healed", he said and made ready to go.

"Well then," she said, "I did not ever transgress except that an amazing man came who had a golden sporan, and as long as he shook the sporan it did not stop showering gold, and I took it from him.

He nodded. "That is not all of it," he said.

At last she told about the box and about the cloak, and that she left him on the island.

"Do you still have these?" he said.

"Yes," she answered.

"Well then," he said, "you must give them to me."

"And if I do not," she said.

"If you do not," he replied, "keep your antlers together with them; because it is not in this manner will you be healed but only when you give them up", and he again made ready to go.

She cried out to him, and she gave up those things. He then took sufficient apple mash and she ate it and the antlers fell from her. There was happiness in the king's palace when the king's daughter was healed, and the king made the man the Commander of his army.

He gave the order for the army to parade before him on that special day.

The army assembled before him and he saw one of his companions, and he gave orders that he be put into prison. He then saw the other one, and ordered him also to the prison. When the parade was finished he praised the army and dismissed them.

His two companions were in prison but they did not know what they had done to the new Commander that he would imprison them, and they were greatly distressed.

The Commander came where they were and he said to one of them, "you look like such and such a person."

"It is I," said he.

And to the other man, "and you are the likes of such and such a person."

"It is I," said he.

"Do you not know me?' said the Commander.

"No," they said."

"It is I," he said, "your companion to whom you were so kind. Come out and you will be second in command to me in the army." And they were very happy.

The Commander married the king's daughter; and the wedding-feast continued for a year and a day; and they sent me home in paper shoes on a pavement of glass.

79 "Mise chuala 's a chunnaic e".
[Retold by Donald Beaton]

Dh'fhalbh Dubhag-tòn-ri-teallaich don traighe a dh'iarraidh maoraich, chan fhac I tràigh no lionadh riamh roimhe, 's nuir thainig an lìonadh mun cuairt di shaoil I gun robh am bràth (deireadh an t-saoghail) air tighinn.

Dh'fhalbh Dhubhag-tòn-ri-teallaich agus ràinig I Pocan-a'-bhaile-fhàsaich. "A bheil thu stigh a Phocan-a'-bhaile-fhàsaich, so am bràth air tighinn?"

"Co chuala na chunnaic e?" arsa Pocan-a'-bhaile-fhàsaich.

"Mise chuala 's a chunnaic e", arsa Dhubhag-tòn-ri-teallaich, "fom bhonnaibh a thainig e."

An sin dh'fhalbh Dhubhag-tòn-ri-teallaich agus Pocan-a'-bhaile-fhàsaich agus ràinig iad Fàsach-a'-bhaile-fhionnaich.

"A bheil thu stigh, Fàsach-a'-bhaile-fhionnaich so am bràth air tighinn?"

"Cò chuala na chunnaic e?" arsa Fàsach-a'bhaile-fhionnaich.

"Mise chuala 's a chunnaic e", arsa Dhubhag-tòn-ri-teallaich, "fom bhonnaibh a thainig e."

Dh'fhalbh Dhubhag-tòn-ri-teallaich agus Pocan-a'-bhaile-fhàsaich agus Fàsach-a'-bhaile-fhionnaichagus ràinig iad Tìerna-Loch-odha.

"A bheil thu stigh a Tìerna-Loch-odha, so am bràith air tighinn." Cò chuala no chunnaic e?" arsa. Tìerna-Loch-odha.

"Mise chuala 's a chunnaic e", arsa Dhubhag-tòn-ri-teallaich, "fom bhonnaibh a thainig e."

Dh'fhalbh Dhubhag-tòn-ri-teallaich agus Pocan-a'-bhaile-fhàsaich agus Fàsach-a'-bhaile-fhionnaich agus ràinig iad Tìerna-Loch-odha agus ràinig iad Gobha-bhaile-bhric.

"A bheil thu stigh a Ghobha-bhaile-bhric so am bràth air tighinn?"

"Cò chuala no chunnaic e?" arsa Gobha-bhaile-bhric.

"Mise chuala 'sa chunnaic e", arsa Dughag-tòn-ri-teallaich, "fom bhonnaibh a thàinig e."

Dh'fhalbh Dhubhag-tòn-ri-teallaich agus Pocan-a'-bhaile-fhàsaich agus Fàsach-a'-bhaile-fhionnaich agus Tìerna-Loch-odha agus Gobha-bhaile-bhric, Minidh agus Ceap agus ràinig iad Daor-am-sgaile.

"A bheil thu stigh a Dhaorad-am-sgaile, so am bràth air tighinn?"

"Cò chuala 's a chunnaic e? arsa Doarad-am-sgaile.

"Mise chuala 's a chunnaic e." arsa Dubhag-tòn-ri-teallaich, fom bhonnaibh, thainig e."

Dh'fhalbh Dhubhag-tòn-ri-teallaich agus Pocan-a'-bhaile-fhàsaich agus Fàsach-a'-bhaile-fhionnaich agus ràinig iad Tìerna-Loch-odha agus ràinig iad Gobha-bhaile-bhric, Minidh agus Ceap agus ràinig iad Daorad-am-sgaile.

"A bheil thu stigh a Dhoarad-am-sgaile, so am bràth-air tighinn."

"Cò chuala 's a chunnaic e?" arsa Doarad-am-sgaile.

"Mise chuala 's a chunnaic e." arsa Dubhag-tòn-ri-teallaich, fom bhonnaibh a thainig e."

Dh'fhalbh Dhubhag-tòn-ri-teallaich agus Pocan-a'-bhaile-fhàsaich agus Fàsach-a'-bhaile-fhionnaich, agus Tìerna-Loch-odha agus Gobha-bhaile-bhric agus Minidh agus Ceap's Daorad-am-sgaile, agus ràinig iad am Fear-a-bha-san-t-sloc.

"A bheil thu stigh Fhir-a-bha-san-t-sloc, so am bràth air tighinn?"

"Cò chuala no chunnaic e?" ars' am Fear-a-bha-san-t-sloc, "so am brath air tighinn?"

"Mise chuala sa chunnaic e," arsa Dubhag-tòn-ri-teallaich, fom bhonnaibh a thainig e."

Dh'fhalbh Dhubhag-tòn-ri-teallaich agus Pocan-a'-bhaile-fhàsaich agus Fàsach-a'-bhaile-fhionnaich, agus Tìerna-Loch-odha agus Gobha-bhaile-bhric agus Minidh agus Ceap's Daorad-am-sgaile, agus Fear-a-bha-san-t-sloc agus ràinig iad Tuthadair-na-h-àtha.

"A bheil thu stigh a Thuthadair-na-h-ath so am bràth?"

"Cò chuala na chunnaic e?" arsa Tuthadair-na-h-àtha.

"Mise chuala sa chunnaic e," arsa Dubhag-tòn-ri-teallaich, fom bhonnaibh a thainig e."

Dh'fhalbh Dhubhag-tòn-ri-teallaich agus Pocan-a'-bhaile-fhàsaich agus Fàsach-a'-bhaile-fhionnaich, agus Tìerna-Loch-odha agus Gobha-bhaile-bhric agus Minidh agus Ceap's Daorad-am-sgaile, agus Fear-a-bha-san-t-sloc, agus Tuthadair-na-h-àtha agus ràinig iad Tuthadair-a'-mhuilinn.

"A bheil thu stigh a Thuthadair-a'-mhuilinn, so am bràth air tighinn?"

"Cò chuala no chunnaic e?" arsa Tuthadair a' mhuilinn.

"Mise chuala sa chunnaic e," arsa Dubhag-tòn-ri-teallaich, "fom bhonnaibh a thainig e."

Dh'fhalbh Dhubhag-tòn-ri-teallaich agus Pocan-a'-bhaile-fhàsaich agus Fàsach-a'-bhaile-fhionnaich, agus Tìerna-Loch-odha agus Gobha-bhaile-bhric agus Minidh agus Ceap's Daorad-am-sgaile, agus Fear-a-bha-san-t-sloc, agus Tuthadair-na-h-àtha agus Tuthadair-a'-mhuilinn, agus ràinig iad an Gearan-bachan-bàn.

"A bheil thu stigh a Ghearain-bhacaich-bàn, so am bràth air tighinn."

"Cò chuala no chunnaic e?" ars' an Gearan-bacach-bàn.

"Mise chuala sa chunnaic e," arsa arsa Dubhag-tòn-ri-teallaich, fom bhonnaibh a thainig e."

Dh'fhalbh Dhubhag-tòn-ri-teallaich agus Pocan-a'-bhaile-fhàsaich agus Fàsach-a'-bhaile-fhionnaich, agus Tìerna-Loch-odha agus Gobha-bhaile-bhric agus Minidh agus Ceap's Daorad-am-sgaile, agus Fear-a-bha-san-t-sloc, agus Tuthadair-na-h-àtha agus Tuthadair-a'-mhuilinn, agus an Gearan-bachan-bàn, 's chaidh iad uile gu leir a bhàthadh anns a' Bràth.

I heard it and I saw it.
[As recalled by Donald Beaton]

Dubhag-tòn-ri-teallaich left to go to the sea-shore to look for mussels; she had not seen a full or ebb tide before, and when the surging water came about her she thought it was the deluge (end of the world) coming.

Dhubhag-ton-ri-teallaich left and she reached Pocan-a'-bhaile-fhàsaich.

"Are you in, Pocan-a-bhaile-fhàsaich, the conflagration is coming."

"Who heard or saw it?" asked Pocan-a-bhaile-fhàsaich.

"I heard and saw it," said Dhubhag-tòn-ri-teallaich, "under my soles it came."

Then Dhubhag-tòn-ri-teallaich agus Pocan-a'-bhaile-fhàsaich left and they reached Fàsach-a'-bhaile-fhionnaich.

"Who heard or saw it?" said Fàsach-a'-bhaile-fhionnaich"

"I heard and saw it," said Dhubhag-tòn-ri-teallaich, "under my soles it came."

Then Dhubhag-tòn-ri-teallaich agus Pocan-a'-bhaile-fhàsaich and Fàsach-a'-bhaile-fhionnaich left and they reached Tìerna-Loch-odha.

"Are you in Tìerna-Loch-odha, the judgment is coming?"

"Who heard or saw it?" said Tìerna-Loch-Odha.

"I heard and saw it," said Dhubhag-tòn-ri-teallaich, "under my soles it came."

Then Dhubhag-tòn-ri-teallaich agus Pocan-a'-bhaile-fhàsaich and Fàsach-a'-bhaile-fhionnaich and Tìerna-Loch-Odha left and they reached Gobha-bhaile-bhric.

"Are you in Ghobha-baile-bhric, the judgment is coming?"

"Who heard or saw it?" said Gobha-bhaile-bhric.

"I heard and saw it," said Dhubhag-tòn-ri-teallaich, "under my soles it came."

Then Dhubhag-tòn-ri-teallaich agus Pocan-a'-bhaile-fhàsaich and Fàsach-a'-bhaile-fhionnaich and Tìerna-Loch-Odha and Gobha-bhaile-bhric left and they reached

Minidh agus Ceap's Daorad-am-sgaile.

"Are you in Minidh agus Ceap's Daorad-am-sgaile? The judgment is coming."

"Who heard or saw it?" said Minidh agus Ceap's Daorad-am-sgaile.

"I heard and saw it," said Dhubhag-tòn-ri-teallaich, "under my soles it came."

Then Dhubhag-tòn-ri-teallaich and Pocan-a'-bhaile-fhàsaich and Fàsach-a'-bhaile-fhionnaich and Tìerna-Loch-Odha and Gobha-bhaile-bhric and Minidh and Ceap's Daorad-am-sgaile left and they reached Tuthadair-na-h-àtha.

"Are you in, Tuthadair-na-h-àtha? The judgment is coming."

"Who heard or saw it?" said Tuthadair-na-h-àtha.

"I heard and saw it," said Dhubhag-tòn-ri-teallaich, "under my soles it came."

Then Dhubhag-tòn-ri-teallaich and Pocan-a'-bhaile-fhàsaich and Fàsach-a'-bhaile-fhionnaich and Tìerna-Loch-Odha and Gobha-bhaile-bhric and Minidh and Ceap's Daorad-am-sgaile and left and they reached Tuthadair-'a-mhuilinn.

"Are you in, Tuthadair-'a-mhuilinn? The judgment is coming."

"Who heard or saw it?" said Tuthadair-'a-mhuilinn.

"I heard and saw it," said Dhubhag-tòn-ri-teallaich, "under my soles it came."

Then Dhubhag-tòn-ri-teallaich and Pocan-a'-bhaile-fhàsaich and Fàsach-a'-bhaile-fhionnaich and Tìerna-Loch-Odha and Gobha-bhaile-bhric and Minidh and Ceap's Daorad-am-sgaile and Tuthadair-'a-mhuilinn left and they reached an Gearan-bachan-ban.

"Are you in, Gearan-bachan-ban? The judgment is coming."

"Who heard or saw it?" said Gearan-bacan-ban.

"I heard and saw it," said Dhubhag-tòn-ri-teallaich, "under my soles it came."

Then Dhubhag-tòn-ri-teallaich and Pocan-a'-bhaile-fhàsaich and Fàsach-a'-bhaile-fhionnaich and Tìerna-Loch-Odha and Gobha-bhaile-bhric and Minidh and Ceap's Daorad-am-sgaile and Tuthadair-na-h-àtha and Tuthadair-'a-mhuilinn and Gearan-bachan-ban and they altogether were drowned in the Judgment.

Sunset over the Firth of Lorne, Oban, Argyll, Scotland

Section Eight - Humour and Satire

Poems and songs of ridicule and satire have a long tradition in Gaelic writing and oral transmission. Rev Allan MacDonald MacKillop demonstrates in his examples that this tradition was alive and well among the Gael. The Highlanders were not above poking fun at themselves as well as anything else which they saw as deserving of their satire or their barbs. In Australia this could include responding to the irritation provoked by popular songs of the day (Ta-ra-ra Boom De Day), refuting an early anti-smoking campaign (*Dìomoladh na Pìob-Thombaca*) or identifying where the Law in Australia showed itself to be an 'ass'. (*Mod Loch-na Lusan*).

An attempt by the Australian government to prevent a man, Egon Kisch (an anti-fascist campaigner from Eastern Europe) whom it regarded as a political undesirable, from landing in Australia, led to a court case where he was given the language test. This was part of a law designed to prevent certain, 'foreign people' from entering Australia and it was part of the obstacle course an unwanted immigrant had to undertake in order to be admitted to the country. This test was generally in English or one of the other major living European languages, although the law did not stipulate which European language was to form the basis of the test. This latter fact gave the government wide scope in manipulating the test in order to deny entry to anyone it deemed as 'undesirable'.

In the case of Egon Kisch, a man who was familiar with several European languages, the government resorted to using Scottish Gaelic as the test language. Kisch failed this but a case in his defence was launched to show that Gaelic was not a "living" European language in the general meaning of that term. This case was successfully argued in the courts much to the disgust of many Gaels in Australia one of whom satirized the whole affair in a poem, '*Mod Loch nan Lusan*'– in Gaelic!

Although the denominational form of worship which many of the Gaels practised might have been regarded as severe by outsiders, it was not beyond a member to make wry observations about ministers and their attitudes to services on occasions as, for example, with *Am Ministir* and *Chi Bhi Searman.*

Gentle ridicule could also be directed even at attitudes to their own language such as in *Aois, Maise agus Cliù na Gàidhlig* and the letter from 'Garunnach'. Although most of the pieces given here relate to public issues, there were also occasional wry observations on the innocent gullability of people as with *A Phòsadh* and *Seun Airson Dèanamh Leanna.*

Distant characters and events proved also to be within the reach of the Gael's barbs. Towards the end of the nineteenth century, for example, the Boer leader Paul Kruger was the subject of one of these satirical poems, *Cò Sud an Cruigeir?*

80 Ta-ra-ra Boom De Day

[le Dòmhnall Mac Ionmhainn junior]

Cha chluinn thu ach ta-ra-ra
'Ga sheinn s a h-uile h-àite
O, 's mise ghabh a ghràin air
"Ta-ra-ra- boom de day."

Tha òran aca 'n dràsda,
Tha gun binn, gun sgoinn, gun chànain,
O rinn e mise a shàrachadh,
"Ta-ra-ra- boom de day."

Gum beir iad air an t-sràid thu,
Ga fheadanaich s ga rànaich,
An t-òraghan fèin gun tamh
Aig "Ta-ra-ra- boom de day."

Chaidh Eoghan mac an Tàillear,
Am bliadhna dh'iarraidh Màiri,
S e 'm freagradh thug i dha-san
Ta-ra-ra boom de day.

Am fear aig an robh pharrot
'S a dh'ionnsaich e dhi Ghàidhlig,
Gun fhacal aice 'n dràsda,
Ach "ta-ra-ra- boom de day."

Thuirt Dùghall mòr san Airde,
'S e marcachd na lair bhàn, rium,
Nach feuch an cuir thu Gàidhlig,
Air "ta-ra-ra- boom de day."

Gun dean mi sin gun dàil dhuit,
O 'n tha sibh uile lathair,
'S e Ghàidhlig th' air ta-ra-ra,
'N làir bhàn, an cù, 's tu fèin.

Tha gobhar aig mac Pharlain
A dh'abair as "ta-ra-ra"
Tha coileach aig Mòr bhàn
Their "ta-ra-ra- boom de day."

Se 'n t'òran rinn mo ghualadh,
Tha ghnàth a ràn s 'm chluasan,
'S chan fhaidh mi cadal suaineach
Le nuallan "Ta-ra-ra boom de day."

Ta-ra-ra- Boom de Day
[by Donald MacKinnon junior]

Today nothing is heard but "Ta-ra-ra"
It is sung everywhere.
O, and I have a loathing of it,
"Ta-ra-ra boom de day."

This song that they have at present,
Is without melody, without taste, without meaning,
And I am wearied by this
"Ta-ra-ra- boom de day."

It confronts you on the street
With its whistling and roaring
Your own organ does not rest
From "Ta-ra-ra boom de day."

Ewen, the Tailor's son, this year
Went to propose to Mary
And this was her response to him,
"Ta ra-ra- boom de day."

The man who had a parrot
Was teaching her Gaelic,
She is still without a word
Except "Ta-ra-ra boom de day."

Big Dugald from this region,
Riding his white mare, said to me,
"You cannot put into Gaelic
Ta-ra-ra boom de day."

I can do that for you without delay
Since you are all present,
The Gaelic for "Ta-ra-ra",
Is "the white mare, the dog and yourself."

Macfarlane has a goat,
It says "Ta-ra-ra"
Fair Marion has a cockerel
Which says "Ta-ra-ra boom de day."

The song is my torment
It is always roaring in my ears,
And I can get no restful sleep
With the howling of "Ta-ra-ra boom de day."

81 Dìomoladh na Pìob'-Thombaca

[le Alasdair Mac Dhomhnuill, Geelong.]

H-ithill iuthill ho hill o,
Chan eil fòghnadh idir dhuit,
'S truagh nach robh thu le d' phìob cham
Greis thall ann an Virginia.

Gheibheadh tu sgapt' air na blàir
'S na h-àiteachan sin iomfhuasgladh
Far am bheil tombac a'fàs
Mar chàl ac' air na h-imirean.

Ach, 'Gilleasbuig òig, a rùin,
'S ann tha smùid dhe d'shimilear,
'S cha tig diocladh air an tràs
Is crùn agad ri iomlaid.

Cha bhi gean ort 's i 'g ad dhith,
'S mi thlachdmhor e gur frithear thu
Mar bhodachan a' chin lèithe
'S gun deud aige le 'n itheadh e.

Cha robh thu ach balach òg
Nuair thòisich thu ri dinneadh innt';
'N diugh ged bhiodh Mac Chrimein beò
'S e ceò na 'cheòl bu ghrinne leat.

Tha Aindrea, do bhràthair òg,
Ro-ghòrach mu na cruinneagan:
Cha'n iarr thusa bean ri d' bheò
No pòg ach ceò na duilleige.

Na'n creideadh tu naigheachd fhìor
M'a rèir, is olc an luibh dhuit i,
Dh'fhàg i d' aghaidh tana geur
Is t' fhiaclan mar am buidheagan.

'S mòr gu'm b'fheàrr dhuit bainne-blàth,
Fion, no càl a shluigeadh tu,
'Dheanadh barrachd feum dha t' fheòil
Na dheanadh ceò is smugaidean.

Dispraise of Pipe Tobacco

[by Alexander MacDonald, Geelong]

"Hithill iuthill ho hill o,
There is never enough for you,
It is a pity you aren't, with your curved pipe,
Across in Virginia for a while.

There you would find it scattered on the ground
And in convenient places
Where tobacco grows
Like kale in the fields.

But my dear young Archie,
Smoke pours out of your chimney,
And will not become less
While you have a crown to barter.

You will never be happy without it,
I am pleasant while you are impatient
Like a little old man already grey
And without tooth with which to eat.

You were only a young lad
When you began to stuff it down;
And today, though McCrimmon were alive,
The smoke, not the beautiful music, would mean more to you.

Andrew is your young brother,
So silly about the pretty girls;
But you have not asked a woman into your life
Instead you have kissed only the smoke of your leaf.

If you trust in reliable news
According to me, the weed is bad for you,
It has left your face thin and sharp
And your teeth stained yellow.

Fresh milk would be better for you;
Swallowing wine, or broth
Would be better for your body
Than would smoke and spittle."

82 Fhreagair Gilleasbuig, 'g a Moladh

"Tha mi 'd chomain, a dhuin' òig,
A dh' òrduich mi 'Virginia!
Tha tombac agam gu leòir,
'S 'n am phòcaid òr 'n a "ghinidhean."

'S i mo leannan-s'a a' phìob chrom
Nach iarr m' a com na ribheanan;
Tha i torach gun bhi trom,
Mo nighean donn gu sgiobalta.

Gur a ciatach, caoimhneil, blàth,
Fialaidh, pàirteach, milis i;
Bidh i còmhla rium 's gach àit,
Is m' fhàillinnean cha'n innis i.

Na 'm biodh tusa, 's do shòrn fuar,
Air a' chuan ag iomramh,
Cha bhiodh tu idir cho luath
Le d'dhuanagan g' a dhiomoladh.

Na 'm biodh tu caithris na h-oidch'
Gun choinnlean no gun tein agad,
Theireadh tu mar thuirt mi 'n raoir,
'S ann oirr tha loinn 's an t-eireachdas.

Feudaidh Aindrea pòsadh tràth
Màiri bhàn no Iseabal;
Nì a' phìob mo chumail-s' blàth,
'S cha chluinn mi ràn nan iseanan.

Theirig thusa do 'n tigh-òsd'
'S dean do leòir a shlugadh ann,
Cuiridh mise suas mo cheò,
Cò 's fhaide beò – an tuig thu mi?

'S iomadh feum 'tha air a' phìob,
Ach chan inns mi uile iad;
Cuimhnichidh mi air an àigh
'Nuair chì mi luath na duilleige."

Archibald's Answer in Praise of Tobacco

"I am obliged to the young man
That ordered me 'Virginia'!
I have plenty of tobacco
It is as gold guineas in my pocket.

I love my curved pipe
And do not ask for young ladies on my breast;
It is substantial without being too heavy,
My tidy brown haired 'maiden'.

It is handsome, genial, warm,
Hospitable, generous, sweet;
It is my company everywhere I go
And it does not tell me my failings.

If it were you, with a cold snout
Rowing on the sea,
You would not, at all, be so quick
With your disparaging little ditties.

If it were you watching in the night
Without stalk of barley, or a fire,
You would say as I said last night
The pipe is beautiful and decent.

Andrew must marry soon
Fair Màiri or Isabel
My pipe will make me an affectionate support
Without me hearing the bawling of children.

You go to the hotel
And satisfy yourself guzzling,
I send up my smoke,
Who is it that lives longest – I ask you?

The pipe has many uses,
I have not mentioned them all;
I recollect the happiness of it
As soon as I see the leaf."

83 Aois, Maise agus Cliù na Gàidhlig

[le Gilleasbuig Mac Dhomhnuill]

O, molamaid a' Ghàidhlig
Thug urram thar gach cànain,
'S i chainnt a bh' aig ar màthair
'S a' chèarn anns an d' rugadh sinn.

Tha seanairean ag ràitinn
Gun robh i anns a' ghàradh,
Nuair choinnich Eubh' ri Adhamh
'S i Ghàidhlig a labhair iad.

Bithidh i aig luchd-seòlaidh
A bhios air muir an còmhnuidh;
'S ann innte labhair Noah
Toirt òrdighean d' am mharaichean.

Ged chrathadh i aig Babel
Mu'n deachaidh tur gu làr;
Thionndaidh rith' a càirdean
A thug bàigh is caidreamh dhi.

O, labhradh anns gach àl i,
Le laoich mo ghaoil 's na blàraibh,
Nach aomadh ri uchd nàmhaid,
'S pìob na màl! 'g a spreigeadh dhaibh.

Tha Calum Cille 'g ràitinn
Gu robh i aig Naoamh Pàdruig;
'S ann innte sgrìobh e 'm bàirlinn
A ghràinich na nathraichean.

Cha d' fhàg e muile-mhàgag
No uiread agus cràigein;
Na h-uile-bhèistean snàigeach,
Thug e bàs gun sagart dhaibh.

O'Connuill a tha 'g ràitinn
Gu robh i feumail dhasan
O 'n shaor i bho an bhàs e
Nuair bha e measg Shasunnach.

Is thug e taing don òg-bhean
A fhritheil aig a' bhòrd da

Nuair labhair I gun foil ris,
"Na òl e, tha neimh ann dhuit!"

Bha i an tigh na Ban-rìgh
'G fòghlum do na pàisdean,
Is b'annsa leò gu h-àraidh
Gun nàire bhi labhairt innt'.

Is tha i an Dunèideann
Co-ionann ris a' Bheurla
Bhon thug am pobull spèis dhi
Stèidhicheadh 's a'chathair i.

Is bha i anns na nèamhan
Aig cinnich agus treubhan
O 'n latha ràinig Abel
Is rè na beatha mhaireannaich.

Nis sguiridh mi de 'm mhànran
Chuir urraim air a' Ghàdhlig,
O 'n tha i uile sàbhailt'
'N tìr an àigh 's na flaitheannaish.

The Antiquity, Beauty and Fame of Gaelic
[by Archibald MacDonald, Grafton, NSW]

Let us praise Gaelic
More honoured than any other tongue
It is the language of our mother
And of the region where we were born.

Our ancestors tell us
That in the garden,
When Eve met Adam
It was Gaelic they spoke.

It will be with sailors
Who are continually on the sea;
And it was in Gaelic that Noah spoke
Giving orders to his crew.

Though it was shaken at Babel
Whose tower completely collapsed;
Her friends turned to her
Giving love and embracing her.

O, it is spoken in every generation
By my beloved hero in battle,
Not yielding to the enemy,
The pipes an incitement to them.

Calum Cille declares
That St Patrick spoke it,
And in it wrote the banishment
That drove out the snakes.

He did not leave a frog
Or so much as a toad;
Nor any creeping beast,
He brought death without a priest for them.

O'Connell* also says
That it was useful to him
Since it saved him from death
When he was among the English.

He gave thanks to the young woman
That attended him at his table,
When she spoke in Gaelic to him
"Do not drink, you will be poisoned!"

It was in the Queen's house**
The children learned it;
And they were especially glad
To be speaking it without embarrassment.

It is in Edinburgh
Equal with English;
The people have taken a liking for it,
Founding a Chair in it.***

Gaelic was in the heavens
In every nation and tribe,
From the day of Abel
And to life everlasting.

Now I will stop my love-song
Laying reverence upon Gaelic,
Since it is completely secure
In that glorious land and in heaven.

*The Irish nationalist Daniel O'Connell (1775-1847) had a marked influence upon the ongoing debate by the British government towards Ireland in the first half of the nineteenth century. He was responsible for achieving some reforms involving the civil rights of the Irish Roman Catholics. Attempts, presumably authorised by the British government, were made to assassinate him.

** Queen Victoria reportedly had some of her children taught the Gaelic language

***A Chair in Celtic was established at Edinburgh University in 1882, after a world-wide subscription was opened. Queen Victoria headed the list of donors.

84 Rann Do Aran Coirce

[le Alasdair MacDomhnuill, Geelong]

"N tusa mir de aran coirce?
Mìle fàilt ort!
Biadh cha deachaidh riamh 'n am chorpsa
Bheireadh bàrr ort.

Tha mi 'n comaine Mhic Aulaidh
Chur 'n am làimh thu
Ged nach d' iarr mi air leat annlann
Im no càise.

Beannachd aig an tè 'rinn t-fhuineadh,
Deadh bhean 'ic Aoidh;
Gum a fad sic' pailteas connaidh
'S min 'n a fàrdaich.

Bu tu-fhèin a' bheò-shlàinte thaiceil,
'S cha b' e cruineachd,
'S trica dh'fhuadaich fuachd is acras
Bho gach uinneig.

Là a ghabhainn mias dhe 'n lite
No coach stapaig,
Rachainn thar nam bean air iteig
Le mòr thapadh.

'S toigh le Sasunnach bhi r' oiceil
'S ròsd bhi aige
'S tusa, 'choirce, riumsa 'chòrdadh
'M bròs no 'n taigeis.

'S iomadh capull 's òigeach ainmeil
Timchioll Glascho
Rinn thu reamhar cnàimheach meamnach,
Crith nan caisteal.

'S Ilionmhor treunlaoch agus gaisgeach
Rinn thu àrach
Eadar Tigh Iain Ghrot is Sasunn,
Goill is Gàidheal.

B’ ann dhiu Fionn, rìgh mòr nan claidhean,
Bruce is Wallace,
Laoich bu tric a ruag an naimhdean,
Roimh am faileas.

Clìu don Tì a rinn cho torrach
Cur an Earraich!
Soraidh bhuan gu tìr nam bonnach
Tìr nam beannachd!

A Song to the Oatcake
[Alexander MacDonald, Geelong]

Are you a piece of oatcake?
A thousand welcomes to you!
I've never eaten anything
That would top you.

I am grateful to you, MacAulay,
Let me shake your hand
Though I don't want to spread it
With butter and cheese!

My compliments to she who baked them,
Otherwise McKay's wife,
Who has enough firewood
And meal in her house.

You, yourself, have enjoyed a lifetime of fitness,
And it was not due to wheat,
And it often drove off hunger and coldness
From every little girl.

The day I would take a dish of porridge
Or a bowl of crowdie,
I could cross the mountains on wings
With great agility.

The Englishman is glutinous
With his roast beef.
But you, my oats, agree with me
About the brose or the haggis.

And many a mare and renowned stallion
Around Glasgow
You made, large-boned and high-spirited
Shaking the castle.

And many a warrior and champion*
You reared
Between John o' Groats and England,
Lowlander and Gael.

Including Finn, great king of the swords,
Bruce and Wallace,
Heroes who often scattered the enemy
By their shadows.

Praise to the God who made you so plentiful
A plant in spring!
Great praise to the land of the bannock,
Blessed land!

*This is probably a reference to Dr Johnson's attempted put down of Scots who, he said, fed their men and their horses the same diet – Oats. The come-back from Boswell was, "Yes! But what horses! And what men!

85 Lìtir - Na Gaeil a's Cainnt an Dùtcha

[le 'Garranach', Geelong, Victoria

Teachdair Rùnaich,

Tha e cuir brisdeach-cridhe nach beag orm a bhi faicinn a liathad Gael 's a tha 'g àicheadh cainnt an dùthcha, agus gun fhios carson. Cainnt as urramaiche cha d'thàinig riabh a beul duine, agus tha cliù, nan la ach a chleachd i cho farsaing ris an t-shaoghal àitichte.

Gu de theireamaid ri Sasunnach na ri Frangach mur a b'urrainn da cànain a dhùthcha a labhairt? Theireadh, dìreach, nach bu mhòr a b'fhiach e, agus gun robh e cosnadh tàir, chan a-mhàin dha fhèin, ach don t-sluagh dom buineadh e.

Innsidh mi aon ni duibh, a Theachdaire, don robh mi fhèin fianuiseach, agus ged do chuir e mìothlachd gu leòir orm, cha b'urrainn mi gun ghàire a' dhèanamh aig a' cheart àm.

Bha mi aon latha am sheasamh air an t-shràid a' bruidhinn ri fear a mhuinntir Mhuile, nuair a thàinig gill' òg a rugadh 's a thogadh anns a'Ghaeltachd far an robh sinn. Bhruidhin mi fhèin ris 's a' Ghàilig, ach e an fhreagairt a fhuair mi-

"Mise caill tha Gaelic mi bi trì blian 's an country," se sin a Theachdaire ri ràdh gun do chaill esan a Ghàilig, le bhi trì bliadhna 's an dùthaich seo. Cha b'urrain mise smid tuille a' ràdh, a's cha do sheas esan ach goirid.

"Ah Dh-a! Eoghain," os am Muileach rium fhèin, "nach moch a ch-c a'chuthag air an fhear ud."

Mata osa mi fhèin, 's fior dhuit, feumaidh gun d' èirich breamasair chor-èiginn da. Sin agaibh smior na fìrinn.

Slàn leibh air an àm.

Is mi 'Ur Seirbheiseach dìleas.

Lìtir bho "Garranach" Geelong.

.

Letter - The Gael and his Mother Tongue
[by 'Disgusted' Geelong, Victoria]

Dear Messenger
I am very broken-hearted that I should see a Highlander disown his native tongue without any reason. No more honourable language ever came out of a man's mouth and its fame is as wide as the inhabited world.

What would we say of an Englishman or a Frenchman not able to speak his own language? We would certainly say that it was not worth much, either for him or for the people to whom he belongs.

I will tell you one thing, Teachdaire, I was a witness to this and, though it gave me much offence, at the same time I could not help laughing.

I was standing on the street one day talking to a man from Mull, when a young boy, who was born and raised in the Highlands, came to where we were. I spoke to him in Gaelic, but the answer I got was-

"Mise caill tha Gaelic bi trì blian 's an country," that is to say, Teachdaire, he had lost his Gaelic within three years of being in this country. I was dumbstruck and he did not stay long.

"Ah God! Ewan," the Mullman said to me, "the cuckoo was not long in c…king [expletive] on that man."

Truly I say to you that mischief must befall him on account of it.

Be courageous in truth. Goodbye at this time.

Your obedient servant

Letter signed ['Garunnach', Geelong]

86 A Phòsadh

[le Domhnall Mac Ionmhainn junior]

Bha Domhnall dubh a dol a phòsadh, ach cha robh fios aige ciod a fhreagradh e do cheisdin a mhinistir, se chaidh e dh'ionnsuidh fear do na foirbheaich. Ràinig e foirbeach.

"Maduinn mhath dhuibh." ars easan. " 'S ann tha mise airson pòsadh, agus cha robh mi riabh aig pòsadh agus biaidh mi air mo nàrachadh, cluinn cha bhi fios agam ciod na freagairtan a's coir dhoimh a thoirt air a Mhinistir."

"Choir' ud, a dhuinne." ars an forfeach, 's fiamh a ghàire air. "Chan eil agadsa air. A h-uile facal a chluineas tu am Ministir ag ràdh abair thusa na dhèidh e facal air an fhacal."

Thug Domhnall taing dha 's dh' fhalbh e.

Sheas a charaid òg suas gum pòsadh.

"Nì seo do raodha Bean a Dhomhuill Dhuibh." arsa am Ministir.

"Nì do raodha Bean a Dhomhuill Dhuibh." arsa Domhnall.

"Uell, uell, uell." arsa a minister.

"Uell, uell, uell." arsa Domhnall.

"Ai, Ai, Ai." arsa am ministir

"Ai Ai Ai." arsa Domhnall.

"Mach an meairleach dubh chan fhaigh e pòsadh an diugh." arsa am ministir.

"Mach an meairleach dubh chan fhaigh e pòsadh an diugh." arsa Domhnall.

"Thug an seo am Ministir crimmag as mo chluais 's chaidh sinn a mach, 's chuir easan an duine coir air dòigh mi, 's chaidh am pòsadh air aoidhaidh.

The Wedding

[by Donald MacKinnon junior]

Dark-haired Donald was going to be married, but he did not know some of the answers to the minister's questions, and went to see one of the elders.

"Good morning to you." he said. "I am to be married, and I have never been at a wedding and I will embarrass myself. Listen to me, I will not know the proper answer to some of the questions the minister will ask me."

"Man", said the elder, and, he was softly laughing, "you don't have to. Every word the minister says you just repeat after him."

Donald thanked him and left.

The young friend stood up to be married.

"Do you, Donald, take this woman as your wife." said the Minister.

"Do you, Donald, take this woman as your wife." said Donald

"Well, well, well." said the minister.

"Well, well, well." said Donald.

"Ai, Ai, Ai." said the minister.

"Ai, Ai, Ai" said Donald.

"Out you black rogue, there will be no marriage today." said the minister.

"Out you black rogue there will be no marriage today." said Donald.

The Minister then took hold of his ear and they went outside, where he 'straightened' Donald out and the wedding then joyfully proceeded.

87 Tha Banntrach òg Ghaidhealach

Tha Banntrach òg Ghaidhealach a fhuair riabh ur airson a bhi boidheach, banail, toileach air pòsadh. Chan eil gin de chloinn aice, ‘s chan eil i ach ochd bliadhna-fichead a dh’aois.

Tha stric mhòr fhearainn aice, moran de thaighean saor, agus cor a’s cuig mile punnd sasunnach ‘s a bhanc, cha phòs i duine ach Gael eadar ochd bliadhna deug a’s da fhichead bliadhna.

Feumaidh e bhi eadar cùig troighean ‘s seachd agus cùig troighean ‘s a deich air àirde agus deas, dìreach air ceannaibh a chnabh.

Thèid i leis do dh’Albhinn na dh’àite air bith a thogras e.

Sgrìobh gu Fàinne-Sholuis. Post Office, Launceston

An deicheamh latha den treasa mìos, 1857.

Advertisement The Gaelic Messenger

A Young Highland Widow

A young Highland widow, modest, and still pretty, is willing to marry. She has no children and she is just twenty-eight years of age.

She has a large farm, many houses in an unencumbered condition and five hundred pounds English in the bank and seeks an unmarried man (must be a Highlander) between eighteen and forty years old.

He must be between five foot seven and five foot ten in height, and skilful; able to earn his keep.

She will go with him to Scotland or any place he chooses.

Write to "Wedding Ring", Post Office, Launceston
10t May, 1857

88 Seun Air Son Dèanamh Leanna

[le Dòmhnall Peutan]

Anns an àm 's robh Righ Seumas VI ag ionnsachadh nan ealaidhean ann an Cillribhinn fo oileineachadh Dheòrsa Bochanain bha gach àrd fhòghlum agus eòlas air an cunntas mar ghisreagan agus mar dhruidheachd, no mar bu bhitheanta leò a' ràdh ris, "An Sgoileireachd Dubh," agus uime sin bha Deòrsa Bochanan le mhòr eòlas air a mheas 'n a bhuidsich.

Bha boirionnach bochd a' cumail tigh-leanna ann an Cillribhinn nach robh idir a' dèanamh gu math anns a' gnothach, agus chaidh i gu Deòrsa Bochanan chum gun cuidhicheadh e i le dhruidheachd.

An dèigh còmhradh dùrachdach a bhi aca ri chèile thuirt Deòrsa rithe nan leanadh i gu cùramach ris an t-seòladh a bheireadh esan di gum biodh i ann an ùine gheàrr beairteach.

Gheall i gun deanadh i sin.

"A Pheigi" ars' an druidh ionnsaichte, "gach àm a thèid thu a' dhèanamh leanna tilg a mach as an tuba sèa làin ladair do dh-uisge, aig an cuairt ri d' laimh chì eadar gach làn ladair do bhraich mhath anns an tuba aig a' cheart am a'tionndadh ri d' laimh dheis eadar gach làn ladair. A thuilleadh air a sin bi cinnteach gun caith thu air ceanghlachan beag seo gun fhuasgladh gun fhosgladh mu d' mhuineal gu latha do bhàis."

Rinn Peigi gach ni mar a dh'aithne dhi, agus ann an ceann bheagan bhliadhnaichean chruinnich i mòr bheairteas.

An uair a fhuair i am bàs chaidh an crios-muineil a thug Deòrsa dhi fhosgladh, agus fhuaradh an taobh a stigh dheth pàipeir air an robh sgrìobhta:

"Ma nì Peigi leann math
Gheibh i dha reic mhath."

A Charm for Making Good Beer
[by Donald Beaton, Queensland]

In the time of King James VI, learning science at St Andrew's under George Buchanan's teaching involved the higher branches of learning and knowledge of arithmetic, charm and magic or, as they commonly say, "The Black Arts," and George Buchanan, with his great knowledge, had a reputation as a wizard.

A poor woman who maintained an alehouse in St Andrew's was not doing very well in her business and she went to George Buchanan in order for him to help her by means of a spell.

After fervently speaking to each other George said to her that if she carefully followed the directions he would give her then she would be wealthy in a short time.

She promised that she would do so.

"Peggy," said the learned philosopher, "every time that you go to make beer throw out of the vat six full ladles of water, and repeat this between each full spoon of good malt you add to the vat, at the right time stirring between every full ladle. Over and above that be certain that you wear this little knot about your breast without untying it until the day you die."

Peggy did every thing that he commanded her, and in only a year she became very wealthy.

When she died the necklace that George had given to her was at last opened, and inside was the paper on which he had written:

"If Peggy will make good beer
She shall get good sales for it."

89 Mod Loch na Lusan

(le a dhìt a Ghàidhlig)
Aoir - Le Fògarrach bho Chaolas-Hirt
[An t-Urramach Ailean MacDhomhnall Mac Philip]

Thig an seo, a mhic mo chridhe
Dean suidhe oir tha thu sgìth
Innsidh mi dhuit sgeula neònach
Air an Lagh 'n uair chaidh e clì.

Siod mar chaidh Mod Loch-na-Lusan
Seo mar chaidh Mod Loch-na-Lusan
Siod mar chaidh Mod Loch-na-Lusan
Nuair dhìt iad a Ghàidhlig.

'S fìor mar dh' aithris an sean-fhacal
"Cam 'us dìreach thig an Lagh";
Ach 's ann cam a thig e daonnan,
Nuair tha ùghdarran gun bhlagh.

Seo mar a thòisich a chomhstrì
Dh'fhàg ar Lagh gun sùgh gun stàth;
Rinn dh'ar dùthaichne ball-bùirde
Cuis-fanaid 'us fella-dha.

Air lath' àraid, mar a tharladh,
Thàinig long a nall thar chuan
Bha h-air bòrd an du-ghall, Eoghin,
Aon nach d'fhuair an fhàilte bhuin.

"Eoghin mhic Kisch", ars Mac-Meamnadh,
"Nach thu fèin a chulaidh-thruais;
Daonnag ag iomain na'n asail-
Gann do h-eanchainn, pailt do chluais.

"Chan eil annad ach droch bhatar,
Chan fhaigh thu cead tigh'n air tìr
'S robh bheag orm fèin an tuaileas
Chualas ort air feagh gach sgir.

Chan èiginn dhomh bhi ga d' fhuadach
Chaoidh ann seo cha seas do bhonn,
Oir mar sgrìobh thu cainnt na'n Gaidheal
Cha ruig thu gu bràth ar fonn.

Na creid idir gur h-e faoineis
Tha mi' 'g altrum na mo bheachd
Siod agad riaghailt ar Cinnich:
Daignicht' ann an Lagh 's an reachd."

Nuair chual' Eoghin guth na Gàidhig
'S beag nach d' chaille e uile neart
D' fhàs e balbh 'us dall 'us bodhar
Thrèig gach cobhair e 'us feart.

Chaidh cuireadh a' chur le cabhaig
Air fear ìnnleachach an gnìomh:
Dhearbhadh gum bu gheal an fitheach
'S gur h-ann dubh bha'n eala riamh.

Thional luchd talla na goilleam
'S thòisich an deasbaireachd theann:
'S gann bhiodh fios aig fear 'g an èisdeach
Cò bha fodha chas na cheann.

Dh' èirich an sin a fear-tagraidh
Bha seasamh air taobh Mhic Kisch.
Phriob e shùil 'us bhuail e bhasibh:
"Fhea'raibh, èisdaibh ruim a-nis!"

" 'S math tha fios air feadh na domhain
Mar thòisich ar Cinneach fèin:
Rinn an Lagh ar sinnsir fhòghradh
As gach fearan fodh na ghrèin.

'S iomadh cèarn bho'n deach a sguirseadh
Eadar Lunnain 's Bail-ath-cliath:
Dream a ghoid an crodh bho'n achadh;
Caorich 's gobhair bho'n an t-sliabh.

Nuair ràinig iad Loch-na-Lusan-
Air dhaibh tigh'n a nall thar chuan,-
Cha robh aon dhuibh labhradh Gàidhlig;
Cha chual iad riamh fiù sa fuaim.

Spàrradh orra mhàin aon chùmhnant:-
Bhi mi-chliùteach le droch-bheart,
Murt 'us mèairle, bràid 'us gadachd,
Ceilig 'us breugan 'us ainneart."

Thug na foirbhich air a chathair
Gu h-aithghearr a mach a' bhinn:-
"Tha Eoghin cho math ri 'r sinnsir;
'S ceart an comhairlich' e dhuinn.

'Se ar barrail thaobh na Gàidhlig-
Gur fad bho na chaill i 'n deò,
'S gur mi-laghail bhi ga h-àireamh
Ann a-measg na cànain beò."

'S iomadh cainnt 'us linn 'us fine
Air an d' thug a Ghàidhlig buaidh,
'S a dh' aindeoin Mod Loch-na-Lusan
Chan eil i fathast san uaigh.

The Egon Kisch Affair
A Satire by an Exile from the Straits of St Kilda
[Rev. Allan MacDonald MacKillop]

My dear sir, come here
Sit, because you are tired
And I will tell you a strange tale
When the Law went wrong.

In that way went Mod Loch-na-Lusan
In this way went Mod Loch-na-Lusan
In that way went Mod Loch na Lusan
When they condemned Gaelic.

It is true as the proverb says
"That justice and the law is blind"
But it is blind indeed,
When its authors are incompetent.

Thus began the battle
That left our law without sense or meaning
Making our country an object of derision
A cause of mockery and ridicule.

On a certain day, so it happened,
A ship came from across the sea
On board was the foreigner, Ewan,
Without a single welcome to this country.

"Ewan MacKisch," said Mac-Meamnadh,
"Are you not an object of pity;
A human with the conduct of an ass-
Dimwitted but with large ears.

You are nothing but a wicked idler,
You have no permission to come ashore
I have learned a little of the scandal
That is everywhere heard about you.

It is not necessary for me to expel you;
Weeping will not do you any good.
Unless you write the Gael's language
You will never reach our land.

Do not believe that it is folly
That I entertain this opinion
You have before you our Nation's rules:
Confirmed in the Law and the statutes."

When Ewan heard the sound of Gaelic
He almost lost all strength
He grew silent and was as blind and deaf,
Alone and without assistance.

An invitation was quickly sent out
For an expert in the subject
To prove that the raven was white
And that swans were never black.

The people gathered chattering in the hall
And the tense dispute began:
And few that heard understood
What it was all about.

Then arose the advocate
Standing beside Mac Kisch
With twinkling eye he clapped his hand
"Men listen now to me!"

"It is well known throughout the world
That the country from which we originated
Made Laws that exiled our ancestors
To every land under the sun.

It is from many regions they came and settled
Between London and Dublin:
People who stole the cattle from the field;
And sheep and goats from the moor.

When they reached Loch-na-Lusan
After coming across the ocean,
Not one of them spoke Gaelic;
Nor had any heard a sound like it.

Only one condition was required of them:-
That they be wickedly infamous,
Or murderers, thieves and rogues,
Or traitors and liars or violent."

An elder then took the chair
The verdict quickly given:-
"Ewan is as good as our ancestors;
And this is our just counsel.

It is our opinion concerning Gaelic-
That it is long since dead
And that it is unlawful now to regard it
Among the living languages."

Many a tongue and generation and clan
Brought victory to Gaelic,
And in spite of Mod Loch-na-Lusan
It is not yet in its grave.

90 Am Ministir

[le Dòmhnal Mac Ionmhainn senior]

Am Ministir, a' meunanach,
A' leughadh a chaibdeil
B' èigin dha bhi stad uaireanan
Chum so a cheiltinn ùainn

Mar obair a dh'aindeòin
Gun thlachd, gun blas,
Oir bha peacaich mun cuairt air
Ro uallach gun smachd.

Ach an dè is an-diugh
Tha 'leughadh agus ùrnuigh
Le beatha agus dùrachd
Le sùrd agus treòir.

91 Cha Bhi Searman

[le Dòmhnal Mac Ionmhainn senior]

Cha bhi searman am màireach
Ged 'se latha na sàbaid bhios ann
An Eaglais Choraci nan Gael.

'S e mi chràdh nach bi sin ann.
Ach bi aimidachd is gàrrtaich
[Balach] 's nighean mar is àbhaist
Oir 'se latha breith na Ban-righ

Victoria an diugh.

Ban rìgh nam Buadh!!!

The Minister
[by Donald MacKinnon senior]

The Minister, yawns,
While reading a chapter;
Having to stop at times
In order to conceal it from us.

It is an unwilling task,
Without satisfaction or savour,
Since sin surrounds him
Too oppressive to control.

But yesterday and today
There were readings and prayers,
With life and sincerity
With preparation and direction.

No Sermon
[by Donald MacKinnon senior]

There will be no sermon tomorrow,
Even though it is Sabbath day,
In the Coraki Highland Church.

I am troubled that it will not take place.
Instead, there will be frivolity and celebration
[Among the boys] and girls, as usual,
Because it is the birth date of the Queen!

It is Victoria's birthday.

Virtuous Victoria!!!

92 Cò Sud an Cruigeir

[le Dòmhnall 'ic Ionmhainn junior]

Cò sud an Cruigeir tha bùireadh cho àrd,
A' buaireadh an t-saoghail le ladarnas dall,
'S a' sèideadh a thrombaid? 's e Duitseach a th' ann,
Gun choir aig' air uaisleachd 's e suarach 'n a chainnt.

Sèist: A chiall, nach e 'm burraidh e, bodach bochd liath,
'Toirt dùbhlain dar dùthaich, an duine gun chiall,
Bu choir dha bhi 'g ùrnuigh le dùrachdas dia 'n,
'S a bhi lùbadh a ghlùintean 'toirt ùmhlachd dar Triath.

An cual' thusa a bhòillich 's e 'g òrduchadh luath
Na Breatunnaich bhrònach a sguabadh don chuan?
"Bidh Boers ro-òirdheirc a' bòsdall le buaidh,
Is mise 'n am Impire dìleas dh'am shluagh!"
Sèist: A chiall, nach e 'm burraidh e … etc

Dean cabhag, a bhodaich, is falaich do cheann
Mun tig ort na Gàidheil, fir iomairt nan lann,
Lem beigleidean stàillinn g' ad bhrodadh gu teann
Gun ùine ort air ùrnuigh no dùbhlan 'thoirt daibh,
Sèist: A chial, nach e 'm burraidh e … etc.,

Tha na Breatunnaich sunndach 'n an giùlan fon airm,
Tha iad mòrchuiseach, òrdachaill, stòlda, 'n an cainnt,
Chan fhuiling iad tàire no tàmailt 'thoirt dhaibh,
Gus an campaich iad òrdail 'am Pretoria thall.
Sèist: A chiall, nach e 'm burraidh e … etc.,

'S na Boers a bha bòsdail is glòrmhor 'n an cainnt,
Bidh an glùintean a' lubadh, 's an sùilean fàs dall,
Nuair a chì iad an ceannard 'g a chrochadh ri crann,
Cha chluinnear 'n sin bòillich, 's thig an an-iochd gu ceann.
Sèist: A chiall, nach e 'm burraidh e … etc.,

Who is this Kruger?
[by Donald MacKinnon junior]

Who is this Kruger that roars so loud
Provoking the world with deceitful boldness,
Blowing his own trumpet? He is Dutch,
Without justice or dignity, his is a despised tongue.

Chorus: He is without sense, the poor grey-haired old man,
Challenging our country, the madman,
He ought to be praying with godly earnestness,
And kneeling in humility before our Lord.

Have you heard his boasting, quickly ordering
The sweeping of the miserable British into the sea?
"Boers are famous for their boasting of victory
I am the true Emperor of the people!"
Chorus: He is without sense … etc.,

Make haste, old man, hiding your head,
Against you come the Gaels, men used to wielding the sword,
With their steel bayonets forcing you back
Without time for prayers or for defying them.
Chorus: He is without sense … etc.,

The British are cheerful, bearing up under arms,
They are heroic, disciplined and restrained in their conversation,
They will not permit meanness or scandal among themselves,
Before they encamp they cross Pretoria in orderly fashion.
Chorus: He is without sense … etc.,

It is the Boers, bombastic in their speech,
Who will be kneeling, with empty dull eyes,
When they will see their leader hanging from a tree
That boasting shall cease, and their oppression come to an end.
Chorus: He is without sense … etc.,

Appendix One Source Material and Context

Section One - Leaving

1 An t-Abrach a Fàghail a Dhùthcha

Source: *An Teachdaire Gaidhealach** Aireamh 5, June 1, 1857, p.5.

Context: The poet laments what has happened in the Highlands generally, and to Lochaber in particular, the poet's own homeland. He extols the way of life of the past under noble chiefs and loyal clansmen. The poet also is clear where the blame for what has happened to the Highlands. The people were innocent of any blame which was partly laid upon some Chiefs and those clearing the land for sporting estates etc.

Author: Eoghan Mac-an-t-Shaoir

Tune: Not provided.

[Anns an Òran seo tha Eoghan Mac-an-t-Shaoir a toirt cunntais fhirinnich dhealbhach air "Nabuigheachd dhileas" nan Gaidheal, agus air a mhòr mheas a bha aig an uachdarain orra anns na h-àmannan a chaidh seachad a nuas gu linn a Phrionnsa. Bha fàraid gu leòir air na Gaeil 's na lathaibh sin gun teagamh, ach a dòcha leis na cinn-feadhna Ghàidhealach, an-diugh, na caoirich Shasunnach le "Meud 's a tha de 'n ghionaich nan cridheachan," agus tha iad a' fògradh nan gael as an dùthaich fon nach eil feum tuillidh aca dhaibh; ach tha bealach eile fosgailte d' ar luchd-dùtcha far am faigh iad fearann gu leòir, agus "nach iarr an Fhèill-Martuinn na Mail orr ni 's mò."]

[In this song Ewen MacIntyre gives a true and graphic account of the clanishness ('Nabuigheachd dhileas') of the Gael, and of the great respect towards their chief in times past and down to the time of the Prince.** Many Gaels, without doubt, would question that today, and it is probable that the Highland chief today is equated to the English sheep "Great of greed, small of heart," and they have ejected the Gael out of his country without any further need of him; but a gate has been opened for our countrymen where they will get plenty of land and "not be asked for increased rent at

Martinmas."]

* *An Teachdaire Gaidhealach* (The Highland Messenger), was a Gaelic language monthly paper which was published in Hobart in 1857 by Charles Wallace Hall (q.v.). The paper lasted ten issues before the failure of Hall's other business ventures sent him into bankruptcy. It had a wide distribution not only all over the Australian colonies, but also in Scotland itself. It provided a venue for Gaelic poetry contributed by Highland immigrants in Australia. It also contained news, stories, older Gaelic poems from famous Gaelic poets, Gaelic sermons, traditional tales and editorials dealing with themes as wide as the supernatural and the dangers of drink.

It also sought to provide a message board for Gaels in all parts of Australia, information about incoming emigrant ships from Scotland, general advice such as how to remit money to family in Scotland, 'agony' advice, how to collect undelivered mail, pep talks to colonists and anything else which it considered helpful to Highland immigrants.

**Bonnie Prince Charlie.

***Machair. The machair was the grassy land between the land proper and the sea particularly on the coastlines of the Outer Hebridean Islands such as those in North and South Uist and Lewis. Sometimes the machair could be reasonably fertile areas but in others they could be sandy or unproductive.

**** Martinmas. Saint Martin's day was held on 11 November each year and, in the nineteenth century, it was the time when rents for leasing of land became due and when, at hiring fairs, farm workers would find out if they would be hired for another year or discharged by the land owner. It was this annual ritual which added a great deal of anxiety and uncertainty for farm labourers and those who rented land.

2 *Naidheachd bho An Teachdaire Gaidhealach*

Source: *An Teachdaire Gaidhealach* Aireamh 2, April 2, 1857, p.8.
Fasachadh na Gaidhealtachd

Source: *An Teachdaire Gaidhealach* Aireamh 6, July 1, 1857, p.8.

Context: News from 'home', as featured in *An Teachdaire Gaidhealach*, kept the Highlanders in Australia up to date regarding what was happening in the Highlands. This section of *Teachdaire* also kept the settlers abreast of other news such as deaths of people back in their home district, news about the movement of church ministers, shinty reports etc.

These 'News Items' laid the blame for the 'clearances' firmly on the heads of the landowners and compliant Clan Chiefs. The law-abiding Highlanders in Sutherland are contrasted with the heartless factors of the landed proprietors who, for their own selfish ends, forcibly removed loyal Highland families.

Luchd-Imric Ghaidhealach

Source: *An Teachdaire Gaidhealach*, Aireamh 8, September 1, 1857, p.8.

Context: Against a background of continuing 'Clearances', and large-scale depopulation taking place, especially in the Scottish Highlands, renewed efforts were being made in Tasmania to assist the new arrivals. Again, the hand of God is seen as directing all of these events to the advantage of the Highlanders.

Author: Editorial

3 Slàn le Beanntan an Fhraoch agus le Gleanndaruail

Source: An Gaidheal 1874, pp.217-218.

Context: Reluctance to leave is overwhelmed by economic necessity.

Author: [Anon]

Tune: Cumha Airdmeànaig)

4 An Gaidheal a' Fàghail a Dhùthcha

Source: *An Teachdaire Gaidhealach*, Aireamh 4, May 1, 1857, p.6 (concluded in *An Teachdaire Gaidhealach*, Aireamh 5, June 1, 1857, pp. 5-6).

Context: This was one of the many poems of its type lamenting the forced expulsion of tenants from their homeland and is one of a series written by Ewan MacIntyre the theme of which deals with his love of Lochaber and his deep distress at being forced to leave. MacIntyre's poems also identify the confusion which existed among those forced to leave their homeland and the shock at the changes which took place in so short a time. He writes as one who accepted that a great calamity had befallen his land; one that had not been the fault of those who had, for generations, dwelt on the land.

Author: Eoghan Mac-an-t-Shaoir (Ewan MacIntyre) was one of several emigrants from the Highlands and Islands of Scotland to Australia who composed multiple poems.

Tune: Not provided.

5 Òran – Slàn Leat Albainn

Source: The Òban Times *Tiom Òbain* October 3, 1885, p.6.

Context: A poem by James MacMillan who, like Ewan MacIntyre, was a regular contributor. of Gaelic material to *An Teachdaire Gaidhealach* and newspapers and journals overseas, principally in Scotland, such as the *Oban Times*, *An t-Ard Albannach* (*The Highlander*), *The Celtic Monthly*, *Cuairtear nan Gleann* and *An Gaidheal*. This is another example of a nostalgia poem comparing Scotland and its flora and fauna favourably against anywhere in the world. The poet seems to have travelled widely leading him to make his comparisons between Scotland and other countries.

Author: James MacMillan

Tune: The song was set to the tune 'Gur tu mo bheann-chomainn'.

6 Cead le Dùthaich nam Beann

Source: *An t-Ard Albannach* 26 June 1875, p.3.

Context: A typical emigration poem bidding farewell to all that was familiar.

Author: Anon.

Tune: Not provided.

7 An latha dh'fhàg Dòmhull Dearbhaig

Source: *Celtic Monthly* Vol. 15, No 3, Dec 1906, pp.45-46.

Context: Looking back over fifty years, the Editor of the *Celtic Monthly* remembers the sad procession of folk from the village who had gathered to bid a sad farewell to a fellow villager about to leave for Australia.

Author: Editor *Celtic Monthly.*

8 *Òran an Eilthirich*

Source: *An Teachdaire Gaidhealach*, Aireamh 8, September 1, 1857, pp. 4-5.

Context: Sadness at leaving Mull after being 'cleared' from the land and bundled onto an Emigration ship.

Author: Angus Beaton

Tune: Not provided.

9 An t-Abrach aig Uaighean a Dhìlsean

Source: *An Teachdaire Gaidhealach*, Aireamh 7, August 1, 1857, p.4.

Context: Eoghan Mac-an-t-Shaoir wrote these verses at Bhraigh-Lochabar on seeing many of his fellow countrymen leaving for Australia. Going past the church (Cill-a-chairioll), they stopped to look at the last resting place of their kin in those ancient graves. This song, as with some others of the poet, was composed in difficult circumstances in Australia and, full of pathos, it reflects his great love of his homeland.

Author: Eoghan Mac-an-t-Shaoir (Ewan MacIntyre)

Tune: Not provided.

10 Guma Slàn do na Fearaibh

Source: Am Baile (Inverness)

Context: The composer, Donald Campbell (1798-1875), born at Dalnaspidal, Glen Garry, He wrote this on the occasion of the emigration of 326 inhabitants, mostly from the Invereshie Estate where some clearances had taken place, on the St George bound for Sydney in 1838. Though the wording of the poem suggests that Donald was one of the emigrants, it appears that he did not leave with the others.

Author: Donald Campbell

Tune: Not provided.

Section Two - The Journey - On the Seas

11 Òran an Eilthirich

Source: *An Teachdaire Gaidhealach,* Aireamh 8, September 1, 1857, pp. 4-5.

Context: The poet, Angus Beaton (q.v.), provides one of the few authentic first-hand contemporary accounts of the immigration process and voyage of Highland steerage migrants who often were 'forced' to leave their homeland and face the terrors of the long trip and the uncertain conditions of a sea voyage to the other side of the world.

["Tha an t-òran a leanas a tabhairt mion chunntas air gach ni a thachair don luchd-imric 's don luing leis an do sheòl an t-ughdair, anns an Fhogaradh, 1852, 'on a dh'fhàg iad a Ghaeltachd gus an d-ràinig iad Astraillia, far an do dhealich e ri a' luchd-dùtcha ionmhainn – cuid diubh, theagamh, nach fhaicear leis tuillidh gu bràth.

Tha an t-òran seo, mar an ceudna, a nochdadh barail an Ughdair air a chearna de Phort Phillip anns na thilgeadh a chrannchur – a gearan gu h-àraidh air a bhi air a chuartachadh le Priomh-Mhuinntir (Aborigines) an àite agus fada fo mhinisteiribh an t-soisgeil. Chan eil gun teagamh, na Teachdairean Spioradail cho lionmhor ann an Astraillia 's a tha anns a Ghaeltachd, ach ged nach eil, cha 'n faod 'ar luchd-dutcha a' misneach a leigeil a sìos airson sin – tha 'm Bìobuill aca agus feudaidh gach neach dhiù a bhi na mhinisteir, na fhardaich s' na theoghlach fein. Tha ran na dha de 'n òran seo a toirt n' ar cuimhne barail Ian Ic-Illeathain, bard Thighearna-Chola, air cul-choilltichibh Ameirica:*, goirid an deigh dha toiseachadh air a chriomaig fhearuinn a cheannaich e a rèiteach:-

'S beag ioghnadh' dhomhsa bhi tùrsach brònach,
'S mi seo a chòmhnuidh an cois nam bean,
Aig abhainn Bhaton a tha mi' tàmhachd,
Gun aon nis fheàrr nam buntata lom,
Mun dean mi àiteach, 's mun d-thoir mi bàr às,
'S choille ghàbhaidh 'chuir as a bonn,
Le neart mo ghàirdean gum bi mi sàraichte,
'S greis air fàillinn mun fàs a chlann."

Tha dochas againn gu bheil mughadh barail aig Aonghas Beatan an diu air Astraillia, na bha aige nuair a chunnaic e a choilltichibh dosrach uaine an toiseach."]

*This a reference to one of the best-known poems by John Mclean, the bard of the Laird of Coll, '*Òran do dh'Aimearaga*' (also known by its title *A' Choille Gruamach - The Gloomy Forest*). McLean, who went to Canada in the 1820's, comments on the gigantic task that faced the settler seeking to clear huge forest spreads before being able to cultivate the land and prepare a crop. Rob Dunbar, commenting on McLean's poem, writes that part of McLean's attitude towards the forest land also stemmed from the evil and threats, real or imaginary, which such a dark forest presented. Angus Beaton, whether through direct acquaintance with McLean's famous poem (composed c1820-21) or whether he was simply stating a common fear confronting new settlers to Australia facing the unknown, draws obvious parallels with some of McLean's lines. McLean, for example, writes "Gu bheil mi 'm ònrachd 'sa choill' ghruamaich." ('I am all alone in the gloomy forest.') with Beaton's lines. 'Tha mi seo aig loch-Elisa, ceud mìle bho shagairt.' ('I am now here at loch Elisa, a hundred miles from a faithful minister proclaiming the truth.). But there is, too, a deeper fear which exists. McLean writes, 'Fo dhubhar nan craobh, cha bhi h-aon again beò;/ Madainn allaidh 'us bèistean ag èigheach 's gach fròig." (Under the trees, none of us will be left alive/With wolves and beasts howling in every lair.", while Beaton complains, 'S olc na coimhearsnach tha agam o 'n a thàinig mi 'n àite/Daoine dubha 's coin-fhiadhaich gur e 'n gnìomh bhi ri mèirle. 'Wicked men surround me since I came to this place, Black men and wild dogs continue to thieve.'

Author: Angus Beaton

Tune: Faill illirin o na h-ug's horo eille,
Faill illirin o na h-ug's horo eille,
Faill illirin o na h-ug's horo eille,
Dhealich sinn air a chladach 's fhad
Ma faic sinn a cheile.

12 Òran Tha 'n Oidche

Source: *The Oban Times* September 26, 1885, p.5.

Context: The poet composed this song while he was in Sydney. It is probable that he is reminiscing about his voyage out to Australia years before and indicates that the love of his homeland still lies on his heart. MacMillan was another of the poets, like MacIntyre, who composed multiple poems.

Author: James MacMillan

Tune: Not provided.

13 An t-Abrach Air Chuan

Source: *An Teachdaire Gaidhealach*, Aireamh 7, August 1, 1857, p.4.

Context: The poet, sailing from his homeland, casts his mind back and determines that he will never forget his native land.

MacIntyre had obviously moved on from Victoria, where his first poems were dated, and writes this one from Byron Bay in New South Wales.

Author: Ewan MacIntyre.

Tune: Not provided.

14 Air Bòrd an t-Saoithich 'Typhoon' ann an Acarsaic Lisboin

Source: In private hands.

Context: The ship, the *Typhoon*, had been dismasted in a storm and had put into Lisbon harbour for repairs. The author of this poem, Rev. Alexander MacIntyre, a well-known Free Church of Scotland minister from the Highlands, travelling to Australia in 1853 to minister to Gaelic-speaking Highlanders, offers his views of the ship and the people sailing on her.

Like many emigrant ships, the *Typhoon* carried three main classes of people - the paying cabin class passengers, assisted emigrants and the steerage class. The poet provides a colourful if, at times, an overly judgmental description of these classes foreshadowing the task any evangelical minister would have in breaking the hard hearts of these people.

Author: Rev Alexander MacIntyre

Tune: Not provided.

15 Losgadh na Luinge *India*

[A Sheòl Ghrianaig, a dhol do Australia,

Mìos-Mheadhoin an t-Samhraidh, 1841]

Source: *Cuairtear nan Gleann*, Mìos – Meadhonach an t-Earraich, No 20, October 1, 1841, pp 235-237.

Context: A first-hand report of the destruction of the immigrant ship, *India*, by fire and the miraculous rescue from the sea, by a passing ship. Of the 214 on board, 18 were lost.

Author: The writer's name was withheld.

16 Sgiorbeaidhean Muladach

Source: *An Teachdaire Gaidhealach* No 8, September, 1857, pp.7-8.

Context: The long trip from Britain to Australia (which could last up to five months) was fraught with many dangers. These included diseases, storms, icebergs and fire at sea. Even when a safe passage was navigated to Australian waters, there were still potential dangers although the ship was within sight of a safe harbour! This was the case when a terrible tragedy took place at Sydney Heads.

Notes: *An Teachdaire Gaidhealach* reported that a ship from Britain, the *Dunbar*, which, after a safe voyage to Australian waters, had sunk after hitting the rocky headland at Sydney Heads with all but one of its 120 passengers and crew being drowned.

The second report concerned the *Champion* which, between Portland Bay and Melbourne, was holed and sank almost immediately, again with a large loss of life.

17 Mu She'oladh Thairis Air Crios-Mheadhoin na Talmhainn

Source: *Cuairtear nan Gleann* Mìos Meadhonach an Earraich, No 38, April 1, 1843, pp41-47.

Context: A first-hand account of the Crossing the Equator ceremony on an immigrant ship. The report details how violent and unpleasant the experience could be for many of those carried by this ship whether assisted or cabin passengers.

Author: Letter was signed 'Sgiathanach', Clachan Chìllmhuire, Toiseach an Earraich, 1843.

Section Three - Looking Back

18 Tuireadh a' Ghàidheal

Source: *An Teachdaire Gaidhealach* Aireamh 9, October 1, 1857.

Context: The poet foresees a time, however, when future generations, who would be educated and knowledgeable, will emerge to right the wrongs done in the past by landlords, compliant government authorities and weak clan chiefs. These generations would be prepared to fight through the courts to obtain justice for the Highlanders. Such reforms as the Crofting Acts of 1886, as well as those introduced since, have given some protection to those Highlanders situated on crofts. But what was lost was not simply access to land, but a whole culture and no amount of Crofting reforms would ever be able to restore this. The more perceptive of the poets writing in their new homeland and, perhaps, most of the settlers themselves, were aware of this and accepted that there would be no return – Cha till, cha till ... etc.

"Rinneadh na rannan seo le Gàidheal, a mhuinntir siorramachd Pheairt air dha, an dèigh a bhi air falbh o dhùthchaich fad mòran bhliadhnaichean, sgrìob a thoirt a dh' fhaicinn, a ris, Athuill a's Bhraidalba; agus beachdachadh air na h-atharraicheanaibh mòra a rinn na h-uachdrain anns na cèarnaibh sin de 'n Ghaeltachd. Sguabadh air falbh an tuath mheasail, chòir, fhialuidh a bha 'g àiteachadh an fhearuinn, fad linntin, 's tha a-nis gach gleann, 's sliabh fo fheidh."

'R'

"These verses were composed by a Highlander whose people came from Perthshire. After having been away from his native-land for many years, he is writing how he saw Athol and Breadalbane on a return visit. He considered the many changes that had been effected by the chief of that region of the Highlands. He observed that the respectable, honest and hospitable people of the north, who had cultivated the land for generations, had all been swept away, and that every mountain and glen were now under deer."

Author: 'a Gàidheal

Tune: Not provided.

19 Fàilte Don Ghaidhealtachd

Source: *The Oban Times* February 17, 1900, p.7.

Context: A typical nostalgic poem – looking back, remembering and longing for the return which the poet now knows is not possible. However, he ends on a confident note relating an old prophecy that the revival of the Highlands will lie in the hands of the overseas descendants of the Gaelic diaspora. Their successors, it was claimed, would return and, with their wealth, once again fill the glens and mountains with poetry and song.

Author: Donald MacKinnon senior

Tune: Not provided.

20 Loch Laggain

Source: *An Teachdaire Gaidhealach,* Aireamh 8, September 1, 1857, p.5.

Context: The love of their country of birth and rearing was expressed often by the settlers in Australia in highly glowing and descriptive verse and prose. Examples of this run through many of the creative works contributed by Highlanders in Australia. Expressions of this sentiment can be found in Beannachd, Loch Laggain and John MacLennan's *Òran Do Mo Dhachaidh.*

Author: Nothing is known of the author other than that he appears to have come from the area of Badenoch. His description of Loch Laggan and the surrounding Bens suggests a close familiarity with these features.

Tune: The poet set the song to the tune 'The Meeting of the Waters'.

*Pattach - The name of a local river which flows into the head of the Loch.

** Fergus the Great (430-501) is said to have been the first King of Dàl Riata (Scotland).

21 Mo Mhàthair

Source: *The Oban Times* 11th December, 1886, p3.

Context: James MacMillan composed this poem many years before this publication date, when he was leaving Scotland for Australia, and the *Oban Times* had published it. In an attached note, MacMillan says he is again submitting it to the *Oban Times.*

Author: James MacMillan.

Tune: Not provided.

Writing from his home in Kanowa, Western Australia on 13th December, 1899, he writes:

"Sir, These verses appeared in the *Oban Times* a number of years ago. I shall be glad if you can find room for them in your paper once again. They are appropriate when so many young men are leaving for the war in South Africa. If they have no other merit they at least go to show with what feeling and veneration a young Highlander regards a good and loving mother on leaving his native land, never to return, or to see that loving mother in this world again. I am etc ... James MacMillan.

It would seem that the *Oban Times* acceded to MacMillan's request as the poem appeared in the *Oban Times* again on 27 January, 1900, p7, just a few weeks after the date of MacMillan's letter.

[This poem was also reprinted in *Mac-Talla* Vol 8, No 32, 16th February, 1900, p8.]

22 Òran Do Mo Dhachaidh

Source: *The Celtic Annual,* 1916, p.82.

Context: John MacLennan, with his wife, returned to Scotland for a visit and this resulted in further compositions. Ill-health prevented him ever again returning, a fact which he reveals in the foregoing poem.

John MacLennan, along with Rev. Allan MacDonald MacKillop (qv), founded the

Gaelic Society of Queensland.

Author: John MacLennan. A native of Gairloch who composed many Gaelic poems and published a book of these.

Tune: The author set his words to the tune 'Muile nam Mòr-bheann'.

*Beinn Eighe is now part of a National Nature Reserve. The village of Kinlochewe is nearby.

23 Camus Oinich

(Cuimhneachain Ionmhainn)

Source: *The Celtic Magazine* Vol. 1, 1875-76, p.253.

Context: The poet reminiscing about his life in Lochaber before migrating to Australia. Memories of his 'idyllic' younger years, his education, his introduction to the bible and his love of Scotland, he concludes, will remain with him until the end of his days.

Author: 'Abrach' Alan Cameron, Melbourne, Victoria.

Tune: Not provided.

*The village of Ballachulish, by Loch Leven, sits at the foot of Glen Coe and is overlooked by Beinn a' Beithir.

24 Sa' Choill Fo Sgìos

Source: *Guth na Bliadhna,* 1921, pp.217-218

Context: The poet composed this while in Sydney. His story, as he relates it in this poem, was the familiar dream of many emigrants. The goal of making a quick fortune in Australia and, returning to the homeland, to live like a lord, was a dream commonly pursued and, just as commonly, rarely realised. The poet's description takes the romance out of goldfield life and pictures it in its starkest and bleakest reality. He also gives expression to his heart-felt home-sickness exacerbated by his acknowledgment that he would now never return.

This poem was actually composed many years before its publication in *Guth na Bliadhna* and relates to the poet's sorry days on the goldfields of Western Australia in the nineteenth century.

Author: James MacMillan

Tune: Not provided.

25 Òran do Thìr m' òige

Source: *The Oban Times* June 30, 1906, p.3.

Context: A lament that the poet will never see his homeland or friends or family again. The passing of thirty-five years since leaving the Highlands has meant that many of his friends will already be in their graves.

Author: James MacMillan

Tune: Not provided.

26 Gràdh Dùtcha

Source: *The Oban Times* October 29, 1898, p.7.

Context: A poem inspired by the anniversary of the author's arrival in the colonies. It provides some autobiographical material along with nostalgic memories of his homeland. The poem hints at the infirmity from which he suffered. It was some kind of disability affecting his mobility.

Author: Alexander MacDonald

Tune: Not provided.

27 Na Tulaichean Boideach

Source: *The Oban Times* June 9, 1900, p.6.

Context: Reminiscences about childhood haunts. Cnoc-nan-long is mentioned and the poet named his Australian home after it. Written at Kanowna, Western Australia, a mining area, he contrasts the dry, drab-brown colonial environment with the beauty, and the colourful setting which had characterised his place of birth in Scotland.

Author: James MacMillan.

Tune: Not provided.

*Cnoc-nan-Long was probably the area the poet grew up in Scotland.

28 Comh-Chomunn Ri Eas Ridhe

Source: *An Gaidheal* Vol. 3, No. 34, 1874, pp.305-307.

Context: The poet draws on common devices in nostalgic poetry using images of a dream and personifying some place or object to which the exile can then express, through conversation, the feelings which he is experiencing. This, and other poems by the same author, were commended by 'Nether Lochaber' (Rev. Alexander Stewart), a well-known figure in the Scottish Gaelic literary world, who encouraged their publication in Scottish journals.

Author: 'Abrach' Alan Cameron

Tune: Not provided.

29 Am Bruadar

Source: *Donald MacKinnon Diary* – In private hands.

Context: A nostalgia poem in the form of a dream of being back in his native land.

Author: Donald MacKinnon senior.

Tune: Not provided.

30 Beannachd – Tiom an Obain

Source: *The Oban Times* October 10, 1896, p.2.

Context: Like many exiles from the Highlands, the poet relied heavily upon subscribing to (or borrowing from others) the few Scottish newspapers, such as *the Oban Times*, which contained some Gaelic material and also allowed 'exiles' like the author, to keep up with events in the Highlands.

Author: Alexander MacDonald

Tune: No tune provided.

31 Am Moladh gu 'Thair an t-Sàl'
Gu Kate M. Powrie, Faisgeadal, Ardnamurchan
Source: *The Oban Times* June 30, 1900, p.7.
Context: The author was so struck with a song which had appeared in *The Oban Times* that he wrote his own poem in response to it as an appreciation of its words and sentiments.
Author: James MacMillan.
Tune: Not provided.

Section Four - The New Homeland - First Impressions

32 A Chuairtair mo Rùm

Source: *Cuairtear nan Gleann* Vol 1, No 11, 1 January, 1841, 251-256.

Context: A long, and very negative, opinion piece by an unnamed letter-writer living in the colony of Tìr Mhan Diemein (Tasmania). The best of land had already been taken up. Water was very scarce and difficult to obtain even from the digging of wells. Land and timber were very poor.

The writer's conclusions cover what he sees as the poor conditions of primary resources such as timber, land and water in that colony. He finishes by strongly advising prospective emigrants not to come there.

Author: Unnamed correspondent to *Cuairtear nan Gleann.*

33 A Chuairtair mo rùm, Mothaichadh iadsan

Source: *Cuairtear nan Gleann* Vol. 1, No. 11, 1 January, 1841, pp. 252-256.

Context: An abbreviated account, for a home audience, of the situation regarding land, water and flora, in Van Diemen's Land (Tasmania). This letter, according to the author, aimed to provide "a true, well-informed and first-hand account about Van Diemen's Island.". Eyewitness accounts by those immigrants from the Highlands and Islands who had settled in Tasmania were sought, especially by homeland newspapers. Government emigration schemes designed to settle the victims of forced clearances, or those just fleeing poverty, were often unhappy with the amount of negative news from settlers which found its way into Highland newspapers. This was especially so as such news, relating to the long and dangerous voyage entailed in travelling to Australia, as well as to the conditions associated with the land, its remoteness, the climate and the aborigines, hardly was the sort to encourage potential emigrants. Emigration societies sought to encourage home newspapers and journals to print only positive news from Highland emigrants. Thus, a mixture of views, derived from personal correspondence, articles, songs and poems, appeared in periodicals and newspapers such as *Cuirtear nan Gleann*, *An Gaidheal*, *An t-Àrd Albannach*, and *the Oban Times.*

Author: Cuairtear withheld the name of the contributor.

34 Fhìr Mo Gràidh

Source: A private letter from Rev Dr A. MacIntosh Mackay, Sydney (in private hands), to a friend in Scotland. Dr Mackay, a prominent minister of the Free Church of Scotland, and Gaelic scholar, had been called by the Gaelic Presbyterian church congregation in Melbourne to fill their vacant pulpit. He went afterwards to fill the vacancy at St George's Free Church congregation in Sydney.

Context: Among other matters, Mackay gives his first impressions of the country seeing it as suitable for widescale settlement by Highlanders. He makes the point, however, that hard work, sober habits and saving is the only way by which these settlers will ever be able to obtain land of their own.

Author: Rev Dr A. MacIntosh Mackay

35 Lìtir – Bho Rob MacDhùgaill

Source: *Cuairtear nan Gleann* Vol. 4, June 26, 1843, pp.113-117.

Context: Extracts from a letter which Rob MacDougall, a newly arrived immigrant, wrote about his first impressions of Australia on his way up country in Victoria to take up employment.

Like many Highlanders who were hired by station owners 'up country' in the new colonies of Australia, this immigrant had to find his own way to the property where he would be employed. However, MacDougall seems to have found the countryside well worth the journey and waxes lyrical about the features of the land.

Author: Rob MacDougall.

36 Do na Gael an Albainn

Source: *An Teachdaire Gaidhealach* Aireamh 2, April 2, 1857, p.8.

Context: The positive message which this sort of letter, and the three which follow it, provided was often used by Emigration agencies in Britain to paint a picture of successful life in the colonies in order to induce other Highlanders to emigrate. Emigration societies were often concerned at some of the negative images of the voyage and of life in the colonies appearing in newspaper letter columns and journals such as *Cuairtear nan Gleann*, and sought to combat this by 'salting' the papers with positive images such as those contained in this and the following letters.

The Highland and Island Emigration Society sought to suppress any negative views of the Australian colonies and actually sponsored the publication of a series of letters from Highland emigrants to Australia which had positive content. This publication, although the original letters were in Gaelic, presented the letters in English which were widely distributed and selectively salted in Highland newspapers such as *the Oban Times* and *The Highlander.*

Author: Pen name only, 'Lìtir bho 'Caraid nan Gaidheal', Ballarat.

37 Tha an Fhàilte Chridheil

Source: Editorial from *An Teachdaire Gaidhealach* Aireamh 8, September 1, 1857.

Context: This is part of an editorial informing readers how well the Australian Gaelic paper, *An Teachdaire Gaidhealach*, had been received in the Highlands and remarking that news was still being received of ongoing examples of 'clearances'. While decrying the cruelty of the land owners for these acts, the writer acknowledges the hand of God behind these events and praises Him for providing a country with so many blessings for the destitute Highlanders.

38 Lìtir – An Sgiathanach ann an Astràilla

Source: *An Teachdaire Gaidhealach* Aireamh 7, August 1,1857, pp.7-8.

Context: A letter published in *An Teachdaire Gaidhealach* presenting the story of a settler and his family who had managed, after a period three years of hard work and frugality, to save enough to leave his shepherding job and obtain a piece of land himself. He holds out his experience as one which the poor highlanders still in the

Highlands and Islands could easily emulate in the new land.

Author: John MacLeod, lately from Skye, Scotland.

*Whitsun and Martinmas were the periods in the year when rents were raised and farm workers were either re-hired or were without work. It was a time of great anxiety for those leasing a farm and for those who were farm labourers. In neither case did the highlander have any security or the power to bargain with his master.

39 Am Bliadhna

Source: *Donald MacKinnon Diary* –In private hands.

Context: The aftermath of a bushfire is tallied by Donald MacKinnon who lists the various consequences of the fire which swept through the district where other families lived.

The tally of death and the destruction of property is quite severe, but it is the loss of his caman which seems to distress MacKinnon the most!

Author: Donald MacKinnon.

40 Lìtir - Bho Donnchaidh Camshron

Source: *Cuairtear nan Gleann* Vol.2, No.23, January 8, 1842, pp.320-321.

Context: The writer provides his experiences and success after just a year in the colony. He foresees that he will be independent within a few years.

This is an example of the type of message which the home government and immigration agencies wanted to see publicised to encourage uprooted Highlanders to accept assisted emigration to Australia.

Author: Letter from Duncan Cameron, Ohoi, New England, New South Wales, 16th June 1841 to a friend in Scotland.

41 Lìtir – Gu *An Teachdaire Gaidhealach*

Source: *An Teachdaire Gaidhealach* Aireamh 10, November 1, 1857, p.5.

Context: This letter offers, perhaps, a more realistic view of 'getting on' in the new country than some of the other 'rags to riches' stories that were publicised. Contrary to the goldrush propaganda, where gold nuggets were there for the picking up, success in the colonies, in reality, relied very heavily upon hard work and sober habits.

Author: 'Calum agus Mise'

42 Òran an Eilthirich

Source: *An Teachdaire Gaidhealach*, Aireamh 8, September 1, 1857, pp. 4-5.

Context: The author of this poem, Angus Beaton, relates how he and many others were cleared from land on Mull and bundled on a ship bound for Australia. In these verses, from his longer poem, he gives his impressions of the remote place he has settled in the Australian colonies and his fear of wild dogs (dingos?) and aborigines.

Author: Angus Beaton

Tune: This song was set by the author to the tune, "Faill illirin ..."

43 'Theab Peilear Burraidh'

Source: Private correspondence between Rev Dr A. MacIntosh Mackay, Ballarat and an unnamed friend in Scotland. In private hands.

Context: Dr Mackay relates an incident when he was almost shot to death by a nervous soldier.

When the Church of Scotland in Australia (the Presbyterian Church) was split in 1846 (following the Disruption of 1843 in Scotland itself), those who left, ministers and people, formed a Free Church which was named the Presbyterian Church of Eastern Australia. Until 1851 Port Phillip (Victoria) was part of the colony of New South Wales under the general name of Eastern Australia. It became a separate colony in 1851 taking the name of Victoria. To change the name of the Church would have required an Act of Parliament and this has not been sought up to the present.

Author: Rev Dr A. MacIntosh Mackay, Minister of the Presbyterian Church of Eastern Australia (Free Church of Scotland), Melbourne Victoria.

*Martial Law – the Ballarat Gold fields had, a short time before, been the scene of violence (the Eureka Stockade) between the soldiers and some miners protesting against, among other grievances, the unjust licence system imposed on them by the authorities. Although it was quickly put down, some of the miners and a few soldiers were killed or wounded. Martial Law was proclaimed and Dr MacIntosh, foolishly, was out and about without a pass.

Section Five - Love, Loss and Relationships

44 An Latha an Diugh

Source: *Donald MacKinnon Diary* – In Private Hands.

Context: The author, although a long-time settler in Australia, still used events and seasons and traditions from his native Coll as his point of reference when going about his normal work at Coraki, New South Wales. These six short pieces were grouped by the editors to demonstrate this theme.

Author: Donald MacKinnon.

45 Gearr-Chunntas Air Trathan Araid Dhe 'M Shaogal

Source: *The Oban Times* September 15, 1900, p.7.

Context: Mr Alexander MacDonald, originally from Sleat, Isle of Skye, was a long-time resident of Geelong, Victoria, since his arrival in Australia many years before. He suffered from an increasingly worsening condition of paralysis of the limbs. A day of respite from his immobility led him to visit an old friend, Samuel MacAulay who, coincidentially, was also suffering from a bout of ill-health. When he found that MacAulay was not at home MacDonald left a note, in Gaelic, chalked onto the doorstep. Each man was adept at poetic composition and the missed visit occasioned the following. When MacAulay returned home he saw the message chalked on his doorstep and composed the first verse of a poem in Gaelic which, some days later, he was able to give to MacDonald. Confined to bed, MacDonald completed the poem began by MacAulay. In the course of relating the incident, Alexander MacDonald provides some autobiographical material and mentions his infirmity and his strong religious faith.

Author: Alexander MacDonald

46 Bliadhna Mhath Ùr

Source: *The Oban Times* January 5, 1901, p.7.

Context: The poet uses an annual celebration in Australia as his point of contact with past memories of such celebrations in the Highlands.

Author James MacMillan

Tune: No tune is given although the theme and the rhythm of the words suggest that the poet had a tune in mind when composing his poem.

47 Diluain an t-Sainnseal (Handsel Monday)

Source: *Donald MacKinnon Diary* – In private hands.

Context: Personal lines by Donald MacKinnon senior, remembering with joy and affection the year of his marriage.

Author: Donald MacKinnon senior.

Tune: Not provided.

*Handsel Monday - In Scotland, the first Monday after New Year's Day is, traditionally, known as Handsel Monday. Gifts (Scottish-Handsels), are usually given out at this time.

48 Fàth Mo Liunnduith

Source: *Donald MacKinnon Diary* – In private hands.
Context: A painful recollection of the death of the poet's wife.
Author: Donald MacKinnon senior.
Tune: Not provided.

49 Alastair an Gaol/Marbhrann do Alastair

Source: In private hands.
Context: The joy of a son's birth/A lament for the son's death.

A freak accident which led to his beloved son's death was the catalyst for the composing of this lament. Although the poet poured out his grief, it was not out of despair or unbelieving resignation. The poem's latter lines show the joyful confidence that father and son will be reunited in the eternal presence of God.

Author: Rev Alan MacDonald MacKillop

Tune: Although no tune is given, this lament was sung by one of Mr MacKillop's family in North Uist. The singer's daughter informed one of the editors of this fact although she could not remember the tune.

Note: The term 'Caochail' (change) was used to signify the state of having died.

*Whitsunday ('Air Latha Caingeis') was the day of the year on which a tenant-at-will was liable to get notice to 'quit his holding', or be evicted. Farm workers, likewise, would be informed whether they were to be re-hired or whether they were given notice to quit their position. The poet makes play on this practice by using the term 'quit' to refer to his son's death on Whitsunday, as Alastair getting "a sharp notice to quit."

The expression A' Bhràthair', used in the first line of the last verse, was the affectionate term by which Mr MacKillop always addressed his son, Alastair.

'Flath-Innis', used in the last verse, was the Celtic pre-Christian name for Heaven and here, Mr MacKillop was using it in its 'classical' Gaelic sense.

50 Marbhrann

Source: *An Teachdaire Gaidhealach* February, 1857, p.4.

Context: The editor of: *An Teachdaire Gaidhealach* appended the following introduction to this poem. "A' Marbhrann a leanas, do Ghaedhal a dh'eug ann an Hobart Town air a cheathreamh-lath-deug de mhìos deireannach na bliadhna 1856, a chuir dar n-ionnsuidh le caraid anns a Bhaile sin."

["This Lament was composed in memory of a Gael who died in Hobart Town on the fourteenth day of last month in the year 1856, and was sent to us by a friend in that Town."]

Author: Pen Name 'Creagan-an-Fhithich'
Tune: Air 'Creag na Ciadain'.

*The name 'The Raven's Rock' is the motto of Glengarry (the same as the MacDonalds of whom Glengarry is a branch) – and is symbolised by a raven perched on a rock.

51 Air a' Chèilidh

Source: *Donald MacKinnon Diary* – In Private Hands.

Context: An example of how bad weather and a social call rationalises the decision to have a day of leisure and idle conversation for a busy farmer.

Author: Donald MacKinnon senior.

52 Òran – Tha Mi Fo Chùram

["A rinnedh le leannain do Thormod Mac Neachdail, Scorrabreachd, an uair a bha e gu seòladh, na òganach treun, sgairteal, as an Eilean Sgitheanach gu Australia. Cha do Phill e air ais gu eilean a' breith, oir chaidh a bhàthadh gu muladach ann an treun a neirt, agus ann an tòiseach a shoirbheis, an uair a chaidh e air maduinn bhlàth ga fhailcedh fèin anns a' chuan."

["Composed by the wife of Norman Nicholson, Scorrybreac, Skye. He had sailed as a brave, vigorous young man, from Skye to Australia. He never returned to the island of his birth because, sadly, he drowned in his prime and at the beginning of his prosperity, when he went to bathe in the sea one warm morning."]

Source: *An t-Àrd Albannach* October 11, 1873, p.3.

Context: Norman Nicholson had gone to Australia to seek his fortune. Sadly, he drowned while bathing in the sea. His wife pines for him while drifting in and out of belief whether or not he is dead and determining to be re-united with him by travelling to Australia herself.

Author: Wife of Norman Nicholson

Note: The drowned man's wife, still on Skye, mentally cannot accept the news of her husband's death. The reference to the image of her "beloved's breast is white", clearly a reference to his dead, drowned body, does not seem to have convinced her and the poem wavers between the reality and the unreality of her husband's death. In her state of delusion, she believed that her husband was still crossing the ocean to Australia. She also fantasised about being reunited with him in Australia although, at times, she does seem to be aware that he has gone ('an exile') to a place where she cannot be i.e. the realm of the dead.

53 Cumha Airson Anabla

Source: In Private Hands.

Context: The author of these words was Rev Allan MacDonald MacKillop. In his younger years in Scotland, Anabella, the subject of this poem, was someone for whom he had great affection and whom he had hoped to marry. When it became clear to him that this would not happen, he accepted an appointment as a missionary to Australia.

He never returned to Scotland and he later married and had a family and spent fifty happy years with his wife and children. However, he never lost the precious memory of his first love, Anabella, and the news of her death led Mr MacKillop to pen this memorial to her.

Author: Rev Alan MacKillop MacDonald.

Tune: No tune is given though the running chorus suggests that it is meant to be sung.

54 Lìtir – Thu'n Caraid

Source: *The Oban Times* June 30, 1906, p.3.

Context: A strong friendship between the poet in Australia and a friend still in Scotland seems to be under strain because of the distance between them. The emigrant in Australia writing to his friend Donald in Scotland asks whether the fact that he has not heard from him means that Donald has forgotten him.

Author: James MacMillan

*The poet also imagines that things must have changed in the Glen where friendship and mutual help had now disappeared with the passage of time. The poet hopes, however, that he is wrong and that the best aspects of the old Highland culture still remain.

He adds that if he is wrong he hopes his friend will forgive him his doubts and that he looks forward to receiving a letter from him.

***The Oban Times* was a Highland newspaper published at Oban, Scotland, partly in Gaelic and partly in English. It carried local news in Gaelic as well as original Gaelic poetry and it was subscribed to by many Highlanders in Australia. It also published many literary contributions from Gaels in Australia and New Zealand.

55 Òran – Do Aonghas Brocair

Source: *The Oban Times* June 11, 1898, p.6.

Context: The subject of this poem had been a noted fox-hunter in the Highlands and Islands in the poet's younger days. The hunter had emigrated to Australia and was now in his declining years. The word 'Brocair' means a fox hunter, in Gaelic. Identification of people was often made by using a person's occupation as a descriptive name.

Author: Alexander MacDonald, Geelong, Victoria

Tune: 'Faigh a Nuas Dhuinn am Botul'

56 Òran – Do Fhloraidh Bheag

Source: *The Oban Times* March 10, 1900, p.7.

Context: The subject may have been a close family friend's child although the sentiments expressed could suggest a favourite child within or without the poet's own family circle.

Author: James MacMillan
Tune: 'Gur i chaileag bhòidheach lagach'.
Note: Although the title mentions these lines as being the first part of the song, no follow-up verses have been located. [eds].

57 Beannachdan Chum Dhomhnull

Source: *The Oban Times* 3 February, 1900, p8.
Context: Selected verses of another, longer, poem by James MacMillan who appears to be responding to a letter he had received, possibly in poetic form, from a friend in Scotland. MacMillan appears puzzled as to how he should understand some of the poem's lines.
Author: James MacMillan
Tune: Not provided.

Section Six - Religion

58 Tha Mill do Neoil.

Source: *Donald MacKinnon Diary* – In Private Hands.

Context: The poet ponders the need for rain and the need for religious revival – each dependent upon God's providence.

Author: Donald MacKinnon

Tune: Not provided.

59 Lìtir a Chum nan Gaidheal a tha Chòmhnuidh

Source: *The Colonist* November 7, 1838, p.3.

Context: This is probably the first piece of printed Gaelic (in an English publication) in Australia. It is an appeal to Highlanders, especially those who have achieved a measure of prosperity in the colony, for funds to build a Gaelic church. William McIntyre was a prominent Free Church of Scotland minister in NSW, and worked among highlanders at Maitland and other places. He was responsible for clearing (albeit with his wife's money), the long-standing debt on St George's Church (PCEA) Sydney.

Author: Rev. William MacIntyre

60 Naigheachdan

Source: Letter from John Macleod to *An Teachdaire Gaidhealach* Aireamh 7, August, 1857, p.8.

Context: MacLeod laments the fact that there is a shortage of Gaelic churches and Gaelic ministers in Victoria.

Author: John Macleod.

61 Aodhaireil O Sheannadh

Source: *Lìtir Aodhaireil O Sheanadh Na h-Eaglais Saoire* ann *am Bhictoria.* [Extract only] from printed letter held by State Library of Victoria, Melbourne, Victoria.

Synod of the Free Church in Victoria

Context: For many of the Highland emigrants, Church and Bible had played a large part in their lives and that of their families in their homeland. The worship concerns of these settlers were thus an important element in the settling process in their new homeland. The subject appears in much of the correspondence and other writing by many of the Highlanders in the colony.

Author: Moderator of the Free Church in Victoria, 1855.

[Eds note: Although the name of the author of this pamphlet does not appear on the Pamphlet itself, the Moderator at this time was Rev. Dr A. McIntosh Mackay and it is probably safe to conclude that he was the author.]

62 Lìtir Don Chuairtear Bho Rob MacDhùgaill

Source: *Cuairtear nan Gleann* Vol.4, June 26, 1843, pp.113-117.

Context: This is a short extract from a longer letter which Rob MacDougall wrote to *Cuairtear nan Gleann* giving details of his first impressions of Melbourne and its buildings and the major Churches operating in that town.

Author: Rob MacDougall

63 Lìtir Mi-Naomhachadh na Sàbaid

Source: *An Teachdaire Gaidhealach* Aireamh 3, April 1, 1857, p.6.

Context: Highlanders were confronted in the colonies with a religious environment far removed from what they had enjoyed in some of the towns and villages in the Highlands. They encountered a society where the Sabbath was not recognised and where drinking was rife among many of the settlers. These aspects of the new frontier shocked many of the Highland settlers. Others of their number, unfortunately, fell into some of the worst evils of the frontier way of life.

Author: 'S.T.' Melbourne, Victoria

64 Lìtir gu a' Charaid

Source: Letter in private hands. A private letter from Rev Dr A. MacIntosh MacKay to unnamed Friend in Scotland.ga

Context: Dr MacKay is presenting his views of the Australian colonies, the opportunities which exist for poor highlanders and, at the same time, presenting a dark picture of excessive use of alcohol and the irreligious character of many of the people. Dr Mackay's letter to a friend in Scotland paints a rather bleak picture of some sections of society. Although the conditions existed for every immigrant family from Scotland to succeed, many were turning aside from civilized living. Mackay adds that irreligion, laziness and a lifestyle akin to that of ignorant savages, better describes many of these settlers all of whom, he wrote, were digging their own pathway to hell.

In Theab burraidh he also makes reference to the lawlessness which still existed in certain areas, which were under martial law, and which almost cost him his life at the hands of a nervous soldier.

Note: Mackay, a prominent minister of the Church of Scotland, and Gaelic scholar, had been called by the Gaelic Presbyterian church congregation in Melbourne to fill their vacant pulpit.

Among other matters, Mackay gives his first impressions of the country seeing it as suitable for widescale settlement by Highlanders. He makes the point, however, that hard work, sober habits and saving their earnings are the only ways by which these settlers will ever be able to obtain land of their own.

Author: Rev Dr A. MacIntosh MacKay.

65 Aran na Beatha

Source: *An Teachdaire Gaidhealach*, Aireamh 3, April 1, 1857, p.6.

Context: Mr Lachlan Mackenzie was a well-known church minister in the Loch Carron district in the Scottish Highlands. In areas where some people had little education, a sermon could be read in what the minister would illustrate by means of story.

Author: Anonymous.

66 An Dìbleach Bochd

Source: *An Teachdaire Gaidhealach* Aireamh 10 November 1,1857, p.3.

Context: A homily on the gospel teaching that even the most wretched of sinners can be washed clean and accepted by God. It portrays a longing for the day when the believer will leave the trials and struggles against a sinful world and be taken to heaven where they will sing eternal praises to God.

Author Ewan MacIntyre.

Tune: Not provided.

67 Deoch Làdir

Source: *Donald MacKinnon Diary* - In private hands.

Context: Another example of the attitude of some Highlanders in the colonies to the excess of drinking which they encountered. The writer demonstrates the link which he saw between excessive drinking and unruly and unlawful social behaviour and the decline in the practice of the Christian religion. He especially lays the responsibility upon the parents to protect their children and not to be a bad example to them.

Author: Donald MacKinnon junior.

68 Cuairt ann an Àit-Adhlacaidh

Source: *The Oban Times* November 5, 1898, p.7.

Context: A message that all, sooner or later, must die and stand before God in judgment. It is an exhortation, too, for people to live their lives while on Earth in accord with this truth.

Author: James MacMillan

Tune: Not provided.

Section Seven - Folklore - Tales and Songs

69 Linntean Dorcha an t-Shaobh-Chràbhaidh

Source: *An Teachdaire Gaidhealach*, Aireamh 5, June 1, 1857.

Context: The editor of *An Teachdaire Gaidhealach*, on more than one occasion, addresses the need for Highlanders in their new land to take advantage of education whereby they would lose their backward, superstitious beliefs.

It is ironic that, despite its teaching nature, the Messenger happily received contributions to its pages which encompassed legends, superstitions and fantasy material without comment or any sign of criticism or rejection of it!

Author: Editorial - *An Teachdaire Gaidhealach.*

70 MacCruimein – Na Cumhadh an Fhògararraich

Source: *An Teachdaire Gaidhealach* Aireamh, 10, November, 1857, pp.3-4.

Context: A lament at the leaving of the Macrimmons* the hereditary pipers to the Macleods of Skye. Probably meant to be symbolic of the way of life that was disappearing from the Highlands and Islands.

Author: 'Mactalla' Rev Duncan MacCalman

Tune: Not provided.

**Macrimmons – The hereditary pipers of the Macleods came from the Macrimmon family who established a school of piping on Skye centuries before. Cha Til Macruimein – (Macrimmon will never return), is a well-known pibroch often played at funerals.

*** Dunvegan Castle is the hereditary seat of the Macleods of Skye.

71 Cù aig Tighearna Dhiùra

Source: *Donald MacKinnon Diary* - In private hands.

Context: A reference to the famous hound of the Duke of Jura which was surpassed only by Bran, Fingal's mighty hunting dog. Fingal was the legendary leader of the Feinne – the Fingalian Warriors - the subject of Ossian's epics

Author: Donald MacKinnon senior.

*Bran was a giant hound which was Fingal's hunting dog.

** Conan (Conan mac Morna) was a warrior and a member of Fingal's Feinne – a circle of warriors loyal to Fingal.

72 A Chrìthionn Seo

Source: *The Celtic Monthly* Vol 11, August 1903, p.210.

Context: Donald Beaton recorded that, when he was growing up on Mull, this verse was a rhyme that children recited when they came across an aspen. The legend relates to the time of Christ's crucifixion and has many variations. In one version aspen trees tremble as a curse for being disrespectful towards the holy family in that they did not bow their branches towards the holy family as the other trees had done. Another version, and the one that Donald Beaton seems to be alluding to here, is that it was from the wood of the aspen tree that the cross on which Christ was crucified was made. For this reason, the tree had been cursed in the aforementioned manner.cc]

Author: Donald Beaton.

73 Fath Ioghnaidh a' Choigrich

Source: *An Teachdaire Gaidhealach*, Aireamh 5, June 1, 1857 agus Aireamh 6, July 1857.

Context: A wonder story with a late religious twist in its tail.

Author Traditional Tale as Retold by 'A True Gael', Geelong.

74 Raonull agus an Collunn Gun Cheann

Source: *An Teachdaire Gaidhealach*, Aireamh 10, November 1, 1857, p.7.

Context: One of the several folk stories about the Raonull, a traditional character.

Author: Traditional Tale as retold by 'A True Gael', Geelong.

75 Raonull agus an Sgiobair

Source: *An Teachdaire Gaidhealach*, Aireamh 10, November 1, 1857, p.7.

Context: Another traditional Gaelic story featuring Raonull.

Author: Traditional Gaelic Tale retold by 'A True Gael', Geelong.

76 Cù Dubh a' Chuain Ghuirm

Source: *The Celtic Monthly* Vol.15, March 1907, pp.114-116.

Context: Donald Beaton, the contributor of this story, was an emigrant whose family was 'cleared' from the Isle of Mull. He was a collector and repository of Gaelic poetry, song and traditional tales and frequently contributed these to Gaelic magazines and newspapers in Scotland. He was also a great champion of the Gaelic language and wrote extensively on ways by which it could survive and thrive in the colony of Australia. His father, Angus Beaton, (qv) also migrated to Australia in 1852 and was himself a considerable Gaelic poet.

Author: Traditional Tale as re-told by Donald Beaton.

77 Chrom an Fhàsaich

Source: *The Celtic Monthly* Vol.15, No.3 December 1906, pp. 45-46.

Context: The author recollects a game which used to be popular in his youth on Mull and which was a means of teaching wrestling. He raises the question, to the editor of *the Celtic Monthly*, whether such games were still played. The answer he gets is a depressing one.

Author: Retold by Donald Beaton.

78 Sgeulachd na Trì Saighdearan

Source: *The Celtic Monthly* Vol. 16, October, 1907, pp.5-7.

Context: The re-telling of a traditional Highland tale featuring magic, bravery and justice.

Author: A Traditional Tale re-told by Donald Beaton.

79 "Mise chuala 's a chunnaic e"

Source: *The Celtic Monthly* Vol. 15, October, 1906, pp.45-46.

Context: A traditional children's continuance tale after the style of Henny Penny etc.

Author: A traditional story retold by Donald Beaton.

Note: *The Celtic Monthly* has a foreword to this contribution as follows.

"The following curious play has been sent us by Mr Donald Beaton, Queensland, who says he heard it last at a Ceilidh in Dervaig, Isle of Mull, fifty-two years ago, and saw it acted at Arisaig, fifty-seven years ago. It is after the style of 'Murachan is Mearachan' or the English rhyme, 'The House that Jack Built.' We are not aware that it has ever been in print before.

Section Eight - Humour and Satire

80 'Ta-ra-ra- Boom de Day'

Source: In private hands.

Context: The poem relates a social irritation, not entirely unknown in modern society, the non-stop repetition of the latest 'pop' tune.

Author: Donald MacKinnon junior.

Tune: Not provided.

81 Dìomoladh na Pìob-Thombaca

Source: *The Oban Times* November 22, 1902, p.7.

Context: A humorous exchange regarding the virtues, or otherwise, of smoking.

Author: Alexander MacDonald.

Tune: Set to the air, 'An Dotair Leòdach 's biodag.'

82 Fhreagair Gilleasbuig – 'G a Moladh

Source: *The Oban Times* November 22, 1902, p.7.

Context: A smoker's response to the anti-smoking campaign.

Author: Alexander MacDonald

Tune: Set to the air, 'An Dotair Leòdach 's biodag.'

83 Aois, Maise agus Cliù na Gàidhlig

Source: *The Oban Times* November 21,1903, p.3.

Context: A tongue-in-cheek recitation of the fame, since the time of creation, of the Gaelic language.

Author: Archibald MacDonald.

Tune: Not provided.

*It was believed that Queen Victoria had some of her children taught Gaelic.

**This was established in 1882. Highlanders and others gave large support to fund-raising campaigns in Australia to help fund the Establishing of the Chair.

84 Rann do Aran Coirce

Source: *The Oban Times* 7 April, 1900, p.7.

Context: Humorous verses on the superiority of the oatcake.

Author: Alexander MacDonald

Tune: Not provided.

85 Lìtir bho 'Garunnach', gu *An Teachdaire Gaidhealach*

Source: *An Teachdaire Gaidhealach* No 4, 1857, p.8.

Context: Reaction to a youth's rapid loss of the Gaelic.

Author: 'Disgusted'.

86 A Phòsadh
Source: *Donald MacKinnon Diary* – In private hands.
Context: Amusing short tale of a gormless groom.
Author: Donald MacKinnon junior.

87 Tha Banntrach Òg Ghàidhealach 'Gairm'
Source: *An Teachdaire Gaidhealach* No 3, April 1, 1857, p.8.
Context: Probably a spoof 'lonely heart' advertisement.
Author: Anonymous advertisement.

88 Seun Airson Dèanamh Leanna
Source: *An Gaidheal* Vol. 2, 1874, p.52.
Context: Traditional tale with a twist ending.
Author: Donald Beaton

89 Mod Loch na Lusan
Source: In private hands.
Context: Egon Erwin Kisch was a multi-lingual, anti-fascist speaker and writer and Czech-Jewish journalist, who was refused entry to Australia when his ship, the Strathaird, arrived in Melbourne on November 13, 1934. As the ship left dock Kisch jumped from the deck onto the quay breaking his leg. However, he was put back on the ship which then sailed to Sydney. Kisch had been invited to Australia to speak at anti-Fascist rallies. The resultant court case over whether the 'dictation test' designed to keep him out of the country was a valid one actually gave Kisch and the anti-Fascist cause a great deal more publicity than would have been the case had the government not resorted to such tactics to keep him out of the Australia. The High Court ruling in favour of Kisch meant that he was freed and continued in the country until 1935 speaking at various rallies denouncing Hitler and Fascism. However, the legal ruling, which relegated Scottish Gaelic to the dustbin, sparked an outcry from Scots and the major Sydney newspapers (among the other Press) were filled with correspondence and arguments on the matter.

In the case of Egon Kisch, a man who was familiar with several European languages, the government resorted to using Scottish Gaelic as the test language. Kisch failed this but a case in his defence was launched to show that Gaelic was not a "living" European language in the general meaning of that term. This case was successfully argued in the courts much to the disgust of many Gaels in Australia one of whom satirized the whole affair – in Gaelic!
Author: Rev Allan MacDonald MacKillop
Tune: Le Fògarrach bho Chaolas-Hirt

90 Am Minister
Source: *Donald MacKinnon Diary* – In private hands.
Context: A wry look at a local minister.
Author: Donald MacKinnon senior

91 Cha Bhi Searman
Source: *Donald MacKinnon Diary* – In private hands.
Context: A holiday for Queen Victoria's birthday – not appreciated by all.
Author: Donald MacKinnon senior.

92 Cò Sud an Cruigeir
Source: *The Oban Times* June 23, 1900, p.7.
Context: This is a jingoistic piece humorously mocking Paul Kruger (1825-1904), the Boer's political leader.
Author: Donald MacKinnon junior
Tune: No tune is given but the presence of a chorus suggests that it was meant to be sung.

Appendix Two

Images Used

1. A Lochaberman Leaving His Country
   (Page 15)
   Loch Leven, Scotland.
   [Photo courtesy of Free Images Pixabay HTML]

15. The Burning of the *India*
    (Page 64)
    The barque *India* (1840) – setting out for its first journey to Australia in 1840.
    [South Australia Immigration Records, South Australia State Library.]

15. The Burning of the *India*
    (Page 65)
    Samuel Elyard, S. (1817-1910) Australian artist of the Burning of the Barque "*India*", off Greenock in the South Atlantic Ocean, 19th July 1841.
    [Photographic Print, State Library of Victoria Filename a14928:346880]

20. Loch Laggan
    (Page 95)
    Loch Laggan, Scotland.
    [Photo courtesy of Alastair Garrow]

23. Ounich Bay
    (Page 107)
    Looking down from Righ Forest on Ballachulish village and across Onich Bay.
    [Photo courtesy of Evelyn Bakker]

23. Ounich Bay
    (Page 107)
    Looking over North Ballachulish and Onich Bay to Garbh Bheinn, under low cloud. This is the highest peak of the Hills of Ardgour.
    [Photo courtesy of Evelyn Bakker]

23. Ounich Bay
(Page 109)
High in the Righ Forest looking over Onich Bay (Loch Linnhe) to the Ardgour Hills.
[Photo courtesy of Evelyn Bakker]

28. Ree Waterfall
(Page 124)
Near the top of the Abhainn Righ Gorge (King's River Gorge) looking down on one of the first of the eight natural 'steps' making up the Righ Waterfall. The Righ River tumbles almost 1,000 feet in a series of eight steps (waterfalls) into the Righ River Gorge.
[Photo courtesy of Evelyn Bakker]

28. Ree Waterfall
(Page 124)
A lower 'step' of the Righ Falls.
[Photo courtesy of Evelyn Bakker]

28. Ree Waterfall
(Page 127)
Another 'step' of the Righ Falls.
[Photo courtesy of Evelyn Bakker]

52 Cliff Falls
(Page 197)
On the Isle of Skye
[Photo courtesy of Evelyn Bakker]

73 The Culloden Memorial Stone
(Page 263)
Culloden Battlefield, Scotland
[Photo courtesy of Evelyn Bakker]

76 Sunset over the Firth of Lorne
(Page 281)
Oban, Argyll, Scotland
[Photo courtesy of Evelyn Bakker]

79 Sunset over the Firth of Lorne
(Page 303)
Oban, Argyll, Scotland
[Photo courtesy of Evelyn Bakker]

Short Biographical List of Contributors to the Anthology

Camshron, Ailean 'Abrach' – Cameron, Allan (1812?-1882) was born in the Lochaber district and was a seasoned traveller before emigrating to Australia. Not much is known of his activities in Australia although he may have been the Allan Cameron who was one of the agents in Tasmania for the distribution of the Gaelic paper *An Teachdaire Gaidhealach* in 1857. He moved across to Melbourne, Victoria and it was from here he appears to have written most of his Gaelic poetry under the pen name 'Abrach'. He was a friend of 'Nether Lochaber' (Rev. Alexander Stewart) who promoted Cameron's work through Gaelic journals and newspapers in Scotland.

Camshron, Donnchadh – Cameron, Duncan (1803-1863) was born at Ardnamurchan. He emigrated to NSW from Tobermory in 1837 on the Brilliant arriving in Sydney January 1838. He became a farmer and died in Grafton NSW in 1863.

MacAmhlaidh, Samuel – MacAulay, Samuel (1828-1907?), born at Glen Bernisdale, Skeabost, Isle of Skye. He emigrated to Australia via coastal ship from Snizort and then from Greenock aboard a Highland and Island Emigration Society (HIES) ship, the Georgiana, in July 1852. After the ship docked in Geelong, Victoria, there was a mutiny when some of the crew refused to sail the ship on to Sydney, insisting instead that they be allowed to go off to the goldfields. The resultant action led to the Captain shooting dead one of the ringleaders and the other rebellious crew injuring the Captain and lashing him to the wheel while they made their escape. MacAulay was a native Gaelic speaker who settled in Geelong where he became a long-standing member of the Comunn na Feinne. He was a friend of Alexander MacDonald (q.v.), but the few lines at the head of an Alexander MacDonald poem is the only example of MacAulay's Gaelic writing which has been located.

Mac-an-t-Saoir, An t-Urramach Alasdair – McIntyre, Rev. Alexander (1806?-1878)

Alexander MacIntyre was born at Rannachan by Strontian a village on the west coast of Argyllshire, and was one of twelve children and one of only five (one brother and three sisters) who survived into adulthood. He received his early education at Strontian and, later, commenced medical training at Edinburgh, but following his conversion to Christ he trained for the ministry. During the period of the Ten Year's Conflict MacIntyre was a staunch supporter of the Evangelical Party and was anti-landlord and anti-establishment, facts which delayed his trials and licensing by his own Presbytery. It was not until 1836, at the age of thirty, that he was licensed in Ross-shire by a Presbytery under the Synod of Glenelg. He refused to accept a call from Strontian, convinced that he had a calling to minister as an evangelist rather than through a settled ministry.

While he was based at the Parish of Kilmallie, Lochaber experienced a period of revival under his preaching. When the Disruption took place in 1843 and many landowners were refusing those who 'came out' the use of buildings and land for church services, MacIntyre ministered initially outdoors and later from a floating church which was towed and anchored in Loch Sunart at Strontian.

In the years 1843-47 he itinerated around Skye, Mull and North Uist. Many of his hearers were driven by the potato famine and poverty to emigrate to Northern New South Wales. During part of 1846 and 1847 he ministered on Prince Edward Island, Nova Scotia for the Colonial Committee of the General Assembly of the Free Church of Scotland, but he returned and resumed his itinerating ministry in the Highlands until 1853 when he offered himself for service in Australia. He sailed (September 1852) aboard the Typhoon to Geelong, Victoria, arriving in March, 1853 and stayed with his brother who had settled there some years before. He then moved to New South Wales and was accepted by the Free Church (a disruption had taken place in Australia in 1846) and worked at Ahalton. In 1858 he returned to Geelong serving the Gaelic Free Church (Presbyterian Church of Eastern Australia) in that place while also itinerating among Gaelic-speaking congregations in other parts of Victoria and also in New South Wales. He continued this type of ministry until his death at Geelong in 1878. His stance in support of the Free Church in Australia (the Presbyterian Church of Eastern Australia) is credited with keeping Highlanders, especially in Victoria, out of the Re-unification of the 1850's and beyond thus ensuring the continued presence of the Free Church in Australia to this day. MacIntyre was a powerful evangelical preacher in Gaelic and English with a passion for 'lost souls' and had a marked affect upon Highland congregations wherever he travelled. While he wrote Gaelic verse himself, he was also the subject of many Gaelic poems, especially in Canada.

Alexander MacIntyre died, unmarried, at Geelong on 9th June 18 1878, aged 71.

Mac-an-t-Saoir, Eoghan – MacIntyre, Ewan, was born in Lochaber. He appears to have been 'cleared' from where he was living in the Highlands and reluctantly emigrated to Australia. The date of his arrival is not known although he was in Victoria by 1857 and may have shifted to NSW. He composed many poems in Gaelic and was active in the promotion of Gaelic schools both in Australia and the Scottish Highlands. (eg see *An Teachaire Gaidhealach*.] Little more is known of this settler.

Mac-an-t-Saoir, An t-Urramach Uilleam – Rev. William McIntyre (1806-1870), born at Kilmonivaig near Fort William, the son of a tenant farmer. He took his M.A. in 1829 at Glasgow and then studied at Divinity Hall, was licensed by the Presbytery of Dunoon and ordained in 1837. He taught school for his brother in Glasgow until Rev. John Dunmore Lang, the pioneering minister of NSW, persuaded him to go to Australia. He sailed as chaplain to the 260 Highlanders on board the Midlothian, arriving in Sydney in December, 1837, where he conducted the first ever service in Gaelic held in the colonies. He served at Scots church, Sydney with Lang as well as teaching theology in the latter's Australian College He also helped run *The Colonist* newspaper, and itinerated among Gaels in the Hunter Valley north of Sydney until accepting a call to a Gaelic ministry at Maitland (1841-46). McIntyre was influential in supporting an Australian 'Disruption' in 1846 siding with the 'Free Church' group, establishing a new Gaelic church at East Maitland which he served (1846-62), and becoming one of the ministers who founded the Presbyterian Church of Eastern Australia (the 'Free Church'). In 1847 he established a Gaelic-speaking 'Free Church' at Ahalton, NSW which was later served by Alexander McIntyre (q.v.). McIntyre married his cousin who was heir to the extensive Australian property of her father, Peter McIntyre, and became financially independent. When he was called to replace Dr A. MacIntosh Mackay (q.v.) at the debt-ridden St George's church in Sydney in 1862, he served the congregation without stipend until his death in 1870 and managed to reduce the debt from a massive £12,000 to less than half that amount before he died. He generously gave of his own money. He edited the Australian Free Church journals *The Voice in the Wilderness* and *The Testimony* as well as publishing prolifically on theological issues.

Always a theological conservative and faithful to the Protestant heritage, his intention to deliver a public lecture on Roman Catholicism led to what is known as the Maitland Riots in 1860 when he and his party were attacked by a mob of Irish Roman Catholics on the way to the Lecture Hall. Although William himself was injured, his brother received even more severe wounds from which he subsequently died.

MacAoidh, An t-Urramach Ollamh A. Mac-an-Toisich – Mackay, Rev. Dr A. MacIntosh (1793-1873) was born at Eddrachilis, Sutherlandshire, the son of a tacksman. He studied at United College, St Andrews (1814-18), then at the Divinity Hall of Glasgow University, which later conferred a LLD on him in 1829 for his substantial scholarly contribution to the Highland Society's Gaelic Dictionary. He also took studies at Edinburgh and Aberdeen universities. Licensed by the Presbytery of Skye he served at Laggan (1825-32) and Dunoon (1832-43). He supported the Evangelical Party in the conflict which led to the Disruption of 1843. Mackay edited the Free Church Gaelic publication *An Fhianuis* (*The Witness*) between 1845 and 1850. He also served as the Moderator of the General Assembly of the Free Church 1849-50. At the age 61 he offered himself for service among the Gaels in Australia. He arrived in Melbourne in December, 1853 and, at first, ministered to scattered Highland groups until he accepted a call to the Gaelic-speaking congregation in the Melbourne suburb of Carlton in 1854. There he built St Andrew's church (opened 1855) at crippling expense (£10,000) especially given that the congregation was a financially poor one. He was Moderator of the Free Presbyterian Church (Free Church) of Victoria 1855-56. Called to Sydney he repeated the exercise there, building St George's Church for the vast sum of £14,000. As a result, the congregation was unable to pay his £600 p.a. stipend and offered a lower amount. Mackay resigned in 1861 and returned to Scotland, ministering at Tarbert on Harris 1862-68. His drawn-out preaching style did not suit the two urban Australian congregations he served and, as a consequence, he was unable to collect large congregations around him.

McCalman, An T-Urramach Dùghall – Rev Dugald McCalman (1830-1880) was born at Ben Auc in Argyllshire. He studied for the ministry of the Free Church of Scotland subsequently being ordained by the Presbytery of Lorn, on the island of Mull. He emigrated sometime before 1854, ministering briefly to Highlanders at Carlton in Melbourne before moving to Portland in the Western District of Victoria. In November 1856 he became Free Church minister at Mosquito Plains (Naracoorte) over the border from Victoria in the far east of South Australia where there were many Gaelic-speaking Highland settlers. This was an extensive parish extending from Edenhope in Victoria to Robe in the south-east of South Australia, and Dugald McCalman travelled regularly to conduct Gaelic services for Gaels at Edenhope, Robe and Penola until such time as those congregations gained ministers of their own. His ministry at Naracoorte extended over twenty-one years. As well as contributing his own Gaelic poetry, Duguld McCalman committed to print some of the traditional material which he had learned when growing up in the Highlands of Scotland.

MacDhòmhnaill, Alasdair – MacDonald, Alexander (1844(?) - 1927) was born at Sleat on Skye and was a Gaelic schoolteacher on that Island before he moved from Portree to Glasgow. After a short sojourn there he emigrated to Australia. At the age of twenty-eight he was teaching school (in English) for the Education Department of Victoria at Geelong in Victoria. He also spent several years working on the goldfields but met with very little profit. He became crippled as the result of a progressive disability although this did not prevent him writing a good deal of light-hearted Gaelic poetry. He was a long-time member of the Highland Society, Comunn na Feinne, based in Geelong, and won several prizes in its annual Gaelic language competitions which it held for poetry and prose. He regularly contributed poems to *The Oban Times* and had been writing Gaelic poetry even before leaving Scotland. He latterly moved to Melbourne and died in 1927 at an advanced age.

MacDhòmhnaill, Gilleasbuig - Archibald MacDonald was born Isle of Skye, and by 1882 was living by the Clarence River at Grafton, some fifty kilometres from the coast, in northern New South Wales. He writes that he had often visited Oban in his youth, and he was a regular reader of *The Oban Times* which he had sent out to him at Grafton. This provided him with some solace for the shortage of Gaelic-speakers where he resided with whom to converse. Nothing more is known about this contributor.

MacDhùghaill, Raibert – MacDougal, Robert (1813-1887) was born in Fortingall, Perthshire, Scotland in 1813. He arrived in Melbourne as an assisted migrant, on the Manlius in February, 1842 and worked as a shepherd. This settler was an adventurous explorer and huntsman who had spent three years in outback Canada hunting for firs. He was a man literate both in English and Gaelic. He wrote *Ceann-Iuil an Fhir Imrich* (*The Emigrant's Guide to North America*). This was originally published in the 1840's but a new version was printed as recently as 1998.

He returned from Canada to Scotland in 1839 where he was active in Gaelic circles and published a Gaelic version of Robert Burns' Tam o'Shanter in 1840 and also some of his own Gaelic poems. His *Ceann-Iull an Fhir Imrich (The Emigrant's Guide to North America)* was published in 1841. He also emigrated to Australia the same year. He settled in Australia and became a renowned cattle breeder publishing his first book on cattle-breeding, *The Australian Herd Book* (1858).

MacDougall married in 1853 Margaret Rankin (1834-1913) and had a family of six (five daughters and one son)

He was a religious man in the reformed faith although his firm Presbyterianism was not always appreciated by others. He became one of the two foremost cattle breeders in Victoria and also served in the Victorian parliament.

MacFionghain, Dòmhnall – Mackinnon, Donald (1800-1884), was born at Grishipoll, Isle of Coll. He was a Gaelic schoolteacher and lay preacher. He married Isabella Forbes of Glenelg in 1834 and the family (including his son Donald q.v.) emigrated to Australia in 1860 where a number of relatives were already established. They first settled at Shoalhaven in NSW where they were tenant farmers for six years and then moved to the Richmond River district where Donald took up land at Oakfield, East Coraki in NSW in 1866. Donald recorded many of his daily activities in a series of diaries, some in Gaelic, and wrote many poems and songs in his native language as well as some in English. He was a deeply religious man but he was also a keeper of Highland traditions and his house became a focal point for Scots, and more particularly for Gaels, in the area. Donald also carried out a welfare role in providing jobs and guidance and material help for new settlers from Scotland.

MacFiongain, Dòmhnall – MacKinnon, Donald (1842-1934), was born on the island of Eigg, son of Donald MacKinnon (q.v.). He was apprenticed to a blacksmith, but accompanied his family to Shoalhaven, NSW in 1860, where his father became a tenant farmer on the estate of a Mr Berry. Sent by his father to inspect the Richmond River district of northern NSW with a view to assessing its potential as an area for the family to take up land of their own, he wrote back to his father:

"Pack up, sell off, pay no more rent to Mr Berry.
This is the new Canaan, this is the Promised Land."

That report is said to have induced not only his own family, but a total of fifty others to move to the Richmond River. Donald junior never married but, like his father, he maintained diaries in Gaelic and wrote prose pieces as well as poetry in Gaelic.

MacLennan, John – Iain dubh Mac Dhòmhnull 'ic Iain (1861?-1948) was born in a clachan at Gairloch, Wester Ross. As a young man his restlessness caused him to travel to, and work in, most of the districts of Scotland, turning his hand to various activities.

Eventually he settled in Glasgow where he shared a house with three other young Highlanders. This group devoted many evenings to the enjoyment of Gaelic songs and stories. MacLennan resolved to emigrate to Canada with some friends, but he fell in love with a beautiful young woman who was about to sail to Australia. He followed her as soon as he could, departing so hastily in 1884 that he had no time to make a farewell visit to family and friends in the Highlands. This was something which he lamented in a song, 'Thug mi gaol dhuit Ian Bhàin', which he composed during his voyage. He discovered an old friend, Alasdair Choinnich, also from Gairloch, aboard the ship. When he disembarked at Brisbane he found a number of settlers from his part of the Highlands already settled in that place. After his arrival he spent some time as a 'swagman', walking the roads in search of work as a farmhand before settling in Brisbane. He was active in Gaelic circles and in attending Gaelic worship services. Together with some friends, including the Rev. Allan MacDonald MacKillop (q.v.), Mr MacKillop, being more literate in Gaelic than Mr MacLennan, rendered good service by correcting MacLennan's Gaelic writings. John MacLennan helped form, along with Mr MacKillop, the Comunn Gaidhealach Bhrisbane. He wrote much Gaelic verse and prose and his work regularly appeared in Highland papers. A small volume of his work *Duanagan agus Sgeulachdan Beaga*, appeared in 1937. He also wrote a volume based upon a second trip to his homeland, although this was largely in English.

MacLeòid, Iain – MacLeod, John (1825?-??) was born at Duirnish on Skye. He was an assisted emigrant on the Highland and Island Emigration Society ship Allison which sailed from Liverpool on 13th September, 1852. He arrived at Geelong, Victoria December 20, 1852. MacLeod was hired as a shepherd by a squatter, Alexander Kennedy, who had a 22,000 acre property "Bough Yards" with 5,000 sheep in the Parish of Guildford, County Talbot in an area outside the official settled districts of Victoria. Nothing more is known of this settler.

Mac 'Ille-Mhaoil, Semas – MacMillan, James, was born at Ardnamurchan. It is not known when he came to Australia. He worked at the gold mines at Kanowna and Coolgardie in Western Australia but he appears to have lived, at times, in some of the other States. He was a prolific contributor of Gaelic poems to publications in Scotland.

Mac Philip, An t-Urramach Ailean MacDhòmhnaill - Rev. Allan MacDonald MacKillop - (1869-1956), was born at Griminish, North Uist, the son of a crofter and fisherman. He was a native Gaelic speaker who, by his own admission, knew only a few sentences in English by his late teens. Nevertheless he was coached by the Free Church minister's daughter and, after several attempts, won a bursary to attend the 'Grammar School of Old Aberdeen' in 1889. After a long period of stop-start study, brought about by illness, lack of money and by his commitment to work for the charitable Ladies Association by teaching at various schools in the Isles, he eventually worked his way through university followed by theological studies under the auspices of the United Free Church. He was licensed by the Presbytery of Aberdeen in 1903, and worked as a probationer but, for various reasons, he saw little prospect of a settled appointment in Scotland. He offered himself for mission work in Australia and, in 1904, left for that country.

He was initially appointed to work in Queensland and then Northern New South Wales. Returning to a ministry in Queensland, he also became involved in pioneering theological studies in that State and later became lecturer in Divinity and Church History at Emmanuel College in Queensland's Theological Hall. In addition, he continued his own education, taking out two degrees through Australian universities. He wrote voluminously on historical, literary, Celtic and antiquarian subjects, as well as engaging himself in contemporary social and political ones being particularly interested in the education of the young. He was a passionate Gaelic scholar and helped found a Gaelic Society in Queensland along with his friend John MacLennan (q.v.). For forty years he conducted Gaelic church services in Brisbane and other centres and also in Melbourne whenever visiting Victoria. He also took part in the Gaelic Society of Victoria where his recitation of Gaelic tales was always warmly received.

He composed Gaelic poetry, both serious and satirical, during his long residence in his adopted country. He was a repository of an immense number of the Gaelic poems and songs composed during the Land Reform troubles in the Highlands and Islands (of which he was a contemporary). Unfortunately only 'Agus, ho, Mhòrag, ho rò, gheibh sinn fearann' seems to have survived in his papers. He married in Australia in 1906 (his wife was Alice Forbes, a direct descendant of Forbes of Culloden), and taught his children many of the traditional puirt na beul which he remembered from his own childhood as well as composing his own, an example of which is included in this anthology. He also wrote and translated many of the traditional tales as amusements for his own children and their friends. A biography of his years in Scotland before leaving for the colonies, *A Goodly Heritage* was published in 1998.

Peutan, Aonghas – Beaton, Angus (18???-1860) worked on the Quinish Estate, Mull. According to one of his own poems he appears to have been 'cleared' from the estate with his family and others from the same area and put on a ship for Liverpool from where in August 1852 they left for Moreton Bay, Australia. Angus seems not to have settled in Queensland and by 1857 he had taken up work on the land in Victoria as a shepherd and hutkeeper. He was known as a bard before leaving Mull and he carried on his art in Australia. It is to his son Donald (q.v.) that we are indebted for the examples, brief as they are, of Angus' verse in Scotland. His longer poem, *Òran an Eilthirich*, gives one of the few authentic contemporary graphic accounts of the voyage to Australia as a steerage passenger and of the deprivations, fears and isolation to which many shepherds and out-station workers were exposed once they reached the colonies. He shared his son Donald's enthusiasm for the Gaelic language and in one of his other poems he expresses his joy when a Gaelic language paper, *An Teachdaire Gaidhealach* (q.v.) was begun in Australia in 1857.

Peutan, Dòmhnall – Beaton, Donald (1835-1907), was born at Dearbhaig, the Quinish Estate, Mull, son of Angus Beaton (q.v.) He showed an early interest in Gaelic traditions, tales and poetry, matters in which he was encouraged by his father. Donald was sixteen or seventeen when he embarked, from Liverpool on 19th August, 1852 with his family, on board the Marmion to Australia. Although the family was disembarked at Portland Bay, Victoria, they eventually made their way to Queensland. Donald spent some time as a 'swagman' moving around Australia leaving Queensland on occasions for health reasons but finally settled at Mackay in Queensland. It was during his wanderings that he was often able to record the oral traditions of other Highland emigrants whom he met on these travels.

Donald was a strong champion on behalf of Gaelic and he proposed group settlement schemes for Gaelic families moving to the Australian colonies (going so far as to advocate the setting up of a Gaelic colony). He pressed for the use of Gaelic as a medium of instruction for the children of Highlanders and worked for the setting up of Gaelic schools in Australia as well as in the Scottish Highlands and Islands.

Donald was very much a tradition bearer and he retained memories of Gaelic lore from his own childhood on Mull, and in later life moved to preserve much of this stock by committing it to print. By then he sensed that Australia was unlikely to produce a thriving and enduring Gaelic culture and he contributed his collected and remembered folk material to Gaelic journals and newspapers. His last letter bears a postscript regretting that his terminal illness was progressing too fast to enable him to write down the story *Turas na feinne do dh'fhearrun na banrigh ruaidh* which he had been anxious to preserve. He died at Mackay, Queensland in 1907 aged 72.

MacKinnon, Donald (senior) 1800-1884

Born	14th July 1800
Where	Grishipoll, Isle of Coll
Married	Isabella Forbes of Glenelg, January 1934
Died	18th August 1884

Donald was a teacher and lay preacher. He emigrated to Australia with rest of his family in 1860.

He first went to Shoalhaven in NSW where he worked for, and leased land from the Berry estate in 1866. He shifted to Richmond River NSW and, after some preliminary scouting, he took up land at Oakfield, East Coracki, NSW.

He became a focal point for other Scots in the area and many of the traditions were maintained.

Donald senior composed Gaelic poetry and prose.

He maintained a strong religious witness.

MacKinnon, Donald (junior) 1842-1934

Son of Donald senior (qv)

Born Isle of Eigg 18th January, 1842.

He was apprenticed as a blacksmith.

Died 9th June 1934

After spending 6 years on the Berry estates (NSW), Donald senior sent his son, Donald junior, to "spy out the land" in another district.

The report was a dramatic one. Donald sent his message:

"Pack up. Sell Off. Pay no more rent to Mr Berry. This is the new Canaan. This is the Promised Land."

This inspired not only Donald senior to shift but also another fifty families who followed the MacKinnon family to the Richmond.

Like his father, Donald junior also maintained diaries in Gaelic and composed Gaelic poetry and prose.

Donald MacKinnon junior died, unmarried, on 9 June 1934.

Online

For more info and to see the photos referred to in this book, find us online at: https://gaelicvoicesfromaustraliainthenineteenthcentury.wordpress.com/

About the Editors

The editors, now retired, met while working at Deakin University - Kerry Cardell in Humanities and Cliff Cummin in Social Sciences.

They share an interest in migrant cultures, specifically looking at how such cultures respond when faced with the challenging circumstances of colonial life and its competing nationalities.

They have researched and written extensively on this subject and only rarely have they engaged in duelling!